The R

D0362482

Havana

written and researched by

Fiona McAuslan and Matt Norman

ROUGH
GUIDES

www.roughguides.com

AUG 1 Q

Contents

Street sellers colour section following p.80

Retro Havana colour section following p.144

Colour maps following p.248

www.roughguides.com

3

Introduction to
Havana

Of all the Caribbean capital cities, Havana is surely the most captivating. A potent mix of Revolutionary history, faded grandeur and a frenetic music scene has been a siren song for centuries and shows no sign of abating. Havana embodies a variety of images, from the tumultuous foam crashing over the Malecón seawall to Chinese bicycles and classic cars sailing along its roads; from age-stricken Baroque architecture rising above the potholed streets to sunsets over ancient city fortifications. Habaneros themselves are no less eclectic and captivating. The ingenuity with which they wring a livelihood colours visitors' interactions with them, from catching a ride in a 1950s cab to staying in a private home.

Though not the cradle of the Revolution (that title goes to the east of the country) Havana is the seat of the country's power and opens a window onto how this outpost of **socialism** functions in a modern world. There is a prevailing sense that Havana should be visited now before this unique synthesis of Revolution, classic cars and 1950s memorabilia disappears – but this runs the risk of viewing Havana as a museum piece, rather than as the dynamic and vibrant city that it is. While the glamorous pre-Revolution world epitomized by hotels built with Mafia money and smoke trails of Chevrolets still has plenty of currency, aspects of modern Havana such as a new bus infrastructure, perfectly renovated plazas and a plethora of new restaurants indicate a city confidently embracing its future.

There is some truth in the tongue-in-cheek Cuban phrase that "there is Havana and then the rest is just countryside". Certainly no other city in Cuba – perhaps even in the whole Caribbean – comes close to being such a cultural and historical metropolis and none so captures the country's essence. Havana

hosts several of the most prestigious arts festivals in the Americas, including the **International Film Festival** and the **International Jazz Festival**. And throughout the year the city's calendar bulges with smaller events: classical recitals, salsa, hip hop and bolero concerts as well as **ballet** and **theatre** seasons – all generally priced to be within reach of most citizens and visitors.

Thanks to its old town, Havana also boasts a **UNESCO World Heritage Site**, a rarity among Caribbean cities. The deep harbour mouth, wide enough to accommodate the fleets of sixteenth-century ships making their way back to Spain, was the fulcrum of life in the city for early colonists – as well as the pirates who preyed upon them – and it is here that the earliest settlements in **Habana Vieja** originated. The restoration of this neighbourhood has been one of Havana's greatest recent triumphs and the compact heart of the city, thickly clustered with **museums** and sights, is the biggest draw for visitors.

Havana's coastal geography is embedded in its psyche. Habaneros orientate themselves by the position of the sea, and the **Malecón** sea wall is not just Havana's most recognizable sight but something that is central to life in the city – every day it is a kaleidoscopic theatre of kissing couples, troubadour trumpeters and fishermen looking for an early-morning haul.

Unlike any other city in the Americas, Havana is a city that is not only best seen **on foot**, but one that is comparatively well set up to do so. Few dual carriageways or multi-lane roads scar the thoroughfares and for a modern city, the level of traffic is refreshingly low. There

▲ Band playing in a Havana bar

Revolutionary icons

There is no getting away from Cuba's long history of rebellions or its cast of characters. In every neighbourhood the same names crop up time and again, in the titles of museums, squares, hospitals, schools and streets. José Martí, Antonio Maceo and Máximo Gómez, all heroes of the nineteenth-century Wars of Independence, as well as Camilo Cienfuegos and Che Guevara, who both fought in the Revolutionary War of the 1950s, have all become almost mythical in status. The State never misses an opportunity to remind its citizens of the ideals they should aspire to emulate: the José Martí statue in Havana's Parque Central is the grand-daddy of them all, the first ever statue of Martí in Cuba, erected in 1905.

can be few cities left where horse-and-carriage and bicycle taxis are afforded as much space as vintage hot rods, jalopies and modern cars. A lack of commercially driven urban development has allowed Havana to retain the beauty of its past – albeit often in famously crumbling form. A host of **architectural styles**, from Baroque, Rococo and eclectic to Art Deco, Modernism and Soviet Brutalism form a vivid archeology of the city.

Further west the living becomes more gracious. **Vedado**, the district that developed in Havana's sugar boom of the eighteenth century, is filled with once-lavish mansions that now house multiple families, minor state organizations and, as in the case of El Hurón Azul (the Union of Cuban Writers' and Artists' headquarters), well-respected music venues. At a remove from the more frenetic action of the city's eastern reaches, this largely residential area has a wide choice of hotels and private homestays (*casas particulares*) that make it the most pleasant area in which to stay.

What to see

First-time visitors tend to gravitate towards the time-warped colonial core of **Habana Vieja**, the oldest district of the city, where the ramshackle seventeenth-century merchants' houses, fortifications,

churches and homes provide an atmospheric introduction to Havana's past. The ongoing restoration of this area has created several world-class museums, chief among them the **Museo Nacional de Bellas Artes**, whose art represents a broader range of work by domestic artists than you will find in the rest of Cuba combined. The **Museo Castillo de la Real Fuerza**, housed in Havana's oldest fortification in the leafy **Plaza de Armas**, provides an intriguing overview of Cuba's naval history. What the **Museo de la Revolución** lacks in visual impact it makes up for in insight into the history of the movement that has so defined modern Cuba.

West of this narrow huddle of streets, and presiding over the junction between Habana Vieja and **Centro Habana**, are the city's two most splendid buildings. The former seat of governance, the **Capitolio** bears uncanny resemblance to Washington D.C.'s Capitol building and is a complex composition of architectural pomp and detail. Adjacent to it, the **Gran Teatro** is equally impressive. Most visitors pause to admire the frieze of stone-and-marble maidens and angels caught in ornate perpetuity on the exterior, yet too few enjoy the programme of world-class **ballet and opera performances** available within. Virtually hidden behind the Capitolio is Centro Habana's greatest draw, the **Fábrica de Tabacos Partagás**, where many of the country's finest cigars are created. Deeper into the warren of Centro Habana is the vividly painted alley **Callejón de Hamel**, which is where you can see traditional **rumba** performed every Sunday.

While Vedado's biggest draw will always be the enduring photogenic appeal of the **Memorial Ernesto Che Guevara** and the **Monumento José Martí**, the restaurants, theatres and music venues of this gentle suburb usually entice visitors to return several times during their stay. The most notable refreshment stop is **Coppelia**, the giant ice-cream parlour housed in a 1960s space-age-style building, where excellent but affordable ice cream is dished up to the masses. Heading west across the Río Almendares, the cityscape grows more expansive and palatial as the stately Avenida 5ta heads into **Miramar**. At first glance there may seem little for visitors amid the august houses, but there is nowhere in Havana that has such a concentration of excellent – almost world-class – restaurants and a wide smattering of nightspots patronized by Havana's new money.

With so much to capture attention within the city itself, one could almost overlook the golden beaches lying close by. The glistening waters and soft sands of **Playas del Este** make for an easy day-trip and perfectly round off a Havana experience.

When to go

Havana has a hot and sunny tropical climate, which is strongly influenced by its proximity to the sea. The average yearly temperature is between 24 and 26°C, though in the winter (Dec–Feb) it can drop as low as 15°C at night. The **dry season** runs roughly from November to April, when it's advisable to pack at least one garment with long sleeves. If you visit Havana in the summer, and more broadly between May and October, considered the **wet season**, expect it to rain on at least a couple of days over a fortnight. September and October are the most

▼ Classic Plymouth Deluxe

Street Art

As with much of Cuban culture, some of the most captivating **artwork** can be found not within the walls of institutions, but on the streets. Calligraphic eulogies to José Martí and the bons mots of Che and Fidel unfurl along city walls, while drab apartment blocks are enlivened with bold murals in bright colours. In recent years urban graffiti has become more prevalent, with foreign and homegrown artists leaving their mark. Keen-eyed visitors will spot iconic images by British street artist **Banksy**, particularly on Obispo in Habana Vieja, while Brazilian graffitist **Nina** has painted her gaggles of wide-eyed children throughout Centro Habana. Perhaps the most arresting mural is in Regla, where a collaboration between Cuban artists and Brazilian spray painters **Os Gemeos** has created a dreamy fairyland near the main square. Catch it while you can – street art is a beautiful but transitory pleasure in Cuba, as the sea air is very corrosive.

threatening months of the annual **hurricane season**, which runs from June to November. Though Havana has suffered some damage in recent years, it holds up relatively well compared with cities on other Caribbean islands and in some Central American countries, even in the fiercest of hurricanes.

The **peak tourist season** in Cuba runs roughly from mid-December to mid-March and all of July and August. At those times prices are highest and accommodation needs to be booked in advance. Compared to the all-out celebrations in other countries, Christmas in Havana is a low-key affair. **New Year's Eve** dovetails with the anniversary of the Revolution on January 1 and so is much more fervently celebrated, often with free street concerts. In both December and February, when the Latin American International Film Festival and International Jazz Festival take place respectively, the city is filled with visiting dignitaries and has a fantastic buzz. Carnival happens in July, though in recent years it has often been cancelled due to lack of funds.

Average temperatures and rainfall in Havana

	Jan	Feb	Mar	Apr	May	Jun	Jul	Aug	Sep	Oct	Nov	Dec
Havana												
Max/min (°C)	18/26	18/26	19/27	21/29	22/30	23/31	24/32	24/32	24/31	23/29	21/27	19/26
Max/min (°F)	64/79	64/79	66/81	70/84	72/86	74/88	76/90	76/90	76/88	76/84	70/81	66/79
Rainfall (mm)	71	46	46	58	119	165	125	135	150	173	79	58

20

things not to miss

It's not possible to see everything Havana has to offer in one trip – and we don't suggest you try. What follows, in no particular order, is a selective taste of the city's highlights: colourful places to stay, the best places to try cigars and renowned festivals. They're arranged in five colour-coded categories to help you find the very best things to see, do and experience. All highlights have a page reference to take you straight into the guide, where you can find out more.

01 Che Memorial Page **96** • No self-respecting visitor should leave before they've captured the ultimate photo opportunity. Pick up a beret at a street market first and strike a classic pose.

02 **Necrópolis de Colón** Page 97 • Wander through Havana's most serene space and admire the grandiose morbidity of the monuments and tombs.

03 **Playas del Este** Page 180 • Head east with the body beautifuls to soak up the sun on Havana's glorious golden beaches.

04 **Casa del Habano at the Hostal Conde de Villanueva** Page 157 • Kick back with a Cohiba in one of the city's most atmospheric cigar emporia, located in a mezzanine attic.

05 **Mercado de la Catedral** Page 158 • With handcrafted cigar boxes, original artwork and sculptures, leather bags and hand-made jewellery on offer, this excellent market is one of the few places in town where you can shop till you drop.

07 Street theatre Page **147** • In Habana Vieja you're never far from an exuberant display from the stilt-walkers, clowns and dressed-up dames who caper through the streets.

06 Museo Nacional de Bellas Artes Page **72** • You could easily spend a whole day lost among the marvels that Cuba's finest art collection has to offer.

08 Fábrica de Tabacos Partagás Page **80** • Women rolling cigars on their thighs may be a well-perpetrated myth, but a tour around this famous factory nevertheless offers a window onto cigar-making and some idiosyncratic Cuban working practices.

09 **Callejón de Hamel** Page **84** • For an alternative Sunday service, head to this tiny painted alleyway for the weekly rumba session.

10 **Commercial art galleries** Page **158** • Havana's commercial galleries showcase the best work from across the country – dip in for a look and you might even come away with a masterpiece to be.

11 **Stay in a casa particular** Page **114** • As an alternative to a hotel, rent a room in a Habanero's house and enjoy great company, excellent home-cooked meals and a look at Havana behind closed doors.

12 Eat in a Miramar paladar Page **132** • Try a meal at atmospheric *La Esperanza*, one of the city's lesser-known paladars, where the magnificent food is matched by the sumptuous décor in this carefully restored 1940s Art Deco house.

13 Edificio Bacardí Page **136** • The Bacardí family's pre-Revolution headquarters is an Art Deco masterpiece. Admire the exquisite detail while lingering over a *Cuba Libre* at *Café La Barrita* inside.

14 Havana International Jazz Festival Page **151** • The chance to catch an impromptu performance in a hotel or bar with one of the heavyweights of Cuba's jazz scene makes this a festival to aim for.

15 Hotel Nacional Page **87** • After a day's sightseeing, the best place to savour a sundowner is under the arches on the airy terrace of this splendid 1930s hotel.

16 Industriales game at Estadio Latinoamericano Page **163** • When Havana's best-loved baseball team are ready to hit home runs, their passionate fans get into carnival mode. Join the party at their 55,000-capacity stadium.

17 **Museo Ernest Hemingway** Page **185** • Preserved just as he left it, Papa's house offers an intriguing look at the minutiae of the great writer's life in Havana.

18 **Vintage American car ride with Gran Car** Page **29** • There's nothing quite as evocative as seeing Havana slide by from the passenger seat of a vintage car. Chevrolets, Buicks and the occasional De Soto will thrill anyone with an eye for a classic.

19 **Festival de Cine** Page **154** • Soak up the buzz, talk to directors and catch the hottest new films at Havana's premier festival.

20 **National Union of Cuban Writers and Artists** Page **145** • If you take pot luck on a night out in the beautiful grounds of the UNEAC building, you might catch a musical luminary like Pablo Milanés strumming his stuff.

Basics

Basics

www.roughguides.com

Getting there

Although Cuba is now firmly established on the Caribbean tourist circuit, there are still not as many direct flights as one might expect. It's easier to get to Havana from Europe or Canada than, say, the US. That said, there are several airlines flying to Havana, and with forward planning you should have little problem picking up a flight to suit your budget.

Airfares always depend on the season, with the highest around mid-December to mid-March and all of July and August. You'll get the best prices during the **low season** – mid-March to mid-April and mid-November to mid-December.

While the majority of flights to Cuba still involve a change somewhere in Europe, the Virgin routes from the UK to Havana are a direct connection. It's always worth comparing prices online. Though Havana now regularly features in the destinations offered by high-street **travel agents**, the experience of smaller agents specializing in Latin America (see p.22) gives them an edge over their better-known rivals. More familiar with the details specific to Cuba, such as airport departure tax and tourist cards (see p.41), they can also usually find the cheapest flights.

Flights from the US, Canada, Mexico and the Caribbean

Since the United States continues to maintain a Cold War-era **embargo** on trade with Cuba, US citizens are not allowed by their government to travel there freely. The basic idea behind the prohibition is to keep the Cuban economy from benefiting from US tourist dollars. That said, it is actually possible for US citizens to go to Cuba, and something like 150,000 of them do so every year.

Canadians are as free to travel to Cuba as to any other country, and travelling via Canada is one of the obvious alternatives for US citizens.

From the US

The majority of US visitors to Cuba go legally by obtaining a **"licence"** from the US Treasury Department. Who qualifies for one of these tends to change quite often due to the ongoing tug-of-war between the US government's conservative and liberal factions over the enforcement of the embargo (for more details, see box below).

If you do succeed in obtaining a licence to travel to Cuba, you can call **Marazul Tours** in New Jersey or Miami (see p.23) about booking a place on one of their permitted charter flights to Havana from New York or Miami. If you don't have a licence, don't bother calling them, as they (and all other

Obtaining permission to travel to Cuba

If you're a US citizen and think you have a case for being granted permission to travel to Cuba, perhaps as a journalist, student or on some sort of humanitarian mission, contact the **Licensing Division**, Office of Foreign Assets Control, US Department of the Treasury, 1500 Pennsylvania Ave NW, Washington D.C. 20220 ☏202/622-2480, ⊛www.treas.gov/ofac. You can also get information from the Cuban government at the **Cuban Interests Section** at 2630 16th St NW, Washington DC 20009 ☏202/797-8518; or the **Cuban Consulate Office** at 2639 16th St NW, Washington DC 20009 ☏202/797-8609. Most of the specialist tour operators in the US should also be able to assist you in getting your licence.

agencies) are prohibited by law from advising you on getting around the restrictions. Marazul Tours runs flights from Miami for US$300 and from New York for US$625. Note that non-US citizens cannot use these routes if they are travelling as tourists or without government approval.

For everyone else who wants to visit Cuba for reasons less acceptable to the US government, like tourism, a degree of ingenuity is required. Usually this means doing little more than **travelling via a third country**, and there are a number of well-established routes to choose from should you decide to do this, including Canada, Mexico and other Caribbean islands. In addition, the Cuban authorities make it easier for US citizens to get around the travel ban by agreeing not to stamp their passports (stamping their tourist cards instead).

If you are a US national, it's important to understand that you will be operating outside **the law** by going to Cuba without a licence. It is probably a good idea to find out exactly what the restrictions are, and the possible consequences to you for ignoring them, before you decide to make the trip.

From Canada, Mexico and the Caribbean

In the low season it is possible to get **APEX fares** (a heavily discounted return airfare ticket that cannot be cancelled) from Montréal or Toronto to Havana on Cubana for as little as US$350, though the average fare is about US$560. While Cubana is the only airline with regularly scheduled flights to Cuba from Canada, there are a number of **charter companies** flying the route. Since the charter operators are not allowed to deal directly with the public, to find out about these flights you must go through a travel agent.

The following are sample fares for round-trip travel from Mexican and Caribbean cities to Havana: Mexico City (US$400); Cancún (US$240); Kingston or Montego Bay (US$420); and Nassau (US$350). Flights to Nassau in the Bahamas are the most direct route from the US for blockade-busting Americans or non-US citizens who want to

move on to Cuba from the States. Note that US citizens cannot use credit cards issued by a US bank to purchase tickets.

A few **specialist operators** offer thematically designed trips, with special-interest itineraries. This is particularly so with US tour operators, as those groups who do organize trips have to be, by definition, engaged in one of the specific activities, like study tours, permitted by the US government; the definition of "studying" in Cuba on one of these tours can be quite broad, however.

Flights from the UK and Ireland

Two airlines have direct scheduled flights to Cuba from Britain. **Cubana**, the national Cuban carrier, has one weekly flight departing from London Gatwick for Havana. Though Cubana tends to offer the least expensive flights on the market, they have, in the past, had a reputation for unreliability. For smooth service and mod cons the best choice is **Virgin Atlantic**, which has direct flights to Havana departing from Gatwick twice weekly. Return fares start from £450–600 including taxes in low season and shoot up to £700–800 including taxes in high season.

Various airlines fly to Havana from European cities, including Madrid, Paris, Amsterdam and Rome, and **non-direct flights** sometimes offer a saving on the cost of a direct flight. **Air France** is the most versatile option, with six weekly flights from London Heathrow to Havana via Paris. Prices range from £550 to £600 for most of the year, with the glaring exception of late December, when a ticket is likely to cost £800 or more. **Iberia** flies daily from London Heathrow and Manchester with a change of plane in Madrid; return fares are between £500 and £600, with similar late-December price rises. Other airlines flying direct from European cities include Cubana, KLM, Martinair and Air Europa.

No airline flies non-stop **from Ireland** to Cuba, and you'll usually change planes in London, Paris or Madrid. Air France flies from Dublin via Paris from €350. Otherwise the best option is to buy a flight from London, Paris or Madrid and arrange a separate transfer.

As you will not be able to get a tourist card from a travel agent in Ireland, your only option is to get one from the **Cuban Embassy** at 2 Adelaide Court, Adelaide Road, Dublin 2 ☎353 1475 0899.

Flights from Australia and New Zealand

Cuba is hardly a bargain destination from Australasia, as there are no direct flights. The least expensive and most straightforward route is **via Tokyo to Mexico City**, from where there are frequent flights to Havana. From Australia, Qantas Airlines has flights from Melbourne and Sydney to Tokyo (where you stay overnight), then on to Mexico City and Havana for A$2780. From New Zealand, Air New Zealand flies from Auckland to Mexico City, with connections on to Havana, starting at around NZ$3550.

RTW flights

If Cuba is only one stop on a longer journey, you might want to consider buying a **round-the-world (RTW) ticket**. Some travel agents can sell you an "off-the-shelf" RTW ticket that will have you touching down in about half a dozen cities; others will have to assemble one for you, which can be tailored to your needs but is apt to be more expensive. Bear in mind, though, that you will not be able to fly from the US to Cuba, or vice versa, meaning you'll most likely have to include another country in the Caribbean or Latin America.

By sea

Out of deference to, or fear of, the US blockade, very few **cruise ships** stop at Cuban ports – those that do are then prohibited from docking in the US for six months.

Six steps to a better kind of travel

At Rough Guides we are passionately committed to travel. We feel strongly that only through travelling do we truly come to understand the world we live in and the people we share it with – plus tourism has brought a great deal of **benefit** to developing economies around the world over the last few decades. But the extraordinary growth in tourism has also damaged some places irreparably, and of course **climate change** is exacerbated by most forms of transport, especially flying. This means that now more than ever it's important to **travel thoughtfully and responsibly**, with respect for the cultures you're visiting – not only to derive the most benefit from your trip but also to preserve the best bits of the planet for everyone to enjoy. At Rough Guides we feel there are six main areas in which you can make a difference:

- Consider what you're contributing to the **local economy**, and how much the services you use do the same, whether it's through employing local workers and guides or sourcing locally grown produce and local services.
- Consider the **environment** on holiday as well as at home. Water is scarce in many developing destinations, and the biodiversity of local flora and fauna can be adversely affected by tourism. Try to patronize businesses that take account of this.
- Travel with a purpose, not just to tick off experiences. Consider **spending longer** in a place, and getting to know it and its people.
- Give thought to how often you **fly**. Try to avoid short hops by air and more harmful night flights.
- Consider **alternatives to flying**, travelling instead by bus, train, boat and even by bike or on foot where possible.
- Make your trips "**climate neutral**" via a reputable carbon offset scheme. All Rough Guide flights are offset, and every year we donate money to a variety of charities devoted to combating the effects of climate change.

With a history of confrontation at sea between Florida-based Cuban exile groups and the Cuban maritime authorities, and the rocky relationship between Cuba and the States in general, sailing into Cuban waters can be problematic. Normal **visa requirements** apply, and you should make sure you have these before you embark on your trip. While it is not currently a legal requirement to notify the Cuban authorities of your arrival, it is common maritime courtesy to do so. You should radio ahead where possible. By law you can only be cleared at a port of entry which also has a marine facility. Most visiting yachts aim to enter at the Hemingway Marina. **Yacht** owners can dock in one of the four hundred berths here, in canals 4.5m in depth and 6m wide. If you are docking you should notify your arrival through VHF channel 16 or 72, or alternatively HF channel 7462 or 7821. It's also worth bearing in mind that facilities for repairing vessels are fairly limited in Cuba.

The possibilities for sailing from the US took a turn for the worse in February 2004, when President Bush passed legislation decreeing that all sailors must apply for a **"sojourn license"** from the Commerce Department. However, as these are not issued to pleasure trips, sailing vacations to Cuba for US citizens are effectively outlawed for now, although under President Obama's more liberal stance towards Cuba this legislation may be less stringently enforced. A good source for information is *The Cruising Guide to Cuba* by Simon Charles. Another useful resource is ⓦwww.noonsite.com.

In Cuba, the best organization to contact for information on entry requirement updates is **Federación Nautical de Cuba**, INDER, Via Blanca y Boyeros ☎7/857-7146, ☏7/833-3459.

Airlines, agents and operators

Airlines

Air France ⓦwww.airfrance.com.
Bahamasair ⓦwww.bahamasair.com.
British Midland ⓦwww.flybmi.com.
Cubana ⓦwww.cubana.co.cu.

Iberia ⓦwww.iberia.com.
(JAL) Japan Air Lines ⓦwww.jal.com or www.japanair.com.
LanChile ⓦwww.lan.com.
Mexicana ⓦwww.mexicana.com.
Qantas Airways ⓦwww.qantas.com.
Virgin Atlantic ⓦwww.virgin-atlantic.com.

Airline offices in Havana

Aerocaribbean Calle 23 no.64 e/ Infanta y P, Vedado ☎7/879-7524 to 25, 832-7584 & 836-5936.
Aeroflot Miramar Trade Center, 5ta Ave. e/ 70 y 80, Miramar ☎7/204-3200.
Aerogaviota Ave. 47 no.2814, e/ 28 y 34, Reparto Kohly, Playa ☎7/204-5603, 203-3066 & 203-0686.
Air Canada José Martí International Airport ☎7/649-7012 & 836-3226.
Air Europa Miramar Trade Center, 5ta Ave. e/ 70 y 80, Miramar ☎7/204-6904.
Air France Calle 23 no.64 e/ Infanta y P, Vedado ☎7/833-2642 to 44.
Air Jamaica Calle 23 no.64 e/ Infanta y P, Vedado ☎7/833-2448 & 833-4011.
Copa Airlines Miramar Trade Center, 5ta Ave. e/ 70 y 80, Miramar ☎7/833-1758 & 833-3657.
Cubana Calle 23 no.64, Vedado ☎7/834-4446 to 49 & 836-4950 & Miramar Trade Center, 5ta Ave. e/ 70 y 80, Miramar ☎7/204-6679 & 204-9647.
Iberia Miramar Trade Center, 5ta Ave. e/ 70 y 80, Miramar ☎7/204-3444 & 833-5041.
LTU Calle 23 no.64, e/ Infanta y P, Vedado ☎7/833-3524 to 25.
Martinair Holland Calle 23 no.64, e/ Infanta y P, Vedado ☎7/833-3730 & 833-3531.
Mexicana Calle 23 no.64, e/ Infanta y P, Vedado ☎7/833-3228 & 833-3130.
Virgin Atlantic Miramar Trade Center, 5ta Ave. e/ 70 y 80, Miramar ☎7/204-0747.

Agents and operators

Blazing Saddles Travels UK ☎020/8424 0483, ⓦwww.cyclecuba.net. The only tour company dedicated solely to cycling trips. Organizes one- and two-week tours to a variety of locations around the island.
Captivating Cuba UK ☎08444/29916, ⓦwww.captivatingcuba.com. Specialist branch of Travelcoast Ltd, offering some resort-based packages and tailor-made tours built around festivals, carnival, painting and cigars.
Center for Cuban Studies US ☎212/242-0559, ⓦwww.cubaupdate.org. Sends expeditions from the US to Cuba on humanitarian missions, such as

administering eye tests and distributing spectacles, and arranges trips for various professionals.

Co-op Travel Care UK ☎0870/112 0085, ⓦ www .travelcareonline.com. Packages to Havana from the UK's largest independent travel agent. Non-partisan and informed advice.

Explore Worldwide UK ☎01252/760 000, ⓦ www.explore.co.uk. Big range of small-group tours, treks and expeditions centred on aspects of Cuba including revolutionary history, salsa and cycling.

Global Exchange US ☎415/255-7296, ⓦ www .globalexchange.org. A non-profit organization that leads "reality tours" for US citizens to Cuba. "Travel seminars" explore local culture, music, health, religion or agriculture; you can also take a class on Cuban rhythms or the Spanish language, or book a place on a bicycle tour.

Intrepid Travel UK ☎020/8960 6333, ⓦ www .intrepidtravel.com. Small-group tours with the emphasis on cross-cultural contact and low-impact tourism with various options including "independent Cuba".

Journey Latin America UK ☎020/8747 3108, ⓦ www.journeylatinamerica.co.uk. Well versed in the various flight deals to Cuba and usually able to dig out some of the best-value flights on the market. Offers reliable and well-planned escorted group tours and individual itineraries.

Marazul Tours US ☎201/319-1054 or 800-223-5334, ⓦ www.marazulcharters.com. Books tickets on charter flights, for officially sanctioned US travellers, to Havana from Miami or New York, and can arrange hotel accommodation as well.

North South Travel UK ☎01245/608 291, ⓦ www.northsouthtravel.co.uk. Friendly, competitive travel agency, offering discounted fares worldwide. Profits are used to support projects in the developing world, especially the promotion of sustainable tourism.

Progressive Tours UK ☎020/7262 1676, ⓦ www.progressivetours.co.uk. The emphasis is on grassroots visits, including study tours designed to provide close contact with Cuban people. Also arranges more traditional but very reasonably priced

one- or two-week hotel-based holidays. The office also issues tourist visas.

STA Travel UK ☎0871/230 8571, US ☎800/781-4040, ⓦ www.statravel.com. Worldwide specialists in independent travel; also student IDs, travel insurance, car rental, rail passes and more. Good discounts for students and under-26s and good prices on Havana flights.

Trips Worldwide UK ☎0800/840 0850, ⓦ www .tripsworldwide.co.uk. Good-value tailor-made trips around Cuba; the speciality is fly-drives starting in Havana.

Worldwide Quest Nature Tours US ☎416/633-5666 or 800/387-1483, ⓦ www.worldwidequest .com. Holidays with ecotourist agendas. Hiking or cycling tours with stays in mountain resorts and lodges in some of the most beautiful Cuban countryside.

Arrival

Havana has a five-terminal international airport, a train station, two interprovincial bus stations and a cruise ship terminal. Passengers arriving at any of these entry points are usually forced to get a taxi into the city, as there are no shuttle services from any of them to central Havana. All passengers on international flights departing from Havana must pay a $25CUC departure tax at the airport.

By air

All international flights land at **José Martí International Airport** (switchboard ☎7/266-4644 & 275-1200; information ☎7/266-4133 & 649-5666), about 15km south of the city centre in the borough of Boyeros. There are three principal terminals, with the vast majority of international passengers arriving at Terminal 3 (☎7/649-0410 & 649-5786), which has information desks, a bureau de change, a few shops and a restaurant. There are **car rental desks** in each of the three terminals.

Since there is no public transport linking the rest of Havana directly with the airport, the chances are you'll have to pay for a **taxi**; there is a taxi rank right outside the terminal and usually taxi touts acting as intermediaries between drivers and punters. These guys are worth latching on to as they can fix you up in the same car with other travellers to split costs, though be prepared to haggle; on the meter the half-hour journey to Habana Vieja, Vedado or Miramar shouldn't cost more than $15–20CUC. The nearest local bus stop is over 2km away on the Avenida de Rancho Boyeros.

Anyone departing Havana on an international flight must pay a **departure tax**, currently $25CUC. This is payable at designated kiosks in the departure hall in Terminal 3 and can only be paid after checking in. **Theft** from luggage during baggage handling is relatively common and if your suitcase or bag is not lockable it is advisable to get it shrink-wrapped. There is a shrink-wrapping service available in the departure hall, costing $5CUC per item. **Customs** allow you to carry up to fifty cigars and two bottles of rum without having to declare them. Anything above these quantities must be accompanied by a purchase receipt. For more information on **customs regulations** consult ⓦwww .aduana.co.cu.

By bus

There are two long-distance bus terminals in Havana. Most tourists from elsewhere in Cuba arrive on the interprovincial **Víazul** buses at the diminutive **Terminal Víazul** (☎7/881-1413 & 881-5652), on Avenida 26 across from the city zoo in Nuevo Vedado. There is an information desk here, a café and some public telephones but precious little else, and the local area is predominantly residential so most people jump straight in a **taxi** on arrival; there are usually several waiting in the bus station car park. On the meter the journey to Habana Vieja should cost around $5CUC, and even less to Miramar or Vedado; in the more likely event that the taxi driver is not using a meter you should be able to negotiate a similar price. One of the few **local buses** that passes the bus station on Avenida 26 is the #P3 but you'll need to change from this to another bus to get anywhere useful. Most Cubans, and some foreigners, travel by the cheaper of the two interprovincial bus services, **Astro**, whose buses pull in at the **Terminal de Omnibus Nacionales** (switchboard ☎7/870-9401; convertible-peso ticket office ☎870-3397; information ☎879-2456), at Avenida de la Independencia (also called Avenida de Rancho Boyeros) esq. 19 de Mayo, near the Plaza de la Revolución. This station is closer to the heart of Havana and a taxi ride to most of the central accommodation options shouldn't cost more than a few convertible pesos. The station is on several local bus routes, including the #P12 to Habana Vieja and the

#P16 to the hotel district in Vedado, while you can pick up the Habana Bus Tour (see below) just a block away.

There are daily **departures** from both bus terminals to the rest of Cuba but foreign passport holders are officially obliged to travel with Víazul.

By train

Trains from other Cuban provinces pull in at the **Estación Central de Ferrocarriles** (☏7/860-9448 & 862-1920) in southern Habana Vieja. Fewer official taxis pass by here than at the bus stations so you may have to ring for one (see p.27 for numbers), or negotiate a price with one of the private taxis usually waiting outside the station. Also always on hand are *bicitaxis* but these are far from ideal if there are two or more of you and you have lots of baggage.

Several **local buses** stop close by to the station, the most useful of which are the #P4 and #P5, both of which pass along roads circling Habana Vieja before cutting into the heart of Vedado via Centro Habana and finally onto Miramar. Catching either of these usually crowded buses in the middle of the day with heavy bags will almost certainly be an uncomfortable experience.

The other train station in Havana is the tiny **Terminal Casablanca** (☏7/862-4888) on the eastern side of the bay. This is the terminal for the Hershey line, Cuba's only electric train service, connecting Havana and Matanzas (see p.77). From here you can walk to the edge of the bay and catch the cross-bay ferry (see p.26) or ring for a taxi.

By cruise ship

Around twice a week **cruise ships** call in at Havana, docking at the **Terminal Sierra Maestra** (☏7/866-6524 & 862-1925), inside the harbour and just a few metres away from the heart of Habana Vieja. There are two rental car offices inside the terminal and numerous hotels and restaurants within easy walking distance.

Getting around

Havana has a poor public transport system, with no metro or municipal train network and an overcrowded bus service. That said, significant improvements have been made in recent years, making buses slightly more accessible to visitors, while a useful tourist bus service has been added to the options available. The regular bus system still presents a number of challenges for newcomers thanks to an idiosyncratic queuing culture, information-less bus stops and a complete lack of timetables. But as most journeys cost less than half a national peso, and with a far more extensive network than the tourist bus service, reaching out to destinations such as Parque Lenin and Santiago de las Vegas, you may be tempted to try your luck. Despite these improved options you will almost certainly find yourself having to use a taxi at least once, though this is not such a bad thing when the car is a 1955 Chevrolet.

By bus

The Habana Bus Tour service, a recently established but invaluable network of tourist buses connecting the most-visited sections of the city, means visitors to Havana now have a user-friendly alternative to traversing the capital by taxi. With a timetabled schedule, bus stops with route maps and a guaranteed seat, this service offers everything that the regular bus system doesn't, albeit for a much greater cost. For $3CUC you can ride all day on any of the three routes (T1, T2 & T3, see colour maps for details) as often as you like. **Tickets** are sold on board.

The two hubs for the network are the Parque Central (T1 & T3) in Habana Vieja and the Plaza de la Revolución (T1 & T2) in Vedado. Though there are designated bus stops, you can flag buses down anywhere on their routes. In theory the service runs daily from 9am to 9pm at half-hourly intervals but in reality this varies and you can sometimes find yourself waiting at a stop for an hour or more, while last buses set off as early as 7pm.

The **regular bus** system, divided between the Metrobús and Omnibus Metropolitanos networks, is at the heart of everyday life in Havana. The **Metrobús** network (see colour maps) has seen the greatest improvements in the last few years, though this fact may surprise first-time users of the service, given the overcrowding and long waits still associated with it. Nevertheless, it is the easier of the two networks to use, with a more regular, less crowded service than existed a few years ago, and you should be able to get anywhere you need using Metrobús exclusively. Its buses are distinguishable by their route names, all beginning with "P". The vehicles themselves, most of them relatively new bendy buses, were imported from China to replace the converted juggernauts known as *camellos* that so characterized public transport in Havana until recently.

The only written information you will find at a bus stop is the numbers of the buses that stop there, and sometimes not even that. The front of the bus will tell you its final destination, but for any more detail you'll need to consult

Cross-bay ferries

Ferries for Regla and Casablanca, both on the eastern side of the bay, leave from a small jetty opposite the Russian Orthodox Cathedral (see p.56) on San Pedro in Habana Vieja. Bikes are not permitted. Departures are roughly every thirty minutes between 6am and 11pm. The cost is 10c in CUP.

the **bus route map** in this guide (see colour maps) or posted inside the bus. Waiting for any bus you'll need to mark your place in the queue, which may not appear to even exist. The customary rule is to ask aloud who the last person is when you arrive at the stop; so, for example, to queue for bus #P5 you should shout "*¿Última persona para la P5?*". When the bus finally pulls up, make sure you have, within a peso, the **right change** – there's a flat fee of 40¢ in national pesos and you won't receive any change no matter the value of the coin or note you pay with.

By taxi

There is a confusing array of different taxi types in Havana but essentially you need to know about the three most common kinds, each detailed below.

State tourist taxis

Though they are not officially the exclusive preserve of tourists, most state-run taxis charging in convertible pesos are referred to as **tourist taxis** or *turistaxis*. They are usually modern cars, commonly Nissans, Peugeots and Mercedes, though some are older Russian Ladas. They should all come equipped with meters but it is common for drivers to have their meters turned off, for legitimate reasons or otherwise, in which case it makes sense to negotiate a price before setting off.

Tariffs vary considerably according to a number of murky factors as well as the size and style of the car, the season and the company itself, but on the whole expect to pay between 55¢ and 65¢ per kilometre. Panataxi tend to be the cheapest. At the other end of the price scale are Gran Car taxis, state-run American classics in pristine condition but usually rented out by the hour (see car rental agencies on p.29).

Private taxis

Just as common as metered state taxis are the privately owned cars, predominantly 1950s American classics or Ladas, which have been converted into taxis by their owners. The local name for these is *máquinas* or *taxis particulares*, but in English they are most accurately referred to as **private taxis**.

Private taxis are licensed either to charge in national pesos or convertible pesos, while some are not licensed at all. There is no way of telling from outward appearances which currency the taxi is licensed to charge, or indeed whether it is a taxi at all, but it is assumed that as a foreigner you will be paying in convertible pesos. Many drivers, whether correctly licensed or not, won't turn down the chance of a convertible-peso fare and are prepared to run the risk of the hefty fine, or bribe, should they be stopped by the police.

Private taxis are not necessarily cheaper than metered taxis and **negotiation** is part of the whole unofficial system; if you don't haggle the chances are you'll end up paying double what a state taxi would cost. For example, most drivers picking up passengers in Habana Vieja would accept $4CUC for the journey to the Plaza de la Revolución or around $6CUC to Miramar. The essential thing is that you **establish a price** before you begin your journey. Be aware also that private taxi drivers may sometimes pick up another passenger en route, effectively but unofficially becoming what is known as a *taxi colectivo*.

Taxis colectivos

Taxis colectivos are usually national peso-charging taxis and more akin to a bus service. These are generally privately owned vehicles, mostly old American classics as these have the most seating, though some are state-run Russian cars. Most characteristically they tend to work **specific routes**. One of the best-known and most useful routes begins on Neptuno in Centro Habana, between the Parque Central and Avenida de Italia. From here, having loaded up their car with as many passengers as possible, drivers usually head for Vedado, via the length of Neptuno, where they turn onto L and head for either Linea or 23. Your best bet of flagging one of these taxis down is on one of these roads, and though there are no markings on any of them to distinguish them as *colectivos*, the giveaway sign is usually any old American car packed with people. You may, however, find it hard to flag one down, since it's unusual for tourists to use

Havana taxi companies

Habanataxi ☏7/648-9086 & 648-9090
Panataxi ☏7/855-5555 & 855-5456
Taxis OK ☏7/877-6666

these taxis, and drivers are sometimes reluctant to pick up non-Cubans.

It is generally accepted in Havana that a trip in a *colectivo* anywhere within the city will cost $10CUP, though as a non-Cuban you may have to negotiate.

Bicitaxis and coco taxis

Havana has legions of **bicitaxis**, also known as *ciclotaxis* – three-wheeled bicycles with enough room for two passengers, sometimes three at a squeeze. Fares are negotiated but don't expect cheaper rates than automotive taxis.

Less common are **coco taxis** (☏7/873-1411), sometimes called *moto taxis*, operated by the state firm Panatrans. They are aimed strictly at the tourist market and offer the novel experience of a ride around town semi-encased in a giant yellow bowling ball, dragged along by a small scooter. Fares have become standardized at 50¢ per kilometre, but there will always be drivers looking to charge unsuspecting tourists a higher rate. There have, however, been a significant number of accidents involving these vehicles.

By rental car

The expense of **renting a car** in Havana means it is generally best avoided, though there are some obvious advantages. If you intend to take day-trips out to the city limits and beyond, or if you are based in Habana Vieja, Centro Habana or Vedado but want to make frequent visits to the excellent restaurants, paladars and nightclubs of Miramar, you may find a rental car preferable to the slow, unreliable and for some places non-existent public transport options.

All **car-rental agencies** in Cuba are run by the state, with international companies like Avis and Hertz non-existent, so you will generally find similar deals wherever you go, though some firms specialize in more upmarket, and therefore more expensive cars. **Prices** – which are rarely less than $40CUC a day and usually between $50CUC and $70CUC – depend more on the type of car you rent. There is an extra $10–15CUC a day for insurance and a deposit of $200CUC to $300CUC.

Demand, especially in high season, usually far outweighs supply, meaning agencies are often very limited in the car and price options they can offer. For the same reason it is often difficult, if not impossible, to book a car in advance. In this respect it is well worth booking before you arrive in Cuba, a more reliable way of ensuring you get a good deal or a car at all.

All agencies require you to have held a driving licence from your home country or an international driving licence for at least a year and that you be 21 or older.

Driving

Driving in Havana can be a bit of a chaotic experience, with many drivers showing scant regard for the rarely enforced highway code.

The first thing to be aware of when driving in Havana is the distinct **lack of road markings**, making most junctions precarious and in some cases downright dangerous. Where **traffic lights** exist, there is often only one suspended high above the road, so keep a keen eye out for them. A permanently flashing yellow light at a junction, either on a standard traffic light or a single light on its own, means you have right of way. A flashing red light at a junction means you must give way.

The quality of the road surface in some neighbourhoods, particularly Centro Habana, is terrible and it's wise to expect **potholes** on most backstreets, though most of the main streets are in decent condition.

See p.229 in "Language" for a brief glossary of driving terms.

You should also be vigilant for the large X signs, announcing a **railroad crossing**, known as a *crucero* in Spanish. These have no barriers and the accepted practice is to slow down, listen for train horns and whistles and look both ways down the tracks before driving across. The crossing you are most likely to encounter is on the airport road, the Avenida de Rancho Boyeros.

If all this weren't enough to contend with during the day, the **absence of street lighting** on all but the busiest city streets means driving at night can become a real nightmare.

There are no metered **car parks** or parking spaces in Havana and you could easily pass a car park without realizing it, as they are often makeshift affairs, sometimes in the ruins of old buildings. The easiest to spot are the state-run versions, usually marked by a *Parqueo Estatal* sign. Both these and private car parks are manned by attendants with whom you may need to establish a price, though at state-run car parks there is often a price list posted. If you're parking overnight, establish a price beforehand and find out when the attendant's shift ends. If the car park is particularly crowded you may be asked to leave your keys in case your car needs to be moved to allow another driver out.

Leaving your car on the street is of course an option, but bear in mind that car crime has been on the rise over the last decade in Cuba and few car rental firms offer insurance covering the cost of your wheels if they are stolen. The police also tend to look less favourably on theft or damage to a vehicle if it is left anywhere other than a garage or a car park.

Gas stations

Gas stations in Havana are few and far between, with just one in Centro Habana and Habana Vieja, right on the municipal border at Paseo del Prado esq. Cárcel. There are several, however, in Vedado and Miramar. Officially, **tourist cars** can only fill up at convertible-peso gas stations, identifiable by the names Cupet-Cimex and Oro Negro, the two chains responsible for running them. They are rarely if ever self-service, and tipping is generally expected. The cost of gas is 95¢ per litre for *especial* (which some rented cars require by law), 75¢ for regular and 45¢ for diesel, still used in one or two models.

Car-rental agencies

Cubacar ☎7/835-0000 & 273-2277, 🌐www
.transtur.cu. Over fifty rental points in the city
including at the Terminal Sierra Maestra in Habana
Vieja (☎7/866-0284).
Gran Car ☎7/881-0992. Classic American cars
rented with chauffeurs. Prices begin at $25CUC an
hour or $125CUC a day.

Havanautos ☎7/835-0000 & 273-2277, 🌐www
.transtur.cu. Run by the same parent company as
Cubacar, so the same pricing structure but with some
alternative rental points, including at Calle 23 y M in
Vedado.
Rex ☎7/835-6830, 🌐www.rex.cu. Fewer branches
and generally more upmarket cars. Has an office in
the Terminal Sierra Maestra in Habana Vieja
(☎7/862-6343).

Addresses

Street names in Havana are generally not preceded by the word calle (street) and
are usually expressed in addresses as a street in between two other streets, whose
names are preceded by e/, an abbreviation of entre (between), thus Obispo e/
Mercaderes y Oficios. However, with streets whose names are numbers or letters,
the first street is usually preceded by the word calle, thus Calle L e/ 23 y 25. If a
building is on a corner, then esq., an abbreviation of *esquina* (corner), is used, thus
Calle L esq. 23. You may also see this written as Calle L y 23. Look out for the
words *altos* and *bajos* appearing in addresses; they indicate top-floor and
ground-floor flats respectively. The abbreviation s/n in an address stands for *sin
número* and means the address has no number.

Following the 1959 Revolution, streets in towns and cities throughout Cuba were
renamed. The old names, however, continued to be used and today most locals
still refer to them. Where a name appears on a street sign it will almost always be
the new name. Wherever addresses are written down they tend to also use the
new name, though some tourist literature has now returned to using the old
names. Where an address incorporating a renamed street appears in this book the
new name will be used with the old name in brackets, unless the new name is so
rarely used as to make it almost obsolete, in which case the new name will be
given in brackets.

New and old street names

New name	Old name
Agramonte	Zulueta
Aponte	Someruelos
Avenida Antonio Maceo	Malecón
Avenida de Bélgica (northern half)	Monserrate
Avenida de Bélgica (southern half)	Egido
Avenida Carlos Manuel de Céspedes	Avenida del Puerto
Avenida de España	Vives
Avenida de la Independencia	Avenida de Rancho Boyeros
Avenida de Italia	Galiano
Avenida Salvador Allende	Carlos III
Avenida Simón Bolívar	Reina
Brasil	Teniente Rey
Capdevila	Cárcel
Leonor Pérez	Paula
Máximo Gómez	Monte
Padre Varela	Belascoaín
Paseo de Martí	Paseo del Prado
San Martín	San José

Health

Providing you take common-sense precautions, visiting Havana poses no particular health risks. In fact, some of the most impressive advances made by the Revolutionary government since 1959 have been in the field of medicine and the free health service provided to all Cuban citizens. Since 1959, vaccination programmes have eliminated malaria, polio and tetanus, and patients from around the world now come to Cuba for unique treatments developed for a variety of conditions such as night blindness, psoriasis and radiation sickness.

No **vaccinations** are legally required to visit Cuba, unless you're arriving from a country where yellow fever and cholera are endemic, in which case you'll need a vaccination certificate. It is still advisable, however, to get inoculations for hepatitis A, tetanus and typhoid. For anyone intending to make frequent visits to Cuba, it is worth bearing in mind that a booster dose of the hepatitis A vaccination within six to twelve months of the first dose will provide immunity for approximately ten years.

It is a sensible idea to bring your own **medical kit** (see box below), painkillers and any other medical supplies you think you might need, as they are difficult to buy.

Food and water

Due to the risk of parasites, drinking tap water is never a good idea in Havana, even in the swankiest hotels. Whenever you are offered water, whether in a restaurant,

paladar or private house, it's a good idea to check if it has been boiled – in most cases it will have been. **Bottled water** is available in convertible-peso shops and most tourist bars and restaurants.

Although reports of **food poisoning** are few and far between, there are good reasons for exercising caution when eating in Havana. Food bought on the street is in the highest-risk category and you should be aware that there is no official regulatory system ensuring acceptable levels of hygiene. Self-regulation does seem to be enough in most cases, but you should still be cautious when buying pizzas, meat-based snacks or ice cream from street-sellers. National peso restaurants can be equally suspect, particularly those in out-of-the-way places.

Dengue fever

Mosquitoes are largely absent from Havana due to regular fumigation. Although Cuba is

---

A travellers' medical kit

The following are some of the items you might want to carry with you:
- Antihistamines
- Antiseptic cream
- Insect repellent
- Plasters/Band-aids
- Imodium (Lomotil) for emergency diarrhoea treatment
- Lint and sealed bandages
- Paracetamol/aspirin
- Multivitamin and mineral tablets
- Rehydration sachets
- Calamine lotion
- Hypodermic needles and sterilized skin wipes
- Thrush and cystitis remedies

not malarial there are occasional outbreaks of **dengue fever**, the most recent one in late 2006, when there were a number of fatalities as a result. There is no vaccine for this viral infection, most common during the rainy summer season, but serious cases are rare. Prevention is the best policy: dengue mosquitoes bite during the day, so avoid dark colours, which attract mosquitoes, and ensure you have effective repellent on exposed skin. Symptoms develop rapidly following infection and include extreme aches and pains in the bones and joints, severe headaches, dizziness, fever and vomiting. Should you experience any of these symptoms, seek medical advice as soon as possible.

AIDS and HIV

The expansion of the sex trade in Havana threatens state control of the disease, but for now at least the risk of contracting **AIDS** in Cuba remains very low. All the usual common-sense precautions of course still apply, while the poor quality of Cuban **condoms** means it's worth bringing your own supply. Note that anyone planning on staying in Cuba longer than ninety days is required upon entry to show proof of their HIV-negative status.

Hospitals, clinics and pharmacies

Don't visit Cuba assuming that the country's world-famous **free health service** extends to foreign visitors – far from it. In fact, the government has used the advances made in medicine to earn extra revenue for the regime, through a system of **health tourism**. Each year, thousands of foreigners come to Cuba for everything from surgery (especially a night blindness operation unique to the island) to relaxation at a network of anti-stress clinics. Such services don't come cheap, and effectively subsidize healthcare for Cubans.

Even with all the government investment in the medical sector, Cuba's health service has been hit hard by the US trade embargo. The worst affected area is the supply of medicines, and some hospitals now simply cannot treat patients through lack of resources.

Hospitals and clinics

There are specific **hospitals** which accept foreign patients and one or two that are exclusively for non-nationals, most of them run by **Cubanacan** and its subsidiary **Servimed** (ⓦ www.servimedcuba.com), an organization set up in 1994 to deal exclusively with health tourism. The only general **hospital for foreigners**, as compared to the various institutions set up for specific ailments and conditions, is the Clínica Central Cira García (☎ 7/204-2880 & 204-2811 50 13, ⓦ www.cirag.cu) at Calle 20 no.4101 esq. 41 in the capital's Miramar district. The Hospital Hermanos Ameijeiras at San Lázaro no.701 e/ Padre Varela y Marqués González in Centro Habana (☎ 7/876-1000), considered the best of its kind in Cuba, has two floors reserved for foreign patients.

If you do wind up in hospital in Cuba, one of the first things you or someone you know should do is contact **Asistur** (☎ 7/866-4499; ⓦ www.asistur.cu), who usually deal with insurance claims on behalf of the hospital, as well as offering various kinds of assistance, from supplying ambulances and wheelchairs to obtaining and sending medical reports. However, for minor complaints you shouldn't have to go further than the **hotel doctor**, who will give you a consultation. If you're staying in a *casa particular*, things are slightly more complicated. Your best bet, if you feel ill, is to inform your hosts, who should be able to call the family doctor, the *médico de la familia*, and arrange a house-call. This is common practice in Cuba where, with one doctor for every 169 inhabitants, it's possible for them to personally visit all their patients.

There is no single **emergency number** for ringing an ambulance, but you can call ☎ 7/838-1185 or 838-2185 to get one. You can also contact Asistur, on their emergency number (☎ 7/866-8339).

Pharmacies

Ninety-five per cent of the **pharmacies** in the city are of little use to non-prescription-wielding tourists. They are desperately low on medicines, another poignant reminder of the effects of the US embargo, and stock a tiny fraction of what you can find in the small number of international pharmacies located in upmarket hotels. The *Comodoro* in Miramar (☎7/204-9385) has the best pharmacy, though the *Sevilla* in Habana Vieja (☎7/861-5703) and *Habana Libre* in Vedado (☎7/838-4593) offer good alternatives. Even in these there is not the range of medicines that you might expect, and if you have a preferred brand or type of painkiller, or any other everyday drug, you should bring it with you. For natural remedies head for the Farmacia Taquechel on Obispo in Habana Vieja (see p.65) or the pharmacy in the Focsa building shopping complex at Calle 17 esq. L Vedado (see p.161).

Medical resources for travellers

US and Canada

Canadian Society for International Health ☎613/241-5785, ⊛www.csih.org. Extensive list of travel health centres.

CDC ☎1-800/232 4636, ⊛www.cdc.gov/travel. Official US government travel health site.
International Society for Travel Medicine ☎1-770/736-7060, ⊛www.istm.org. Has a full list of travel health clinics.

Australia, New Zealand and South Africa

Travellers' Medical and Vaccination Centre ☎1300/658 844, ⊛www.tmvc.com.au. Lists travel clinics in Australia, New Zealand and South Africa.

UK and Ireland

Hospital for Tropical Diseases Travel Clinic ☎0845/155 5000, ☎020/7388 9600 (Travel Clinic), ⊛www.thehtd.org.
MASTA ☎0870/606 2782, ⊛www.masta-travel-health.com.
Travel Medicine Clinic ☎028/9031 5220.
Tropical Medical Bureau ☎1850/487 674, ⊛www.tmb.ie.

Money

In Cuba there are two units of currency, the Cuban peso (CUP) and the Cuban convertible peso (CUC). While Cuban salaries are paid in Cuban pesos (*pesos cubanos*), the vast majority of foreign visitors use convertible pesos (*pesos convertibles*), divided into centavos and, like the Cuban peso, completely worthless and unobtainable outside of Cuba. The colour and images on convertible peso banknotes are distinct from those on regular pesos and the notes clearly feature the words "pesos convertibles." The banknote denominations are 100, 50, 25, 10, 5 and 1, while there are 50¢, 25¢, 10¢ and 5¢ coins. At the time of writing 1 convertible peso ($1CUC) is worth 24 national pesos ($24CUP), equivalent to £0.67, €0.75 or US$1.08. For years until 2004 the exchange rate between the convertible peso and the US dollar was fixed at $1CUC to US$1, but since that year a hefty tax of around ten percent has been levied on all exchanges of US dollars to convertible pesos. This tax has effectively been reflected in the exchange rate, making a dollar worth less in Cuba now than it was before 2004.

The Cuban peso, which is also referred to as the **national peso** (*peso nacional* or *moneda nacional*), is also divided into 100 centavos. Banknotes are issued in denominations of 50, 20, 10, 5, 3 and 1. The lowest-value coin is the worthless 1¢, followed by the 5¢, 20¢, 1-peso and 3-peso coins, the last adorned with the face of Che Guevara.

This confusing dual-currency system has its own vocabulary, consisting of a collection of widely used terms and slang words (see Language, p.226). The first thing to learn when trying to make sense of it all is that both national pesos and convertible pesos are represented with the dollar sign ($). Sometimes common sense is the only indicator you will have to determine which of the two currencies a price is given in, but the most commonly used qualifiers are *divisas* for convertible pesos and *moneda nacional* for Cuban pesos. Thus one national peso is sometimes written $1MN. However, many Cubans refer to either currency as pesos, in which case you may have to ask if they mean *pesos cubanos* or *pesos convertibles*.

Traveller's cheques, credit/debit cards and ATMs

Hard currency is king in Havana, and although you'll generally be OK using **credit cards** in the upmarket hotels, restaurants and touristy shops, when dealing with any kind of private enterprise, from paladars to puncture repairs, anything other than cash isn't worth a centavo. Wherever you are it pays to always have at least some money in **cash**, particularly given that power cuts are common in Cuba and sometimes render credit cards unusable. By bringing your money (though not US dollars) in cash or Traveller's cheques, you will avoid the ten percent commission levied on all credit and debit card transactions and withdrawals. **Scottish** and **Northern Irish** banknotes and coins cannot be exchanged in Cuba.

Traveller's cheques

Although **Traveller's cheques** are easily exchangeable for cash in many banks and bureaux de change (*cambios*), subject to a small commission of 2.5 to 4 percent, a significant number of shops and restaurants refuse to accept them, and US-dollar Traveller's cheques will be subject to an additional ten percent tax. Complicating matters further, most banks and *cambios* require a receipt as proof of purchase when cashing Traveller's cheques. Also, make sure that your signature is identical to the one on the original cheque submitted: cashiers have been known to refuse to cash cheques with

Pricing and the dual currency system

The general rule for most visitors is to assume that everything will be paid for with **convertible pesos**. Ninety-nine percent of state-run hotels, most state-run restaurants, most bars, nightclubs and music venues and the vast majority of shop products are priced in convertible pesos, though you can use **euros** in one or two restaurants and other establishments. You'll be expected to pay for a room in a *casa particular*, a meal in a paladar and most private taxis in cash with convertible pesos, though there is occasionally some flexibility.

Entrance to most cinemas and sports arenas, rides on local buses, street snacks and food from agromercados are all paid for with **national pesos**, while some shops away from the touristy areas and streets stock products priced in national pesos too. There are also goods and services, such as stamps and, most notably, long-distance transport, that can be paid for with either currency. Sometimes this means the national peso charge applies only to Cubans, while non-Cubans pay the equivalent in convertible pesos, as is the case with tollgates on roads and museum entrance fees. However, in some instances tourists are merely advised rather than obliged to pay in convertible pesos, and by doing so occasionally enjoy some kind of benefit, such as being able to bypass a waiting list or queue. It should be noted, however, that though foreign passport holders are generally obliged to pay for hotel rooms in convertible pesos, it is perfectly legal for a non-Cuban to use national pesos in most circumstances where the currency is valid, despite the funny looks or contrary advice you might well receive.

It's best to carry convertible pesos in **low denominations**, as many shops and restaurants simply won't have enough change. Be particularly wary of this at bus and train stations or you may find yourself unable to buy a ticket. If you do end up having to use a $50CUC or $100CUC note, you will usually be asked to show your passport for security. The slightest **tear** in any banknote means it is likely to be refused.

---

seemingly minor discrepancies like, for example, an "I" dotted in a different place.

Credit/debit cards and ATMs

Credit cards – though predominantly only Visa and MasterCard – are more widely accepted than Traveller's cheques for purchases, but **debit cards** such as Maestro and Cirrus are not accepted at all, so a Visa debit card is your only real option. No cards issued by a US bank are accepted in Cuba and nor is American Express or Diners Club, regardless of the country of issue. For most Cubans, plastic remains an unfamiliar alternative to cash, and you should be careful not to rely exclusively on your credit or debit card as a form of payment.

The number of **ATMs** in Havana is slowly increasing but there are still relatively few and most of them only accept cards issued by Cuban banks. Among those that do accept foreign cards, very few take anything

other than Visa, and again none accept cards issued by US banks. Most ATMs display stickers stating clearly the cards they accept. Those that take foreign cards are generally found in top-class hotels, branches of the Banco Financiero Internacional and the Banco de Crédito y Comercio, or one or two CADECA *casas de cambio*.

As with all transactions involving a foreign credit or debit card in Cuba, the amount you withdraw or spend in convertible pesos will be converted into US dollars to allow your bank or card issuer to then convert US dollars to your home currency (so, at the current exchange rate, if you withdraw $100CUC it will appear as US$108 on your transaction receipt). When using ATMs, there will also be a commission charge, details of which should appear on the withdrawal slip issued with your cash. Credit cards are more useful for obtaining **cash advances**, though be aware of the interest charges that these will incur. For most cash advances you'll need to deal with a bank clerk. There is no longer a minimum withdrawal when dealing with a bank clerk, and a maximum limit of $5000CUC.

Banks and exchange

Banking hours in Havana are generally Monday to Friday 8am to 3pm; to exchange money outside of these hours you'll need to seek out a hotel with a bureau de change (see below).

Foreign currency transactions are commonly dealt with by the government body CADECA, which runs its own *casas de cambio*, often in white kiosks at the side of the road. They are also in buildings that look more like banks, including a branch at Obispo no.257 e/ Aguiar y Cuba in Habana Vieja where you can use a credit or debit card. These *casas de cambio* are also where to change convertible pesos into national pesos. No commission is charged for these transactions and there is no minimum or maximum quantity restriction. Opening hours are generally Monday to Saturday 9am to 6pm and often Sunday 8.30am to 12.30pm.

Black market salesmen often hang around outside *casas de cambio* and may offer a favourable exchange rate for buying national pesos or, sometimes more tempting, the opportunity of buying national pesos without having to queue. Although dealing with a black market salesman is unlikely to get you into any trouble, it should generally be avoided as it could result in a prison sentence for the Cuban. You may also be approached by people on the street offering to exchange your money, sometimes at an exceptionally good rate. This is always a con.

The Banco Financiero Internacional is the most efficient and experienced at dealing with foreign currency transactions and has a number of branches in Havana. Also generally reliable is the Banco de Crédito y Comercio, which has a wider spread of branches. Be warned that some banks are only equipped to deal with national pesos, and are therefore useless as far as foreign visitors are concerned. Also note that you'll need to show your passport for any transaction at a bank.

Most of the larger **hotels** have *cambios*, where you can exchange money, with more flexible hours than the banks – the *cambios* at the *Hotel Sevilla* in Habana Vieja (daily 8am–8pm) and the *Hotel Nacional* in Vedado (daily 8am–noon & 1–8pm) are two of the only places in the city where you can withdraw or exchange money late in the evening or on a Sunday. Commission for changing foreign cash to convertible pesos ranges from two to four percent.

Financial difficulties

For any kind of money problems, including insurance claims, most people are directed to **Asistur** (ⓦwww.asistur.cu), set up specifically to provide assistance to tourists with financial difficulties, as well as offering advice on a number of other matters, legal and otherwise. Asistur can arrange to have money sent to you from abroad as well as providing loans or cash advances. The main branch is on the Paseo del Prado no.208–212 esq. Trocadero (Ⓣ7/866-8920, 866-8339 & 866-8527, ⓔasisten@asistur.cu) on the Habana Vieja–Centro Habana border. If you have a problem with your credit card or if it gets stolen, go to the Centro de Tarjetas Internacional at Calle 23 e/ L y M (Ⓣ7/833-4466), underneath the Habana Libre in Vedado, where they can cancel cards and access details of recent card transactions.

The media

All types of media in Cuba are tightly censored and closely controlled by the state. While this means that the range of information and opinion is severely restricted and biased, it has also produced media geared to producing (what the government deems to be) socially valuable content, refreshingly free of any significant concern for high ratings and commercial success.

Newspapers and magazines

There are very few **international newspapers** available in Cuba, a couple of Spanish and Italian dailies being the only ones that appear with any regularity. Away from the more sophisticated hotels you're unlikely to find even these, and tracking down an English-language newspaper of any description is an arduous, usually unrewarding task. The growing number of **bookshops** sometimes stock non-Cuban newspapers and magazines, though editions are often months, or even years, out of date.

The main **national newspaper**, *Granma* (Ⓦ www.granma.cu), openly declares itself the official mouthpiece of the Cuban Communist Party. The stories in its eight tabloid-size pages are largely of a political or economic nature, usually publicizing meetings with foreign heads of state, denouncing US policy towards Cuba, or announcing developments within sectors of industry or commerce with some arts coverage. Raúl Castro's speeches or Fidel Castro's musings are often published in their entirety and the international news has a marked Latin American bias. Articles challenging the official party line do appear, but these are usually directed at specific events and policies rather than overall ideologies. Hotels are more likely to stock the weekly *Granma Internacional* (50¢). Printed in Spanish, English, French, German, Italian, Turkish and Portuguese editions, it offers a roundup of the week's stories. There are two other national papers: *Trabajadores*, representing the workers' unions, and *Juventud Rebelde*, founded in 1965 as the voice of Cuban youth. Content is similar, though *Juventud Rebelde*, in its Thursday edition, features weekly listings for cultural events and has more articles that regularly critique social issues.

Among the most cultured of Cuba's **magazines** is *Bohemia* (Ⓦ www.bohemia .cu), Cuba's oldest surviving periodical, whose relatively broad focus offers a mix of current affairs, historical essays and regular spotlights on art, sport and technology. The best of the more specialized publications are the bimonthly *Revolución y Cultura*, concentrating on the arts and literature, and the tri-monthly *Artecubano*, a magazine of book-like proportions tracking the visual arts. There are a number of other worthy magazines, such as *La Gaceta de Cuba*, covering all forms of art, from music and painting to radio and television; *Temas*, whose scope includes political theory and contemporary society; and *Clave*, which focuses on music.

Radio

There are eight national **radio** stations in Cuba, but tuning into them isn't always easy, as signal strength varies considerably from place to place. You're most likely to hear broadcasts from **Radio Taíno** (Ⓦ www .radiotainocubasi.cu), the official tourist station, and the only one on which any English is spoken, albeit sporadically. Playing predominantly mainstream pop and Cuban music, Radio Taíno is also a useful source of up-to-date tourist information such as the latest nightspots, forthcoming events and places to eat.

Musically speaking, other than the ever-popular sounds of Cuban *salsa*, stations rarely stray away from safe-bet US, Latin and European pop and rock. The predominantly classical music content of

Radio Musical Nacional is about as specialist as it gets.

Of the remaining stations there is little to distinguish one from the other. The exception is **Radio Reloj**, a 24-hour news station with reports read out to the ceaseless sound of a ticking clock in the background, as the exact time is announced every minute on the minute.

National Cuban radio stations and frequencies

Radio Arte (FM). Dramas and documentaries.
Radio Enciclopedia (1260MW/94.1FM). Strictly instrumental music drawn from various genres.
Radio Habana Cuba (106.9FM). News and chat in a number of languages.
Radio Musical Nacional (590MW/99.1FM). Internationally renowned classical music.
Radio Progreso (640MW/90.3FM). Music and drama broadcast daily 3–6pm.
Radio Rebelde (670 and 710MW/96.7FM). Sport, current affairs and music.
Radio Reloj (950MW/101.5FM). National and international news 24hr a day.
Radio Taíno (1290MW/93.2–93.4FM). Tourist station playing popular Cuban and international music.

Television

There are four national **television channels** in Cuba: Cubavisión, Telerebelde, Canal Educativo and Canal Educativo 2, all commercial-free but with a profusion of public service broadcasts, revolutionary slogans and daily slots commemorating historical events and figures. None of them broadcasts 24 hours and sometimes, particularly on Sundays, they do not begin transmitting until late in the day, though usually they are running by 9am.

Surprisingly, given the sour relationship between Cuba and the US, **Hollywood**

films are a staple on TV, sometimes preceded by a discussion of the film's value and its central issues. The frequent use of Spanish subtitles makes them watchable for non-Spanish speakers. Cubavisión shows most of the films, and for years has broadcast two of them, usually well-known blockbusters, on Saturday nights starting around 10pm.

Cubavisión also hosts another long-standing Cuban television tradition, the staggeringly popular **telenovela** soap operas, both homegrown and imported (usually from Brazil or Colombia). There are also several weekly music programmes showcasing the best of contemporary Cuban music as well as popular international artists. Saturday evenings are the best time to catch live-broadcast performances from the cream of the national salsa scene.

Telerebelde is the best channel for **sports**, with live national-league baseball games shown almost daily throughout the season, and basketball, volleyball and boxing making up the bulk of the rest. As the names suggest, both Canal Educativo channels are full of educational programmes, including courses in languages, cookery and various academic disciplines.

Officially, **satellite TV** is the exclusive domain of the hotels, which come with a reasonable range of satellite channels, though you won't find BBC or VOA. Cuba's international channel is Cubavisión Internacional, designed for tourists and showing a mixture of films, documentaries and music programmes.

The best places to look for **programme times** are in the pages of *Granma* and, for Cubavisión Internacional, *Opciones*. The plusher hotels usually carry a TV schedule magazine for the satellite channels.

Culture and etiquette

There are a few cultural idiosyncrasies in Cuba worth bearing in mind. Cubans tend to be fairly conventional in their appearance, and view some Western fashions, especially scruffy traveller garb, with circumspection, mainly because Cubans in similar dress (and there are a number around in Havana) are seen as anti-establishment. Anyone with piercings or dreadlocks may find themselves checked rigorously at customs and occasionally asked to show their passport to the police.

Many **shops** restrict entrance to a few people at a time, and although as a tourist you may bypass the queue, you'll win more friends if you ask "*¿el último?*" (who's last?) and take your turn.

Service charges of 10–12 percent are becoming increasingly common in state restaurants and in smarter paladars. It is mandatory to pay this, so it's wise to check whether it will be included before ordering, as it is not always stated on the bill. In state restaurants where it is not included you should tip at your discretion; in paladars tips aren't expected but always welcome. You should normally tip when you use a state-run taxi; if you do catch a privately run *maquina* taxi, tipping is not expected as your fare goes wholesale the driver and as a tourist it will probably have been negotiated. A tip can sometimes open previously closed doors, like viewing the interior of a private building or an otherwise closed museum. It's also customary to tip the attendant in a hotel toilet, should there be one, with at least some loose change.

Public toilets

Public toilets are few and far between in Havana, and even fast-food joints often don't have a washroom. The best places for public toilets are hotels, as generally these are regularly cleaned and well maintained. But even these sometimes suffer from a lack of **toilet paper** – carry your own supply in case. No plumbing system, be it in a *casa particular* or hotel, can cope with waste paper, so to avoid blockages remember to dispose of your paper in the bins provided. In Habana Vieja there is a public toilet at Mercaderes e/ Amargura y Plaza Vieja.

Travel essentials

Costs

Havana is not a particularly cheap place to visit, but with some considerable effort it is possible to get by on a low budget. Most visitors stick to using convertible pesos for all their spending, in which case you can expect to need a **minimum weekly budget** of $220CUC, based on sharing a double room in a *casa particular*, eating in cheaper restaurants and at your *casa particular*, travelling by Habana Bus Tour and taxi and choosing the cheapest nightspots. On the other hand, if you stay in any of the hotels bar the cheapest half dozen, eat at a decent spread of restaurants throughout the week and go out every other night to the higher-profile music and club venues, expect a spend closer to $600CUC. If you are determined to keep costs to a minimum you should aim to do as much of your spending as possible with national pesos, in which case it's possible to get by on the equivalent of around $110CUC per week.

Though **museum entrance** costs are generally low, often only a convertible peso or two and in some cases free, most places charge a larger sum to take photos (typically $2–$5CUC) and as much as $25CUC to enter with a video camera.

Crime and personal safety

Regrettably, crimes against visitors are on the rise in Havana (including some violent crime), so it pays to be careful. In the vast majority of cases, the worst you're likely to experience is incessant attention from *jineteros*, *jineteras* and hustlers, but a few simple precautions will help ensure that you don't fall prey to any petty crime.

Some travellers have reported **thefts from luggage** during baggage handling both on arrival and departure, so consider carrying valuables in your hand luggage, using suitcase locks and having bags shrink-wrapped before check-in.

The most common assault upon tourists once you've arrived into Havana itself is **bag-snatching** or **pickpocketing**, so always make sure you sling bags across your body rather than letting them dangle from one shoulder, keep cameras concealed whenever possible, don't carry valuables in easy-to-reach pockets and always carry only the minimum amount of cash. A common trick is for thieves on bicycles to ride past and snatch at bags, hats and sunglasses, so wear these at your discretion. Needless to say, don't leave bags and possessions unattended anywhere, but be especially vigilant on beaches, where it can take a skilful thief a mere moment to be off with your possessions. While there's no need to be suspicious of everyone who tries to strike up a conversation with you (and many people will), a measure of caution is still advisable. There has been a marked increase in bag-snatching in Centro Habana (and some isolated cases of **violent muggings**), so be particularly vigilant during the day and avoid walking around the area at night.

Other than this, watch out for **scams** from wily street operators. Never accept the offer of money changers on the street, as some will take your money and run – literally – or give you a roll of notes that on closer inspection proves to be just rolled-up paper. You should also avoid using unregistered taxis and never take a ride in a cab where "a friend" is accompanying the driver. Although you're unlikely in this scenario to suffer a violent attack, you may well find yourself pickpocketed. This is a particularly common trick on arrival at the airport, where you should be extra vigilant.

Some **hotels** are not entirely secure, so be sure to put any valuables in the hotel security box, if there is one, or at least stash them out of sight. Registered *casas particulares* are, as a rule, safe, but you stay in an unregistered one at your peril. If you have a **rental car**, be aware that these can sometimes be seen as easy pickings. Take all the usual sensible precautions: leave nothing visible in your car – including items you may consider worthless like maps or snacks – even if you're only away from it for a short period of time. Furthermore, thieves may break into and damage cars to take radios, wing mirrors or spare parts. To avoid this, always park in a car park, guarded compound or other secure place. Car rental agencies will be able to advise you on those nearest to you, or, failing that, ask at a large hotel. *Casas particulares* owners will also be able to tell you where to park safely.

If the worst happens and you suffer a **break-in**, call the rental company first as they should have supplied you with an emergency number. They can advise you how to proceed and will either inform the police themselves or direct you to the correct police station. You must report the crime to be able to get a replacement car and for your own insurance purposes. There have also been occasional reports of attacks by hitchhikers, so if you are going to pick people up exercise caution.

You should always carry a photocopy of your **passport** (not the passport itself), as the police sometimes ask to inspect them.

Police

Habana Vieja's police headquarters are in the mock-colonial fort at Tacón e/ San Ignacio y Cuba. The main station in Centro Habana is at Dragones e/ Lealtad y Escobar (☏7/866-3707). In an emergency ring ☏106.

Emergencies

Should you be unfortunate enough to be robbed and want to make an insurance claim, you must report the crime to the **police** and get a **statement**. Be aware, though, that the police in Cuba are generally indifferent to crimes against tourists – and may even try to blame you for not being more vigilant. You must insist upon getting the statement there and then, as there is little chance of receiving anything from them at a later date. Unfortunately, the chance of your possessions being recovered is equally remote.

After seeing the police, you may find it more useful to contact **Asistur** (Prado no. 208 e/ Trocadero y Colón, Habana Vieja ☏7/866-4499, ⓦwww.asistur.cu), the

Jineterismo

The complex and contentious issue of **jineterismo**, a Cuban-coined term, is reflected in the rather hazy definition and use of the word itself. In general, the pejorative term *jinetero* refers to a male hustler, or someone who will find girls, cigars, taxis or accommodation for a foreign visitor and then take a cut for the service. He – though more commonly this is the preserve of his female counterpart, a *jinetera* – is often also the sexual partner to a foreigner, usually for material gain. In the eyes of Cubans, being a *jinetero* or *jinetera* can mean anything from prostitute to paid escort, opportunist to simply a Cuban boyfriend or girlfriend. As an obvious foreign face in Havana you will often be pursued by persistent *jineteros* and *jineteras*.

Immediately after assuming power, Castro's regime banned prostitution and, officially at least, wiped it off the streets. The resurgence of the tourist industry has seen prostitution slink back into business but the exchange of services is not always straightforward. Many Cubans are desperate to leave the country and see marrying a foreigner as the best way out, while others simply want to live the good life and are more than happy to spend a few days pampering the egos of Westerners in order to go to the best clubs and restaurants and be bought the latest fashions.

Legislation introduced in 2003 has given police the right to stop tourists' cars and question Cuban passengers they suspect to be *jineteros*, and *casas particulares* must register all Cuban guests accompanying foreigners (foreigners themselves are not penalized in any way).

24-hour assistance agency, which can arrange replacement travel documents, help with financial difficulties and recover lost luggage. In the case of a serious emergency, you should notify your foreign consul (see p.42).

Women travellers

Though violent sexual attacks against female tourists are virtually unheard of, female visitors to Havana should brace themselves for a quite remarkable level of attention. Casual sex is a staple of Cuban life and **unaccompanied women** are generally assumed to be on holiday for exactly that reason, with protestations to the contrary generally greeted with sheer disbelief. The nonstop attention can be unnerving, but in general, Cuban men manage to combine a courtly romanticism with wit and charm, meaning the persistent come-ons will probably leave you irritated rather than threatened. It's worth knowing, too, that some of your would-be suitors are likely to be *jineteros*.

If you are not interested, there's no surefire way to stop the flow of comments and approaches, but decisively saying "no", not wearing skimpy clothing and avoiding eye contact with men you don't know will lessen the flow of attention a little. You could also resort to wearing a wedding ring. However, it's as well to remember that even a few hours of friendship with a Cuban man can lead to pledges of eternal love. Flattering though such a pledge may be, it's most likely nothing to do with your personal charms but because **marriage to a foreigner** is a tried-and-tested method of emigrating.

Electricity

The **electricity** supply is generally 110V/60Hz, but always check, as in some hotels it is 220V. Some hotels also have adaptors which guests may borrow. Private houses are sometimes prey to scheduled power cuts for both electricity and gas, an energy-saving device introduced during the Special Period to help conserve limited fuel resources. If you stay in a tourist hotel you are unlikely to be affected by this.

Entry requirements

Citizens of most Western countries must have a ten-year passport, valid for two months after your departure from Cuba, plus a **tourist card** (*tarjeta del turista*), essentially a **visa**, to enter Cuba. Tourist cards are valid for a standard thirty days, though for Canadians they are valid for ninety days, and must be used within 180 days of issue. Although you can buy one from the Cuban Consulate, usually available instantly, some tour operators, airlines and travel agents can sell you one when you purchase your flight. As well as a completed application form and the relevant payment you'll need a photocopy of the main page of your passport and confirmation of your travel arrangements, specifically a return plane ticket and an accommodation booking. The charge in the UK is £15, in Canada between CAN$20 and CAN$30, in Australia A$35 and in New Zealand NZ$44.

On arrival in Cuba, at immigration control, you will have to fill in an **International Embarkation and Disembarkation Form**, detailing the address of where you initially intend to stay. Although you are permitted to put the name of a registered *casa particular* or a friend's house, you will pass through immigration much more smoothly if you enter the name of a state hotel – rarely is this ever checked. Be aware that if you don't have any address you may be forced to pay on the spot for three nights' accommodation in a hotel of the state's choosing. You will not be permitted entry to Cuba without an onward or return plane ticket.

Once in Cuba, you can **renew a tourist card** for another thirty days for a fee of $25CUC. To do this either consult one of the *buros de turismo* found in the more upmarket hotels or go to the immigration office in Nuevo Vedado at Factor esq. Final (Mon–Fri 8.30am–3pm) – arrive early and expect delays. You must pay your $25CUC fee in special stamps, which you can buy from banks. When renewing your visa you will need details (perhaps including a receipt) of where you are staying.

Should you wish to stay longer than sixty days as a tourist (120 if you are Canadian) you will have to leave Cuban territory and return with a new tourist card. Many people do this by flying to Mexico and getting another tourist card from the Cuban Consulate there.

Embassies and consulates

There are no consulates or embassies in Cuba for Australia or New Zealand; citizens are advised to go to either the Canadian or UK embassies.

Canada Embassy, Calle 30 no.518, Miramar ☎7/204-2516 & 204-2382, ⨍204-2044.
South Africa Embassy, Ave. 5ta no.4201 esq. 42, Miramar ☎7/204-9671 & 204-9676, ⨍204-1101.
UK Embassy, Calle 34 no.702–704, Miramar ☎7/204-1771, ⨍204-8104.
US Special Interests Section, Calzada e/ L y M, Vedado ☎7/833-3551 to 59 & 833-3543, ⨍833-2095.

Cuban consulates and embassies abroad

Australia Consulate-General, Ground Floor, 128 Chalmers Street, Surry Hills, Sydney ☎02/9698 9797, ⨍8399 1106.
Canada Embassy, 388 Main St, Ottawa, Ontario K1S 1E3 ☎613/563-0141. Consulate-General, 4542–4546 Decarie Boulevard, Montreal H4A 3P2 ☎514/843-8897 ⨍845-1063.
Ireland Embassy, 2 Adelaide Court, Adelaide Rd, Dublin ☎353/1475 0899.
UK Embassy and Consulate, 167 High Holborn, London WC1 ☎020/7240 2488; 24hr visa and information service ☎0891/880 820.
US Cuban Interests Section, 2630 16th St NW, Washington DC 20009 ☎202/797-8518. Consulate Office, 2639 16th St NW, Washington DC 20009 ☎202/797-8609.

Insurance

Travel insurance is vital in case of accident or serious illness in Havana (particularly given the expense of Cuban medical expertise), and handy in case of theft or loss of belong- ings. Before paying for a new policy, however, check whether you are already covered: some all-risks home insurance policies may cover your possessions when overseas, and many private medical schemes include coverage when abroad.

When securing baggage cover, make sure that the per-article limit – typically under £500 – will cover your most valuable possessions. If you need to make a claim, you should keep **receipts** for medicines and medical treatment, and in the event you have anything stolen, you must obtain an official statement from the police.

Internet

Getting **internet access** in Havana is still not particularly easy or cheap. Cybercafés are few and far between, and finding somewhere with a reliable, fast connection a considerable challenge. The **hotels** offer the fastest and most robust connections but their rates can be exorbitant, commonly charging between $6CUC and $10CUC an hour. Those hotels best equipped for internet use are the *Florida*, *Inglaterra* and *Parque Central* in Habana Vieja, the *Meliá Cohiba* and *Habana Libre* in Vedado and the *Meliá Habana* in Miramar.

ETECSA, which runs the national telephone network, operates what it calls **Telepuntos** and **Minipuntos**, where you can get online (see box below), although often with a painfully slow connection. Minipuntos are large walk-in phone booths, some of which also have a couple of computer terminals offering internet access. Telepuntos centres, of which there are only two in Havana, are much larger, contain around ten internet terminals and offer a number of other services, including fax facilities, sale of prepaid phone cards and telephone cabins. Some of their services are offered in national pesos, but foreign visitors are likely to be charged in convertible pesos and may be

Telepuntos and Minipuntos

Minipunto Calle 23 esq. P, Vedado ☎7/838-1225.
Minipunto Ave. 3ra esq. 70 ☎7/202-9522.
Telepunto Obispo no.351 esq. Habana, Habana Vieja ☎7/866-0111.
Telepunto Aguila no.565 esq. Dragones, Centro Habana ☎7/866-4646.

required to show a passport for internet access. Currently, charges in Telepuntos and Minipuntos are 10¢ per min with a minimum charge of $6CUC, giving you an hour online.

Having always been keen to control the flow of information to the Cuban public, the government has, unsurprisingly, restricted its citizens' access to the web. However, though private home internet connections are illegal, Cubans can now go online in Telepuntos and Minipuntos. They also have access to Cuba-based email accounts, and there is an increasing number of homes in Havana with online addresses, most notably *casas particulares*, though those with computers are still in a significant minority. All hotels now have email addresses but most restaurants do not.

Laundry

There are few public laundry services in Cuba. Most people do their own or rely on the hotel service, although if you are staying in a *casa particular* your landlady is likely to offer to do yours for you for a small extra charge.

Mail

There's a good chance you'll get back home from Havana before your postcards do. Don't expect **airmail** to reach Europe or North America in less than two weeks, while it is not unknown for **letters** to arrive a month or more after they have been sent. **Theft** is so widespread within the postal system that if you send anything other than a letter there's a significant chance that it won't arrive at all. You should also be aware that letters and packages coming into Cuba are sometimes opened as a matter of government policy.

Stamps are sold in both convertible and national pesos at post offices (from white-and-blue kiosks marked Correos de Cuba) and, for convertible pesos only, in many hotels. Convertible peso rates are reasonable at 75¢ for a postcard or letter to the US or Canada, 85¢ to Europe and 90¢ to the rest of the world. However, if you request **national peso stamps**, which you are entitled to do, at between 40¢ and 75¢ for postcards and marginally more for letters, it can work out over fifteen times cheaper.

There are **post offices** in Habana Vieja, Centro Habana, Vedado and Miramar, normally open Monday to Saturday from 8am to 6pm. The branch at Paseo del Prado esq. San Martín in Habana Vieja has poste restante facilities – letters or packages should be marked *lista de correos* and will be held for about a month; you'll need your passport for collection. A more reliable alternative is to have mail sent to a hotel, which you need not necessarily be staying in, marked *esperar*, followed by the name of the addressee. They will usually hold mail for at least a week, often longer, even for non-guests. Some of the larger hotels offer a full range of postal services, including DHL and the Cuban equivalent Cubanacán Express, usually at the desk marked Telecorreos.

Maps

The maps in this guide should be all you need but if you do decide to purchase a locally produced version, the best map shop in the city is El Navegante at Mercaderes no. 115, e/ Obispo y Obrapía in Habana Vieja (☏7/861-3625).

Opening hours and public holidays

Cuban offices are typically open for business Monday to Friday 8.30am to 5pm, with many of them closing for a one-hour lunch

National holidays

January 1 Liberation Day. Anniversary of the triumph of the Revolution.
May 1 International Workers' Day.
July 25–27 Celebration of the national rebellion.
October 10 Anniversary of the start of the Wars of Independence.
December 25 Christmas Day.

break anywhere between noon and 2pm. **Shops** are generally open Monday to Saturday 9am–6pm, sometimes closing for lunch, while the shopping malls and department stores stay open as late as 8pm. Sunday trading is increasingly common, with most places open until noon or 1pm. Hotel shops stay open all day. Banks generally operate Monday to Friday 8am to 3pm.

Theoretically, **museums** are usually open six days a week (Mon–Sat or more usually Tues–Sun) from 9am to between 5pm and 7pm, with an hour (or two) for lunch. Those open on Sunday generally close in the afternoon. However opening hours – particularly for smaller establishments – are not an exact science, and you may arrive to find them closed for no discernable reason.

Phones

The chances are that it will be cheaper to use your mobile phone than a payphone to ring abroad from Cuba, though US travellers may encounter added complications. However, if you are making a call to a Cuban number then it's much more economical to use a payphone.

Mobile phones

Cubacel (☎5/264-2266, ⓦwww.cubacel.com), which is part of ETECSA, the national telecommunications company, is the sole **mobile phone service provider** in Cuba, and if you intend to bring your own handset to Cuba you should check first whether or not your service provider has a roaming agreement with them. Most of the major European, Australasian and Canadian operators now have such agreements. In 2009 US President Obama lifted restrictions on US telecommunications firms, allowing them to establish roaming agreements with Cuban companies and to develop the necessary cable and satellite facilities to

enhance communications links between Cuba and the US.

Renting or buying a mobile phone

The alternative to bringing your own handset is to rent or buy one in Cuba, which may be a necessity if your service provider does not have a roaming agreement with Cubacel or you have the wrong kind of mobile phone, though this is less likely now that the Cubacel network supports both GSM and TDMA phones. You can rent a mobile phone from Telepuntos (see box, p.42) or the Cubacel office at Calle 17 y C in Vedado. They offer temporary as well as permanent contracts to visitors and residents alike, but you are more likely to use the **pay-as-you-go** deals using prepaid cards. The prepaid service costs a daily rate of $3CUC for line rental and call rates within Cuba are between 40¢ and 60¢ per minute. You will also be charged to receive calls, though at slightly lower rates. International call rates are currently $2.45CUC to Canada, $2.70CUC to the US and $5.85CUC to Europe, Australia and New Zealand. Prepaid cards are not widely available so make sure you stock up at the provider's office. **Mobile phone numbers** begin with a 5 in Cuba.

Payphones

There are, broadly speaking, two kinds of **payphones** in Havana. The most common kind are blue and don't accept coins, only Chip **prepaid phone cards**. For sale in convertible pesos in denominations of $5CUC, $10CUC and $20CUC, you'll need a Chip card to make an international call from a public telephone. Chip cards are available from post offices, hotels, national travel agents, some banks, Minipuntos and Telepuntos (see box, p.42).

There are also national-peso payphones; they are grey and those with a digital display are just as reliable as their convertible-peso charging counterparts. Most are coin-operated and accept 5¢, 20¢ and 1 peso coins, but some accept Propia prepaid phone cards, charged in national pesos and available in 3, 5 and 7 peso versions. Though this type of phone card is rarely sold in hotels, information offices or touristy

---

Useful numbers

Directory enquiries ☎113
International dialling code for calls to Cuba ☎53
International operator ☎012
National operator ☎00 and ☎011

Infotur offices and buros de turismo

Habana Vieja Obispo e/ Bernaza y Villegas ⑦7/866-3333 & 863-6884, ⑥obispdir @enet.cu; daily 9am–6pm.

Miramar Ave. 5ta y 112 ⑦7/204-7036, ⑥miramar@enet.cu; daily 10am–6pm.

Playas del Este Ave. 5ta e/ 468 y 470, Guanabo ⑦7/796-6868, ⑥guanadir@enet.cu.

Buros de turismo Obispo esq. San Ignacio, Habana Vieja ⑦7/863-6884; Terminal 3, José Martí International Airport, ⑦7/642-6101; Terminal Víazul, Ave. 26 y Zoológico, Nuevo Vedado ⑦7/883-4729.

shops, you can usually buy them at Telepuntos and they will save you a lot of money if you make regular calls to numbers within Cuba. There are still one or two of the older, rustier versions of these national-peso payphones, which only accept 5¢ coins, have no digital display and are very temperamental. There are national-peso phones in Telepuntos but otherwise they are usually found in places where tourists are unlikely to see them, especially in public buildings like hospitals. It should be noted that international calls on any kind of national-peso phone are impossible.

National rates for payphones are reasonable, starting at 5¢ per min for calls within the same province (see opposite for international rates).

Making a call

To make a **local call** from Havana simply dial the phone number you require. To make a **national call** dial ⑦0 followed by the area code and number and this will give you a direct connection. However, some interprovincial calls are only possible through the operator. If you're consistently failing to get through on a direct line, dial ⑦00 or 011. To ring a Cuban mobile phone from a land line you'll also need to prefix the number with ⑦0.

International calls made from Cuba are charged at exorbitant rates and it is usually cheaper to call from your own mobile phone. The cheapest method is to call from a payphone, as opposed to calling from a hotel – often up to fifty percent more expensive – or a private phone, which can be both confusing and expensive. For international calls without operator assistance, possible from the newer convertible-peso payphones but only on a relatively small proportion of private phones, dial the international call prefix, which is ⑦119, then the country code, the area code and the number.

Currently, a payphone call to the US **costs** $2.45CUC per min; to Canada $1.90CUC per min; to Central America and the Caribbean $2.40CUC per min; to South America $3.20CUC per min and to the rest of the world $3.80CUC per min. However, calling the US from Cuba is subject to a US-based tax, an extra cost of 24.5¢ per min not included in the officially listed call rates. A call connected via the international operator from a payphone incurs even higher call rates, roughly between $1.50CUC and $2CUC more expensive than the standard rate, though a call to Europe and Australia made in this way is charged at a wallet-emptying $8.75CUC per minute.

You cannot make direct overseas phone calls from a private phone in a house in Cuba; instead you must go through the international operator (⑦012). This has its own special complicated procedure and will involve calling reverse charge at exorbitant rates – use a payphone if at all possible.

You may see **telephone numbers** in Havana written as, for example, "866-7711 al 18", meaning that when you dial the final two digits you may have to try all the numbers in between and including 11 and 18 before you get through.

Time

Cuba is on Eastern Standard Time in winter and Eastern Daylight Time in summer. It is five hours behind London, fifteen hours behind Sydney and on the same time as New York.

Cuban Tourist Board offices abroad

Canada 440 Blvd Rene Levesque, Suite 1105, Montréal H2Z 1V7 ☏514/875-8004,
✉montreal@gocuba.ca; 1200 Bay St, Suite 305, Toronto M5R 2A5 ☏416/362-0700,
🌐www.gocuba.ca.
UK 154 Shaftesbury Ave, London WC2H 8JT ☏020/7240 6655, ✉tourism@cubasi
.info (Mon–Fri 10am–7pm).

Tourist information

The Cuban tourist information network **Infotur** (🌐www.infotur.cu) has three proper offices and a number of smaller *buros de turismo* around Havana, including desks in hotel lobbies (see box, p.45). The friendly staff are generally willing to help with all sorts of different queries, though they do try to steer visitors towards the state-run tourist apparatus. They sell a few basic guides and maps, book organized excursions and hotel rooms and provide information on concerts and restaurants. As a state-run venture, Infotur does not officially supply information on paladars or *casas particulares*, though the staff are sometimes willing to help with their own recommendations. Similarly, though they can help you with car rental or the tourist bus service, it is not strictly within their remit to provide information on public transport.

Despite these limitations, however, Infotur remains the best place to go for practical information, and to pick up the useful free monthly listings booklet *Guía La Habana*. There is a desperate shortage of printed tourist, travel and listings information, with public transport maps and paper timetables all but non-existent and the copies of *Guía La Habana* usually in short supply. Given this it makes sense to go online in Havana to get information. Though there are numerous Cuban **websites** featuring tourist information on Havana, all of which are of course state-maintained publications and accordingly uncritical, two of the best websites for up-to-date listings and reliable recommendations for the latest goings-on in the city are foreign sites: The H and Cuba Absolutely (see box below).

Travellers with disabilities

Most of the upmarket hotels are fairly well equipped for **disabled travellers**, each with at least one specially designed room and all the necessary lifts and ramps. Elsewhere in Havana, however, there are very few amenities or services provided. Transport may prove the biggest challenge: the crowded public buses are not modified for wheelchair users, while the tourist buses do not have ramps. Using a taxi is the best option, as accessible car rental is difficult to find. Several taxi companies have people carriers that can accommodate wheelchair users.

Useful websites

🌐**www.bienvenidoscuba.com** Limited but useful monthly listings and practical information for tourists.

🌐**www.cubaabsolutely.com** Excellent, well researched and well written site covering almost everything going on in Havana.

🌐**www.cubatravel.cu** The official website of the Cuban travel industry.

🌐**www.habananuestra.cu** The website of the Oficina del Historiador de la Ciudad is an excellent resource, with an invaluable section on all the latest cultural events in Habana Vieja.

🌐**www.thehmagazine.com** A well-informed site with monthly listings for music, art, dance, theatre, literature and film.

The City

The City

www.roughguides.com

Habana Vieja

T here is no other area in Havana that gives such a vivid and immediate
sense of the city's history as **Habana Vieja** – or Old Havana. Cobbled
plazas, colonial buildings hewn from stone, leafy courtyards, countless
churches, sixteenth-century fortresses and architecture famously ravaged
by time and climate are all remarkably unmarred by modern change or growth.
However, the very lack of urban development between the 1960s and 1990s,
which allowed the historical core to be so untouched, was ironically the same
force that allowed for the area's subsequent decay.

The **restoration projects** that began in the 1990s and turned a spotlight on
Habana Vieja are still visibly underway today, and while classic streets like
Obispo and Mercaderes have been given a new lease of life, this has inevitably
created a more sanitized version of the old town's former self. Yet much of the
rawness of the past remains; dip down the side streets for a vision of the Habana
Vieja of yesteryear, with neighbours chatting over wrought iron window grills
and the interiors of schoolrooms glimpsed in former merchants' mansions.

Habana Vieja is made for exploring **on foot**, with the main sightseeing area
relatively compact. Although the narrow streets and eclectic architecture lend a
sense of wild disorder, it's actually very easy to navigate thanks to the arrangement of its streets on a straightforward grid system. The **Plaza de Armas** is at
the heart of the historic part of the old city and is the logical starting point for
touring the district, with numerous options in all directions, including the
prestigious **Plaza de la Catedral** three blocks away to the north and the larger
but equally historic **Plaza Vieja** five blocks to the south.

For the other unmissable sights head from the Plaza de Armas up **Obispo**,
Habana Vieja's busiest street, to the **Parque Central**. The wide streets and
grand buildings on this western edge of Habana Vieja differ in feel from the rest

The Oficina del Historiador de la Ciudad

The enormous task of restoring and reconstructing Habana Vieja from the ruin and
rubble is planned out and directed by an institution set up specifically for the purpose,
the **Oficina del Historiador de la Ciudad**. The work and influence of this venerable
institution is everywhere in Habana Vieja, its distinctive blue-and-white signs marking
the sites of future and ongoing projects, while it has overseen the building or
rebuilding of almost every hotel, museum, shop and restaurant in the area since the
1990s. It publishes a bi-monthly magazine and a website known as **Opus Habana**;
check either for almost anything going on in Habana Vieja, including details of all the
temporary exhibitions at the museums as well as conferences, musical performances
and cinema listings (listings on the website are in the "Cartelera" section).

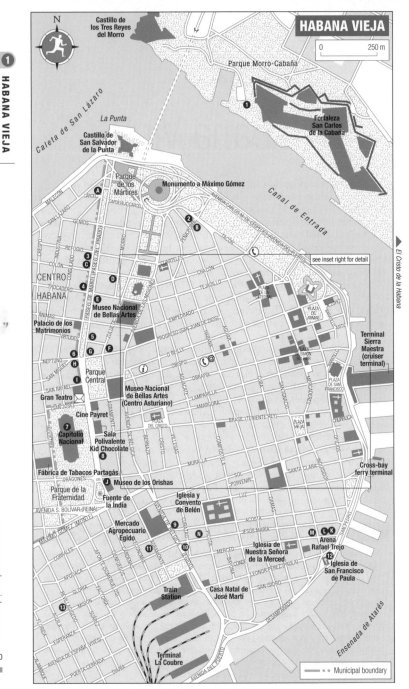

HABANA VIEJA

N

0   250 m

Castillo de
los Tres Reyes
del Morro

Parque Morro-Cabaña

①

Fortaleza
San Carlos
de la Cabaña

Caleta de San Lázaro

La Punta

Castillo de
San Salvador
de la Punta

Canal de Entrada

Parque
de los
Mártires

Monumento a Máximo Gómez

②
Ⓑ

see inset right for detail

Ⓐ

CENTRO

HABANA

③
Ⓒ

④

Ⓓ

Ⓔ
Museo Nacional
de Bellas Artes

PLAZA
DE LA
CATEDRAL

PLAZA
DE
ARMAS

Palacio de los
Matrimonios

⑤

Ⓖ

Ⓕ

Terminal
Sierra
Maestra
(cruiser
terminal)

⑥

Ⓗ

ⓘ

PLAZA
DE SAN
FRANCISCO

Parque
Central

Ⓘ

Museo Nacional
de Bellas Artes
(Centro Asturiano)

PLAZA
DE SIMÓN
BOLÍVAR

Gran Teatro

Cine Payret

PLAZA
VIEJA

⑦

Capitolio
Nacional

Sala
Polivalente
Kid Chocolate

⑧

Fábrica de Tabacos Partagás

Ⓙ Museo de los Orishas

Cross-bay
ferry terminal

Parque de la
Fraternidad

Fuente de
la India

Iglesia y
Convento
de Belén

Mercado
Agropecuario
Egido

⑨

Ⓝ

Ⓜ **Ⓛ Ⓚ**
Arena
Rafael Trejo

⑪

⑩

Iglesia de
Nuestra Señora
de la Merced

⑫
Iglesia de
San Francisco
de Paula

Train
Station

Casa Natal de
José Martí

⑬

Ensenada de Atarés

Terminal
La Coubre

━ ━ ━ Municipal boundary

▶ *El Cristo de la Habana*

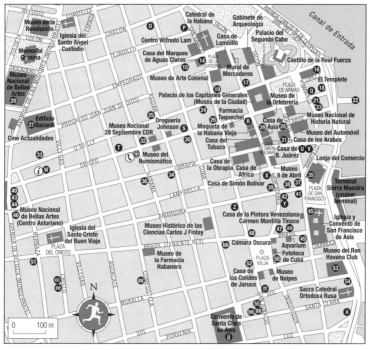

ACCOMMODATION		RESTAURANTS		BAR & CAFÉS		CLUBS & LIVE MUSIC VENUES	
Ambos Mundos	R	Al Medina	28	Bar Asturias	5	Basilica Menor de	
Armadores de Santander	ii	Anacaona	J	Bar Bilbao	25	San Francisco de Asis	45
Los Balcones	gg	A Prado y Neptuno	6	Bar Dos Hermanos	54	Casa de la Cultura	
Beltrán de Santa Cruz	ff	La Barca	18	Bar Havana Club	53	Julián del Casal	13
Caribbean	C	Bar Cabaña	2	Bar Monserrate	46	Chico O'Farrill	
Casa de Aurora y Julio	K	El Baturro	10	La Bodeguita del Medio	15	Snack Bar	0
Casa de Daniel Carrasco Guillén	ee	Bodegón Onda	V	Café La Barrita	27	Disco Galicia	11
Casa de Eugenio Barral García	M	La Bodeguita del Medio	15	Café El Escorial	50	Iglesia de San Francisco	
Casa de Evora Rodríguez	A	Café El Mercurio	35	Café Habana	39	de Paula	12
Casa de Fefita y Luis	A	Café del Oriente	37	Café O'Reilly	24	Museo Nacional	
Casa de Juan y Margarita	W	Café Taberna	47	Café de Paris	26	de Bellas Artes	20
Casa de Martha y Yusimi	N	Castillo de Farnés	44	Cafetería Bellas Artes	20	Oratorio de	
Casa de Mery	T	Cafetería El Corojo	17	Cafetería El Corojo	X	San Felipe Neri	34
Casa de Migdalia Caraballé Martin	hh	Don Ricardo	O	El Cañonazo	Q	Salón El Gijonés	5
Casa de Nelson	L	Doña Blanquita	3	Casa de las Infusiones	29		
Casa de Pablo Rodríguez	dd	El Floridita	40	La Casa del Café	21		
Casa Riquel	cc	Hanoi	51	Cremería El Naranjal	30		
Chez Nous	bb	Jardín del Eden	Z	Dulcería San Felipe	41		
El Comendador	V	Jardín del Oriente	38	El Floridita	40		
Convento de Santa Clara de Asís	jj	La Julia	33	El Gallo	36		
Conde de Villanueva	X	El Mesón de la Flota	Y	Lluvia de Oro	32		
Florida	S	La Moneda Cubana	19	La Logia	7		
Los Frailes	aa	La Mulata del Sabor	55	El Louvre	I		
Hotel del Tejadillo	P	Los Nardos	8	La Marina	49		
Inglaterra	I	La Paella	U	Los Marinos	22		
El Mesón de la Flota	Y	El Paseo	G	Museo del Chocolate	42		
Palacio O'Farrill	O	El Patio	14	El Patio	14		
Park View	D	Plaza de Armas	R	Plaza de Armas	R		
Parque Central	G	El Pórtico	G	El Pórtico	G		
Plaza	F	Prado	D	Puerto de Sagua	9		
Raquel	Z	Roof Garden "Torre del Oro"	E	Taberna del Galeon	23		
San Miguel	B	Santo Angel	48	Taberna de la Muralla	52		
Santa Isabel	Q	El Templete	16	Torrelavega	31		
Saratoga	J	Los Vitrales	4				
Sevilla	E	La Zaragozana	43				
Telégrafo	H						
Valencia	U						

of the old town, and belong to an era of reconstruction in Havana heavily influenced by the United States, most strikingly in the **Capitolio** building. The late nineteenth and early twentieth centuries saw many colonial buildings demolished and replaced with flamboyant palaces, imposing Neoclassical block buildings and some of the finest hotels ever built in the city, many of them still standing today. Some of the most impressive museums are here, including the **Museo de la Revolución** and the **Museo Nacional de Bellas Artes**, Cuba's best and biggest art collection.

The southern half of Habana Vieja has so far been largely unaffected by the huge restoration projects and contains only a couple of small museums, most notably the **Casa Natal de José Martí**. This mostly residential district displays a more potent dose of the battered charm that gives the old city so much of its unique character.

A word of warning: Habana Vieja is not only a magnet for *jineteros* but is also the **bag-snatching** centre of the city, with an increasing number of petty thieves working the streets, so take the usual precautions.

Plaza de Armas and around

The oldest and most animated of Habana Vieja's squares, the **Plaza de Armas** is where Havana established itself as a city in the second half of the sixteenth century; it has been dominating life in the neighbourhood ever since. Based around an attractive leafy core, the plaza is often seething with tourists, while live music wafts from *La Mina* restaurant in the corner. Next door there is a shop selling water ($1CUC) filtered through a seventeenth-century water filter imported from Spain. The three brick streets and, uniquely, the single wooden one that make up the outer border are dominated every day (save Monday) by Havana's biggest and best secondhand **book market** (see p.159).

In the square's northeastern corner, the incongruous classical Greek architecture of **El Templete**, a curious, scaled-down version of the Parthenon in Athens, marks the exact spot of the foundation of Havana and the city's first Mass in 1519. The building itself was established in 1828; the large ceiba tree which now stands within its small gated grounds is the last survivor of the three that were planted here on that inaugural date. Inside the tiny interior (daily 9am–6.30pm; $1CUC), two large paintings depict these two historic ceremonies, both by nineteenth-century French artist Jean Baptiste Vermay, whose work can also be seen inside the Catedral de la Habana.

For most of the nineteenth century, the Plaza de Armas was the political heart of Havana and boasted distinguished examples of colonial architecture. Today, several of these historic buildings house museums, most notably the Museo de la Ciudad.

Museo de la Ciudad

The robust yet refined **Palacio de los Capitanes Generales** on the western side of the plaza was the seat of the Spanish government from the time of its inauguration in 1791 to the end of the Spanish-American War in 1898. It's now occupied by one of Havana's best museums, the **Museo de la Ciudad** (daily 9am–6.30pm; $3CUC, $4CUC with guided tour), which celebrates the original building itself as well as the city's colonial heritage in general. Highlights on the ground floor include a fantastic nineteenth-century fire engine and a collection of horse-drawn carriages. Upstairs, among rooms that have been restored to their original splendour, is the magnificent Salón de los Espejos (Hall of Mirrors), lined with glorious gilt-looking mirrors, ornate candlestick holders and three huge, ostentatious crystal chandeliers. Next door is the slightly less striking Salón Verde, also known as the Salón Dorado (Golden Hall), where the governor would receive guests amid golden furniture and precious porcelain. Completing the triumvirate of the building's most impressive rooms is the sumptuous Salón del Trono (Throne Room), which, with its dark-red, satin-lined walls, was intended for royal visits, though no Spanish king or queen ever visited colonial Cuba.

Palacio del Segundo Cabo

In a corner of the plaza, at Tacón and O'Reilly, is the **Palacio del Segundo Cabo**, dating from the same period as the Palacio de los Capitanes Generales and similarly characterized by elegant, stern-faced architecture. It served its original purpose as the Royal Post Office for only a few years, and has been used by a host of institutions since, including the Tax Inspectorate, the Supreme Court of Justice and the Cuban Geographical Society; currently the building acts as the headquarters of the **Instituto Cubano del Libro** (Cuban Book Institute). The least accessible of the plaza's buildings, there is nevertheless usually someone on hand to accompany you into the courtyard for a gander at the august Baroque architecture, where the ageing stone archways shoulder an iron-girdered balcony complete with wooden shutters and colourful portals. You can also wander beyond the entrance if you pay to visit the discreet, single-room **art gallery**, the **Sala Galería Raúl Martínez** (Mon–Sat 9am–6pm; $1CUC), which holds temporary exhibitions, usually of modern art. Many of the artists whose work is hung here have illustrated books published by the Instituto Cubano del Libro. In the entrance hall are posted details of readings, workshops and conferences that periodically take place inside. There are also two relatively well-stocked **bookshops** (see p.159) selling predominantly Spanish and Cuban titles.

Museo Nacional de Historia Natural

The **Museo Nacional de Historia Natural** (Tues 10am–4pm, Wed–Sun 10.30am–6pm; $3CUC, $4CUC with guide), on the corner of Obispo and Oficios, is, on an international scale, an unremarkable and rather diminutive natural history museum. Nevertheless, it is one of the biggest and best of its kind in Cuba, and one of the only museums in Habana Vieja suitable for children. There are models and video displays around the first section of the ground floor, charting a brief history of life on earth. In the rooms beyond, light-and-sound effects bring the mammals of the five continents to a semblance of life, but the lack of any background scenery makes the cluttered displays feel a bit flat. Upstairs the displays of Cuban species are mildly interesting, though display cabinets are insensitively high for children. The most unusual of the species here is the prehistoric *manjuarí* fish, though there are also examples of the *jutía carabalí* (a large indigenous tree rat) as well as iguanas, bats and various birds. In an adjoining building, the *sala infantil* offers a space for kids with crayoning tables, games, story books and a somewhat macabre stuffed-baby-animal petting area.

Museo de la Orfebrería

A few doors along on Obispo, just beyond what are technically the confines of the square on the other side of Oficios, is the **Museo de la Orfebrería** (Tues–Sun 9am–6.30pm; $1CUC), worth a twenty-minute scoot round. This building was a colonial-era workshop for the city's prominent goldsmiths and silversmiths and now displays some of their work, as well as interesting gold and silver pieces from around the world. There are all kinds of objects on display, from pocket watches and walking sticks to ceremonial swords and vases. Look out in particular for the fantastic, ostentatious old clocks and, upstairs, silver roosters from Peru. A jewellery shop is also located in the same building (see p.161).

Castillo de la Real Fuerza

Due north of the plaza, just across O'Reilly, the **Castillo de la Real Fuerza** is a heavy-set sixteenth-century fortress surrounded by a moat. Built to replace a more primitive fort that stood on the same site but was destroyed by French pirates in 1555 (see p.202), this impressive building never really got into its role as protector of the city. Set well back from the mouth of the bay, it proved useless against the English who, in 1762, took control of Havana without ever coming into the firing range of the fortress's cannon. Today the six-metre-thick stone walls make an atmospheric setting for the **Museo Castillo de la Real Fuerza** (Tues–Sat 9.30am–5pm, Sun 9.30am–12.30pm; free). Opened in 2008 under the auspices of the Oficina del Historiador de la Ciudad, this display of Cuba's naval history is an excellent addition to Habana Vieja's museums.

The first room is littered with interesting relics mainly found on or near the site, like pre-Columbian stone axes, a bayonet clumped with rust and a fascinating model of the castle itself. These are a good warm-up act for rooms further into the castle's depths, which are stuffed with **treasure** culled from the colonies and destined for Spain. Fat silver discs as big as dinner plates and 22-carat gold bars almost a foot long, bearing marks from the mines of Lima and Potosí, glitter in one display cabinet while another is filled with Spanish marriage necklaces and other jewellery. Elsewhere, the museum's attention is turned to the **ships** themselves. All labels are in Spanish but the scale models of galleon ships, alongside comprehensive exhibits detailing life on board for sailors, can be easily appreciated without them.

In the castle's upper level there are more model boats, including some modern liners, but the real draw is the rooftop view over the eastern bay and also the bell tower, complete with the original bell used to warn Habaneros of approaching pirates. Cresting the tower is a copy of the Giraldilla weathervane – a bronze statue of a woman, named after the Giralda tower in Seville, which is that city's symbol. The original is now in the Palacio de los Capitanes Generales, following its deposition in the 1926 hurricane.

Gabinete de Arqueología

Half a block north from the Plaza de Armas on Tacón is the **Gabinete de Arqueología** (Tues–Sat 9am–5pm, Sun 9am–1pm; $1CUC), primarily of interest to archeology enthusiasts as the range of exhibits is slightly disappointing. The ground floor is the showcase for colonial artefacts found in churches and old houses around the capital, including some seventeenth- and eighteenth-century doors and two huge sugar cauldrons as used in the old refineries, but overall this floor contains little that you can't see better examples of in other Havana museums. The museum really earns its name in the upstairs rooms, where archeological finds from Cuba and Latin America include 5000-year-old ceramic figurines from Ecuador and a skull from the Siboney culture, the oldest peoples to have inhabited Cuba.

Around the corner on O'Reilly, a splendid colonial building is being transformed into a future must-see sight, the **Museo del Habano**. This is set to become a comprehensive showcase for Cuba's world-famous cigar industry which, amazingly, has until now been represented in the diminutive Casa del Tabaco on nearby Mercaderes (see p.59).

Oficios

The oldest street in the city, **Oficios**, heads south from the Plaza de Armas and is lined with colonial residences, several of which now house small museums. At no.16 is the **Casa de los Árabes** (Tues–Sat 9am–5pm, Sun 9am–1pm; free or donation), a former religious school. The building, constructed in the seventeenth century, is one of the most striking single examples of the Moorish influence on Spanish – and therefore Cuban – architectural styles. It tends to outshine the sketchy collection of Arabian furniture and costumes found in its corridor-room, which is set up like a Marrakesh market and features fabrics and rugs hanging from the walls and ceilings.

Across the street, and of wider appeal, is the **Museo del Automóvil** (Tues–Sat 9am–5pm, Sun 9am–1pm; $1CUC) where, among the two dozen or so cars parked inside, dating mostly from the first half of the twentieth century, the 1902 Cadillac is one of the most attention-grabbing. The 1981 Chevrolet donated by the Peruvian ambassador and a number of other models deliver a rather succinct history of the automobile, which one can't help feeling should be more comprehensive given the number of old cars still on the streets in Cuba.

Plaza de San Francisco and around

Two blocks beyond the car museum, Oficios opens out onto the **Plaza de San Francisco**, opposite the colourful **Terminal Sierra Maestra**, where the two or three luxury cruisers that include Cuba in their Caribbean tour come to dock. With the main port road running the length of its west side and two of its main buildings given over to offices, the square is the most open and functional of Habana Vieja's main plazas and attracts fewer sightseers than its nearby counterparts. The surrounding architecture, however, exercises a commanding presence, particularly the impressive five-storey **Lonja del Comercio** on the north side. This corpulent construction looks like a classical Roman theatre but was in fact built in 1909. It originally served as the Chamber of Representatives but now houses the Brazilian Embassy and various commercial companies in its refurbished interior, an office complex better suited to Wall Street than Habana Vieja.

Taking up the entire southern side of the square is the **Iglesia y Convento de San Francisco de Asís**, built in 1739 on the site of an older structure, which from 1579 was one of the most prestigious religious centres in Havana, a kind of missionary school for Franciscan friars who set off from here for destinations throughout Spanish America. Wonderfully restored in the early 1990s, the monastery now contains the neatly condensed **Museo de Arte Religioso** (daily 9am–6pm; $2CUC, or $3CUC with English-speaking guide, $2CUC extra to take photos), featuring wooden and ceramic figurines of the saints, church furniture and pottery found on the site. The real pleasure, however, comes from wandering around the beautifully simple interior, admiring the solid curves of the north cloister, and climbing the wooden staircase up the 46-metre-tall bell tower for magnificent **views** across the bay and over most of Habana Vieja.

At Oficios no.162, opposite the entrance to the church, is the **Casa de la Pintora Venezolana Carmen Montilla Tinoco** (Mon–Sat 9.30am–5pm; free), a delightful colonial townhouse restored in the mid-1990s from scratch by Tinoco, a Venezuelan artist and friend of Fidel Castro. Used for exhibitions of Cuban and overseas artists alike, Tinoco's own surreal and sometimes morbid paintings hang on the interior balcony. Outside, on the far wall of the patio garden, is a huge ceramic mural by renowned Cuban artist Alfredo Sosabravo, made up of hundreds of leafy and mollusc-like shapes to represent Cuban flora and fauna.

Museo del Ron Havana Club

A couple of blocks south from the Plaza de San Francisco along the port road is one of Havana's flashiest museums, the **Museo del Ron Havana Club** (Mon–Thurs 9am–5pm, Fri 9am–4pm; $7CUC), a showpiece for the country's sizeable rum industry. Tracing the history and production methods behind this 400-year-old liquor, the lively tour (with guides who also speak English, French, German and Italian) offers one of the city's few modern museum experiences, with slick presentation and interactive exhibits. Passing through darkened atmospheric rooms, the tour is designed to follow the rum-making process in sequential order, charting the transformation of sugar cane into Cuba's national drink.

The tour begins with an introductory five-minute film, with a pidgin-English translation, followed by rooms displaying various pieces of historical and contemporary machinery, including a *trapiche*, used in the colonial era to press sugar cane. There's a great model of a sugar mill factory, complete with a train chugging around the outside, which you can admire from an overhead gangway. Further on, you can smell the odours from bubbling tanks full of fermenting molasses, see distillation and filtration apparatus and step inside the moody barrel-lined cellars. The tour finishes up in a fully functioning replica of a 1930s **bar**, where you are given a sip of the brew itself. There is also a shop selling the full range of Havana Club rums plus, slightly unexpectedly, a pleasant little art gallery exhibiting the work of contemporary Cuban artists. In the same building is *Bar Havana Club* (see p.134), a more sociable, atmospheric option to the museum bar, which also serves food and has its own entrance, meaning you can come here outside of museum hours.

Sacra Catedral Ortodoxa Rusa

Standing out like a sore thumb on the Avenida del Puerto and a dead ringer for a fairytale fortress, the **Sacra Catedral Ortodoxa Rusa Nuestra Señora de Kazán** (daily 9am–5.45pm; free), to give it its full name, is one of the most unexpected sights in Habana Vieja. Modelled on Byzantine architecture, full of cylindrical shapes and topped with five bulbous domes, this Russian Orthodox cathedral, the first and only one of its kind in Cuba, was inaugurated on October 19, 2008. Such a strikingly unique building in Havana makes it difficult to resist the temptation to look inside but, perhaps surprisingly, the interior is memorable mostly for its simplicity. It nevertheless deserves a visit, if only for a few minutes.

The starkness of the white-walled, white marble-floored nave, accessed via the pleasant little courtyard up the steps at the rear, is punctuated by three golden chandeliers and a gleaming gold, flat altar, full of painted saints and angels, but otherwise there is very little to avert your gaze. There are thought to be between five and ten thousand Russians in Havana, most of whom moved here during the 1960s and 1970s, a time of enthusiastic economic and cultural exchange between Cuba and the Soviet Union. Having gone through a frosty period in the 1990s, relations are warming again between the two countries and, significantly, the cathedral was visited by the Russian President Dimitri Medvedev in November of 2008, while the inauguration ceremony was attended by a large Russian delegation led by Patriarch Kirill I, now head of the Russian Orthodox Church.

Plaza de la Catedral and around

The **Plaza de la Catedral**, in northeastern Habana Vieja, is one of the most historically and architecturally consistent squares in the old city. Perfectly restored and pleasantly compact, it's enclosed on three sides by a set of symmetrical eighteenth-century aristocratic residences. The first houses were built on the site – which was swampland when the Spanish found it – around the turn of the sixteenth century. It wasn't until 1788 that the Plaza de la Ciénaga (Swamp Square), as it was then known, was renamed the Plaza de la Catedral, after the Jesuit church on its north face was consecrated as a cathedral.

The striking yet relatively small **Catedral de la Habana**, hailed as the consummate example of the Cuban Baroque style, dominates the plaza with its swirling detail, curved edges and cluster of columns. Curiously, however, the perfect symmetry of the detailed exterior was abandoned in the design of the two towers, the right one noticeably and unaccountably wider than the left. The less spectacular cathedral interior (Mon–Fri 10.30am–3pm, Sat 10.30am–2pm; free) bears an endearing resemblance to a local church. It features a set of lavishly framed portraits by French painter Jean Baptiste Vermay (copies of originals by artists such as Rubens and Murillo), commissioned by Bishop José Díaz de Espada in the early nineteenth century to replace those works he considered to be in bad taste. Other than these and an unspectacular altar, featuring imported silverwork and sculptures completed in 1820 by the Italian artist Bianchini, the three naves are relatively empty. This is due in part to the removal of one of the cathedral's principal heirlooms, a funeral monument to Christopher Columbus said to have contained his ashes, which now stands in the cathedral in Seville, where it was taken when the Spanish were expelled from Cuba in 1898. For $1CUC you can climb the spiral stone staircase to the top of the **bell tower**, where the views take in the Capitolio and the other side of the bay.

Museo de Arte Colonial

Opposite the cathedral, the Casa de los Condes de Casa Bayona, built in 1720, houses the **Museo de Arte Colonial** (daily 9am–7pm, doors close at 6.30pm; $2CUC, guided tour $1CUC extra, $2CUC to take photos). Its comprehensive collection of well-preserved, mostly nineteenth-century furniture and ornaments offers more insight into aristocratic living conditions during the later years of Spanish rule in Cuba than any other building on the plaza. The predominantly European-made artefacts were collected from colonial residences around the city and include elaborately engraved mahogany dressers and a petite piano. One room is full of colourful *vajillas*, plates engraved with the family coat of arms of counts and marquises from Cuba. It was customary in colonial aristocratic circles to give one of these *vajillas* to your hosts whenever visiting the house of fellow nobility. The museum also features some fine examples of the brightly coloured stained-glass arches, known as *vitrales*, a classic of colonial Cuban design used to crown doorways and windows.

The rest of the plaza

Leaning against one of the stone pillars under the arches on the east side of the plaza is a life-sized **bronze statue** by José Villa Soberón of Antonio Gades, one of the greatest Spanish ballet dancers and choreographers of modern times, to whom the revival of Flamenco is attributed. Gades was also a committed communist and passionate supporter of the Revolution: Fidel Castro awarded him the Order of José Martí, one of Cuba's highest honours, shortly before his death from cancer in 2004. His ashes are also interred in Havana.

Sharing the northwestern corner with the cathedral, and host to the *El Patio* restaurant (see p.126), is the **Casa del Marqués de Aguas Claras**, the most sophisticated of the plaza's colonial mansions. Thoroughly deserving of a visit (though you'll have to eat at the restaurant to do so) it features a serene fountain-centred courtyard, encompassed by pillar-propped arcs and coloured-glass portals. Next door, occupying the other half of the west side of the plaza, is the **Galería Victor Manuel**, a well-stocked arts and crafts shop. Across from here, the **Casa de Lombillo** (Mon–Fri 9am–5pm & Sat 9am–1pm) dates from 1741 and was originally home and office to a sugar-factory owner. Much of it is closed to the public, but via the door on Empedrado you can pop inside and take a peek at the patio or scale the broad staircase.

At the end of Callejón del Chorro, a short cul-de-sac on the southwestern corner of the plaza, is the low-key **Taller Experimental de Gráfica** (Mon–Fri 9am–4pm; free), where a small selection of artwork, more innovative than most of what's on offer around this area, is exhibited in front of the large workshop where it is produced. The **Centro de Arte Contemporáneo Wifredo Lam** (Mon–Sat 10am–5pm; $2CUC), at San Ignacio esq. Empedrado, in the shadow of the cathedral, has a much larger though often quite bare gallery showing equally off-centre contemporary art, including photography, painting and sculpture. All exhibitions are temporary; previous shows have included huge, bizarre-looking amalgamations of modern household objects.

Mercaderes

Bookended by the Plaza de la Catedral and the Plaza Vieja is **Mercaderes**, the most heavily trodden and interesting route between these two old squares, full of small museums and simple but pleasing distractions. Along with Oficios this is one of the two oldest streets in Havana and almost every building on this six-block street, some dating back to the seventeenth century, has now been restored or renovated, making it one of the most historically evocative

▲ Mural de Mercaderes

pedestrian precincts in Habana Vieja. The most densely packed sightseeing section is south of Obispo, where there is a museum, gallery, hotel or café occupying almost every building. Halfway along is the diminutive **Plaza de Simón Bolívar**, surrounded by small museums and featuring an ideally located café, perfect for a drink in the shade.

The Mural de Mercaderes

On the block nearest to the Plaza de la Catedral along Mercaderes is the giant **Mural de Mercaderes**, portraying 67 figures from the history of Cuban arts and politics. Pictured as a group standing outside and on the balconies of a classic colonial Cuban building, they include Carlos Manuel de Céspedes (nineteenth-century revolutionary), José de la Luz y Caballero (nineteenth-century philosopher), Jean Baptiste Vermay (French painter whose work appears in the cathedral and in El Templete on the Plaza de Armas) and José Antonio Echeverría (1950s student leader and revolutionary).

Maqueta de la Habana Vieja

Two blocks from the mural, at Mercaderes no.114, is the **Maqueta de la Habana Vieja** (daily 9am–6pm; $1CUC), an enthrallingly detailed model of the old city, including the bay and Habana del Este. Made up of some 3500 miniature buildings, the cityscape took three years to construct and occupies the larger part of the single room you can visit here. You should be able to pinpoint a few hotels, the main squares and the largest buildings, like the Capitolio. Each scheduled viewing is accompanied by a lighting sequence meant to replicate a day in the life of Habana Vieja and comes complete with the sounds of birdsong and car horns; if you listen carefully enough you should be able to make out the voice of someone offering to sell you a box of cigars.

Casa del Tabaco and Casa de Asia

A few doors along from the Maqueta de la Habana Vieja, at Mercaderes no.120, a narrow staircase leads up almost directly from the street to the **Casa del Tabaco** (Tues–Sat 9am–5.15pm & Sun 9am–12.45pm; free or donation), a surprisingly small collection of smoking memorabilia given Cuba's heritage in this industry. Stretched over five pokey rooms are modest collections of ashtrays, pipes and snuff boxes as well as a slightly more substantial set of twentieth-century lighters in all kinds of shapes and designs, from miniature telephones to a dinky piano and a machine gun. Among the haphazardly displayed collections is a *humidor* donated by Fidel Castro featuring an engraving of Machu Picchu in Peru. Sure to outshine this mostly disappointing collection when it opens will be the Museo del Habano on O'Reilly (see p.54).

Across the street, at no.111, is another museum, the **Casa de Asia** (Tues–Sat 9am–4.45pm & Sun 9am–12.45pm; free or donation). Its long narrow rooms hold a hotchpotch of items from numerous countries, with many pieces donated by their respective embassy in Cuba. The diversity of what's on display means that most visitors will find at least one thing to catch their eye, whether it's the samurai-style sword from tenth-century Laos, the model boats from Bangladesh or the metal statuette of the Hindu deity Shiva Nataraja. A separate set of rooms has been allotted to the Chinese collection, the most comprehensive here, with some of the artefacts donated by the descendants of Chinese immigrants to Cuba, who came in their thousands to the island during the nineteenth century (see box, p.82).

Plaza de Simón Bolívar and around

One block from Obispo on Mercaderes, a mixed group of museums and galleries huddles around the **Plaza de Simón Bolívar**, a delightful and cosy little square consisting of exuberant gardens squeezed up against the surrounding buildings and criss-crossed by pathways. A statue of Simón Bolívar, the nineteenth-century Latin American independence hero (see box, p.62), looks down from a plinth and at the back of the square are the tables of a café based over the other side of **Obrapía**, the street hugging the square's northern border and dissecting Mercaderes. Of the encircling group of museums the **Casa de Africa** contains the most visually arresting exhibits, while the **Casa de Simón Bolívar** has the most coherent theme, the story of its namesake's life. The **Casa de la Obrapía** and the **Fundación Guayasimín** are as interesting for the buildings themselves as for the museums within them.

Casa de Benito Juárez and Fundación Guayasimín

Facing the plaza from the Obrapía side is the occasionally worthwhile **Casa de Benito Juárez** (Tues–Sat 9.30am–4.30pm, Sun 9am–12.30pm; free or donation), also known as the Casa de México. The museum holds some paintings and a few pre-Columbian artefacts from various regions of Mexico, but the permanent collection occupies just one room of this relatively large building; the two rooms set aside for temporary exhibitions of Mexican photography, painting or craftwork tend to be the more interesting sections but are not always in use. The rest of the place is quite empty and not set up to receive visitors. The **Fundación Guayasimín**, on the same block at Obrapía no.111 (Tues–Sat 9.30am–4.45pm, Sun 9am–12.45pm; free or donation), feels even more bare but can claim a more palpable subject matter. Established in 1992, the house used to double up as a studio and gallery for the Ecuadorian painter Oswaldo Guayasimín, a friend of Fidel Castro who died in 1999. Upstairs are a bedroom and a dining room that were set up for Guayasimín, though he never actually used them. Examples of the artist's work are found throughout the place, including a portrait he made of Castro for his seventieth birthday.

Casa de Africa

The standout museum in the vicinity of the Plaza de Simón Bolívar is the **Casa de Africa**, at Obrapía no.157 between Mercaderes and San Ignacio (Tues–Sat 9.15am–4.45pm, Sun 9am–1pm; free), a three-floor showcase for African and Afro-Cuban arts, crafts and culture. Many of the tribal artefacts, traditional art works, sculptures and statues here once belonged to Fidel Castro, most of them given to him by leaders of the African countries he has visited.

Visitors tend to be ushered upstairs first, despite the most arresting exhibits being on the ground floor. These include two fantastic life-size wooden sculptures of large birds from the Ivory Coast, bronze statues of tribal warriors in combat from Burkina Faso and a marvellous sculpted depiction of a royal procession from Benin, featuring a pipe-smoking chieftain being carried on a hammock. The middle floor showcases musical instruments – the numerous drums, lutes, lyres, harps, flutes and whistles here drawn from the personal collection of Fernando Ortiz, a renowned twentieth-century Cuban scholar of Afro-Cuban culture, whose desk sits incongruously in one corner. On the top floor is a mixed selection of furniture and ornamentation, such as a multi-headed wooden carving from Mozambique supposed to represent family members engaged in their daily activities, and a set of engraved elephant tusks.

Casa de la Obrapía

Opposite the Casa de Africa, and distinguished by its ornately framed front entrance, is the more eclectic **Casa de la Obrapía** (Tues–Sat 10.30am–5.30pm, Sun 9am–1pm; free or donation), an expansive seventeenth-century mansion with a spacious central patio and now a somewhat underused museum space. Effectively two museums under one roof, there are only a couple of rooms on the ground floor that are open to the public, both devoted to **Alejo Carpentier** (1904–80), Cuba's most famous novelist; the threadbare displays include the Volkswagen Beetle he used when he lived in France.

The house itself is more distracting than this ground-floor museum and the more substantial set of exhibits upstairs better compliment an appreciation of the interior architecture, partly rebuilt by the Marquis of Cárdenas de Monte Hermoso during this era. The Rococo and Renaissance-style furniture in the master bedroom include an impressively grand bed and a cot designed to resemble an old boat, while another room contains Chinese furniture featuring some particularly elaborate chairs. Many of the rooms are impressively complete, as is the record of its occupants, represented by a huge family tree going back as far as the early sixteenth century. The heavily scented Ylang Ylang tree growing in the central patio was imported from Asia and is a rarity in Cuba. Essential oil is distilled from the flowers and used to make scents by the Habana 1791 perfume shop close by (see p.162).

Up on the roof, which has been deemed structurally unstable and closed in recent years, are the old slave quarters, set along an outdoor corridor in distinctly low-ceilinged rooms. The only room you can go inside up here contains photos of the house before and during its restoration in the 1970s and 1980s, alongside a few plates, bowls and other colonial household artefacts found on site during the pre-restoration excavations.

Casa de Simón Bolívar

Around the corner, facing the plaza at Mercaderes no.156, the **Casa de Simón Bolívar** (Tues–Sat 9am–4.30pm, Sun 9am–12.30pm; free or donation) details the life and times of the Venezuelan known as "El Libertador de las Américas" (see box, p.62). Significant or symbolic events in Bolívar's life – such as his birth, baptism and first sexual experience – are rendered via a series of often comically cartoonish clay models. He is also shown in battle and dancing with a black general in what was then a deliberate act of solidarity. Display screens in a separate room go into more depth, with useful written explanations in English, and there are also prints of some great paintings from the period that provide a lively visual context. You can also take a look around the excellent gallery upstairs, which includes portraits by Cuban and Venezuelan artists of Bolívar, as well as a reproduction of Picasso's *Guernica* made from coloured fabric.

Museo 9 de Abril

A few more steps along Mercaderes towards the Plaza Vieja is what looks like a shop, with the original 1950s sign outside. As the sign indicates, this was once an *armería*, or gun store, but is now the **Museo 9 de Abril**, a one-room **hand-weapon museum** (Mon–Sat 9am–6pm; free) lined with display cabinets full of pistols, machetes, rifles, knives and various other weapons. It is more renowned, though, as a monument to what happened here on April 9, 1958 when, following calls for a general strike led by Fidel Castro, four rebels were killed trying to raid the store. There are photos of those killed as well as a few documents and newspaper articles from the time of the killings.

Simón Bolívar and Latin American independence

One of the few men in history to have had a country named after him, and honoured throughout Latin America for the prominent role he played in the independence struggles of the early nineteenth century, the bicentenary of **Simón Bolívar**'s birth in 1983 confirmed him as one of the region's most enduring icons, revered in Cuba as much as anywhere.

Born into an aristocratic family on July 24, 1783, in Caracas, Venezuela, Bolívar was orphaned by the age of nine, his father having died when he was only three and his mother six years later. At the age of sixteen he was sent to Europe, where he saw out the final years of his formal education. He returned to Venezuela a married man, but his wife, the daughter of a Spanish nobleman, died of yellow fever within a year of the wedding. Grief-stricken, he returned to Europe and immersed himself in the writings of Montesquieu, Jean Jacques Rousseau and other European philosophers. It was under such influences in Paris and Rome that Bolívar developed a passion for the idea of American independence.

He returned once again to Venezuela in 1807, in time to witness the effects of the Napoleonic invasion of Spain the following year. Suffering enormous domestic problems, Spain was forced to loosen its grip on the colonies, providing independence movements all over Spanish America with the perfect opportunity for an insurrection. Over the next twenty years, all mainland South American countries broke free of their colonial shackles and declared themselves independent, leaving the Spanish clinging onto Cuba and Puerto Rico as the last vestiges of a once-vast empire.

Bolívar was to be the single most influential man during these **Wars of Independence**, involved personally in the liberation of Venezuela, Colombia, Ecuador, Peru and Bolivia. His military career began in 1811 when he enrolled himself in the army of the recently declared independent Venezuela. The Spanish were soon to claim back their lost territory and during the ensuing war Bolívar fought hard in six battles to regain control of the capital in 1813, where he assumed the political leadership of the separatist movement. The fighting was far from over, however, and it wasn't until 1821, following numerous military manoeuvres, exile in Jamaica and Haiti and the expansion of his ambitions to incorporate the freeing of the whole northern section of Spanish South America, that Bolívar was to see his vision of a truly independent Venezuela a reality.

Perhaps the most important and heroic of all the military campaigns that he waged during these eight years was the taking of New Granada (modern-day Colombia). Against all the odds he led an army of some 2500 men through the Andes, enduring icy winds and assailing the seemingly unnegotiable pass of Pisba. When Bolívar and his men descended into New Granada the colonial army was completely unprepared, and on August 10, 1819, after victory at the battle of Boyacá, they marched triumphantly into Bogotá.

Despite his prominent role in leading five South American countries to independence, Bolívar never achieved his goal of creating a federation of South American nations, and the high esteem he is held in today contrasts with how tarnished his reputation was when he died, due to the unpopularity of his attempts to establish strong central governments in those same five nations.

Plaza Vieja and around

Despite its name, **Plaza Vieja**, at the southern end of Mercaderes, is not the oldest square in Havana, having been established at the end of the sixteenth century after the creation of the first city square, the Plaza de Armas. It became the "Old Square" when the nearby Plaza del Cristo was built around 1640, by which time Plaza Vieja had firmly established itself as a centre for urban activity, variously used as a marketplace and festival site. Most of its beautifully restored,

▲ Plaza Vieja

porticoed buildings, however, were built in the eighteenth and nineteenth centuries, long after its foundation.

Today, more than any of the other principal old town squares, it reflects its original purpose as a focus for the local community, with some of the buildings around its colourful borders still home to local residents and others occupied by educational and cultural institutions. This has been one of the most redeveloped spots in Habana Vieja over the last decade, now repaved and distinguished with a central fountain, a museum, a redeveloped arts centre and primary school, and some decent shops, restaurants and cafés. Two of the remaining edifices yet to be restored are being transformed into a planetarium and, on the corner of Muralla and Inquisidor, what is sure to be a stunning hotel, bringing back to life the early twentieth-century *Palacio Cueto*.

The most diverting activity on offer around the square is a visit to the **Cámara Oscura**, offering telescopic tours of the surrounding urban landscape, while the only museum on the square, the **Museo de Naipes**, has an odd choice of subject for the location (playing cards) but is engagingly presented. Along the same south side of the square there is a clothes boutique and, in an eighteenth-century mansion on the corner of San Ignacio and Muralla, a dignified retail complex called **La Casona**. Until relatively recently this arch-laden building was full of arts and crafts stores; it now contains a courtyard café, a commercial gallery and a gift shop. The building itself, properly known as the **Casa de los Condes de Jaruco**, was remodelled in 1737 and is said to be one of the most important examples of eighteenth-century Cuban residential architecture, with its numerous stained-glass *vitrales* and interior friezes. In this corner of the square you'll also find the best place for a **drink** around here, the *Taberna de la Muralla* (see p.134), which serves food as well.

For many visitors the Plaza Vieja is as far south in Habana Vieja as they are likely to wander, as the neighbourhood beyond is markedly short on specific sights. However, for a true taste of the old town as it was prior to the current tourism boom this part of the city is worth investigating. For more on what you can see there see pp.69–70.

Cámara Oscura

In the northeastern corner of Plaza Vieja, where Mercaderes crosses Brasil, is the **Cámara Oscura** (daily 9am–5.30pm; $2CUC), a captivating ten-minute tour of Habana Vieja and the bay through a 360-degree-rotating telescopic lens. At the top of the seven-storey Gómez Vila building, built in 1933 and one of only two post-colonial edifices on the square, this impressive piece of kit can pick out sights and scenes from all over the old city in entertainingly close detail. On the same side of the square, at Mercaderes no.307, is the **Fototeca de Cuba** (Tues–Sat 10am–5pm; free), an undersized and underused Cuban photography gallery with two rooms of temporary exhibitions.

Museo de Naipes

Occupying the oldest building on Plaza Vieja, on the corner of Muralla and Inquisidor in the southeastern corner, the **Museo de Naipes** (Tues–Sat 9.30am–4.45pm, Sun 9am–1pm; free) takes a cursory but colourful look at the evolution and culture of playing cards. Decks of cards from around the world and down the years are neatly laid out in display cases, grouped into loose themes such as commerce and culture, and accompanied by related paraphernalia. Many of the decks are from Spain, not surprisingly since most of what is here was donated by the Fundación Diego de Sagredo, a Madrid-based cultural and architectural institution, who part-funded the museum's creation. Some of the graphic design adorning the cards is quite eye-catching, such as with the "Modern Painters" deck from the US, with the four suits represented by the works of Wassily Kandinsky, Joan Miró, Paul Klee and Ernst Ludwig Kirchner, or the Spanish deck split into the football teams of Real Madrid, Barcelona, Athletico Bilbao and Real Betis.

Aqvarivm

About half a block east of Plaza Vieja, on Brasil between Oficios and Mercaderes, is the tiny **Acuario de Habana Vieja** (Thurs–Sat 9am–5pm, Sun 9am–1pm; $1CUC), officially known as **Aqvarivm**. Its dimly lit interior contains eight rather unspectacular fish tanks, each teeming with fish from all over the world. The rarest species here – and certainly the strangest in appearance – is the prehistoric *manjuarí*, looking every bit the living fossil that it is, with its elongated body and protruding jaws lined with three sets of teeth.

Museo de la Farmacia Habanera

In between Plaza Vieja and the residential Plaza del Cristo is the **Museo de la Farmacia Habanera** (daily 9am–6.30pm; free), at Brasil (also called Teniente Rey) e/ Compostela y Habana. This is the old **Farmacia La Reunión**, a huge pharmacy established in 1853 that stayed in business until the Revolution in 1959. Recently restored to the impressive splendour of its heyday, it features an extravagantly adorned ceiling and walls lined with finely carved wooden cabinets brimming with hundreds of porcelain jars, which would once have contained the medicinal mixtures sold here. Some of the nineteenth-century laboratory apparatus used to make these mixtures is exhibited to the rear of the building. Among the medicine bottles, pestles and mortars are some fascinating mad-scientist contraptions, such as the *champione*, used to treat skin inflammations via steam. There are still concoctions for sale here (mostly natural medicines, all made in Cuba), and some herbs and spices too.

Obispo

Linking the Plaza de Armas with the Parque Central to the west is the shopping street of **Obispo**, one of the few streets in Habana Vieja to have been almost completely redeveloped since the mid-1990s. Crowded with foreign visitors and Cubans alike, Obispo is one of the city's most animated thoroughfares, brimming with a lively mix of street vendors, open-front bars, neighbourhood hairdressers, tourist shops, secondhand bookstalls, hotels, restaurants, and numerous front-room galleries and workshops. Away from the city's shopping malls this is the best place in Havana for browsing, with shops including the music store Longina, three bookshops and an excellent arts-and-crafts store, Galería Manos (for reviews of these shops see pp.158–160).

Near the Plaza de Armas end of Obispo is a small group of quick-stop distractions. On the corner of Aguiar, the **Droguería Johnson**, a 1950s pharmacy that's now in reconstruction, should, once it's finished, contrast nicely with the older **Farmacia Taquechel** (daily 9.30am–6.30pm) a couple of blocks further down, between San Ignacio and Mercaderes. Founded in 1898 and restored in 1996, this fully functioning but clearly tourist-focused pharmacy specializes in natural medicines and displays admirable attention to period detail – from the shelves of porcelain medicine jars down to the cash register, there isn't a piece out of place. Next door is the hotel *Ambos Mundos* (see p.110), **Ernest Hemingway**'s base in Cuba for ten years from 1932 and allegedly where he began writing *For Whom the Bell Tolls*. The hotel's rooftop garden is one of the best places for a **drink** in the old city and is open to non-guests. On the way up to the roof in the original 1920s cage-elevator, stop off on the fifth floor and visit Room 511 (daily 10am–5pm; $2CUC), where Hemingway stayed. The original furniture and even his typewriter have been preserved, and there's usually a guide on hand to answer any questions.

Museo del Numismático

Half way along Obispo, in a grandiose, pillar-fronted building at no.305 between Habana and Aguiar, is the **Museo del Numismático** (Tues–Sat 9.15am–4.45pm & Sun 9am–1pm; $1CUC, free for under 12s), whose collection of coins, medals and banknotes over two floors is more interesting than you might think, acting as a window on events and personalities in Cuban history. Downstairs are displays of medals and orders of merit, awarded for distinguished civil and military achievements in Cuba, from the eighteenth century to the present day. Noticeably, the pre- and post-1959 regimes chose José Martí, the great nineteenth-century Cuban patriot, to represent their highest orders of merit. Upstairs, alongside a potted history of world coinage, is a comprehensive collection of Cuban banknotes including colonial-era examples as well as notes from the early 1900s issued by the National Bank of Cuba.

Museo Nacional de los Comités de Defensa de la Revolución 28 de Septiembre

On the same block as the Museo del Numismático is the catchily named but disappointingly sparse **Museo Nacional de los Comités de Defensa de la Revolución 28 de Septiembre** (Tues–Sun 9am–5pm; $2CUC). Something of a missed opportunity, rather than using the space for an illumination of the fascinating role of the Committees for the Defence of the Revolution (see box p.66) instead it's a rag-tag collection of miscellaneous revolutionary paraphernalia and disjointed information backed up with screeching denouncements of

Committees for the Defence of the Revolution

Cuba's Committees for the Defence of the Revolution (CDRs) were established on September 28, 1960 in a speech by Fidel Castro in which he announced that there should be "Revolution in every neighbourhood", a slogan which quickly became the CDR motto.

Operating on a pyramid structure, each neighbourhood block has its own committee, the head of which reports to the zone committee and so on up through municipality, province and finally national-level congress. Membership is available to anyone aged 14 and over and there are currently some 7.6 million members.

Through a far-reaching system of individual groups, the CDRs have three broad objectives: to promote the support of socialism among the masses; to promote and institute social programmes; and to promote the goals of the Revolution. One of their greatest achievements was their part in the drive to eradicate illiteracy in the 1960s. Today their work ranges from promoting health campaigns and co-ordinating hurricane evacuations, to talking truants into returning to school and organizing political rallies and demonstrations. Meetings also function as grassroots forums for social and political debate, with complaints and suggestions for policy change formulated and then passed through the channels of communication to congress.

CDRs also monitor counter-revolutionary activity within the community and it is this omnipresent social control that often attracts the most unfavourable evaluation of their role in Cuban life. Membership is nominally voluntary, though careful surveillance of anyone who doesn't join means even dissenters are prudent to sign up. Incidences of neighbours denouncing one another to the local CDR has made these local institutions largely accountable for the miasmic paranoia ingrained in the Cuban psyche and a common belief that you should always watch what you say out loud. Not surprisingly perhaps, the term cederista (CDR member) is sometimes used to mean nosy parker. Cuba's critics cite the CDR as evidence of a repressive state system but Cuba maintains that constant vigilance, in which the CDR plays a pivotal role, is essential to the national security of a country that has endured fifty years of belligerent foreign policy from its closest neighbour.

the US blockade. The most interesting display is the collection of vintage screen-printed public information posters, which the CDR prints and distributes through local neighbourhoods.

Parque Central and Paseo del Prado

Just beyond the western end of Obispo is the grandest square in Habana Vieja. Flanked by some of the old city's most prestigious hotels, and mostly shrouded in shade, the **Parque Central** straddles the border between Habana Vieja and Centro Habana, and lies within shouting distance of one of Havana's most memorable landmarks, the **Capitolio Nacional**. Though the traffic humming past on all sides is a minus, the grandeur of the surrounding buildings, characteristic of the celebratory early twentieth-century architecture in this section of town, lends the square a stateliness quite distinct from the residential feel which pervades elsewhere in Habana Vieja.

The attention-grabber is undoubtedly the **Gran Teatro**, between San Martín and San Rafael, an explosion of balustraded balconies, colonnaded cornices and sculpted stone figures striking classical poses. The theatre complex is made up of two parts: the nineteenth-century theatre building itself and the former Centro Gallego, or Galician Centre, which was built around the theatre in 1915 at the same time as the exterior. It's well worth taking a guided tour ($2CUC; ask at the ticket booth midway between the two entrances to be allocated a guide) to marvel at the sumptuous Neoclassical interiors of both buildings. Particularly stunning is the recently restored double marble staircase in the former Centro Gallego, which is now largely used for ballet rehearsals and lessons (see p.148 for details of performances).

Next door is the renowned **Hotel Inglaterra** (see p.111), the oldest hotel in the country, founded in 1856; past guests include Antonio Maceo, widely considered the bravest general in Cuban history, who lodged here in 1890 during a five-month stay in Havana. The pavement café out front belonging to the hotel, *La Acera de Louvre*, is one of the few places around the park where you can sit and take it all in.

Cutting through the park's western edge is the **Paseo del Prado**, one of the prettiest main streets in the old town. Also known as the Paseo de Martí, but more often simply as El Prado, its reputation comes from the boulevard section north of the park, beginning at the *Hotel Parque Central* and marching down to the seafront. A wide walkway lined with trees and stone benches bisects the road, while on either side are the hundreds of columns, arches and balconies of the mostly residential neo-colonial buildings, painted in a whole host of colours. Look out for the illustrious **Palacio de los Matrimonios** on Animas – showered in sculpted stone detail, it looks ready to receive royal guests but is in fact one of the city's many wedding ceremony buildings, the popular Cuban alternative to a church. Encouragingly, despite its position in the city's touristic centre, El Prado still belongs to the locals and is usually overrun with newspaper sellers and children playing ball games.

Capitolio Nacional

Just beyond the southwestern corner of the Parque Central, and visible above the Gran Teatro on the same corner, looms the familiar-looking dome of the **Capitolio Nacional** (daily 9am–7pm; $3CUC, $4CUC with guided tours, $2CUC for photos). Bearing a striking resemblance to the Capitol Building in Washington D.C. (though little is made of this in Cuban publications), its solid, proudly columned front dominates the local landscape. It is arguably the most architecturally complex and varied building in the country, and any doubters will be silenced once inside, where the classical style of the exterior is replaced with flourishes of extravagant detail and a selection of plushly decorated rooms. Built in just three years by several thousand workers, it was opened in 1929 amid huge celebrations. Since 1960 the building has functioned as the headquarters of the Ministry for Science, Technology and the Environment but is today principally a tourist attraction.

The sheer size of the magnificent, polished entrance hall, known as the **Salón de los Pasos Perdidos** (The Room of Lost Steps), leaves a lasting impression, but it's the two resplendent main chambers with their breathtaking gold-and-bronze Rococo-style detail, the seat of the House of Representatives and the Senate prior to the Revolution, that are the centrepieces for visitors. There are a number of other captivating rooms, such as the ornate Italian Renaissance-style Salón Baire, the Biblioteca Martí (supposedly a replica of the Vatican library) and, following this, a corridor full of interesting photos portraying the history of the building, including its construction and inauguration. Only one floor is open to the public and tours are surprisingly short, but there's an excellent, albeit slightly incongruous arts-and-crafts shop to keep you occupied a little longer.

Behind the Capitolio, just inside the Centro Habana border on Industria, is the **Fábrica de Tabacos Partagás**, the largest and most famous cigar factory in Havana. See p.80 for details.

Parque de la Fraternidad

The network of lawns dissected by paths and roads immediately to the south of the Capitolio is the **Parque de la Fraternidad**, the biggest expanse of open land in Habana Vieja and the city's largest transport hub. Alive with buses, taxis and people, only a few of them stopping to sit on the park's benches, the sense of commotion here overrides all else. With so much traffic and so many roads to cross, few visitors bother spending much time in the park itself, though there are a couple of curiosities and, on the eastern side, the magnificent **Hotel Saratoga** (see p.112) and the quirky **Museo de los Orishas**, a museum set inside a cultural centre for Afro-Cuban religion.

Once known as the Campo de Marte and used as a drill square by the Spanish colonial garrison stationed in Havana, it wasn't until 1928 that the park took its current form and name, constructed as part of the sixth Pan-American Conference which took place in Havana. This was when the park's centerpiece – a huge, encaged ceiba tree – was planted, the **Arbol de la Fraternidad Americana**, using soil brought from every country that attended the conference. In addition, busts of some of the continent's most revered leaders were installed including Abraham Lincoln, Simon Bolívar and Benito Juárez, the first indigenous president of Mexico.

The park's other showpiece is stranded on what has effectively become a traffic island, on the Prado side of the park; a monument known as the **Fuente de la India**, one of the symbols of the city. Erected in 1837, an Amerindian woman in a feather headdress sits atop this marble monument holding the city's coat of arms, flanked by four fierce-looking fish. The woman is **La Noble Habana**, who, according to popular legend, greeted the Spanish colonialists who first arrived at the port in 1509 with a gesture that appeared to refer to the bay and uttered the word "habana" – thus spawning the name of the city.

Museo de los Orishas

Housed within the **Asociación Cultural Yoruba de Cuba** headquarters, a focal point and meeting place for the capital's Santería community, is the

▲ View of Capitolio Nacional and Parque de la Fraternidad

Santería and Catholicism

Walking the streets of Havana you may notice people dressed head-to-foot in white, a bead necklace providing the only colour in their costume. These are practitioners of **Santería**, the most popular of Afro-Cuban religions, and the beads represent their appointed *orisha*, the gods and goddesses at the heart of their worship.

With its roots in the religious beliefs of the Yoruba people of West Africa, Santería spread in Cuba with the importation of slaves from that region. Forbidden by the Spanish to practise their faith, the slaves found ways of hiding images of their gods behind those of the Catholic saints to whom they were forced to pay homage. From this developed the syncretism of African *orishas* with their Catholic counterparts – thus, for example, the Virgen de la Caridad del Cobre, the patron saint of Cuba, embodies the *orisha* known as Oshún, the goddess of femininity, in part because both are believed to provide protection during birth. Similarly, Yemayá, goddess of water and queen of the sea – considered the mother of all *orishas* – is the equivalent of the Virgen de Regla, whom Spanish Catholics believe protects sailors. Other pairings include San Lázaro, patron saint of the sick, with Babalu-Ayé, Santa Bárbara with Changó, and San Cristóbal with Aggayú.

Museo de los Orishas (Mon–Sat 9am–5pm; $10CUC for one person, $6CUC per person if there's more than one, free for children under 12) or "Museum of the Gods". Located between Máximo Gómez (also called Monte) and Dragones, at the southern end of the Paseo del Prado, this quirky set of exhibits brings to life Afro-Cuban deities with 31 full-size terracotta statues, each one set in its own representative scene. While the pantheon of Afro-Cuban gods is made up of some 401 *orishas*, only the best-known among them are represented here. With the assistance of the on-hand English-speaking guide, this is both a straightforward and fascinating insight into the main deities, as well as some of the practices, which form the basis of this earthy, colourful faith.

Each model in the museum is full of personality, but among the most memorable are Naná Burukú, a squat old lady with a shark-fin haircut, holding a baby; powerful and muscular Changó, god of war, fire and thunder, holding an axe above his head against a dramatic red sky; and buxom Yemayá, goddess of the sea and of motherhood, standing proudly against a backdrop of painted waves. At the foot of each model is a vase, a basket, a fan or some other object used to worship that particular deity. Most of these objects were collected in West Africa where Antonio Castañeda, the director and founder of this private collection, lived for ten years. Castañeda is himself a Cuban *babalao*, a high priest of Santería and among those who conduct religious ceremonies here outside of museum opening hours. These ceremonies are strictly private affairs but there are activities often open to the public, including **dance perform-ances** (see p.149); details can be found on the noticeboard in the entrance hall. There's also a restaurant-cum-cafeteria called *Ojeun*, serving a mix of African and Cuban food.

Southern Habana Vieja

South of the Parque de la Fraternidad and, by extension, the neighbouring street of Muralla, the tourist sights almost instantly die out and Habana Vieja takes on a residential character, dotted with churches, food markets, *casas particulares* and a couple of old convents. Aimless wandering is the best way to enjoy this area: the narrow, crowded streets offer an undiluted taste of life in Old Havana. One or two places of interest provide visits with a bit of structure –

most prominently this district's only museum of note, the **Casa Natal de José Martí**, and the **Convento de Santa Clara de Asís**, the most accessible of the religious buildings. Also breaking up the overwhelmingly residential architecture of the area are local neighbourhood churches, like the surprisingly grand **Iglesia de Nuestra Señora de la Merced** on the corner of Merced and Cuba or, a couple of blocks to the southeast, stranded in the middle of the port road, the **Iglesia de San Francisco de Paula**, both only sporadically open.

Casa Natal de José Martí

Two blocks east of the Parque de la Fraternidad is the Avenida de Bélgica, a main road leading down to the most tangible and best-kept tourist attraction in this part of town, the **Casa Natal de José Martí** (Tues–Sat 9.30am–5pm, Sun 9am–1pm; $1CUC), on the corner of Leonor Pérez. This modest two-storey house was the birthplace of Cuba's most widely revered freedom fighter and intellectual, though he only lived here for the first three years of his life. Though dotted with the odd bit of original furniture, the rooms of this perfectly preserved blue-and-yellow house don't strive to recreate domestic tableaux, but instead exhibit photographs, documents, some of his personal effects and other items relating to Martí's tumultuous life (see box, p.71). The eclectic set of Martí memorabilia includes a plait of his hair, his bureau and a watch chain given to him by pupils of a Guatemalan school where he taught. There are images of his arrest, imprisonment and exile on the Isla de Pinos (now the Isla de la Juventud), and details of his trips to New York, Caracas and around Spain. The endearing simplicity of the house means it will take no more than fifteen minutes to see everything here.

Convento de Santa Clara de Asís

Among all the old churches and convents you'll inevitably come across when walking around southern Habana Vieja, there is only one properly set up to receive visitors – the **Convento de Santa Clara de Asís** (Mon–Fri 8.30am–5pm; $2CUC). From the street, the plain high walls belie the attractive interior, full of plant-filled patios and wooden balconies. Occupying two entire blocks, its entrance is on Cuba between Sol and Luz; only limited sections of the building are open to the public and there is an air of desertion about the place. Founded in 1643 as the first convent in Havana, it operated as such right up until 1922, when the nuns moved to the southern suburb of Luyanó. Today it functions principally as the offices and workshops of the Centro Nacional de Conservación, Restauración y Museología, which works to restore historical artefacts and buildings. You can visit two of the three cloisters but don't expect to see any real evidence that this place functioned as a convent for nearly three centuries.

A series of locked doors and private rooms limits visitors mostly to the convent's outdoor areas, though the occasionally available non-English-speaking guides can extend these boundaries a little further. Most enticing is the unexpectedly leafy courtyard of the main cloister, crisscrossed with paths and an oasis of green in the middle of this concrete-filled part of town. The few historic relics on show can be found in the cavernous hall on the left just inside the main entrance. A hatch in the hall's floor reveals steps leading a short way down into a tiny **crypt** where, in small boxes, lie burial remains first found underneath the convent chapel in excavations made in the early 1980s. The smaller second cloister has been converted to a kind of hostel (see p.111), available to tourists.

It doesn't take long for most people who spend any time touring round Cuba to start wondering, if they don't already know, who **José Martí** is. Almost every town, large or small, has a bust or a statue of him somewhere, usually at the centre of the main square. Born José Julián Martí y Pérez to Spanish parents on January 28, 1853, this diminutive man, with his bushy moustache and trademark black bow tie and suit, came to embody the Cuban desire for self-rule. He was a figurehead for justice and independence, particularly from the extending arm of the US, throughout Latin America.

An outstanding pupil at the San Anacleto and San Pablo schools in Havana, and then at the Instituto de Segunda Enseñaza de la Habana, Martí was equally a man of action, who didn't take long to become directly involved in the separatist struggle against colonial Spain. Still a schoolboy when the first Cuban War of Independence broke out in 1868, by the start of the following year he had founded his first newspaper, *Patria Libre*, contesting Spanish rule of Cuba. His damning editorials swiftly had him pegged as a dissident, and he was arrested a few months later on the trivial charge of having written a letter to a friend denouncing him for joining the Cuerpo de Voluntarios, the Spanish volunteer corps. Only 16 years old, Martí was sentenced to six years' hard labour in the San Lázaro stone quarry in Havana. Thanks to the influence of his father, a Havanan policeman, the sentence was mitigated and the now-ailing teenager was exiled to the Isla de la Juventud, then known as the Isla de Pinos, and finally exiled to Spain in 1871.

Martí wasted no time in Spain, studying law and philosophy at the universities in Madrid and Zaragoza, all the while honing his literary skills and writing poetry, his prolific output evidenced today in the countless compendiums and reprints available in bookshops around Cuba. By 1875 he was back on the other side of the Atlantic and reunited with his family in Mexico. Settling down, however, was never an option for the tireless Martí, who, wherever he was, rarely rested from his writing or his agitation for an independent Cuba. Returning to Havana in 1877 under a false name, he began a series of moves that was to take him to Guatemala, back again to Havana, back to Spain for a second period of exile, Paris, Caracas and New York, where he managed to stay for the best part of a decade. His years in New York were to prove pivotal. Initially swept away by what he perceived to be the true spirit of freedom and democracy, he soon came to regard the US with intense suspicion, seeing it as a threat to the independence of all Latin American countries.

The final phase of Martí's life began with his founding of the **Cuban Revolutionary Party** in 1892. He spent the following three years drumming up support for Cuban independence from around Latin America, raising money, training for combat, gathering together an arsenal of weapons and planning a military campaign to defeat the Spanish. In April 1895, with the appointed general of the Revolutionary army, Máximo Gómez, and just four other freedom fighters, he landed at Playitas on Cuba's south coast. Disappearing into the mountains of the Sierra Maestra, just as Fidel Castro and his rebels were to do almost sixty years later, they were soon joined by hundreds of supporters. On May 19, 1895, Martí went into battle for the first time and was shot dead almost immediately. Perhaps the strongest testament to José Martí's legacy is the esteem in which he is held by Cubans on both sides of the Florida Straits, his ideas authenticating their vision of a free Cuba and his dedication to the cause an inspiration to all.

Museo Nacional de Bellas Artes

Divided between two completely separate buildings, two blocks apart, the **Museo Nacional de Bellas Artes** (Tues–Sat 10am–6pm, Sun 10am–2pm; $5CUC for one building, $8CUC for both, $2CUC for guided tour, under 15s free) is the most impressive and spectacular of Havana's museums and by far the largest art collection in the country. The museum stands head and shoulders above the vast majority of its city rivals, presented and put together with a degree of professionalism still quite rare for this kind of attraction in Cuba. The large and rather plain-looking Art Deco **Palacio de Bellas Artes** on Trocadero, a two-minute walk north along Agramonte from the Parque Central, is where the entire collection had been housed since 1954 but is now the showcase for exclusively Cuban art. This is a detailed examination of the history of Cuban painting and sculpture, including everything from portraits by Spanish colonists to Revolution-inspired work, though pre-Columbian art is notably absent. Artists from the rest of the world are represented in the **Centro Asturiano**, on the east border of the Parque Central, with an impressive breadth of different kinds of art, including Roman ceramics and nineteenth-century Japanese paintings.

No English translations have been provided for any of the titles in either building, which can be a hindrance to fully appreciating some of the works on display, particularly in the ancient art section where it is not always clear what you are looking at. Both buildings have **bookshops** where you can buy good quality, Spanish-only guides to their collections ($12CUC each), invaluable if you have an interest in the context and background of the paintings.

Palacio de Bellas Artes

No other collection of Cuban art, of any sort, comes close to the range and volume of works on display in the Palacio de Bellas Artes, beautifully lit and, refreshingly, air-conditioned. Although spanning five centuries, its collection has a far higher proportion of twentieth-century art, though given the dearth of colonial-era painting around the island the museum can still claim to best represent the country's artistic heritage.

The best way to tackle the three-floor, chronologically ordered collection is to take the lifts up to the top floor and walk around clockwise. Hall One is dedicated to colonial-era painters; its abundance of relatively ordinary, and frankly not particularly skilful, portraits of Cuban nobility and formulaic religious pictures makes this area less engaging than others. One of the few attention-grabbers is *Embarque de Colón por Bobadilla* (*Deportation of Columbus by Bobadilla*) by **Armando García Menocal** (1863–1941), straddling Halls One and Two and striking for its large size and sharp colours. For the most historic works, check the gantry that runs most of the length of Halls One and Two where you can see **Dominique Serres**'s animated drawing of the 1763 English capture of the capital, including the strange sight of the Union Jack flying from the ramparts of El Morro.

Halls Three and Four, taking up the rest of the top floor, leap straight into modern art from the twentieth century. In Hall Three is the most famous of the paintings by one of the first Cuban exponents of modern art, **Victor Manuel García** (1897–1969). His *Gitana Tropical* (*Tropical Gypsy*), an evocative yet simplistic portrait of a young native American woman, is a widely reproduced national treasure. Hard to miss and as striking as anything else in this section is *El Tercer Mundo* (*The Third World*) by one of the Cuban greats, **Wifredo Lam** (1902–82); the provocative and disturbing image exemplifies the influence of Picasso on the artist.

Walking counter-clockwise from the lift on the second floor takes you through Halls Five to Eight and the last fifty years of art on the island. Halls Five, Six and Seven cover the 1950s, 1960s and 1970s respectively, while Hall Eight incorporates all works produced since 1979, including some installation art and modern sculptures. It's in Hall Eight where pop art meets the Cuban Revolution in the work of **Raúl Martínez** (1927–95), whose José Martí heads mimic Andy Warhol's Marilyn Monroes. Styles become increasingly diverse as the paintings become more recent: in the bewildering *Esta es la Historia* (*This is History*) by **Gilberto de la Nuez** (1913–93), the history of Cuba is told all in one image.

It's worth having a drink at the **cafeteria** on the ground floor just to sit beside the pleasant open courtyard, where there are a few modern sculptures dotted about. Before leaving, check the notice board in the entrance hall for upcoming events in the museum, often in its 248-seat theatre.

Centro Asturiano

In contrast to the simplicity of the Palacio de Bellas Artes, the Centro Asturiano, the building housing the international collections of the Museo de Bellas Artes, is a marvel to look at in itself. Stately and grandiose, plastered with balcony-supported columns and punctuated with carved stone detail, the building's foyer is its most captivating feature. Thick pillars and a wide marble staircase announce the entrance to the museum, while looming above are spacious balustraded balconies from which you can admire the stunning stained-glass ceiling.

The exhibits are divided up by country of origin, the largest collections by Italian, French and Spanish artists, on the fifth, fourth and third floors respectively. It's a good idea to start on these higher floors, where you'll find the more varied and interesting collections.

Up on the fifth floor, the **Italian** collection is the most interesting and certainly more historically impressive than the rather mundane **British** rooms, home mainly to eighteenth- and nineteenth- century portraits. One of the few eye-catchers among the smaller **German**, **Dutch** and **Flemish** collections, hung around the spacious balcony on this floor, is *Kermesse* by Jan Brueghel (the younger), one of the only internationally famous artists in this section. The painting depicts a peasant scene with all sorts of debauchery going on, a focus typical of his work.

Most of the fourth floor is dedicated to the **ancient art** of Rome, Egypt, Greece and Etruria, including vases, amphorae, busts, numerous religious figurines and most notably the coffin from a 3000-year-old tomb. On the same floor is the relatively engaging **French** collection spanning the seventeenth to nineteenth centuries, with battle scenes, harbour landscapes, portraits and religious paintings.

On the third floor, the **Asian** collection is a small room of exclusively nineteenth-century Japanese paintings. The most comprehensive single collection is the nearby **Spanish** one, though little stands out. There's a high proportion of religious paintings, particularly from the seventeenth-century Murillo school, along with paintings by Eugenio Lucas Velázquez (1817–70), with his penchant for the melodramatic encompassing bullfights and street scenes.

Down on what is referred to in museum maps as the ground floor (though its entrance is halfway up the main staircase) are the skimpier, more haphazard **Latin American** and **US** collections. Among the small assortment of US imports are a portrait of George Washington and some splendid pictures of the North American great outdoors.

Museo de la Revolución

Facing the Palacio de Bellas Artes from the north, with the entrance a couple of blocks further down on Refugio between Agramonte (Zulueta) and the Avenida de las Misiones, next to a small piece of the old city wall, is Havana's most famous museum, the **Museo de la Revolución** (daily 10am–5pm; $5CUC, $2CUC extra for guided tour). Triumphantly housed in the sumptuous presidential palace of the 1950s dictator General Fulgencio Batista, the museum manages to be both unmissable and overrated at the same time. The events leading up to the triumph of the Revolution in 1959 are covered in unparalleled detail, but overall the museum lacks a clear narrative and your attention span is unlikely to last the full three storeys. Visitors work their way down from the top floor, which is the densest part of the museum. Rooms are grouped chronologically into historical stages, or *etapas*, from *Etapa Colonial* to *Etapa de la Revolución*, though the layout is a bit higgedly-piggedly in places, making it unclear in some rooms what point in the timeline you have reached.

The Revolutionary War and the urban insurgency movements during the 1950s were surprisingly well documented photographically and it's at this stage of the story that the exhibits are most engaging. Among them are the classic photos of the campaign waged by Castro and his followers in the Sierra Maestra and also the sensationalist **Memorial Camilo-Che**, a life-sized wax model of revolutionary heroes Camilo Cienfuegos and Che Guevara in guerrilla uniform striding out of the jungle. However, even serious students of Cuban history may overdose on models of battles and firearms exhibits also found in this section.

Much of the second floor is given over to tiresome depictions of battle plans and the "construction of Socialism", bringing the story up to the present. It's the interior of the building itself, built between 1913 and 1917 during the much-maligned "pseudo-republic" era, that is most captivating on this floor. There's the gold-encrusted Salón Dorado, the lavish dining room of the old palace when it was occupied by General Batista, the dignified furnishings of the Presidential Office, used by all the presidents of Cuba from 1920 to 1965, and the wonderfully colourful **mural** on the ceiling of the Salón de los Espejos.

Joined to the building but located outside to the rear of the museum in the fenced-in gardens of the palace is the **Granma Memorial**, where the boat which took Castro and his merry men from Mexico to Cuba to begin the Revolution is preserved in its entirety within a giant glass case. Also here are military vehicles, whole or in bits depending on which side they belonged to, used during the 1961 Bay of Pigs invasion, and a poignant pink marble monument to those who died in the revolutionary struggle. A flame rising from a single Cuban star is surrounded by the words "Gloria eternal a los heroes de la patria nueva" (Eternal glory to the heroes of the new fatherland).

La Punta and around

La Punta, the paved corner of land at the entrance to the bay, capping one end of the official border between Habana Vieja and Centro Habana, can be considered the outer limit for sightseeing tours in this part of town. Just above the junction of the busy Malecón and the Avenida Carlos Manuel de Céspedes, its position is less than enchanting, though it still attracts groups of chattering locals and youngsters who gather to throw themselves off the Malecón into the rocky pools that jut out from the sea wall here.

The landmark attraction at La Punta is the **Castillo de San Salvador de la Punta** (Tues–Sat 9.30am–5.30pm, Sun 9am–1pm; free), a sixteenth-century fortress occupying most of this space and one of the oldest military fortifications in the city. Construction of the fort began in 1589 at the same time as that of El Morro, and together they formed the first and most important line of defence of the city. Having undergone years of excavations and renovations, the fort finally reopened in 2002 but there is little sense inside the place that you are viewing the results of a massive project. The restorations are impressively immaculate but the simplicity of the original design means exploring the place is over too soon. The fortress consists of little more than several rectangular rooms with a few token exhibits from the colonial era around a desolate central courtyard, all sealed in by the ramparts from where there are modest views along the Malecón and over to El Morro, but which are empty save for a few cannon.

Monumento a Máximo Gómez and around

The wide-open space between La Punta and the rest of Habana Vieja is dominated by heavy traffic on the road that encircles the Neoclassical **Monumento a Máximo Gómez**, before winding down into the tunnel that joins the two sides of the bay. Although one of the grandest memorials in Havana, the statue is relegated to no more than a fleeting curiosity for most visitors because of its traffic-island location, although you can cross the road for a closer look. Dedicated to the venerated leader of the Liberation Army in the nineteenth-century Cuban Wars of Independence, the statue has the general sitting on a horse held aloft by marble figures representing the People.

To the southwest, sandwiched between El Prado and the road encircling the monument, is the pretty little **Parque de los Mártires**, marking the spot where the notorious prison, the Cárcel de Tacón, built in 1838, once held such political prisoners as José Martí. It was mostly demolished in 1939, and all that remains are two of the cells and the chapel in what is little more than a large concrete box.

Parque Morro-Cabaña

While many visitors omit the sights of the **Parque Morro-Cabaña** (daily 8am–11pm; $1CUC), across the bay from Habana Vieja, from their itinerary, those who do make it this far are rewarded by the uncrowded sights of an impressive, sprawling complex of castles and fortifications that, along with the two fortresses in Habana Vieja, comprised the city's colonial defence system. A stalwart part of the Havana skyline, dominating the view across the entrance channel into the harbour, the ordered surrounds of this military park provide an insight into a number of key events in the city's history. Beyond the forts, further into the bay, a gargantuan statue of Christ, **El Cristo de La Habana**, was one of the last public works completed before Cuba was taken over by Fidel Castro and his revolutionary, and subsequently atheist, government.

The easiest way to **get to** this eastern side of the bay is to take a taxi ($3CUC) from Habana Vieja. You can also catch the Habana Bus Tour from the Parque Central – get off at the first stop after the tunnel on the route to Playa Santa María del Mar. Once in the Parque Morro-Cabaña, it's a one-kilometre walk towards the harbour from the fortifications to the Cristo de La Habana. If you're heading directly to the statue from Habana Vieja, consider taking the pleasant **ferry** ($0.10CUP) that leaves every 30min from Avenida del Puerto e/ Sol y Luz, two minutes' walk south from Plaza San Francisco and the main Sierra

Maestra Terminal. There are a number of **restaurants** and **bars** in and around the two fortresses. The best of them, *La Tasca* (see p.127), just off the road between the two, is right down by the water's edge and makes a delightful spot for lunch or dinner.

Castillo de los Tres Reyes Magos del Morro

Crowning the rocky cliffs directly across from La Punta is the imposing **Castillo de los Tres Reyes Magos del Morro** (daily 8am–8.30pm; $5CUC, $6CUC with guide, extra $2CUC for lighthouse, free for children under 12), more commonly known as El Morro. This castle was built between 1589 and 1630 to form an impeding crossfire with the Castillo de San Salvador de la Punta on the opposite side of the bay, a ploy that failed spectacularly when the English invaded overland in 1762 and occupied the city for six months.

Today the castle has an eerie, just-abandoned feel, once you get beyond the bar, shop and the exhibition room laid out with scale models of Cuban forts just off the central courtyard. The cavernous billet rooms and cannon stores are empty but in near-perfect condition, while the easy-to-follow layout and the peaceful, uncluttered spaces of the fortress lend themselves to wandering around at your own pace. Particularly fine are the broad castle ramparts studded with rusted cannon and offering splendid views on all sides. A highlight of a visit here is the set of even greater views from the summit of the **lighthouse**, built on the cliff edge in 1844, over two centuries after the rest of the fortress had been completed.

The architects of *Los Doce Apostoles*, an attractive seafood **restaurant** in the shadow of the fort, down near the rocky shore, contrived to take no advantage of either, with a roof over its rustic patio obscuring sight of the fortress and adjacent buildings blocking out all views across the water. Nevertheless, it's a pleasant spot and the food – mostly fish, shrimp and lobster – is reasonably priced. For a drink with views of the city out over the Florida Straights, choose the neighbouring **bar**, *El Polvorín*, with its sea-facing terrace and cool tavern interior.

Fortaleza San Carlos de la Cabaña

Situated roughly 500m further into the bay from El Morro, the **Fortaleza San Carlos de la Cabaña** (daily 10am–10pm; $5CUC before 6pm, $8CUC after 6pm, guide $1CUC extra, free for children under 12) needs a half day to do it justice. Despite containing a much larger number of things to see and do within its grounds, its wide open spaces, benches and trees, along with a garden area, make it the more relaxing of the two forts. Built to be the most complex and expensive defence system in the Americas, the fortress was started in 1763 as soon as the Spanish traded the city back from the English. However, its defensive worth has never been proved, as takeover attempts by other European powers had largely died down by the time it was finished in 1774.

You can see why it took so long to finish after touring the extensive grounds, akin to a small village complete with a chapel, spacious lawns, several more recently installed cafés and restaurants, and impeccable cobbled streets lined with houses where soldiers and officers were originally billeted – now a miscellany of workshops, touristy arts-and-crafts stores and a number of small **museums**. Among these one- and two-room museums is a weaponry and armoury collection, a set of colonial-era furniture once in practical use at the fortress and a commemoration of the 1961 Bay of Pigs invasion and the 1962 Cuban Missile Crisis, featuring some dramatic photographs from the time. The **Ceremonia del Cañonazo**, in which soldiers in nineteenth-century uniforms fire the canon at 9pm every evening, is entertaining enough to stick around for.

▲ El Cristo de La Habana

El Cristo de La Habana

A kilometre from the Fortaleza San Carlos de la Cabaña, nearer the harbour, on the hill above the picturesque village of Casablanca, is **El Cristo de La Habana** ($1CUC, free if you have visited Parque Morro-Cabaña and retained your ticket). Marta Batista, wife of the dictator, commissioned this seventeen-metre-high Christ figure – sculpted from Italian marble by Jilma Madera in 1958 – in one of the couple's last contributions to the city before departing. Although impressive close up, where you can ponder the massive scale of the sandalled feet and the perfectly sculpted hands, said to weigh a ton each, there's precious little to do on the hillside other than admire the views over Havana. The best perspective on the statue itself is from Habana Vieja, especially in the evening, when you can gaze across the bay and enjoy its floodlit grandeur.

The only other diversion in Casablanca is the **Hershey train** terminus, one end of Cuba's only electric train service (the other end is in the provincial capital of Matanzas). This is not an official tourist attraction and is regularly used by Cubans travelling in between the six stations that make up the line. The classic, lovable little mid-twentieth century trains, however, are a great way to take a slow, relaxing ride through picturesque landscape to Canasí (see p.184), Jibacoa (see p.183) or all the way to Matanzas, just over the border to the east of Havana province, which takes about three hours and costs just under $3CUC.

Centro Habana

For many visitors the crumbling buildings and bustling streets of **Centro Habana**, crammed between the hotel districts of Habana Vieja and Vedado, are glimpsed only through a taxi or bus window en route to the city's more tourist-friendly areas. Yet this no-frills quarter has a character all of its own, as illuminating and fascinating as anywhere in the capital. Overwhelmingly residential, its late eighteenth- and nineteenth-century neighbourhoods nevertheless throb with life, particularly **El Barrio Chino**, Havana's Chinatown, and there's no better place to really savour the essence of the city, particularly because here it's not on display but up to you to discover.

That said, this part of town is for the most part not that attractive on the surface. Full of broken sewage systems, potholed roads and piles of rubbish, Centro Habana has not yet enjoyed the degree of investment and rejuvenation that Habana Vieja has, save for the **Malecón**, where there are at last visible signs of part of the famous seafront promenade returning to its former glory – several of its buildings having enjoyed facelifts in recent years. For now, one of the biggest draws for visitors is the **Callejón de Hamel**, a unique side street close to the Vedado border, which has evolved into a lively hub of Afro-Cuban activity. Elsewhere, Centro Habana's most impressive sight is the **Iglesia del Sagrado Corazón**, a glorious Neo-Gothic church rarely visited by tourists.

As an alternative to the Malecón for a route between Habana Vieja and Vedado, consider taking a wander through the neighbourhood immediately east of the Avenida de Italia. This patchwork grid of virtually traffic-less streets – bordered by San Lázaro, Zanja, Padre Varela and the Malecón – is full of kids playing in the road, laundry drying on nineteenth-century balconies, makeshift bicycle repair shops, the occasional farmers' market and some of the city's most entertaining street art and graffiti, all set to the soundtrack of locals chatting in open doorways. Do take basic safety measures, though, if you plan to wander (see p.39).

West of El Prado

In contrast to the tightly knotted side streets that define both Centro Habana and Habana Vieja, El Prado (also called Paseo Martí), the official border between the two city boroughs, is an expansive road clogged with cars, *bicitaxis* and sightseers wandering admiring the dramatic medley of Neoclassical and Baroque architecture that defines the area. The **Fábrica de Tobacos Partagás**, set back behind the Capitolio Nacional, is the star attraction here but also spare

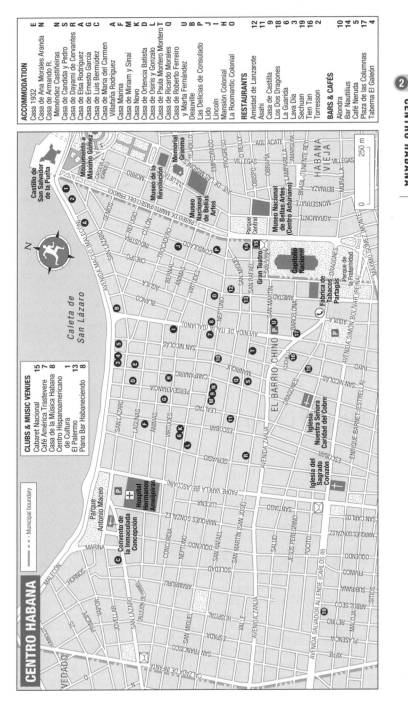

CENTRO HABANA

CLUBS & MUSIC VENUES
Cabaret Nacional	15
Café América Trastevere	7
Casa de la Música Habana	8
Centro Hispanoamericano de Cultura	1
El Palermo	13
Piano Bar Habaneciendo	8

ACCOMMODATION
Casa 1932	E
Casa de Ana Morales Aranda	N
Casa de Armando R. Menéndez Castiñeiras	S
Casa de Candida y Pedro	R
Casa de Dayami de Cervantes	A
Casa de Elsa Rodríguez	G
Casa de Ernesto García	C
Casa de Luis Bermúdez	
Casa de María del Carmen Villafaña Rodríguez	A
Casa Marina	F
Casa de Miriam y Sinaí	M
Casa Novo	K
Casa de Ortencia Batista	D
Casa de Osiris y Gonzalo	L
Casa de Paula Montero Montero	T
Casa de Ricardo Morales	Q
Casa de Roberto Ferreiro y Marta Fernández	U
Deauville	B
Las Delicias de Consulado	P
Lido	J
Lincoln	I
Mansión Colonial	H
La Roomantic Colonial	O

RESTAURANTS
Amistad de Lanzarote	12
Asahi	11
Casa de Castilla	9
Los Dos Dragones	18
La Guarida	6
Lava Dia	3
Sechuan	19
Tien Tan	16
Torresson	2

BARS & CAFÉS
Alondra	10
Bar Nautilius	14
Café Neruda	5
Plaza de las Columnas	17
Taberna El Galeón	4

time to dip into **Galería La Acacia** (Tues–Sat 10am–5pm; free) at no.114 on San José, one street behind El Prado, where contemporary artwork is presented in a pleasantly expansive space.

Fábrica de Tabacos Partagás

Behind the Capitolio (see p.67) stands the **Fábrica de Tabacos Partagás** (Mon–Sat 9–11am & noon–2pm; tours every 15min; $10CUC), one of the country's oldest and largest cigar factories, founded in 1845 and employing some 750 workers. The rich smell of tobacco seduces you as soon as you cross the threshold of the factory, which churns out twelve brands of *habanos*, including such famous names as Cohiba, Monte Cristo, Romeo y Julieta, Bolívar and Partagás itself. Though steeply priced compared to most museum entrance fees, the 45-minute tours here are easily among the most fascinating things to do in the city, with English-speaking guides taking you through the various stages of production – drying, sorting, rolling and boxing – all performed in separate rooms over four floors.

The second floor is used as a cigar-making school, from where, after a nine-month course, those who graduate will move upstairs and join the 250 expert workers making some of the finest cigars in the world. It's on this top floor where the sea of specialist rollers, sixty percent of them women, are expected to produce on average over one hundred cigars a day, depending on the brand and style of cigar they are working on. During their eight-hour shifts they are read to, from a newspaper in the morning and from a book in the afternoon – a tradition dating back to the nineteenth century. There's a very genuine sense here of watching an uncontrived, everyday operation, with most of the workers almost oblivious to the stares of tourists and the tour guide's commentary. The factory also has an excellent shop where you can pick up all the brands made here.

El Barrio Chino

About two blocks south of the Partagás factory, the grand entrance to **El Barrio Chino**, Havana's version of Chinatown, is likely to confuse most visitors, as it's placed three blocks from any visibly ethnic change in the neighbourhood. The entrance, a rectangular concrete arch with a pagoda-inspired roof, is south of the Capitolio Nacional, on the intersection of Amistad and Dragones, and marks the beginning of the ten or so square blocks which, at the start of the twentieth century, were home to some ten thousand Chinese immigrants. Today only a tiny proportion of El Barrio Chino, principally the small triangle of busy streets comprising Cuchillo, Zanja and San Nicolás – collectively known as the **Cuchillo de Zanja** – three blocks west of the arched entrance, is discernibly any more Chinese than the rest of Havana. Indeed, the first thing you are likely to notice about El Barrio Chino is a distinct absence of Chinese people, the once significant immigrant population having long since dissolved into the racial melting pot (see box, p.82). The Cuchillo de Zanja itself does, however, feature its own tightly packed little backstreet food market and is lined with eccentric-looking restaurants, where the curious mixture of tastes and styles is as much Cuban as Asian. Though many of these are aimed squarely at claiming the tourist dollar, Tien Tan (see p.128) is one that stands above the rest with ex-pat Shanghai chefs creating original dishes.

Street sellers

There is limited private enterprise in Havana but what there is exemplifies the resourcefulness of Habaneros. Throughout the city you'll find people making a living from refilling disposable lighters, re-patching bicycle tubes or selling home-made clothes from their front rooms and doorways. Exploring the world of the street sellers reveals a lesser-seen view of Havana and is one of the most rewarding pastimes the city has to offer.

60.00 60.00

RELOJERO

Watch-repair stall ▲

Bookstall on the Plaza de Armas ▲

Art by a Habanero painter ▼

Granizado wagon, Obispo ▼

Havana's hidden world of commerce

When the state legalized a small number of private enterprise in response to the economic difficulties of the "Special Period" in the 1990s, it spawned a new generation of **market stalls** and **cottage industries**. Endless recycling is a key feature – watches are mended rather than replaced, broken **jewellery** is taken to a streetside *joyero* and there is a roaring trade in spare car parts. Bicycle-repair stalls and lighter-refill stations exhibit a similar thriftiness, repairing and reusing objects that in other parts of the world would be simply discarded. Very little is ever thrown out in Havana.

Similarly the **artisans' markets** are a fount of innovation. With limited resources at their disposal, those making a living selling to visitors are forced to be ingenious. If you look closely, you'll see that much of what's on sale is made from raw materials that Habaneros can either find for free or barter for on the black market. Jewellery made from seed pods and snail shells, silver forks and spoons scavenged from hotels' dead stock and bent into bracelets, coasters made from varnished cigar labels – ten a penny if you have a friend who works in the factory – and sculptures carved from cheap coconut wood all make for attractive souvenirs.

In the more workaday neighbourhoods, the goods are aimed at a home-grown market. Sellers here lay out eclectic collections of odds–and–ends in their porches: hair accessories, alarm clocks and electrical parts jostle with frilly children's dresses – most of these clandestine imports, often acquired through relatives visiting from Miami. DVDs and CDs, always pirated, are among some of the most common finds in Vedado and Centro Habana.

Artwork

If you see **art** that catches your eye in a gallery, it's worth pursuing a private sale direct through the artist by heading to their studio to view their work. Several of Havana's most established artists live and work in the suburbs, like the surrealist painter Sandra Ramos, who operates from Playa, and conceptual artist Alejandro González Méndez, from Vedado.

For something more accessible – and cheaper – head to Habana Vieja and choose from the colourful works spilling out of artists' front rooms and in the main *fería* market itself. Most of the works are executed in bright acrylics and while they tend to be more garish representations of nubile Cuban women, Cuban countryside or Korda's famous Che image, you can occasionally find some real gems.

An interesting adjunct to this is the trade of **tattoo artists**. Once seen as a symbol of state rebellion, tattooing is now quasi-legal: practitioners pay a subscription to the Asociación Hermanos Saíz (a state-run youth-arts association) and operate from their own homes. The Vanishing Tattoo website (Ⓦwww.vanishingtattoo .com) has a list of Havana's best-known tattoo artists and their work.

For both artists and tattooists, getting materials to work is a job in itself. **Carrying goods** for relatives to sell is a common way for items like artists' materials to enter the country. Travel agents in Miami's Little Havana will also often waive the price of a ticket in return for "courier" services for American Cubans prepared to carry materials to those waiting for it in Cuba.

▲ Handcrafted wooden fish

▼ An artist's studio

▼ Habanero artist and his works

Ice-cream seller ▲

Agromercado Egido ▼

Popcorn for sale ▼

Food

Among the most successful of the private enterprises set up in the 1990s are the farmers' markets or **agromercados**. Once they have fulfilled their state quotas, farmers are permitted to sell their surplus crop in these markets. Given the lack of fresh fruit and veg in Havana's supermarkets, the sight of it piled high comes as a refreshing surprise. Among the best are Vedado's largest, on 19 y A; and Egido, Habana Vieja's flagship venue on the corner of Avenida de Bélgica and Apodaca.

Some of the best culinary treats that Havana has to offer are available from the street stalls, which usually operate to a high standard of cleanliness. Perhaps the best street treat of all is to buy a paper cone of warm roasted peanuts for $1CUP from the *maniceros* (peanut sellers) who wander along the Malecón plying their wares.

Snacks and drinks

▶▶ **Churros** sugar-covered doughnuts

▶▶ **Coquito acaramelado** caramel-covered coconut ball

▶▶ **Fritura** fritters made of ground corn and seasoning

▶▶ **Granizado** a crushed ice and sugar drink, like a Slush Puppy

▶▶ **Guarapo** sugar cane juice

▶▶ **Maní** roasted peanuts, usually sold in a paper cone

▶▶ **Maní molido** peanut butter bars

▶▶ **Papa rellena** balls of deep-fried mashed potato with a seasoned mincemeat centre

▶▶ **Rositas de maíz** popcorn

▶▶ **Torrejas** eggy sweet bread in syrup

▶▶ **Torticas** shortbread biscuits

▶▶ **Turrón de maní** fritters made of ground corn and seasoning

▲ El Barrio Chino

San Rafael and Galiano

In pre-Revolution days, **San Rafael and Galiano** (also known as Avenida de Italia), which intersect one another a block north of Barrio Chino, were famed as Havana's most prestigious shopping destination. Such was the siren call of shops like Woolworths Ten Cent, Flogar, and the famous El Encanto department store, which boasted the patronage of Lana Turner and Errol Flynn, that the crossroads of the two streets earned the sobriquet *La Esquina del Pecado*, or "Corner of Sin", after all the men who would gather there at closing time to whistle and murmur *piropos* (witty, flirtatious remarks) to the beautiful shop girls as they left work. When El Encanto burned down in 1961, (a CIA arson attack, according to ex Agency man Philip B. Agee) three months before the Bay of Pigs invasion, it marked for many the end of Havana's giddy consumer culture.

Five decades later and general neglect coupled with the effects of the US trade blockade has left the area sorely dilapidated. Instead of swanky shop fronts the area is now peppered with a selection of rather brash hard-currency stores and murkily lit peso shops.

Rather than unearthing great retail finds, the real pleasure of this area is spotting the vestiges of its glamorous past in the old shop signs and elaborate tiled frontages that dazzle amid the ruins. In particular look out for the beautiful yellow-and-blue shop front at no.38 e/Virtudes y Concordia and the Hotpoint mosaic on San Rafael esq. Industria.

China and Cuba

When the Spanish Frigate *Oquendo* disgorged its cargo of 206 indentured labourers from Guangdong into the Havana docks in 1847, it was the first step in a long association between **China** and Cuba. Following the abolition of slavery, between 50,000 to 130,000 Chinese were recruited to work in the island's sugar fields. Although nominally signed to a voluntary eight-year contract, conditions were often as hard as slavery – many workers even died during the voyage while others finished work in debt to plantation owners for food and clothes.

Those who chose to stay in Cuba at the end of their stretch had been joined between 1860 and 1875 by a second wave of Chinese-born immigrants from the US, fleeing anti-Chinese sentiment and repressive legislation introduced in California. It was upon the newcomers' comparative wealth that **Chinatown** was founded, with the former indentured workers forming the basis of a workforce to man the laundries, restaurants and small factories that the US Chinese quickly established. By the nineteenth century, Havana's Chinatown was the largest in Latin America. The Chinese were an important plinth for the emerging Cuban republic, with many fighting in the Wars of Independence against Spain.

Ranks were further swelled around 1912 by a third wave of Chinese who arrived from mainland China during the early years of Su Yat Sen's revolutionary republic, with the total number of Chinese reaching around forty thousand in the 1950s. Victims of racial discrimination under Batista, it's no surprise that many Chinese were inspired by the rebels' call to arms under Castro. Several who joined the revolutionary fight hold senior positions in the government today including Armando Choy, who heads the project to clean up the polluted Havana Bay and modernize the Port of Havana.

Following the Revolution many other Chinese left for the States rather than see their businesses nationalized. Chinatown diminished, shrinking from the 44 blocks it once occupied to the reduced area of today around Cuchillo de Zanja. The tide started to turn once more in 1995, with a **regeneration programme** kickstarted when the Chinese government presented Cuba with the materials to create the Chinatown gate that now stands on Dragones.

Today Chinese culture in Havana quietly holds its own. Lectures on Chinese culture are given in teashops, Tai Chi schools pepper the neighbourhood, Chinese New Year is celebrated annually and the bi-weekly Chinese character newspaper, *Kwong Wah Po*, is painstakingly handset on an ancient press. There are also plans for a museum to Chinese culture. However, China's influence in Cuba is perhaps most evident in the national bus network and plethora of household goods that are now imported as part of burgeoning trade agreements between the two nations.

Iglesia Nuestra Señora Caridad del Cobre and Iglesia del Sagrado Corazón

Four blocks southwest of the Galiano and San Rafael intersection, occupying the length of the block between Manrique and Campanario, is the simple though appealing **Iglesia Nuestra Señora Caridad del Cobre** (Tues–Sun 7am–6pm). Construction of the church began in 1802 and involved the joining of two existing churches, but its restoration in the 1950s has given it a distinctly modern feel, with the soft light and dusty-coloured stone walls engendering an atmosphere of soothing tranquillity. Circular portholes with stained-glass windows featuring star-shaped designs line the walls and are clearly relatively recent additions.

A block south on Manrique and five blocks west on Simón Bolívar, the **Iglesia del Sagrado Corazón** (daily 8am–noon & 3–5pm, mass daily at 8am & 4.30pm), towers above a block of worn-out neo-colonial apartment buildings. Built between 1914 and 1923, this is arguably the most magnificent church in the country. Its unlikely location in the grime of Centro Habana, with heavy traffic passing by outside, contrasts effectively with its Neo-Gothic splendour and makes a wander through its imposing entrance irresistible. Inside, a second surprise awaits, as the church's interior is infinitely more impressive than that of the much more heavily visited cathedral in Habana Vieja: the cavernous vaulted roof of the three naves is supported by colossal columns and the huge central altar incorporates a dazzling array of detail. Wherever you look, something catches the eye, from the skilfully sculpted scenes etched into the central pillars to the stained-glass windows at different levels on the outer walls.

The Malecón and around

The most picturesque way to reach Vedado from Centro Habana or Habana Vieja is to stroll down the **Malecón**, the city's famous seawall, which snakes west along the coastline from La Punta for about 4km. It's the city's defining image, and ambling along its length, taking in the panoramic views, is an essential part of the Havana experience. But don't expect to stroll in solitude: the Malecón is the capital's front room and you won't be on it for long before someone strikes up a conversation. People head here for free entertainment, particularly at night when it fills up with guitar-strumming musicians, vendors offering cones of fresh-roasted nuts, and star-gazing couples, young and old alike. In recent years it's grown in popularity for the city's expanding clique of gays and transvestites, who put its sinuous length to good effect as a nightly catwalk and meeting place, especially the area close to the *Hotel Nacional*. In the daytime it's crowded with schoolchildren (intent on hurling themselves into the churning Atlantic), wide-eyed tourists and wrinkled anglers.

The Centro Habana section, referred to on street signs as the *Malecón tradicional*, has been undergoing tortoise-paced renovations for over a decade now. Lined with colourful neo-colonial buildings, it's the oldest, most distinct and characterful section in the city, though – potholed and sea-beaten – it looks much older than its hundred or so years. Construction began in 1901, after nearly a decade of planning, and each decade saw another chunk of wall erected until, in 1950, it finally reached the Río Almendares. Today there are a few places worth stopping in for their enjoyable sea views. The best of these is *Castropol* (see p.172), *Taberna El Galeón* (see p.134) and the *Lava Día* tapas bar at no.405 (see p.128).

Parque Antonio Maceo

A few blocks from Vedado the Malecón passes in front of the **Parque Antonio Maceo**, often referred to simply as the Parque Maceo, an open concrete park marked in the centre by a statue of Antonio Maceo, the Cuban general and hero of the Wars of Independence. The only other monument of any sort in the park is the **Torreón de San Lázaro**, a lonely little solitary turret, little more than a curiosity but built in 1665, making it 250 years older than the park itself. Once part of the city's defence system, it's now stuck in the corner of the park where Marina intersects with the Malecón. There's a small playground here and the park attracts scores of screaming kids and chattering adults every evening, the best time to visit one of the most attractive public spaces in Centro Habana.

Just south of the park across San Lázaro and next door to the best hospital in the country, the towering Hospital Hermanos Ameijeiras, is the **Convento de la Inmaculada Concepción**, which warrants at least a quick peek inside. The chapel usually has its doors open to the street and is in fine condition, made all the more appealing by the number of Cubans putting it to use. This is very much a working building, its location by the side of the hospital ensuring a relatively frequent line of people coming in to say prayers. There's a resplendent blue-and-gold central altar and marble pillars topped with bronze sculpted detail lining the walls, all bathed in the calming light shining through the stained-glass windows and reflecting off the beige-and-white paintwork throughout.

Callejón de Hamel

Four blocks west on San Lázaro from the Parque Maceo, a wide alleyway known as the **Callejón de Hamel** has been converted into an intriguing and cultish monument to Afro-Cuban culture. Often featured in Cuban music videos, this bizarre backstreet is full of shrines, cut into the walls and erected along the sides, brimming with colour and a mishmash of decorative and symbolic images. The backdrop is an abstract **mural** painted by local artist Salvador González. Both poet and artist, González first started working on the street in 1990, as a private initiative to visually enrich one of the most blighted areas in Centro Habana. You'll find his mystical and esoteric painted verses intertwined among the murals, which now spill over onto nearby apartment block walls and sculptures created from scrap metal. A few chairs and tables make up a tiny café at one end and the alley also features a small studio workshop selling smaller pieces of art done by González. The best time to visit is on a Sunday from around 11am, when it becomes a venue for **Santería ceremonies**. The participants of these mini street festivals dance passionately to the rhythm of rumba in a frenetic atmosphere, accentuated by chants invoking the spirits of the *orishas*. The alley's popularity unfortunately means it has become slightly contrived, but this is still an excellent chance to experience one of the most engaging expressions of Santería.

3

Vedado

The cultural heart of the city, graceful **Vedado** draws the crowds with its palatial hotels, contemporary art galleries, exciting (and sometimes incomprehensible) theatre productions and live music concerts, not to mention its glut of restaurants, bars and nightspots. Loosely defined as the area running west of Calzada de Infanta up to the Río Almendares, Vedado is less ramshackle than other parts of the city and more intimate. Tall 1950s buildings and battered hot rods parked outside glass-fronted stores lend the downtown area a strongly North American air, contrasted with the classical ambience of nineteenth-century mansions; the general impression is of an incompletely sealed time capsule where the decades and centuries all run together.

Vedado is fairly easy to negotiate, laid out on a grid system divided by four main thoroughfares: the broad and handsome boulevards the Avenida de los Presidentes (also called Calle G) and Paseo, running north to south, and the more prosaic Linea and Calle 23 running east to west. The most prominent sector is modern **La Rampa** – the name given to Calle 23 immediately west from the Malecón, as well as the streets just to the north and south. Presenting a rather bland uniformity that's absent from the rest of Vedado, it's a relatively small space, trailing along the eastern part of the Malecón and spanning just a couple of streets inland. A little to the south of La Rampa proper is the elegant **Universidad de La Habana**, attended by orderly students who personify the virtues of post-Revolution education.

Southwest of the university is the **Plaza de la Revolución** with its immense monuments to twin heroes José Martí and Ernesto "Che" Guevara. Although generally considered part of Vedado, Plaza de la Revolución (also known as Plaza) is actually the municipality to which the Vedado neighbourhood belongs, and with its huge utilitarian buildings has a flavour quite distinct from the other parts of Vedado. The uncompromisingly urban landscape of the plaza itself – a huge sweep of concrete – is a complete contrast to the area's other key attraction, the atmospheric **Necrópolis de Cólon**, a truly massive cemetery.

In the part of Vedado north of Calle 23 up to the Malecón, west to the Río Almendares and east roughly as far as the Avenida de los Presidentes, the backstreets are narrow and avenues are overhung with leaves. Many of the magnificent late- and post-colonial buildings that line these streets – built in a mad medley of Rococo, Baroque and Neoclassical styles – have been converted into state offices and museums. Particularly noteworthy is the **Museo de Artes Decorativas**, an exhausting collection of fine furniture and *objets d'art*. Further west from the Malecón, dotted around Linea, Paseo and the Avenida de los Presidentes, are several excellent galleries and cultural centres. Not to be missed is the **Casa de las Américas**, a slim and stylish Art Deco building that was set up to celebrate Pan-Americanism.

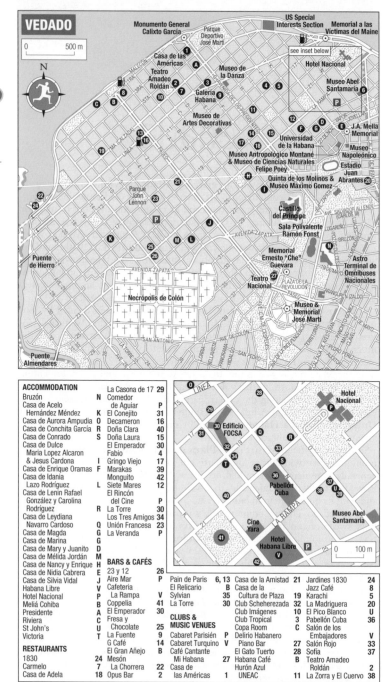

VEDADO

0 — 500 m

N

Monument General Calixto García

Parque Deportivo José Martí

US Special Interests Section

Memorial a las Víctimas del Maine

Casa de las Américas ❶ Ⓐ

Teatro Amadeo Roldán ❷ Ⓐ

Museo de la Danza

Galería Habana ❸ ❼ ❾

❹ ❺

see inset below

Hotel Nacional

Museo Abel Santamaría ❻

Museo de Artes Decorativas

❶❶

❷❹ ❽ Ⓕ Ⓖ

Ⓔ **J.A. Mella Memorial**

Museo Napoleónico

Universidad de la Habana

❶❼ ❶❹ ❶❺

Museo Antropológico Montané & Museo de Ciencias Naturales Felipe Poey Ⓗ

Estadio Juan Abrantes ❷⓿

Quinta de los Molinos & Museo Máximo Gomez Ⓘ

Parque John Lennon ❷❸

❷❶

Castillo del Príncipe

Sala Polivalente Ramón Fonst

Ⓙ

Puente de Hierro

❷❷ ❷❹

Ⓚ Ⓜ Ⓛ

❷❺ ❷❻

Memorial Ernesto "Che" Guevara

Astro Terminal de Omnibuses Nacionales

AVENIDA ZAPATA

Teatro Nacional

❷❼

Necrópolis de Colón

Museo & Memorial José Martí

Puente Almendares

Inset (below)

LINEA

❷❽

Hotel Nacional

❷❾

Edificio FOCSA

❸⓿ ❸❶

Ⓞ Ⓡ

❸❷ ❸❸

Ⓣ ❸❹

Ⓢ

❸❺

❸❻

Pabellón Cuba

❸❼ Ⓤ

❸❽ ❸❾

Museo Abel Santamaría

❹⓿

Cine Yara

❹❶

Hotel Habana Libre Ⓟ

Ⓥ

❹❷

0 — 100 m

La Rampa and around

Halfway along the Malecón's length is the twin-towered *Hotel Nacional* – near an artificial waterfall – marking the start of **La Rampa** (The Slope), the road into the centre of Vedado. Once the seedy pre-revolutionary home of Chinese theatres, casinos and pay-by-the-hour knocking shops, La Rampa is now lined with airline offices and official headquarters, its seedy side long gone (or at least well hidden).

Set on a precipice above the Taganana cave (see box, p.88) and with a magnificent view of the ocean, the world-famous landmark **Hotel Nacional** is home to a princely tiled lobby and an elegant colonnaded veranda looking out to sea across an expanse of well-tended lawn commandeered by tame guinea fowls. The perfect cinematic backdrop for a *mojito*, it was built in 1930 and quickly became a favourite with visiting luminaries – amongst them Ava Gardner, Winston Churchill, Josephine Baker and John Wayne – and since its refit in 1992 has added the likes of Naomi Campbell and Jack Nicholson to its clientele (see p.113 for accommodation details).

Edificio FOCSA

Considered variously as a feat of engineering or a monolithic eyesore, the giant Y-shaped luxury apartment block **Edificio FOCSA** looms over the heart of Vedado like a giant chunk of honeycomb. When built in 1956 this was the second-tallest concrete building in the world; it exemplified modern living with a cinema, supermarket, shops and even a television studio within. According to Alfredo José Estrada in his book *Havana: Autobiography of a City*, by the 1960s the building was known as "*edificio coño*" (roughly equivalent to the "Oh my God!" building) because of the stunned reaction of visiting country bumpkins. Following the Revolution, it housed Soviet personnel whose lack of respect, according to locals, resulted in widespread disrepair. By the early 1990s vultures nested in crumbling eyries and a snapped cable in the deteriorated elevator resulted in a fatal accident in 2000. The state stepped in with a repair programme that has restored much of the building's former glory. Today FOCSA has one of Vedado's better shopping complexes at ground level while *La Torre* restaurant (see p.129) on the 33rd of the building's 35 floors boasts panoramic views over the Malecón and beyond.

Memorial a las víctimas del Maine

Just to the north of the *Hotel Nacional* stands the striking **Memorial a las víctimas del Maine**. It was erected in memory of 260 crew members of the US battleship the *Maine*, which was blown up in Havana harbour on February 15, 1898, and so is studiously ignored by Cuban maps and guidebooks.

Following the Revolution, crowds attacked the monument, toppling and destroying the heavy iron eagle that once perched on the top (the wings are displayed in the Museo de la Ciudad, while the head is in the US Special Interests Section canteen). The present government has stamped its presence with the terse inscription: "To the victims of the *Maine*, who were sacrificed by imperialist voraciousness in its zeal to seize the island of Cuba from February 1898 to 15 February 1961."

Taganana cave

You can enter the Taganana cave (Mon–Sat 9am–5pm; free) through the *Hotel Nacional* grounds, where a small display charts the history of the cave and its rocky outcrop. The cave was named after a character created by Cuban novelist, poet and freedom fighter Cirilo Villaverde, whose story placed the fictional Indian Taganana there after seeking refuge from pursuing conquistadors. The natural cave and its vantage point overlooking the seafront were capitalized upon by the Spanish, who built the Santa Clara battery on it in 1797 and then in 1895 positioned two cannons here for use during the Wars of Independence. Following the war, the battery was expanded and converted into military barracks, which remained until the 1930s, when the area was earmarked for a showcase hotel. A final moment of glory for the cave came during the Missile Crisis in 1962, when Che Guevara and Fidel Castro decamped here with suitable military artillery in preparation for an air defence of the capital.

US Special Interests Section and Plaza Anti-Imperialista

A few blocks back to the east down the Malecón at Calzada y L is the **US Special Interests Section** (☎7/833-3551 & 834-4400), the organization that has acted in lieu of a US embassy since diplomatic relations between Cuba and the US ended in 1961. Around the side of the building there are usually queues of hopeful Cubans waiting to apply for a US visa.

Almost obscuring the building is the **Plaza Anti-Imperialista**, a huge sweeping space under a series of metal suspension arches like the ribs of a giant carcass. Many of the supports are covered in plaques bearing the names and quotes of Cubans and non-Cubans who have supported the country's struggle for self-determination and independence over the last century or so. Also known as Plaza de la Dignidad, this open-air auditorium was hurriedly constructed in 2000 as a forum for Fidel Castro's protestations and invective during the furore surrounding the flight to the US (and eventual return) of schoolboy Elián Gonzáles. In January 2006 North American diplomats began displaying messages about human rights on an electronic ticker tape on the side of the building facing the plaza. What the US termed an attempt to break Cuba's "information blockade" Fidel Castro denounced as a "gross provocation". Later that year the Cuban authorities retorted by erecting 138 black flags, each decorated with a white star facing the ticker tape. They are said to symbolize Cubans who have died as a result of violent acts against the country by unsympathetic regimes since the Revolution began in 1959. The flags, which are sometimes replaced with the national flag, are an impressively sombre sight – which also conveniently mask the messages from view, though these are now, following a thawing in relations, more likely to be international news headlines than anti-Castro propaganda.

Museo Abel Santamaría

Tucked away just east of La Rampa on the corner of unassumingly residential Calles O and 25 is one of Havana's smallest but no less intriguing museums, the **Museo Abel Santamaría** (Mon–Fri 10am–5pm, Sat 10am–1.30pm; free). It was here in 1952 that Abel Santamaría, his sister Haydee Santamaría, Fidel Castro and others planned the attack on the Moncada barracks. Following the unsuccessful attack, Abel was captured and tortured to death upon Batista's orders. In tribute to him his apartment has been preserved as it was on his final days living there. The simply decorated living room and sparse kitchen have little to associate them with the ill-fated revolutionary, but the 1950s furnishings and fittings have an intrinsic interest, not least because they serve to illustrate to anyone familiar with current Cuban interiors how little advance in interior design there has been since this era.

Coppelia

In the middle of a park spanning a whole block between Calles 21 and 23 is Havana's mighty ice-cream emporium, **Coppelia** (Tues–Sun 11am–11pm, closed Mon), the flagship branch of this national chain. Looking like a giant space pod, with a circular white chamber atop a podium, the multi-chamber restaurant was designed in 1966 as an eating place with prices within the reach of every Cuban. Serving over a thousand customers a day, it's hugely popular with locals, who regularly wait in line for ice cream for over an hour – though, contrary to its egalitarian ethics, there is now a separate fast-track parlour to the left of the main entrance catering for those paying in convertible pesos. Cuban film buffs will recognize the park from the opening scenes of Tomás Gutiérrez Alea's seminal 1993 film, *Fresa y Chocolate*. To appreciate the space-age architecture fully go up to *La Torre* restaurant (see p.129) for a panoramic view.

Universidad de La Habana

Regal and magnificent, the **Universidad de La Habana** (ⓦ www.uh.cu) sits on the brow of the Aróstegui Hill, three blocks or so south of La Rampa, overlooking Centro Habana. Founded in 1728 by Dominican monks, the university originally educated Havana's white elite; blacks, Jews, Muslims and mixed-race peoples were all banned, though by an oversight surprising for the time, women weren't, and by 1899 one-seventh of its students were female. It counts among its alumni many of the country's famous political figures, including Cuban liberator José Martí, independence fighter Ignacio Agramonte, and Fidel Castro, who studied law here in 1945. Originally based in a convent in Habana Vieja, it was secularized in 1842 but did not move to its present site, a former Spanish army barracks, until 1902, spreading out across the grounds over the next forty years. Today, the university is an awesome collection of buildings and home to some of the city's most unusual **museums**.

The rubbly pile of oversized grey and whitewashed concrete blocks, near the foot of a sweeping stone staircase capped by twin observation points, is actually the **Memorial a Julio Antonio Mella**, a modern tribute to this former student, political agitator and founder of the Communist Party, thought to have been murdered for his beliefs. Off to one side, a bust captures his likeness while the words on the main column are his: "To fight for social revolution in the Americas is not a utopia for fanatics and madmen. It is the next step in the advance of history." At the top of the stairs, beyond the lofty entrance chamber, lavishly fêted with Corinthian columns, lies the Ignacio Agramonte courtyard, with a central lawn scattered with marble benches and bordered on four sides by grandiose faculty buildings.

The scene of countless student protests, including one led by Julio Antonio Mella in 1922, the university was long seen as a hotbed of youthful radicalism. Guns were stashed here during the Batista administration, when it was the only site where political meetings could take place unhindered. The present administration, however, keeps the university on a firm rein and firebrand protests are no more, though its politicized past is evoked in some quirky details scattered

▲ Universidad de La Habana

throughout the grounds. These include the original American tank captured during the civil war in 1958 and placed here by the Union of Young Communists as a tribute to youth lost during the struggle, and, opposite, an "owl of wisdom" made of bits of shrapnel gleaned from various battle sites. Still a respected seat of learning, the university today has a rather serious air: earnest students sit on the lawn and steps in front of faculty buildings locked in quiet discussion, while inside a library-like hush reigns.

Museo de Ciencias Naturales Felipe Poey and
Museo Antropológico Montané

To the left of the main entrance is the **Museo de Ciencias Naturales Felipe Poey** (Mon–Fri 9am–noon & 1–4pm; $1CUC), the most bewitching of all the university buildings, with a beautiful central atrium from which rises a towering palm twisted with vines. Named after an eminent nineteenth-century naturalist, and with the musty atmosphere of a zoologist's laboratory, the dimly lit room holds an assortment of stuffed, preserved and pickled animals. The highlight is the collection of Polymita snails' shells, delicately ringed in bands of egg-yolk yellow, black and white, while other notables are a (deceased) whistling duck, a stuffed armadillo and Felipe Poey's death mask, incongruously presented along with some of his personal papers. Parents and their offspring may wish to check out the children's corner and pet the stuffed duck, squirrel and iguana.

Those unmoved by the charms of taxidermy can press on up the right-hand staircase along the cloistered balcony to the **Museo Antropológico Montané** (Mon–Fri 9am–4.30pm; free), home to an extensive collection of pre-Columbian pottery and idols from Cuba and elsewhere. Though padded out with apparently indiscriminately selected pieces of earthenware bowls, the collection contains some excellently preserved artefacts, like the Peruvian Aztec pots adorned with alligator heads and the fierce stone figurine of the Maya god Quetzalcoatl, the plumed serpent, tightly wrapped in a distinctive clay coil design. Star attractions include a **Taíno tobacco idol** from Maisí in

Guantánamo; roughly 60cm tall, the elongated, grimacing, drum-shaped idol with shell eyes is believed to have been a ceremonial mortar used to pulverize tobacco leaves. Also fascinating is the delicate reproduction of a Haitian two-pronged **wooden inhaler** carved with the face of a bird, which the Taíno high priest would use to snort hallucinogenic powder in the Cohoba ceremony, a religious ritual for communicating with the dead. These priests would also cure illness, possibly with the aid of a **vomiting stick**, such as the one on display made from manatee ribs, by inserting it into the throats of the afflicted to make them vomit up impurities of the soul. Although from different countries, the inhaler and vomiting stick correspond in shape and design and are thought to come from similar cultures. Finally, check out the stone axe found in Banes, Holguín, which is engraved with the stylized figure of Guabancex, a female deity governing the uncontrollable forces of nature, her long twisted arms wrapped around a small child.

Museo Napoleónico

Just behind the university on San Miguel no.1159, the **Museo Napoleónico** boasts an eclectic array of ephemera on the French emperor, spread over four storeys of a handsome nineteenth-century house. The collection was gathered at auction by Orestes Ferrara, an Italian ex-anarchist who became a colonel in the rebel army of 1898 and subsequently a politician in Cuba. Ranging from state portraits, *objets d'art* and exquisite furniture to military paraphernalia and sculpture, it should appeal to anyone with even a passing interest in the era. The museum is currently closed for renovation.

Central Vedado

West of the university grounds lies **central Vedado**, quieter than the boisterous La Rampa area and more scenic than Plaza de la Revolución. To walk through these silent, suburban streets, once the exclusive reserve of the wealthy, is one of the richest pleasures Havana holds, the air scented with sweet mint bush and jasmine. At night, the stars, untainted by street lamps, form an eerie ceiling above the swirl of ruined balconies and inky trees. No less attractive in the daytime, with few hustlers it is also one of the safest areas to stroll, and the added attraction of several museums will give extra purpose to a visit.

Museo de Artes Decorativas

Housed in a mansion at Calle 17 no.502 e/ E y D, a fifteen-minute walk west from the university, the beautifully maintained **Museo de Artes Decorativas** (Tues–Sat 10.30am–6pm, Sun 9am–noon; $2CUC, $3CUC with guide, $3CUC extra with camera) contains one of the most dazzling collections of pre-Revolution decorative arts in Cuba. Built towards the end of the 1920s, the house was the private estate of the Count and Countess of Revilla de Camargo, who fled Cuba in 1961, whereupon it was appropriated by the state as the ideal showcase for the nation's cultural treasures. With its regal marble staircase, glittering mirrors and high ceilings, it is a perfect backdrop for the sumptuous, if overwrought, collection of Meissen and Sèvres china, *objets d'art*, and fine furniture – a tantalizing glimpse of Vedado's past grandeur. The nine rooms are themed according to period, style and function, with some significantly more distinct and coherent than others, particularly those that most faithfully replicate their original purpose, when the house was lived in, such as the largely unaltered bathroom. Guides are knowledgeable and friendly but tend to bombard you with information, and with such a massive collection in so small a space you may feel more comfortable setting your own agenda and seeing the rooms unattended.

To the left of the grand entrance hall, the **Salón Principal** (Main Room), richly panelled in gold and cream, is full of lavish Rococo ornaments, like the pair of stylishly ugly eighteenth-century German dog-lions, while the Chinese Room next door is dominated by large, intricately screen-printed wooden panels. Upstairs, the rooms are gathered around a majestic balconied hall, among them a fabulous marble bathroom with a marble bath tub inset in the wall. Don't miss the fascinating framed photographs hanging in the upstairs hallways depicting over-the-top banquets and high-society social functions that took place in the house itself in the 1940s and 1950s, alongside pictures of the stashed treasures discovered in the basement in 1961 after the owners had fled the country. Allow time, also, to visit the **gardens** behind and at either side of the mansion, where the unceremoniously presented statues, slightly overgrown alcoves, waterless fountains and less-than-perfect landscaping display a more withered elegance than the interior of the building, but where the flight of the original owners and the abandonment of their wealth is most strikingly apparent.

Parque John Lennon

For an ambling detour, head further up Calle 17 until you reach Calle 6 and the **Parque John Lennon**, so named for the sculpture, created in 2000 by José Villa Soberón, of the eponymous musician seated on one of the park benches. It's a pretty good likeness and more or less life-sized. Although Lennon never came to Cuba, the Beatles have always been wildly popular here, so much so that it's not uncommon to hear people claiming to have learnt English through listening to their songs. Perhaps proving his popularity, Lennon's trademark circular glasses have been prised off by souvenir hunters several times and now the sculpture is protected at night by an armed guard. Every year on December 8 – the anniversary of Lennon's death – there is a combination vigil and jamming session, though recent years have seen attendance dwindle from former crowds to a mere handful of devotees.

Museo de la Danza

A few blocks away to the north from the Museo de Artes Decorativas, on the corner of Linea and the Avenida de los Presidentes, is the **Museo de la Danza** (Tues–Sat 10am–6pm, Sun 9am–1pm; $2CUC, $5CUC extra with camera). Charting the history of the ballet in Cuba but with a subsidiary international focus, the Museum of Dance crams an immense amount of exhibits into a small colonial house and struggles slightly to maintain a clear focus. The common thread, however, is **Alicia Alonso**, Cuba's most famous prima ballerina, and every effort has been made to relate exhibits to her, no matter how tenuous the link. That said, twentieth-century Russian ballet, and particularly **Anna Pavlova**, is given its own spotlight, with an embroidered cape worn by Pavlova, photos of her and a poster from a 1917 production of *El Gallo de Oro* (*Le Coq D'Or*) in which she starred all on display. Some of the best exhibits are found in the museum's back room where original preliminary sketches for costumes and stage sets are exhibited. The final and largest rooms are devoted entirely to Alonso and the **Ballet Nacional de Cuba**, which was founded by Alonso herself, her husband Fernando and his brother Alberto in 1948 and is widely recognized as one of the top ballet companies in the world.

Galería Habana

A short detour west along Linea from the Museo de la Danza to Calles E y F brings you to the unprepossessing doorway, at the base of an apartment block, of one of Havana's longest standing and most respected art spaces: **Galería Habana** (Mon–Fri 10am–4.30pm, Sun 9am–1pm; free; ⓦ www.galerihabana .com). Established in 1962 to showcase Cuban talent, several of the country's most celebrated artists are represented here. With white walls and marble floor, the airy and minimal gallery perfectly frames the work of masters like the late **Wifredo Lam**'s Afro-Cuban Surrealism and **Pedro Pablo Oliva**'s dreamy mysticism. Younger contemporary artists include the collective **Los Carpinteros**, whose architectural installations mix sly humour and social commentary. Exhibitions change every three months, with many pieces offered for sale. Those with several thousand euros to spare can also snap up a slice of Cuban art history for themselves at November's **Subasta Habana** auction (ⓦ www .subastahabana.com), which the gallery runs annually at the *Hotel Nacional*.

Casa de las Américas and around

Towards the Malecón from Linea on the Avenida de los Presidentes, at the junction with Calle 3ra, you'll find the **Casa de las Américas** (Mon–Thurs 10am–5pm & Fri 10am–4pm; free; ☎7/838-2706, ⓦ www.casadelasamericas .org), housed in a dove-grey Art Deco building inlaid with panes of deep blue glass. Previously a private university, it was established as a cultural institute in 1959 – with its own publishing house, one of the first in the country – by the revolutionary heroine Haydee Santamaría to promote the arts, history and politics of the Americas. Since then, its promotion and funding of visual artists, authors, playwrights and musicians has been successful enough to command respect throughout the continent and to attract endorsement from such international literary figures as Gabriel García Márquez.

Today it hosts regular conferences, concerts and talks, many of which are open to the general public and a few of which take place outside of the building's regular opening hours. The monthly programme of events is published on the website and is also available from the reception hall or the Librería Cayuela, the building's small bookshop. It's worth ringing in advance before you visit as attendance at some events is by prior arrangement only. Outside of these events, visitors are restricted either to the bookshop, the ground-floor reception area that sometimes hosts small art exhibitions or, most worthwhile of all, the **Galería Latinoamericana** (Mon–Thurs 10am–5pm, Fri 10am–4pm; $2CUC). This lovely little under-stated gallery tucked away on the first floor stages high-quality bi-monthly exhibitions, showcasing anything from painting and sculpture to photography and film-poster art from other Latin American countries. The Casa de las Américas operates another gallery, the **Galería Mariano** (Tues–Sat 10am–5pm; $2CUC), ten blocks away at Calle 15 no.607 e/ B y C, where exhibitions tend to be of ornamental arts and handicrafts from all over Latin America and the Caribbean.

Within view of Casa de las Américas on the Malecón is the aristocratic **Monumento General Calixto García**. Set in a walled podium, it's an elaborate tribute to the War of Independence general who led the campaign in Oriente, and shows him dynamically reining in his horse surrounded by friezes depicting his greatest escapades, which would warrant closer inspection were it not widely used as a public toilet.

Avenida de los Presidentes and around

Bisecting Vedado from broadly north to south, the **Avenida de los Presidentes** (also called Calle G), is one of the suburb's main arteries connecting the Malecón area to the southern side of Municipio Plaza. Between the sea and Calle 27 the avenue is at its most beautiful, with a wide boulevard lined with lawns, benches and trimmed topiary bushes, and statuesque houses rising amid the trees on either side. Sculptures, statues and tributes to an assortment of presidents are interspersed along its length.

On a white plinth near the northern end are the remains of a statue of Cuba's first president, **Tomás Estrada Palma**, one of the two presidents for whom the avenue is named. Torn down in a wave of anti-American feeling in 1959 as a response to his role in signing the Cuban-American Treaty that leased Guantánamo Bay to the US government, all that remains of the statue are his feet.

Further along, the tributes become more international. Among those non-Cubans honoured are Chile's socialist president and friend of Fidel Castro, Salvador Allende, and Mexican president and national hero Benito Juárez. Perhaps less expected is the statue of US president Abraham Lincoln, in the grounds of the Abraham Lincoln School on the west side of the avenue between Calles 17 and 19.

The second of the avenue's original presidents is at the southern end of the boulevard. Framed by several metres of impressive curved marble colonnade adorned with Neoclassical figures, the statue of **José Miguel Gómez** is redolent of bombastic pomp and self-glorification. Cuba's second president, whose term was dogged by accusations of corruption, was also removed from his plinth in the early 1960s, though he was mysteriously returned to it in 1999.

Castillo del Príncipe

At the foot of the José Miguel Gómez memorial the wide pedestrian-friendly boulevard comes to an abrupt halt; to explore further those on foot must negotiate the narrow dust track that runs alongside the busy flow of traffic heading over the brow of the Aróstegui hill. Almost completely obscured by trees and shrubs lining the sharp banks of the hill to the right is the **Castillo del Príncipe** (closed to tourists). Something of a curiosity, if only because of its notable absence from official tourist literature and maps, the castle was built by the Spanish military engineer Don Silvestre Abarca, who also designed the Fortaleza San Carlos de la Cabaña (see p.76). Perhaps taking advantage of the latterday panoramic view over the Vedado woods down to the sea, the sprawling pentagon, surrounded by a dry moat, was built on the precipice between 1767 and 1779.

The castle's various bulwarks, warehouses and offices provided ample space for the thousand soldiers billeted there in the late eighteenth century. Though it never proved its mettle when under attack, the castle's fortifications – not to mention underground dungeons and galleries – were formidable enough to warrant its conversion into one of Havana's most notorious prisons in the early nineteenth century. The tables were turned in the early years of the Revolution when counter-revolutionaries, including several captured during the Bay of

Pigs invasion, were incarcerated here. The prison was subsequently converted into its rather esoteric present-day use as a ceremonial unit for the armed forces in the 1970s.

Quinta de los Molinos and Museo Máximo Gómez

At the southeastern foot of the Aróstegui hill, Avenida de los Presidentes intersects with Avenida Salvador Allende (also known as Carlos III), which heads east towards Centro Habana. Set back from this traffic-clogged avenue are the romantic remains of the **Quinta de los Molinos** tobacco mill estate, currently closed for renovation. Built in 1836 as a Spanish governor's summer residence, the elegant villa takes its name from the royal snuff mills, or *molinos*, which operated here in 1791. It is also celebrated as the site of the city's first aqueduct, the sixteenth-century *Zanja Real*, the remnants of which are behind the villa and once powered the mill.

To the rear of the building is the **Museo Máximo Gómez** (also currently closed), dedicated to General Máximo Gómez, leader of the Liberation Army in the nineteenth-century Wars of Independence, who moved here in 1899 after the first War of Independence. The 1.5 square kilometres of grounds surrounding the house are full of faded charm with ponds brimming with lily pads. Once re-opened, this should prove to be one of the pleasantest spots in the area in which to linger. The **Hermanos Saiz Cultural Association** runs music and arts events from its venue *La Madriguera* at the back of the site. The outdoor space is a magical spot for seeing contemporary acts amid Havana's young Bohemians (see p.142).

Plaza de la Revolución

At the southwest corner of the Quinta de los Molinos grounds, the Avenida de los Presidentes becomes Avenida de Ranchos Boyeros and continues south for about a kilometre to the **Plaza de la Revolución**. The plaza comes as a bit of a let-down at most times, revealing itself to be just a prosaic expanse of concrete

▲ Memorial Ernesto "Che" Guevara in Plaza de la Revolución

bordered by government buildings and the headquarters of the Cuban Communist Party. It's much better to visit on May Day and other annual parade days, when legions of loyal Cubans, ferried in on state-organized buses from the *reparto* apartment blocks on the city outskirts, come to wave flags and listen to speeches at the foot of the José Martí memorial. Tourists still flock here throughout the year to see the plaza's twin attractions: the **Memorial Ernesto "Che" Guevara** and the **Memorial José Martí**.

Memorial and Museo José Martí

Although widely seen as a symbol of the Revolution, the star-shaped **Memorial José Martí** had been in the pipeline since 1926 and was completed a year before the Revolution began. Its 139-metre marble super-steeple is even more impressive when you glance up to the seemingly tiny crown-like turret, constantly circled by a dark swirl of birds. Near the base sits a seventeen-metre sculpture of José Martí, the eloquent journalist, poet and independence fighter who missed his chance to be Cuba's first populist president by dying in his first ever battle against the Spanish on April 11, 1895. Carved from elephantine cubes of white marble, the immense monument captures Martí hunched forward in reflective pose.

Behind the statue, the stately ground floor of the tower houses the exhaustive **Museo José Martí** (Mon–Sat 9am–4.30pm; museum $3CUC, museum and lookout $4CUC, cameras $1CUC extra), which charts Martí's career mainly through letters and photographs (for more on Martí see p.71). The lavish entrance hall, its walls bedecked with Venetian mosaic tiles interspersed with Martí's most evocative quotes, certainly befits a national hero and is the most impressive aspect of a museum that tends to stray off the point at times. The museum's most eye-catching exhibit is close to the entrance to the first room: a replica of Simón Bolívar's diamond-studded sword, which was given to Fidel Castro by Venezuelan President Hugo Chávez in 2000.

In the second room hang photographs of Martí in Spain, Mexico and North America along with an assortment of artillery, most notably Martí's six-shooter Colt revolver engraved with his name, and the Winchester he took with him into his only battle

A temporary exhibition space in the fourth room showcases work by local artists, while music *peñas* with local crooners singing boleros and the like take place in a small function room on the first and third Saturday of the month.

When you've finished in the museum, an elevator here leads to the top floor to the highest **lookout point** in Havana – on a clear day you can see the low hills in the east and out as far as Miramar in the west. The room is divided into segments corresponding to the five spines of its star shape, so you can move around to take in five separate views.

Memorial Ernesto "Che" Guevara

On the opposite side of the square to the north, the ultimate Cuban photo opportunity is presented by the **Memorial Ernesto "Che" Guevara**, a stylized steel frieze replica of Alberto "Korda" Gutierrez's famous photo of Guevara, titled *Guerrillero Heróico* – the most widely recognized image of him. Taken on March 5, 1960 during a a memorial service for victims of the La Coubre freighter explosion on Calle 23, the photo, with Guevara's messianic gaze fixed on some distant horizon and hair flowing out from beneath his army beret, embodies the unwavering, zealous spirit of the Revolution. It was only in 1967, after his capture and execution in Bolivia that the photo passed into iconography, printed on T-shirts and posters throughout the 1970s as an enduring symbol of rebellion. The sculpture that you see now on the wall of the Ministry of Interior building, where Guevara himself once worked, was forged in 1993 from steel donated by the French government.

Korda, who died in 2001, famously received no royalties from the image, and even gave the image's wide dissemination his blessing. As a lifelong supporter of the Revolution and Guevara's ideals, he believed that spreading the image would allow Guevara's ideals to spread alongside it, which neatly allows for the image's commercial use in Cuba itself.

Necrópolis de Colón

Five blocks northwest from Plaza de la Revolución along tree-lined Paseo, there's a worthwhile detour to the left at the Zapata junction: the **Necrópolis de Colón** (daily 8am–5pm; $1CUC), one of the largest cemeteries in the Americas. With moribund foresight the necropolis was designed in 1868 to have space for well over a hundred years' worth of corpses, and its neatly numbered "streets", lined with grandiose tombstones and mausoleums and shaded by large trees, stretch out over five square kilometres. A tranquil refuge from the noise of the city, it is a fascinating place to visit – you can spend hours here seeking out the graves of the famous, including the parents of José Martí (he is buried in Santiago), celebrated novelist Alejo Carpentier, Alberto "Korda" Gutierrez, and a host of revolutionary martyrs.

The main avenue sweeps into the cemetery past tall Italian marble tombstones, including a copy of Michelangelo's *Pietà*. Particularly noteworthy is the **mausoleum**, just behind the main avenue on Calle 1 y Calle D; draped with marble maidens depicting justice and innocence, it holds the remains of a group of medical students executed in 1871 on the charge of desecrating the tomb of a Spanish journalist.

▲ Necrópolis de Colón

In the centre of the necrópolis is the Romanesque **octagonal chapel**, opened in 1886. Masses are held every day at 8am but the chapel is also open at varying times during the day. You should seize the chance to peek inside and admire the luminous German stained-glass windows and, towering above the altar, Cuban artist Miguel Melero's fresco *The Last Judgement*, which has Christ presiding over winged devils and other reprobates as they plummet to their peril.

Close to hand, at Calle 1 e/ F y G, always engulfed by a cornucopia of flowers and guarded by an attendant, the **tomb of Amelia Goyri de la Hoz** and her child is an arresting sight. A Havanan society woman, Goyri de la Hoz died in childbirth on May 3, 1901, and was buried with her child, who survived her by only a few minutes, placed at her feet. During a routine exhumation the following year, she was supposedly found to be cradling the child in her arms. The story spread immediately. Goyri de la Hoz was dubbed *La Milagrosa* (The Miracle Worker) and the event was attributed to the power of a mother's love working beyond the grave. Soon *La Milagrosa* was attributed with universal healing powers, and to this day supplicants queue round the block to have their wishes granted. A strict etiquette controls the ritual: to stand a chance of success you must first knock on the tombstone three times with the brass handles to alert the saint within, then cover the tomb with flowers before mentioning the wish and, finally, leave without turning your back.

In the southern half of the cemetery, marked by large plots of as yet unused land, veterans of the Revolution, including luminary figures Celia Sánchez, July 26 Movement leader and companion to Fidel Castro, and poet Nicolás Guillén, lie in an extensive and faintly austere pantheon house just off the main avenue. A little way behind this, those who accompanied Fidel Castro on the yacht *Granma* and were slain in the first revolutionary battle at Alegría de Pío repose in slightly more ornate style.

Miramar and the western suburbs

Miramar and the western suburbs is Havana's alter ego, home to the flashiest neighbourhoods in the city, replete with sleek Miami-style residences, swish new business developments and brash five-star hotels. Among the last sections of the city to be developed before the Revolution, this is where the wealth was then concentrated, and it's slowly trickling back through the city's growing clique of international investors and wealthy foreign residents. That's not to say, however, that this area does not suffer the same problems that afflict the rest of the capital. As you travel south through these expansive boroughs, the hallmarks of wealth gradually fade altogether, with mansions replaced by apartment blocks, dogs instead of security guards and increasingly potholed roads. Nevertheless, a gentler pace of life exists throughout the western suburbs, calmed by the broad avenues and the abundance of large drooping trees.

Though there is an **aquarium**, one or two small museums and plenty of wonderful houses and embassies to gawp at, most visitors to this part of the city come here for the **nightlife** and **entertainment**, particularly the famous **Tropicana** cabaret (see p.144), as well as for the area's swanky international **restaurants** and its upmarket **paladars**, offering between them the most diverse and sophisticated eating options in Havana. You'll have to go all the way to the western extremities to find the only proper beach but even then you'll have to pay to enjoy it as it forms part of the grounds of **Club Habana**, a private members' sports and social club.

The whole area west of the **Río Almendares** is occasionally mistakenly referred to as Miramar, but this is in fact the name only of the oceanfront neighbourhood closest to Vedado, the two linked together by a tunnel under the river. Most of this western section of the city, including Miramar and its even leafier neighbour **Kohly**, belongs to the sprawling borough of **Playa**, stretching out for some 15km along the coast as buildings become increasingly thinly spread and the neighbourhoods decreasingly distinct. To the south of Playa are the poorer boroughs of **Marianao**, where Tropicana is located, and semi-rural **La Lisa**, a visit to either of which requires a car or at least a scooter if you are to make the most of them, given their isolated attractions and their position at the all-but-forgotten end of the public transport system. There are, however, a number of buses connecting Habana Vieja and Vedado to Playa (the #P4, #P5 and #P10, for example), while the Habana Bus Tour from the Plaza de la Revolución runs all the way to its far western end.

Miramar

Most visitors venturing over the Río Almendares from the heart of the city find little reason to travel beyond the nearest, most distinct and feature-packed of the western suburbs, **Miramar**. Havana's highest concentration of top-class restaurants and paladars in the city is here, a large number of them within 25 blocks or so of the river, where most of Miramar's visitor attractions are located. Tranquil streets link the busier thoroughfares of Avenidas 1ra, 3ra, 7ma and most prominently 5ta, which continues all the way to the far western end of Playa. The area is also home to troops of top-ranking government officials and host to over eighty foreign embassies and consulates, most of them occupying the countless ranch-size mansions that dominate the leafy avenues. Though the embassies are in great nick many of the once-magnificent houses in between them are in disrepair and the area is not completely free of decay, with derelict buildings and ruined pavements adding to the sense that the neighbourhood has seen better times. Nevertheless, a sense of wealth remains, even if it is a little misleading, the abundant greenery helping to cover the creeping cracks.

In an area as thick with diplomats as this there is an unsurprising lack of street life compared to the boroughs east of the river. In fact, embassy guards outnumber pedestrians in places and it can all seem a bit insipid. Be aware too that the blocks are relatively long in Miramar and an aimless wander can easily turn into a tiresome trek. The best way to avoid this is to aim directly either for one of the area's set of excellent eateries, many of which are located close to bars, cafés and shops, or for specific sights, such as the **Acuario Nacional de Cuba** and its exciting dolphin shows or the impressive scale model of the city, the **Maqueta de la Habana**.

Museo del Ministerio del Interior

About a kilometre from the mouth of the tunnel on Avenida 5ta, on the corner of Calle 14, is the **Museo del Ministerio del Interior** (Tues–Fri 9am–5pm, Sat 9am–3.30pm; $2CUC, $3CUC with guide, $5CUC for photos), the museum of the Cuban secret services. Housed in two airy Miramar mansions, much of the museum is devoted to charting the conflict between the secret services and alleged US attempts to undermine the Revolution. Many of the exhibits comprise billboards written in Spanish, so non-Spanish speakers will find considerably less of interest, though there is still enough here to warrant a quick spin around, should you be in the area.

The first of the two houses contains the most engaging rooms. As memorable as anything else here are the exhibits relating to the countless assassination attempts made on Fidel Castro since 1959 by Cuban-American groups and the CIA. These include explosive devices and weapons hidden in a cuddly toy and a cereal box. There are also details of the ongoing covert operations of the CIA in Cuba, complete with confiscated explosives smuggled in by suspected members of the Cuban-American National Foundation and evidence of several terrorist attacks. Illuminating, though incongruous, are the displays devoted to Elián González, which chart the furore which gripped the country in 2000 when the US- and Cuban-based sides of his family, and by proxy the two nations themselves, fought over custody of this 5-year-old boy. Much of the rest of the museum, however, is quite humdrum.

Within a block of the museum is one of Havana's best cigar emporiums, complete with restaurant and bar, the **Casa del Habano Quinta y 16** (see p.157).

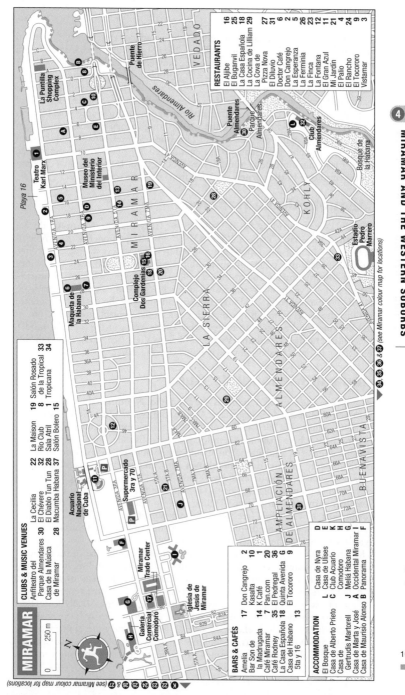

Playa 16

Providing one of the disappointingly few open spaces that face the ocean in Miramar is scrappy but endearing **Playa 16**, not exactly a beach but more a small oceanfront park. Just off Avenida 1ra, between Calle 14 and Calle 16, this rocky natural platform, about the size of a football pitch, is dotted with rock pools where waves have spilled over into the gnarled ground, while parts of it have been paved over and cement benches installed. On calm days it's one of the more relaxing spots for catching a breeze and is the most accessible place in the whole of the city for a dip in the water, though when the sea is rough you are better off popping over the road to *Don Cangrejo*, a restaurant complex with its own swimming pool (daily 10am–6pm; $5CUC) open to non-diners (see p.131 for restaurant review). You can buy food at Playa 16 itself, from a cafeteria tucked into one of the corners, set back from the concrete shore.

Maqueta de La Habana

Six blocks west of Playa 16, at Calle 28 e/ 1ra y 3ra, the **Maqueta de La Habana** (Tues–Sat 9.30am–5.30pm; $3CUC) is a scale model of the whole of Havana, with tiny, Monopoly-house-sized replicas of every single building. Built as an aid to the offices of city planning and development, the city's various eras of construction are colour-coded: colonial buildings are brown, twentieth-century pre-revolutionary structures are ochre, post-revolutionary ones are cream. With a scale of 1:1000 it is colossal, and much of the detail in the centre is difficult to see, although the unwieldy telescopes available for public use in the viewing gallery above do remedy this a little. You can see a similar model, the **Maqueta de la Habana Vieja**, in Habana Vieja (see p.59), although this one tends to draw smaller crowds, making viewing easier.

Acuario Nacional de Cuba

A good bet for a fun few hours is the **Acuario Nacional de Cuba**, 1.5km west of the Maqueta de la Habana, at Avenida 3ra esq. 62 (Tues–Sun 10am–6pm; $7CUC adults, $5CUC children; Ⓦwww.acuarionacional.cu), an outdoor marine park where mammals, reptiles, birds and fish are showcased in wildly varying degrees of animation. You should time your visit to coincide with one of the twenty-minute **dolphin shows**, the unquestionable highlight here, which take place three times a day (11am, 3pm & 5pm), featuring as many as eight highly trained dolphins, or the less spectacular but enjoyable twice-daily **sea lion shows** (noon & 4pm). Failing that, stop here for lunch at the on-site **restaurant**, *El Gran Azul* (see p.131 for review), where, usually at 1.30pm, you can enjoy an underwater dolphin show from your table, viewed through a huge window set below the surface of the water.

Much of the rest of the park can seem a bit lifeless after one of these shows and away from the larger enclosures, where turtles, pelicans and sea lions usually attract the most attention, there are signs of neglect. Dozens of fish tanks, ordered to represent different aquatic environments, demonstrate equally well the various stages of paint corrosion, with many of the tanks totally featureless save for the fish themselves. The largest specie of fish on display is the relatively small cat shark, of which there are several, but even they are contained in a cramped, mouldy, uninspiring looking tank. With so many shortages of materials in Cuba these shortcomings are perhaps understandable and certainly worth taking account of on a visit here.

Miramar Trade Center and around

Three blocks west of the aquarium, sandwiched in between Avenidas 3ra and 5ta, is the **Miramar Trade Center**, a complex of office buildings and retail outlets surrounded by five of the city's best equipped hotels, between them providing the best reason for a visit here with numerous eating, drinking and shopping options. These include one of the city's best **shopping malls**, the Galería Comercial Comodoro (see p.161).

Over Avenida 5ta from the Trade Center, and in stark contrast to that modernist construction, is the Byzantine-style dome of the **Iglesia de Jesús de Miramar**, one of the largest churches in Cuba. Built between 1948 and 1953 it is of little historical significance, though the lofty central nave capped with an impressive altar is worth a peak if the church happens to be open.

Kohly

South of Miramar, running along a more attractive and open stretch of the Río Almendares, is hillier, greener, **Kohly**, a more downmarket neighbourhood with fewer attractions to offer the visitor but home to the city's largest green space, the **Parque Almendares**. This riverside park sits in the shadow of the Puente Almendares, the bridge spanning this part of the river and joining Kohly to Vedado. There is scant reason to stray more than a few blocks from the river in this compact little corner of the borough, with the only other obvious and substantial draw, the **Club Almendares** leisure complex, lying just beyond the river banks a short walk from the park.

Parque Almendares

Right on the edge of Kohly is the only decent-sized city park in Havana, the **Parque Almendares**. Running for about 400m along the river, its tangle of palms, giant weeping figs and pine trees coats much of the park in a dense woodland, filling it with dappled light and an almost eerie enchantment, especially at dusk. This moody charm is enhanced by wishing wells, twisting pathways and iron benches but is tempered by scuffed lawns and abandoned buildings, along with other signs of neglect. At weekends and during holidays it's a popular spot frequented by local families, with salsa reverberating through the park emanating from speakers arrayed around the parking lot.

As well as providing a welcome expanse of greenery, Parque Almendares has several activities to choose from. This is an ideal place for a picnic, particularly as the park's sole café, situated in the centre (Tues–Sun 10am–5pm), is somewhat sparsely stocked. The river, though dirty, makes a good venue for **rowboats** (Tues–Sun 10am–6pm, Cubans $5CUP, non-Cubans $1CUC for 60min), while a **crazy golf** course (Tues–Sun 10am–5pm, $1CUP), playground, **pony rides** (no fixed times, $5CUP) and an aviary make the park one of the better attractions in Havana for children.

The park is the landscaped section of a much larger forested area known as the **Bosque de la Habana**, extending over two kilometres along the river, most of it quite wild with no obvious paths. Plans to develop the woodlands and make them more visitor-friendly have been in the offing for well over a decade but for now the woods offer a slice of the countryside right in the heart of the city.

▲ Bosque de la Habana

Club Almendares

Just out of sight of the park, around a corner a couple of hundred metres up the road and set back from the river, are the verdant grounds of the **Club Almendares** complex. Featuring bars, restaurants, a swimming pool (daily 10am–6pm; $10CUC entry which includes $8CUC worth of food and drink), a games room with pool tables (daily 6pm–6am; $3CUC per hour) and a nightclub, this is a fairly slick operation by Cuban standards and one of the more secluded outdoor spaces in Havana outside of the hotels. This commercial enterprise is in fact linked to the *El Bosque* hotel (see p.113 for hotel review), and is the best place in Kohly for a bite to eat either at the patio pizzeria *La Pérgola* (daily 11am–11pm) or the more formal *El Lugar* restaurant (daily noon– midnight). Club Almendares is gaining a reputation as one of the best salsa venues in the city, with dance classes taking place in the day, though these are predominantly the preserve of dance students on specially packaged holidays. At night it hosts *El Chévere* (see p.142), one of the most respected nightclubs for serious salsa enthusiasts.

Club Habana and Marina Hemingway

Several kilometres west of Miramar are the two most developed coastal attrac- tions in the western suburbs. The best one for a day-trip is **Club Habana**, where a beach, several swimming pools, a bar, a good-quality restaurant and some excellent sports facilities provide more than enough to occupy you from breakfast until dinner. Less compact and neatly arranged is **Marina Hemingway**, where the real draw is the set of organized excursions and the diving and fishing trips that set off from here.

The best way to get to either place is on the **Habana Bus Tour**, with the marina marking the final stop on route T2 (see p.25 & colour map). Metrobus #P4 will get you within a kilometre of the two sites. If you have your own transport just follow Avenida 5ta all the way to the seafront neighbourhood of Flores, an eight-kilometre drive from the tunnel under the Río Almendares. On the way to these coastal playgrounds, on Avenida 5ta, is the **Isla del Coco** theme park (see p.174).

Club Habana

Club Habana (daily 7.30am–9pm; daily rates $10CUC Mon–Fri, $15CUC Sat & Sun; ☏7/204-5700 & 204-3300) is an upmarket leisure and business complex based in and around an enormous stately mansion. Most significantly, it is also the site of Havana's only proper city **beach**. Prior to the Revolution this was the Havana Biltmore Yacht and Country Club, whose members were drawn predominantly from the Cuban aristocratic classes and the wealthy US business community. Today it maintains an air of exclusivity with membership costs prohibitively high for most Cubans and some of the best sports facilities in the whole city.

At 200m in length the palm-lined sandy beach is a real treat compared to anything else this close to the city centre and is usually sparsely populated, not surprisingly given the entrance cost. With several half-decent eateries on site and three **swimming pools** this is the best place in Havana to spend a whole day of pure undisturbed escapism. The palatial clubhouse is prosaically dominated by business facilities but does feature a wall of intriguing photographs depicting the club and its members pre-1959, plus the formal *El Chelo* **restaurant**, which offers reasonably priced seafood and an atmospheric little cellar-style **bar**, *La Bodeguita*. For full details of all sports facilities see p.169.

Marina Hemingway

A kilometre further west along the coastal road from Club Habana, just beyond the small suburb of Jaimanitas, is the **Marina Hemingway**, at Ave. 5ta y Calle 248 in Santa Fe (☏7/204-5088). As well as hosting international fishing tournaments, the marina offers open-water fishing trips, several non-fishing **organized excursions** by boat and a diving club (for details on all of these see pp.165–166). The large site, set along four parallel canals each a kilometre in length, contains shops, hotels, restaurants and a four-lane **bowling alley** (daily 11am–10pm; $3CUC Tues–Fri, $3.50 Sat & Sun) but none are particularly impressive and while the marina is a good spot for lunch if you're in the area, these facilities, scattered haphazardly around the marina and some long past their best, don't by themselves justify a trip all the way out here from the city centre; the diving and fishing trips, however, do.

Marianao and La Lisa

Though between them they account for over a quarter of a million of Havana's total population, large parts of the boroughs of **Marianao** and particularly **La Lisa** don't feel like the city at all. Extending from Playa's southern border they filter into the provincial countryside and both lack distinguishable focal points but they do contain some of Havana's most spectacular nightlife venues. The **Tropicana** is the most famous of them all and is in the north of Marianao, 3km from the Puente Almendares in Kohly. The other most notable nightspot in these parts is **Macumba Habana**, in La Lisa (for reviews of both nightclubs see pp.142 & 144), forming part of the Complejo La Giraldilla, the best-equipped place in either of these two boroughs to sustain a day-trip. If you're in the area you could pop into the **Museo del Aire** (Tues–Sun 10am–5pm; $2CUC) at Ave. 212 e/ 29 y 31, where the collection of over two dozen aeroplanes and helicopters, most of them once in the service of the Cuban Air Force, warrant only a quick look.

Complejo La Giraldilla

A four-kilometre drive south of Club Habana, most of it along Calle 222, will take you from Avenida 5ta to the **Complejo La Giraldilla** (daily 10am–4am), at Calle 222 y 37, a complex with pool, bar, restaurant and live music spread around the rooms and gardens of an isolated Neoclassical mansion. Set in semi-rural surroundings and perfect for a day of outdoor lounging, the house was built in 1925 in what would then have been a country estate. The elegant interior of the house and its colourful gardens are slightly offset by the clumsier size and layout of the adjacent nightclub and music venue, **Macumba Habana** (see p.142 for review), occupying an enormous patio before a large stage. Nevertheless, an afternoon spent by the twenty-five-metre **pool** here (daily 10am–6pm; $5CUC, children $2CUC, includes two drinks) is barely affected by this incongruity and perfectly complimented with lunch in the elegant, reasonably priced Cuban-cuisine **restaurant**, serving buffalo steak among its specialities. A cigar shop and atmospheric wine cellar, where you can also drink and dine, complete this neatly packaged venue.

Listings

Listings

Accommodation

Havana offers the visitor what may at first appear a rather stark choice in terms of accommodation, with the majority of **hotels** charging upwards of $100CUC per night for a double room throughout the year, and in high season (roughly Dec–March & July–Aug) closer to $150CUC on average. The alternative, besides the tiny number of cheap hotels, most of which are very basic, is to pay around $30CUC a night to stay in someone's house, that is to say a **casa particular**, the nearest thing Havana has to bed and breakfasts. However, this is far from a choice between shelling out for luxury and "roughing it". The ever-increasing number of *casas particulares* and their steadily improving standards means there is a broad range of choice – a significant number now offer three-star or even four-star hotel-standard comfort at a fraction of the price. Finding your ideal *casa particular* can be problematic, since they are legally restricted to renting out just two rooms and can easily get booked up, though many now have email addresses, through which you are advised to make bookings.

The top-end hotels offer some of the best dining in the city but the food in the cheaper establishments is rarely as good as the home-cooked meals on offer at most *casas particulares*, usually charged at an additional $6–10CUC for dinner and $3–5CUC for breakfast, though some houses include breakfast as part of the basic cost.

Many visitors choose to stay in **Habana Vieja**, handy for a number of the key sights and well served by restaurants and bars. The massive restoration project in Habana Vieja tossed up new hotels here at a phenomenal rate, with around twenty built or restored in this relatively small city district since the late 1990s and several more currently in construction. *Casas particulares* have also blossomed here and there are said to be over a hundred now legally renting rooms. Much of **Centro Habana** is close enough to Habana Vieja for those wanting to be close to the central sights, but you should be prepared for grimier streets. Quieter, leafy **Vedado** is a more relaxed place to stay, although you'll need transport to make the trip to Habana Vieja. The slick, towering hotels and the luxurious *casas particulares* in **Miramar** are a bit inconvenient for sightseeing, but if money is no object and Western-style luxury a priority, this is the best the city has to offer.

Accommodation prices

Rates are for the cheapest available double or twin room during high season – usually mid-December to mid-March and all of July and August. During low season, some hotels lower their prices by roughly 10–25 percent. Booking in advance online will often secure a significantly lower price.

Hotels

Hotels in Havana are run either partly or wholly by the Cuban state and the quality depends largely on which of these you choose. The vast majority of newly built hotels in Habana Vieja are operated by the Habaguanex chain (Ⓦwww.habaguanexhotels.com), which is generally the most reliable of the Cuban-run companies. Among the other major Cuban names is Gran Caribe (Ⓦwww.gran-caribe.com), which operates the majority of classic hotels in the city like the *Hotel Nacional* and the *Hotel Inglaterra* (but whose standards have slipped, making the star ratings for most of its hotels misleading). Also of note are Cubanacán (Ⓦwww.hotelescubanacan.com) and Islazul (Ⓦwww.islazul .com), both offering serviceable mid-range accommodation; and Gaviota (Ⓦwww.gaviota-grupo.com), which has recently taken sole possession of some of Miramar's hotels that were formerly joint-owned with foreign companies.

If smooth service of an international standard is your priority, you'll want to stay at hotels co-owned by international companies, such as the Sol Meliá (Ⓦwww .solmeliacuba.com) and NH Hoteles (Ⓦwww.nh-hotels.com) chains. Be prepared to pay accordingly – prices for a double room can be as high as $250CUC a night. However, it is always worth trying to negotiate an **off-peak rate**, as several of these hotels are prepared to offer reduced-rate rooms when not fully booked.

Many of the most handsome hotels in Habana Vieja are charismatic colonial-era properties previously owned by Spanish and Cuban aristocrats. Many of these were known as **hostales** (not to be confused with hostels) until a recent rebranding exercise saw most of them officially designated as hotels. Both the existing and the ex-*hostales* are similar to Western boutique hotels in that they are usually smaller than the big corporate hotels, generally consisting of between ten and thirty rooms, though they're not necessarily cheaper than larger hotels and are certainly not independently owned. They offer all the facilities you would expect to find in a good-quality hotel, including decent restaurants, concierge services and shops.

Habana Vieja

Ambos Mundos Obispo no.153 esq. Mercaderes ℡7/860-9530, Ⓦwww.hotelambosmundos -cuba.com. Once long-time host to Ernest Hemingway, this classy 1920s hotel, bang in the heart of the Habana Vieja tourist circuit, features a stylish, sofa-filled and much-visited piano-bar lobby, an art gallery, the original metal cage elevator and a fantastic rooftop terrace. Rooms are simple but comfortable with restrained furnishings, TV and mini-bar and around half have balcony windows. $160CUC.

Armadores de Santander Luz esq. San Pedro ℡7/862-8000, Ⓔcomercial@santander.co.cu. A splendid hotel, tucked away in a secluded corner of Habana Vieja and housed in a stately Neoclassical building that faces the harbour on the port road. Several of the rooms are spread around a delightful second-floor terrace. There's a saloon bar, a pool-table room and a first-floor restaurant

with views of the bay through its floor-to-ceiling windows. $160CUC.

Beltrán de Santa Cruz San Ignacio no.411 e/ Muralla y Sol ℡7/860-8330, Ⓔreserva @bsantacruz.co.cu. Located in the heart of the old city but on one of the less tour-group-trodden streets, this handsomely converted town house – with balconied hallways, wide stone staircase and arch-lined courtyard – has a relaxed vibe. $130CUC.

Caribbean Paseo del Prado no.164 e/ Colón y Refugio ℡7/860-8233, Ⓔreserva@lido caribbean.hor.tur.cu. Plain and uninspiring but one of the cheaper options around the Habana Vieja-Centro Habana border, within easy walking distance of the Parque Central. The rooms are a bit pokey and many have no windows. $54CUC.

El Comendador Obrapía no.55 e/ Oficios y Baratillo ℡7/867-1037, Ⓔreserva @habaguanexhvalencia.co.cu. Agreeable sister hotel of the *Valencia* located next door, this restored colonial building has less of the polished elegance characteristic of hotels in Habana Vieja and more of a countrified feel, with stone floors, ferns lining the wood-railed balconies and a number of intimate little spaces. $130CUC.

Conde de Villanueva Mercaderes esq. Lamparilla ☎7/862-9293, ⓔcomercial @cvillanueva.co.cu. Also known as the *Hostal del Habano*, this is a cigar smoker's paradise with its own cigar shop, a low-ceilinged, bunker-like smokers' lounge and the freedom to smoke anywhere you want on the premises. Despite its relatively small size it manages to squeeze in a number of other alluring communal spaces, including a fantastic cellar-style restaurant and a courtyard brimming with exuberant plantlife. $160CUC.

Convento de Santa Clara de Asís Cuba e/ Sol y Luz ☎7/861-3335, ⓔreaca@cencrem.cult.cu. A convent-turned-hotel suited more for backpackers than holidaymakers, with three of the nine basic but cheerful rooms holding six beds each, though there are better-equipped smaller double rooms. The rooms are located in the less leafy of the two accessible cloisters and there are fans instead of a/c. The current charge, whichever room you stay in, is $25CUC per person.

Florida Obispo no.252 esq. Cuba ☎7/862-4127, ⓔreservas@habaguanexhflorida.co.cu. An impressive restoration of an early nineteenth-century aristocratic residence and expanded since the original reconstruction to incorporate an adjoining building, the *Hotel Marqués de Prado Ameno*. There's a perfect blend of modern luxury and colonial splendour with marble floors, iron chandeliers, birds singing in the enchanting stone-columned central patio and potted plants throughout. $160CUC.

Los Frailes Brasil (aka Teniente Rey) no.8 e/ Mercaderes y Oficios ☎7/862-9383, ⓦwww.hotellosfrailescuba.com. Unique in character, this moody little place is themed on a monastery, with staff dressed as monks. The low-ceiling staircase, narrow central patio and dim lighting work well together to create a serene and restful atmosphere, while the rooms are very comfortable. $130CUC.

Hotel del Tejadillo Tejadillo no.12 esq. San Ignacio ☎7/863-7283, ⓔcomercial @habaguanexhtejadillo.co.cu. Just a block and a half from the cathedral, this is one of the least fancy but more undisturbed of the converted colonial mansions. There's a

pleasant ground-floor bar and a dinky central patio around which most of the rooms are arranged, some of them equipped with kitchenettes, while many are windowless. $130CUC.

Inglaterra Paseo del Prado no.416 esq. San Rafael, Parque Central ☎7/860-8594, ⓔreserva@gcingla.gca.tur.cu. This classic nineteenth-century hotel, one of the best-known in Cuba, is in a superb location on the lively Parque Central. Unfortunately it has lost much of its shine and could do with some serious refurbishment, particularly in some of the rooms. However, the atmospheric interior is full of genuine colonial hallmarks and the pavement café is one of the most sociable spots in the city. $120CUC.

El Mesón de la Flota Mercaderes e/ Amargura y Brasil (aka Teniente Rey) ☎7/863-3838, ⓔreservas@mflota.co.cu. Similar in size and character to a traditional inn and the cheapest of the colonial-conversion hotels in Habana Vieja, the five en-suite rooms at this *hostal* are all spacious and attractive with twin beds, TV and mini-bar. Located within a block of Plaza Vieja, the whole ground floor is a rustic and noisy Spanish restaurant (see p.126). $106CUC.

Palacio O'Farrill Cuba no.102-108 esq. Chacón ☎7/860-5080, ⓦwww.hotelofarrill.com. Unexpectedly grand given its location on a very ordinary street, the *Palacio O'Farrill* is dominated by looming arches and Neoclassical pillars, the tallest of them surrounding a skylight-topped courtyard and others lining the balustraded hallways above, where most of the smartly furnished rooms are found. $160CUC.

Park View Colón esq. Morro ☎7/861-3293, ⓔreserva@parkview.co.cu. Unusual in Habana Vieja, this is a relatively regular, modern high-rise hotel, though more sophisticated than its equivalents in Centro Habana. There are great views across the city from its seventh-floor restaurant. $90CUC.

Parque Central Neptuno e/ Paseo del Prado y Agramonte (aka Zulueta), Parque Central ☎7/860-6627, ⓦwww.nh-hotels.com. The largest hotel in Habana Vieja, this luxury five-star draws in business travellers with its five conference rooms and justified reputation for good service. However, its elegant interior, particularly the leafy lobby, breaks the business-hotel mould. Rooms are sumptuously comfortable, plus there are two classy restaurants, a gym and a marvellous roof terrace featuring a café and swimming pool. $270CUC.

Plaza Agramonte (aka Zulueta) no.167 esq. Neptuno ☎ 7/860-8583 to 89, ⊛www .hotelplazacuba.com. A classic Havana hotel that celebrated its centenary in 2009 but one where standards have dropped of late. The magnificent lobby, complete with fountain, mosaic floor and beautifully sculpted ceilings, has maintained its charm, as has the rooftop bar with its captivating views, but complaints of dirty or badly maintained rooms and poor service have become common in recent years and staying here has become something of a gamble. $120CUC.

Raquel Amargura esq. San Ignacio ☎ 7/860-8280, ⓔreservas@hotelraquel.co.cu. Handsome and sleek with Art Deco touches, this is a surprisingly upmarket establishment given its sidestreet location. A cage elevator, metal chandeliers and a glass ceiling revealing the first floor contribute to the sophisticated finish. $160CUC.

San Miguel Cuba esq. Peña Pobre ☎ 7/862-7656, ⓔcomercial@sanmiguel.co.cu. The only hotel in Habana Vieja facing the bay and the sea, views of which are best enjoyed from the rooftop terrace café. The building itself is rather plain, but lavishly framed mirrors are among several ostentatious touches. $160CUC.

Santa Isabel Baratillo no.9 e/ Obispo y Narciso López, Plaza de Armas ☎ 7/860-8201, ⊛www .hotelsantaisabel.com. One of the most exclusive and best-located of Habana Vieja's hotels, right on the central plaza. Behind this eighteenth-century building's graceful exterior is a refined interior featuring an arched courtyard and fantastic period furnishings in all the rooms. $240CUC.

🏃 **Saratoga** Paseo del Prado no.603 esq. Dragones ☎ 7/868-1000, ⊛www.hotel -saratoga.com. The super-plush Saratoga is the latest Habana Vieja classic to be brought back from the dead, having gained fame in the 1930s. Dripping with lavishness and old-world style, the interior feels like a Humphrey Bogart movie set, with sleek bars and ritzy lounge areas. There's an impressive set of modern facilities too, including a rooftop pool, a gym and a solarium. Rooms feature pseudo-antique furnishings and have DVD players and internet connections while free wi-fi is available throughout the hotel. $275CUC.

▲ Interior of Saratoga

Sevilla Trocadero no.55 e/ Paseo del Prado y Agramonte (aka Zulueta) ☎ 7/860-8560, ⓔreserva@sevilla.gca.tur.cu. A large, refined and historic hotel, dating from 1908 and built in an eclectic mix of architectural styles. It possesses one of Havana's most spectacular top-floor restaurants, the *Roof Garden*, and the old town's largest pool. Rooms are spacious, well-equipped and comfortable. $201CUC.

Telégrafo Paseo del Prado no.408, esq. Neptuno ☎ 7/861-1010, ⓔreserva@telegrafo.co.cu. Though officially a renovated nineteenth-century hotel, so little of the original structure has remained that this attractive four-star is in fact one of the most modern constructions on the Parque Central. At its heart is the eclectically designed ground-floor atrium café incorporating the building's original high-brick arches into its chic, if slightly quirky look, bathed in a distinct glow from the glass roof four storeys up. Rooms are very comfortable but less stylish than the hotel's elegant exterior might suggest. $160CUC.

Valencia Oficios no.53 esq. Obrapía ☎ 7/867-1037, ⓔcomercial@habaguanexhvalencia.co.cu. Plain but pleasant rooms in a beautiful building that feels more like a large country house than a small city hotel. Attractions include a cobbled-floor courtyard with hanging vines. Shares its facilities with *El Comendador*, located next door. $130CUC.

Centro Habana

Deauville Ave. de Italia (aka Galiano) esq. Malecón ☎7/866-8813, ℮reservas@hdeauville .gca.tur.cu. The only seafront hotel in this part of town, on the traditional section of the Malecón, this plain high-rise has rooms with great views and is one of the few places around here with a swimming pool, albeit a very small one. Completely renovated in 2008 and 2009, it now offers the brightest and best-appointed hotel rooms among the relatively modest selection in Centro Habana. Room prices here change particularly frequently. $80CUC.

Lido Consulado no.210 e/ Animas y Trocadero ☎7/867-1102 to 06, ℮reservation@lido caribbean.hor.tur.cu. Located on a run-down street in a lively local neighbourhood, this hotel has dark rooms and rickety furniture, but is a good, inexpensive option, considering how close it is to Habana Vieja. $41CUC.

Lincoln Virtudes no.164 esq. Ave. de Italia (aka Galiano) ☎7/862-8061, ℮carpeta@lincoln.co .cu. One of the more distinctive budget hotels, a handsome though austere building dating from 1926, with reasonably equipped though unsophisticated rooms and good views over some of the grittier parts of the city, especially from the roof terrace. $46CUC.

Vedado

Bruzón Bruzón no.217 e/ Ave de Rancho Boyeros y Pozos Dulces ☎7/877-5683. One of the few hotels where rooms are charged in both national pesos (to Cubans only) and convertible pesos, the *Bruzón* has clean, basic rooms and is close to the Astro bus station. Breakfast is $5CUC extra. $36CUC.

🏃 **Habana Libre** Calle L e/ 23 y 25 ☎7/834-6100 & 838-4011, ⓦwww.hotelhabana libre.com. This stylish Vedado landmark, with stunning atrium and exterior mosaic by Amelia Pelaez, has three restaurants, a terrace pool, a business centre and good-quality rooms with all mod cons. A great choice even if some amenities have seen better days. $150CUC.

🏃 **Nacional** Calle O esq. 21 ☎7/836-3564, ⓦwww.hotelnacionaldecuba.com. One of Havana's best looking hotels, with the air of an Arabian palace. Though some amenities and rooms could do with a bit of an overhaul to make it world class, the swimming pools, health and fitness facilities,

cabaret and open-air garden terrace make this a fine choice. $170CUC.

Meliá Cohiba Paseo e/ 1ra y 3ra ☎7/833-3636, ⓦwww.solmelia.com. This modern hotel close to the western end of the Malecón caters predominantly for the business visitor, with uniformed bellhops, indoor fountains and a mini-mall. The tasteful but unimaginative rooms are full of mod cons and fine views over Vedado. $225CUC.

Presidente Calzada no.110 esq. Ave de los Presidentes ☎7/838-1801, ℮comerc@hpdte .gcatur.cu. *The Presidente* is Vedado's most charismatic hotel. Many of the original features from the hotel's inauguration in 1928 remain, and the small lobby is a delight, with marble flooring and enormous teardrop chandeliers. The rooms' decor complements the general feel with antique furniture, views over the city and marble bathrooms, though the buffet is unlikely to be the highlight of your stay. $140CUC.

🏃 **Riviera** Paseo y Malecón ☎7/836-4051, ⓦwww.hotelhavanariviera.com. Built by the Mafia in the 1950s as a casino hotel, the *Riviera* retains much of that era's style. Many original features – like its long, sculpture-filled lobby, rooms boasting original furniture and Copa Room cabaret – capture the retro vibe. $130CUC.

St John's Calle O no.206 e/ 23 y 25 ☎7/833-3740, ℮jrecepci@stjohns.gca.tur.cu. A pleasant mid-range hotel with an attractive lobby and friendly staff. Facilities include a 24-hour lobby-bar and rooftop pool. $84CUC.

Victoria Calle 19 no.101 esq. M ☎7/833-3510, ⓦwww.hotelvictoriacuba.com. Small and extremely friendly, with only 28 rooms and attentive service, the *Victoria* feels like a private hotel, and features a small swimming pool. $100CUC.

Miramar and the western suburbs

El Bosque Ave. 28A e/ 49A y 49C, Kohly, Playa ☎7/204-9232, ℮reservas@kohly.gav.tur.cu. In a leafy suburb overlooking the eponymous Bosque de la Habana wood, this affordable hotel is the perfect retreat from the thick of the city. Some of the basic but well-maintained rooms have views over the wood itself. Amenities include a pool and a shuttle bus ($3CUC) to Habana Vieja three times a day. $50CUC.

Club Acuario Marina Hemingway, Playa ☎204-6769 & 204-7628, ℮reserva@hmar .mh.cyt.cu. The best of the hotels at the marina lines the banks of two of the four canals here and has a large swimming pool, decent rooms, a good reputation for service and reasonable food. Couldn't be further from the city centre but perfect for fishing and diving trips. $100CUC.

Comodoro Ave. 3ra no.84 esq. 84, Miramar, Playa ☏ 7/204-5551. The selection of well-designed rooms and bungalows, sea views and a shopping mall are tainted by the sometimes sluggish service and below-average standards at the *Comodoro*. Don't be deceived by brochure claims to a beach: it's artificial and basically a large sandpit – though the excellent pool, which winds around the complex, partly makes up for this. $100CUC.

Meliá Habana Ave. 3ra e/ 76 y 80, Miramar, Playa ☏ 7/204-8500, @ www.solmelia.com. Very professional hotel in the heart of the business district. The impressive marble reception area, well-stocked international restaurants, smoking room and huge pool make this excellent, stress-free lodging for visiting VIPs. $220CUC.

Occidental Miramar Ave. 5ta e/ 72 y 76 Miramar, Playa ☏ 7/204 3584, @ www.occidental-hoteles .com. Despite its uninspiring façade, the sleek interior and smooth, professional service make this an excellent choice. Facilities include a business centre, an excellent gym, squash and tennis courts and huge pool. Rooms have all mod cons including wi-fi, and there's a choice of three restaurants. There's a free bus service to the centre, leaving four times a day. $130CUC.

Panorama Ave. 3ra y 70, Miramar, Playa ☏ 7/204 0100, @ comercial@panorama.co.cu. A cosmopolitan and stylish high-rise hotel featuring a marble lobby decked with greenery. A fitness centre, pre-pay wi-fi throughout the hotel, a piano bar and a huge pool with a bar make for a stress-free stay. $120CUC.

Casas particulares

Havana boasts a fantastically broad range of **casas particulares**, from sumptuous boutique-style houses to dingy and cramped places, many of the latter found in Habana Vieja and Centro Habana. All areas, however, possess their fair share of top-class establishments, many on a par with hotels. Though looking for *casas particulares* on the grimier streets of Havana can be a disconcerting experience, behind many of the battered building exteriors are surprisingly grand interiors and comfortable homes. Nevertheless, particular kinds of houses do tend to predominate in certain neighbourhoods; homes in **Centro Habana** and **Habana Vieja**, for example, are almost exclusively in apartments rather than houses and are often located up steep flights of stairs with little or no outdoor space. By contrast, **Vedado** houses, among them some of the city's most elegant nineteenth and early twentieth-century residences, tend to be larger and quieter, often with gardens and patios. **Miramar**'s *casas particulares* are in a league of their own, with several offering independent apartments complete with dining areas and living space and, in some cases, swimming pools. You can expect to pay at least $5–10CUC on top of the usual rates for the privilege though.

Prices are negotiable in all areas, depending on how long you intend to stay and how hard you are prepared to bargain. Meals, including breakfast, are charged as extra in almost all *casas particulares*. Any drinks supplied with your room's fridge that you consume will also be added to your bill, with most houses charging around $2CUC a bottle. All payments are always in **cash** only.

Facilities in casas particulares

There are no power **showers** in Cuban homes: with few exceptions the facility will be an idiosyncratic home-wired electric shower supplying a tepid trickle.

While hotel voltage is 220v, in Cuban homes the **electricity** supply tends to be 110v – so bear that in mind when packing items like hair straighteners.

Casas particulares and the law

The laws governing *casas particulares* change in a frequent and often bizarre-seeming fashion. Basically, this is done so that the government can maintain control of the income that Cubans make from private enterprise – though the party line is that it's to ensure that quality of life is not supplanted by private enterprise. For example, changes to the law have decreed that families may now only let "spare" rooms not otherwise being used as family living quarters. This effectively puts out of business a lot of smaller *casas particulares* which could have cleared out a family bedroom for the duration of a guest's stay. Similarly, in 2008 a crackdown on houses renting more than two rooms saw many previously tolerated "mini hotels" closed down.

Of the host of other new and seemingly minor legal caveats, the ones most likely to affect you decree that proprietors can only rent a maximum of two rooms and can no longer rent a whole apartment or house unless it has a connecting door to the owners' living quarters. Also, guests cannot have more than two people per room unless they're parents with children under the age of 16.

In addition to registered *casas particulares*, there are many that operate illegally without paying taxes. You are not breaking the law by staying in one, and they can be as viable an option as their registered counterparts, if usually no cheaper. If you do stay in this type of accommodation and encounter a problem, however, you will get little sympathy from the authorities.

Legal *casas particulares* should have a sticker of a green or blue icon (a little like a capital I) with the words "arrendador inscripto" on their front door. The law requires proprietors to record the names and passport numbers of all guests, and you are expected to register as soon as you arrive.

It's a good idea to **book in advance**, but be aware that it is common practice amongst landlords to take a booking even when already fully booked, allow you to turn up and then escort you to another *casa particular* from which they will collect a commission. Useful resources for booking include ⓦwww.casaparticular .info and ⓦwww.cubacasas.net, which allow you to reserve *casas particulares* online.

Listed in each section below are the buildings or streets in each area where clusters of *casas particulares* can be found, increasing your chances of finding a vacant room on spec without having to trudge around whole neighbourhoods.

Habana Vieja

Among the best places for a choice of *casas particulares* in one spot is the yellow, nine-floor apartment building at Prado no.20 e/ San Lázaro y Cárcel, within which there are six apartments renting rooms, and at the junction where streets Cuba and Santa Clara meet, opposite the Convento de Santa Clara de Asís.

Los Balcones San Ignacio no.454 e/ Sol y Santa Clara ☎7/862-9877. A plush first-floor apartment that could pass for a colonial art museum with its polished and perfectly preserved vintage furniture and decor. Run by an elderly couple, there are two high-standard bedrooms with their own balconies and large bathrooms, though neither is en suite. $30–35CUC.

Casa de Aurora y Julio Merced no.14 (altos) e/ San Ignacio y Oficios ☎7/863-0536. Just off one of the quieter sections of the port road and with views of the harbour from the living room balcony, there's a sense of calm and space here not available in much of Habana Vieja. The light and airy interior, beautifully maintained, combines modern furnishings with the old house fixtures. Both the rented rooms are clean, comfortable and look fresh. $25–30CUC.

Casa de Daniel Carrasco Guillén Cristo no.16, 2do piso e/ Brasil (aka Teniente Rey) ☎7/866-2106, ⓔcarrascohousing@yahoo.com. There are two large double bedrooms for rent in this grand and cavernous old apartment. Arched doorways, a sculpted ceiling in the living room and balcony views of the Plaza del Cristo all add to the colonial appeal.

Avoiding the accommodation touts

The biggest drawback of staying in *casas particulares* is that you might have to run the gauntlet of the **touts**, also known as *jineteros* or *intermediarios*. Ostensibly, these are locals who work as brokers for a number of houses. In return they collect a commission, usually $5CUC per night, which will inevitably be passed on to the punter, either raising the cost of your room or at the very least compromising your chances of negotiating a lower rate. Be aware that they will often demand their commission from any *casa particular* to which they have taken customers – even when they have done little more than give you directions. There is no way to avoid the attention of these people outright and it can be incredibly frustrating when you feel besieged by people hassling you at every turn. There are, though, several ways to avoid falling prey to touts and thus having your accommodation bill increased unnecessarily:

Always book ahead. If you are approached by touts on the street, state that you have already organized accommodation, but don't disclose where. Often touts will arrive at your chosen house first and tell the owners that they have sent you themselves.

One of the best ways of finding a *casa particular* in another town is by referral. Most *casa particular* owners have a network of houses in other towns which they will recommend, and will often phone and make a reservation for you, or at the very least give you that house's card, though they may themselves charge a commission for this referall. *Casas particulares* all have business cards that they give out to visitors. It's worth asking other travellers for cards and recommendations, as presenting a card on arrival will often secure a reduction and allow you to avoid the touts. If possible, avoid searching for the *casa particular* of your choice while loaded with your bags.

If you need to ask for directions, ask for the street by name rather than the house you want to get to. Another trick to watch for is that *intermediarios* will pretend to direct you to the house of your choice but will actually take you to a totally different house where their commission is better or more reliable.

There is also a modern, neat and self-contained apartment for rent with two double en-suite rooms, custom-built on the roof terrace, justifiably priced at $5CUC per night extra. $25–35CUC.

Casa de Eugenio Barral García San Ignacio no.656 e/ Jesús María y Merced ☎7/862-9877, ✉fabio.quintana@infomed.sld .cu. Deep in southern Habana Vieja, this exceptional *casa particular* is spotlessly clean and contains an impressive collection of flawless antiques. It's a large apartment, run by hospitable landlords, with a garden roof terrace that's a terrific spot for lounging. The two four-star-hotel-standard double bedrooms are exquisitely furnished and include a/c and mini-fridge. $30–35CUC.

Casa de Evora Rodríguez Prado no.20, 9no piso e/ San Lázaro y Cárcel ☎7/861-7932, ✉evorahabana@yahoo.com. Striking penthouse apartment bursting with potted plants, in a relatively modern yellow high-rise on the Habana Vieja-Centro Habana border. Occupying the entire floor, there are fabulous ocean views from the commodious

guest rooms, while from the huge balcony on the other side, which has room enough for two tables and a couple of rocking chairs, unforgettable views stretch across the old city and the bay. Evora lived in Canada for three years and speaks perfect English. $30–35CUC.

Casa de Fefita y Luís Prado no.20, apto. B, 5to piso e/ San Lázaro y Cárcel ☎7/867-6433, ✉fefita_luis@yahoo.com. Situated on the fifth floor of this superbly located apartment block, a stone's throw from the Malecón and within walking distance of the heart of Habana Vieja, this *casa particular* has two simple en-suite rooms for rent, both with great views across the bay plus a windowed terrace balcony perfect for long breakfasts. $30CUC.

Casa de Juan y Margarita Obispo no.522, apto. 5 e/ Bernaza y Villegas ☎7/867-9592, ✉eislerlavin @yahoo.es. On the busiest street in Habana Vieja, close to numerous bars, shops and restaurants, the appeal of this fourth floor apartment, rented in its entirety to guests by the carefree landlord, is in the location. One of the two simple rooms has a balcony looking over the street. The door to the building is just inside a clothes shop entrance, next door to the tourist information office. $30–35CUC.

Casa de Martha y Yusimi Jesús María no.312 (bajos) e/ Picota y Curazao ℡7/867-5005, ℮delfin.marrero@infomed.sld.cu. An apartment within an apartment, on the ground floor, right near the train station. One of the best choices for self-caterers, with a kitchenette, a small dining table and enough space to have friends round. The owners offer you complete independence but equally you are welcome to share with them the communal, plant-lined central patio and ample living room space. $25–30CUC.

Casa de Mery Obispo no.354 e/ Habana y Compostela ℡7/867-3795, ℮lacasademery @gmail.com. Another *casa particular* right in the thick of the action on bustling Obispo and again the central location is the deal breaker, along with the below-average pricing, while the plain, unadorned room is well kept but has an air of functionality about it. More striking is the grandeur of the front room with its thick marble columns and large panelled windows, through which there are views along the street. No meals are offered here. $25CUC.

Casa de Migdalia Caraballé Martín Santa Clara no.164, apto. F e/ Cuba y San Ignacio ℡7/861-7352, ℮casamigdalia@yahoo.es. Opposite the Convento de Santa Clara, this large, airy apartment contains two double rooms and another with three single beds, all benefiting from plenty of natural light thanks to the large, shuttered, street-side window. It's very popular, so reservations are recommended. $30CUC.

Casa de Nelson Merced no.14 e/ Oficios y San Ignacio ℡7/860-3987, ℮nelsonsarduy@enet .cu. Lovingly run and looked after, this pristine *casa particular* has an upbeat feel about it, due in part to its affable owner, but also to its colourful interior. Immaculately tiled and painted in pastel greens and pinks throughout, the homely guest rooms are neatly arranged and come with impeccably clean and fresh en-suite bathrooms, all of which makes up for the tiny windows. $25–30CUC.

Casa de Pablo Rodríguez Compostela no.532 e/ Brasil (aka Teniente Rey) ℡7/861-2111. A spacious upstairs colonial apartment with a huge two-part lounge leading into a radiant patio corridor where the two bedrooms are

located. There's also a lovely roof terrace suitable for sunbathing. Pablo, who has owned this house since 1962, speaks good English. $30CUC.

Casa Riquel Cristo no.12, 2do piso, e/ Brasil (aka Teniente Rey) ℡7/867-5026, ℮casariquel @cubacaribemail.com. Attractive and lofty second-floor apartment in a neo-colonial building constructed in 1912, within half a block of lively neighbourhood park Plaza del Cristo. In contrast to the charming main room with its tall arches, stained-glass windows and chandelier, simple furnishings characterize the two bedrooms, a triple and a double, both with their own decent bathrooms (though only the triple is en suite). Big breakfasts, for an extra $3–4CUC are a plus, as is the gregarious landlady Raquel and her husband Ricardo. $25–30CUC.

Chez Nous Brasil (aka Teniente Rey) no.115 e/ Cuba y San Ignacio ℡7/862-6287, ℮cheznous@ceniai.inf.cu. This magnificent *casa particular* is a real knockout. Majestic from the outside, it is no less impressive within, dignified by perfectly preserved nineteenth-century furnishings and eye-catching features such as the Romanesque bathroom. Two superb balconied rooms are on the first floor, while from the central patio a spiral staircase leads up to the fabulous roof terrace, where there's another very comfortable, contrastingly modern room with en-suite bathroom and its own porch. $30–30CUC.

▲ Typical casa particular building

Centro Habana

In the fourteen–storey apartment block at Malecón no.51 esq. Carcel there are four high-standard apartments. One of the best-connected houses in Centro Habana is the Casa de Miriam and Sinai, from where you can always arrange alternative accommodation if it's fully booked .

Casa 1932 Campanario no.63 (bajos) e/ San Lázaro y Lagunas ☎7/863-6203, ©casahabana@gmail.com. It's the distinctive-ness of its Jazz Age character that makes this tightly packed ground-floor apartment stand out. A treasure trove of Art Nouveau furnishings, there's a film-set quality about the interior design and the leafy central patio, with its wrought-iron, stained-glass gate, and the two bedrooms with their dark-wood beds, wardrobes and chests. The selection of antiques includes a 1930s cash register and a gramophone – and there are sufficient modern comforts too, including TV, fridge and a/c in both en-suite bedrooms. $30–35CUC.

Casa de Ana Morales Aranda Neptuno no.519, apto. 3 e/ Campanario y Lealtad ☎7/867-9899, ©ana.morales@infomed.sld.cu. A comfortable second-floor flat where the huge, stylish bedroom comes with a streetside balcony. The owners are friendly and speak English. $30CUC.

Casa de Armando R Menéndez Castiñeiras Neptuno no.519, apto. 4 e/ Campanario y Lealtad ☎7/862-8400, ©neptuno519@yahoo.es. This quiet flat, tucked away at the back of an apartment building, is furnished with real consistency and artistic style. Much of the well-preserved Art Deco furniture has been here since the 1940s. An extremely likeable, laid-back option run by an astute landlord. $30CUC.

Casa de Candida y Pedro San Rafael no.403 (bajos) e/ Manrique y Campanario ☎7/867-8902, ©candidacobas@yahoo.es. Two double rooms in a down-to-earth ground-floor flat with a dinky hidey-hole patio near the back of the house. Notable for its very informal, family atmosphere. $25–30CUC.

Casa de Dayami de Cervantes San Martín (aka San José) no.618, e/ Escobar y Gervasio ☎7/873-3640, ©lchavao@infomed.sld.cu. Guests are given the run of the upstairs floor, which features a roof terrace at either end, a kitchen-diner and two neat and cosy bedrooms, in this homely two-level apartment. The owners are a friendly family, one of whom speaks English. $25–30CUC.

Casa de Elsa Rodríguez Malecón no.51 esq. Cárcel, apto. 9, 9no piso ☎7/861-8127, ©elsamalecon@yahoo.es. Wonderful, out-of-the-ordinary, artistic apartment up on the ninth floor of a mid-twentieth century seafront building that towers over its neighbours. Both of the spacious en-suite guest rooms have excellent views and are neatly furnished, with memorable touches such as Art Deco armchairs and Art Nouveau glass lampshades. The walls of the elegant communal areas are lined with an eclectic set of original paintings while a comfy, conservatory-style side-room next to the lounge has perfect views of the fortifications on the eastern side of the bay. $35CUC.

Casa de Ernesto García Lealtad no.159 e/ Animas y Virtudes ☎7/861-2753, ©garciaruiz @yahoo.es. There are two excellent rooms here, one effectively an apartment within an apartment, made up of a smartly equipped lounge, bedroom with TV, a/c and safety deposit box, and bathroom but no kitchen. The separate entrance offers complete independence, while the option of sharing the rest of this lovely ground-floor family residence with the affable owners also exists. $25–30CUC.

Casa de Luis Bermúdez San Lázaro no.880 e/ Soledad y Marina ☎7/879-1304. This well-looked-after ground-floor apartment on the Vedado side of Centro Habana offers one room with a double bed and another with two singles. The plastic roof over the central patio casts a soothing light in the sun and complements the grace with which the place has been decorated by its friendly owners. $25–30CUC.

Casa de María del Carmen Villafaña Rodríguez Malecón no.51 esq. Cárcel, apto. 3, 3ro piso ☎7/861-8125. There are two large, cool rooms for rent in this spacious seafront home, one of the most relaxing places to stay in the area. The slanting windows taking up almost an entire wall in the huge front room allow great views along the Malecón and make the place feel like the viewing deck of a ship. Really stands out from the Havana norm. $35CUC.

Casa Marina Escobar no.112 e/ Animas y Lagunas ☎7/867-3014. Spacious and airy house where much of the interior is on a grand scale, from the imposing hallway to the upstairs and downstairs terraces, the latter of which faces the two en-suite rooms for rent. Neither room has a/c but the ceiling fans are usually sufficient given their terrace-side location and high ceilings. $25–30CUC.

🏃 **Casa de Miriam y Sinaí** Neptuno no.521 e/ Campanario y Lealtad ☎7/878-4456, ⓔsinaisole@yahoo.es. A fantastic, smartly furnished first-floor apartment with an enchanting central patio filled with rocking chairs and plants. Two comfortable double bedrooms (one with balcony), with safety deposit box and en-suite bathroom, run by one of the friendliest landladies in the city and her sociable English-, Italian- and German-speaking daughter. $30CUC.

Casa Novo Concordia no.406 e/ Escobar y Gervasio ☎7/863-1434, ⓔporronovo@yahoo .com. Two compact en-suite rooms with a/c, TV and fridge in an upstairs flat with a narrow balcony where you can sit and take in the Centro Habana street life. Run by a doctor and journalist couple, who speak a decent standard of English and whose family have been living here since 1934. $25–30CUC.

🏃 **Casa de Ortencia Batista Perseverancia** no.69 (altos) e/ San Lázaro y Lagunas ☎7/861-1334. You won't find a better-kept, zestier apartment than this in Centro Habana. Freshly painted and tiled throughout, the one spacious and very private double bedroom on the second floor has an excellent bathroom, complete with bath tub, its own little balcony and direct access to a delightfully cosy roof terrace with views of the ocean. $30–35CUC.

Casa de Osiris y Gonzalo Concordia no.423 (altos) e/ Gervasio y Escobar ☎7/862-5337, ⓔosirismiro@infomed.sld.cu. A first-floor apartment in an archetypal nineteenth-century Centro Habana building, featuring high ceilings, stained-glass windows and an outdoor balcony-corridor linking the place together, halfway along which the one room for rent is located. It has a double and a single bed, a shiny en-suite bathroom and a fridge but is otherwise unadorned. An iron spiral staircase at the back of the flat leads to a run-down roof terrace. The owners, a middle-aged couple, have a dog. $25–30CUC.

Casa de Paula Montero Montero San Rafael no.313 e/ Rayo y San Nicolás ☎7/862-7452. Two simple and clean, if slightly dark, double rooms with their own bathrooms in a ground-floor apartment where the owners have combined with neighbouring *casas*

particulares to offer excursions to other provinces. $25–30CUC.

Casa de Ricardo Morales Campanario no.363, apto. 3 e/ San Miguel y San Rafael ☎7/878-4456, ⓔmoralesfundora@yahoo.es. Ideal for anyone looking for privacy and security, as the owner of this thoughtfully decorated, first-floor apartment (fitted with an alarm), is happy to give guests the run of the place. Has a spacious, well-equipped kitchen, one comfy double bedroom and a homely lounge-diner with a TV, large sofa, balcony and decorative items from Mexico. $30CUC.

Casa de Roberto Ferreiro y Marta Fernández San Martín (aka San José) no.253 e/ Ave. de Italia (aka Galiano) y Aguila ☎7/860-9199. One of the best options if you're looking to rent a whole private apartment for two, this cushy little pad features three pristine rooms, including a compact kitchen and a bathroom, all neatly painted and freshly tiled. The pleasant owners live downstairs and have their own separate front door. $25–35CUC.

Las Delicias de Consulado Consulado no.309, apto. B e/ Neptuno y Virtudes ☎7/863-7722. The big selling point at this former paladar, located just a block and a half from the Parque Central, is the excellent food served up in the balconied dining room. One of the two rooms for rent is surprisingly large, given the slightly cramped apartment, and well fitted out, with TV, fridge, two beds and a small walk-in wardrobe. $25–30CUC.

Mansión Colonial Campanario no.164 e/ Animas y Virtudes ☎7/864-6828, ⓔmariabar.chb @gmail.com. A quirky house with two twin rooms for guests and a kitsch line in interior design with pink bed spreads, white furniture, plastic fruit, satin-red drapes and flowery touches all over the place. One of the rooms has its own separate dining room attached, while there is a walled-off kitchen on the central patio set up specifically for visitors, making this a good option for self-caterers or those on a longer stay. There is also a roof terrace and occasionally parked outside is the owner's shiny purple '56 Chevy. $30CUC.

La Roomantic Colonial Amistad no.178 (altos) e/ Neptuno y Concordia ☎7/862-2330, ⓔtamarapuig@yahoo.es. Charming hosts the Puig family have made this relatively humble but well-run *casa particular*, three blocks from Habana Vieja, a relaxing and enjoyable place to stay. Guests have a whole floor to themselves as the family stays upstairs. The two simple, spotless double bedrooms have comfortable beds, large shuttered windows providing plenty of light and dinky en-suite bathrooms. $25CUC.

Vedado

There are thirteen or so apartments running *casas particulares* in the fabulous 1930s apartment block opposite the *Hotel Nacional* (Calle 21 no.4 e/N y O). Most of the apartments are good quality and excellent value and the building, with an impressive Rococo atrium and a cranky lift, is a sumptuous bonus. Good opportunities also abound on Calle K, a wide tree-lined street five minutes away from the *Habana Libre* and La Rampa. There are various *casas particulares* in the apartment block halfway along e/ 25 y 27, as well as some lavishly furnished houses.

Casa de Acelo Hernández Méndez Calle 17 no.1105 e/ 14 y 16 ☎7/831-1377. This mint-green mansion on a quiet side street has two rooms, each with bathroom, a/c and fridge. The splendid grounds include a sundeck, mini pool and a beautiful patio with a barbecue oven. Breakfast and dinner are available for a few convertible pesos extra and English, French and Italian are spoken by the accommodating owners. Parking available. $30–35CUC.

Casa de Aurora Ampudia Calle 15 no.58 (altos) e/ M y N ☎7/832-1843. Two double a/c rooms, one with its own living room and en-suite bathroom, in this beautiful colonial house within a stone's throw of the Malecón. Two expansive balconies each have fantastic sea views. Aurora, Luis and Aurora's son Nelson are among the friendliest and most helpful owners in the city. Delicious and inventive meals cooked by ex-chef Luis are an added pleasure. $25–30CUC.

Casa de Conchita García Calle 21 no.4 e/ N y O, apto. 74 ☎7/832-6187. One of the most popular choices in this beautiful Rococo block (see above), with two very clean and modern rooms tended to by a friendly and helpful host. If Conchita has no spaces she will be able to direct you to the best of the rest in the building. $30CUC.

Casa de Conrado Calle 21, no.15 e/ N y O ☎7/832-1263, @marcogarcia@cubarte.cult.cu. One immaculate en-suite room in front of the *Hotel Capri* with a/c, fridge and CD

player. Friendly host. Breakfast and laundry service also offered. $30CUC.

Casa de Dulce María López Alcaron & Jesús Cardona Calle E no.654 e/ 27 y 29 ☎7/832-1633 @jcardona@correodecuba.cu. This clean and pleasant house has two rooms with private bath. One of the rooms doesn't have a/c and is $5CUC cheaper. The hospitable hosts offer breakfast. $30CUC.

Casa de Enrique Oramas Calle J no.512 e/ 23 y 25 ☎7/833-5913. Well positioned on a quiet street in central Vedado, this house offers a self-contained room with its own entrance, private bathroom, fan, stereo and off-road parking. $25CUC.

Casa de Idania Lazo Rodríguez Calle 25 no.1061 e/ 4 y 6 ☎7/830-9760, @dnsid@ccme.com.cu. Two bedrooms on a beautiful tree-lined Vedado street. Twin beds with a fridge make one room ideal for those sharing, while the second has a double bed. Each has its own bathroom and there's a shared patio. $25–30CUC.

Casa de Lenin Rafael González y Carolina Rodríguez Calle 21 no.4 e/ N y O, apto. 61 ☎7/832-4422, @sandelis@hotmail.com. Three rooms – two en suite – in an airy apartment opposite the *Hotel Nacional* (see p.113). $25–30CUC.

Casa de Leydiana Navarro Cardoso Calle N, no. 203 (bajos), e/ 19 y 21, ☎7/ 835-4030, @carloshf@infomed.sld.cu. Every effort has been made to equal hotel service and mod cons in the two rooms here, with fridges stocked with mini-bar treats, television, fan and faux colonial furniture. There's a large terrace overlooking the Edificio FOCSA on which to take breakfast. $30CUC.

Casa de Magda Calle K, no.508 (bajos) e/ 25 y 27 ☎7/832-3269. The elaborate baroque furniture, chandeliers and china lions adorning this house, with two rooms to rent, are worthy of a decorative arts museum. Each room has a/c and its own bathroom. The largest of the two is particularly splendid, with a king-sized mahogany bed and matching wardrobe. A wide porch out front is perfect for people-watching. Some English is spoken. $25CUC.

Casa de Marina Calle K no.508 (altos) e/ 25 y 27 ☎7/832-1629. Two expansive rooms in this airy first-floor apartment. The walls are lined with accomplished paintings by the owner's son. Each room has a/c, a large bathroom and a regal faux-Napoleonic bed. $25–30CUC.

Casa de Mary y Juanito Calle K no.503, apto 1 e/ 25 y 27 ☎7/832-9989, @jluiscu@hotmail .com. There is a distinctive South Beach Miami feel to this very well-maintained apartment. The two large rooms each have a fridge and en-suite bathroom with natural light. A good choice for a family or two couples travelling together, as the rooms are adjacent and set apart from the rest of the apartment. The house-proud hosts speak English. With the exception of a solitary goldfish, there are no pets. $25CUC.

Casa de Mélida Jordán Calle 25 no.1102 e/ 6 y 8 ☎7/836-1136, @melida.jordan @gmail.com. A big, stylish house set back from the road and surrounded by a marble veranda overlooking a garden filled with roses and ferns. Both of the rooms are beautifully furnished and have a private bathroom. The largest room has twin beds and the other has a double, although an extra bed can be added. English is spoken and there are various extra services available. A superb choice. $30–35CUC.

Casa de Nancy y Enrique Calle 25 no.705 bajos e/ D y E ☎7/830-5411. This large plain room is in a pleasant house on a quiet central Vedado street. The private bathroom is not en suite. $25–30CUC.

Casa de Nidia Cabrera Jovellar (aka 27 de Noviembre) no.359 e/ L y M apto 21 1er piso ☎7/878-0305. One medium-sized room to rent in this pleasant apartment very close to the University of Havana. As a bonus you can just see the sea from the balcony. The owners speak English. $30CUC.

Casa de Silvia Vidal Paseo no.602 e/ 25 y 27 ☎7/833-4165, @silviavidal602 @yahoo.es. An ornate stained-glass window at the top of the marble staircase and mahogany period furniture make this one of the city's most regal *casas particulares*. The two double rooms, one with an extra bed for a child, each has its own bathroom. The lush garden and conservatory are an added bonus. $30CUC.

Miramar and the western suburbs

Miramar's fantastic houses are widely spread throughout the area so if you are looking for a room on spec, pursuing your search by car is the best option. Several of the area's best houses prefer not to be listed but are still identifiable from the blue and white sticker on their

gates. There is a good concentration north of Avenida 5ta roughly between the Río Almendares and Calle 28. Should the ones listed be full, owners can advise you of others in the area.

Casa de Alberto Prieto Calle 4 no.103, Miramar, Playa ☎7/203-5111, @a.prieto@laposte.net. A smart, self-contained apartment with space for three couples. Comes with a kitchen, a dining room and two bathrooms, there's a fantastic roof terrace and the owner speaks English and Italian. Prices depend on how many rooms are rented. From $30CUC.

Casa de Gertrudis Martorell Ave. 7ma no.6610 e/ 66 y 70, Miramar, Playa ☎7/202-6563, @reservas@habitacionhabana .com. Suitable for groups of four to six, this modern deluxe establishment offers a perfect marriage of high-class comfort and facilities with restrained, subtle decoration and furnishings. The whole top floor, complete with a huge terrace, is for guests and features three bedrooms with king-size beds and original paintings by renowned Cuban artists. Knocks the socks off most hotels for sheer luxury but comes at a price. $200CUC for whole floor, $150CUC for one room.

Casa de Marta y José Calle 6 no.108 apto 6 e/ 1ra y 3ra. ☎7/209-5632. A friendly place with two rooms, each with bath. A balcony with a sea view and fantastic home-cooked meals make this a fine choice. $40–50CUC.

Casa de Maurisio Alonso Calle A no.312 apto. 9 e/ 3ra y 5ta, Miramar, Playa ☎7/203-7581, @masexto@infomed.sld.cu. The major selling point of this stylish retro pent-house apartment is its view over the ocean and Havana. One of the three well-appointed and spacious rooms has its own bathroom, while the other two share one. Fresh orange juice every morning, and city tours are just some of the services offered by the very friendly English-speaking owner. $40CUC.

Casa de Nyra Ave 3ra no.1607 e/ 16 y 18, Miramar, Playa ☎7/202-4028. Stylish South Beach-inspired apartment with a marble floor leading out to a fantastic patio and garden. There are three rooms each with a mini-bar, fan and a/c; one is en suite while the other two share a second bathroom. $35–40CUC.

Casa de Ulises Calle 8 no.503 e/ 5ta y 31, Miramar, Playa ☎7/203-7468. Two self-contained apartments with off-road parking set amid mansions on a lovely street. A sun deck and a tranquil garden with rocking chairs add to the appeal. $35CUC.

6

RESTAURANTS AND PALADARS

6

Restaurants and paladars

Although not a city particularly famed for its cuisine, Havana offers the most varied eating scene in Cuba, with a reasonable supply of well-priced international and local **restaurants**, although their settings are often more notable than the food. Dining at the top of a high-rise tower with panoramic city views or in one of the quirky eateries typical to the city often compensates for the somewhat staid and repetitive menus. Cuba's economic situation and subsequent fluctuations in the food supply mean that restaurants and hotels can sometimes run short on ingredients. Perhaps in compensation for this, portion sizes tend to be massive.

For food and service, the best restaurants tend to be in Miramar and the western suburbs, where you'll find imaginative, fairly sophisticated menus as well as attentive service. There are numerous state-approved privately owned restaurants, known as **paladars** (*paladares* in Spanish), most of them concentrated around Miramar and Vedado, dishing up good-value portions of mostly Cuban fare – and the competition between them ensures good quality. Technically they are licensed for up to twelve covers but many seat more than this.

There are also plenty of **ethnic** restaurants in Havana, though foreign food is generally inauthentic and of a poorer standard than *comida criolla*, as Cuban cuisine is known. The most common are Chinese, Italian and Spanish, though you'll also find Turkish, Lebanese, Japanese and French cuisine represented. Of these, Italian tends to be the most authentically reproduced, particularly in some of the plushest hotels in Miramar.

Vegetarians will find decent but predictable choices at most places (pizza and omelettes feature heavily), although Havana now has several good vegetarian restaurants. Vegans are generally better off in paladars, where ordering off-menu is easier and most places serve rice, black beans and root vegetables such as potato and malanga. On the whole, it's best to stick to the hotels or your *casa particular* for **breakfast**, as elsewhere the choice is a bit patchy (for a list of the better breakfast venues see box on p.124). A worthwhile option for an inexpensive **lunch** is to grab a snack from one of the **street stalls** dotted around Habana Vieja, Centro Habana and Vedado, which sell tasty fritters and pizza slices for just a few Cuban pesos.

Restaurants and paladars in the main tourist centres offer meals for about $5–12CUC. Unfortunately, **overcharging** is rife, so to avoid this, always ask to see a menu that has prices listed alongside the dishes. Paladars in particular are prone to adjusting their prices according to the type of customer, although it's not an unheard-of practice in state restaurants as well. Additionally, watch out for touts who will try to guide you to a restaurant and then collar a commission from the owners, which will be passed on to your bill.

Standard **opening hours** for state restaurants and paladars are from noon to midnight. However, official published opening hours should be treated with caution and it's not unusual to find places closing early, and occasionally not opening at all, for an impromptu reason. For this reason it is often a good idea to **ring in advance** before eating out.

For **self-catering** see pp.155–156.

Restaurants

Contrary to popular perception, there are enough fine state restaurants in Havana, many of them in the top-end hotels, to eat exceptionally well throughout your stay, though it will be expensive to do so. What Havana lacks most is mid-range establishments that represent value for money. It's true to say that the majority of the restaurants, particularly those in the main visitor areas of Habana Vieja, Centro Habana and Vedado, are of a pretty low standard when judged against their international counterparts.

Generally speaking, of the three most central areas, Centro Habana has the worst-quality restaurants, Habana Vieja the most diverse selection of ethnic cuisine, and Vedado the best of the hotel restaurants. Further afield, Miramar and the western suburbs have a growing clutch of fine restaurants where you'll pay anything up to $30CUC for a main course.

The **dress code** for restaurants is relaxed or smart casual, though it's wise to take enough clothing to fend off the often fearsomely cold air conditioning. **Smokers** enjoy a free reign in Cuba and there are few totally smoke-free restaurants in Havana, although a growing number now offer a non-smoking area.

Paladars

Havana's paladars offer some of the city's most memorable meals, with the quality in Vedado and Miramar far better than in Habana Vieja and Centro Habana. It's worth noting that some paladars have no written menu. If you are presented with a **verbal menu**, be clear about what the price is before you order. Even those establishments with written menus will usually offer a few extra dishes like shellfish, beef and certain seafood options that are not listed due to their illegality (generally speaking only state restaurants are authorized to sell these products).

Opening hours

Opening hours for all the establishments listed are noon until midnight unless otherwise stated.

Breakfast venues

Cafeteria La Rampa Hotel Habana Libre, Calle 23 esq. L, Vedado. A good choice of breakfast platters in this US-style diner, from traditional Cuban, featuring pork and rice, to the full American breakfast for $10CUC. Breakfast served all day.

Jardín del Oriente Amargura e/ Mercaderes y Plaza de San Francisco, Habana Vieja. An attractive garden café in the heart of Habana Vieja, sinking back into a narrow courtyard. The short list of simple, good-value breakfasts consists mostly of eggs and breads. Breakfast served 8–10am.

El Pórtico Hotel Parque Central, Paseo del Prado esq. Neptuno, Habana Vieja. The marvellous lobby café at this five-star hotel, full of classic colonial charm, serves top-notch continental breakfasts of cakes, croissants, toast and fruit for $7.50CUC or all of the above plus smoked salmon, eggs, bacon, ham, chorizo, cheese, milk and yoghurt for $12CUC. Breakfast served 8am–noon.

Prado Hotel Park View, Colón esq. Morro, Habana Vieja. Breakfast with views all the way over to Vedado from this seventh-floor hotel restaurant. When there are a sufficient number of guests a breakfast buffet is laid on, available to non-guests for $5CUC per person. Breakfast served 7–10am.

La Veranda Hotel Nacional, Calle O esq. 21, Vedado. The buffet breakfast in the basement of this fabulous hotel is unbeatable for sheer scale and choice, with everything you would hope to see in a classic English or American breakfast plus loads of extras including cereal, fruit and sweets. All-you-can-eat for $13CUC. Breakfast served 7–10am.

Habana Vieja and Parque Morro-Cabaña

Restaurants

A Prado y Neptuno Paseo del Prado (aka Paseo de Martí) esq. Neptuno ☎7/860-9636. Always buzzing with punters and the place to come for some of the best pizzas ($5–13CUC) in the city. There's a good selection on the menu, with plenty of pasta and seafood, but the pizzas are the sensible choice here. Well suited to large, noisy groups.

Al Medina Oficios no.12 e/ Obispo y Obrapía ☎7/867-1041. The only Lebanese restaurant in the city, though main dishes such as *Pollo Musukán* and *Samac Libanés* sound more Middle Eastern than they taste. More unique are the mixed meze combinations ($10CUC and $15CUC), which include falafel, fatoush, tabbouleh and less-than-authentic hummus. You can dine inside, where there's a wooden-beam ceiling, brick archways and glass lanterns, or in a canopied courtyard.

Anacaona Hotel Saratoga, Paseo del Prado no.603 esq. Dragones ☎7/868-1000. The eclectic and upmarket international menu, comprising such treats as sushi, oysters and foie gras among its appetizers, is a welcome break from the norm and certainly sets this stylishly decorated hotel restaurant apart. That said, it seems to have overstretched itself a little and the most typically Cuban options, like the lobster and shrimp, are actually the best bet. Most main dishes are between $13CUC and $26CUC.

La Barca Ave. Carlos Manuel de Céspedes (aka Ave. del Puerto) esq. Obispo ☎7/866-8807. Sister restaurant to the outstanding *El Templete* next door, the cooking here is not nearly as refined but is less expensive and more traditionally Cuban, making it a good place to try classics like skewered lobster and shrimp ($10CUC) or Creole-style smoked pork ($12CUC). The breezy open-air location on the port road is enhanced by views of the fortifications on the east side of the bay.

Bar Cabaña Cuba no.12 esq. Peña Pobre ☎7/860-5670. This low-brow café-restaurant, one of the few eateries anywhere near La Punta, is essentially a sightseeing pit-stop. Simple $5–7CUC set meals of grilled pork and chicken are offered in its cheaper upstairs section, where a window seat affords pleasant views over the bay. Open 10am–11pm.

El Baturro Ave. de Bélgica (aka Egido) e/ Merced y Jesús María ☎7/860-9078. Restaurant near the train station, with a Spanish-tavern look and Cuban food. You may be offered the three-course set meals and while these are recommended and reasonable value ($15–23CUC), they cost more than a meal from the standard menu, which waiters here sometimes claim doesn't exist. This is the best place for lunch and escaping the heat on a tour of southern Habana Vieja. Open 11am–11pm.

Bodegón Onda Hotel El Comendador, Obrapía no.55 esq. Baratillo ☏7/867-1037. At the end of a side street and overlooked by many visitors to the area, this dinky tapas joint should be more popular than it is, given the decent quality and excellent value of its two or three set meals (all priced under $5CUC) and small selection of tapas. The standard of cooking is higher than much pricier places nearby and the now departed Spanish chef appears to have left his mark; the bean and chickpea stew is particularly successful. Open noon–4pm.

La Bodeguita del Medio Empedrado e/ San Ignacio y Cuba ☏7/867-1374. One of the city's most famous Ernest Hemingway haunts, this restaurant is always packed to the rafters with tourists but for good reason. The labyrinthine network of rooms, the vibrant atmosphere and walls caked in scribbled messages and photos of celebrity customers make it a must-visit. The food comes in a distinct second but it isn't bad and surprisingly good value for such a tourist trap, with classic creole pork, beef and seafood dishes and one or two less typical offerings, like swordfish, all for between $9CUC and $16CUC.

Café El Mercurio Plaza de San Francisco ☏7/860-6188. The comfy booths and the rich flavours here make this a good option if you're hungry but don't have a delicate palate. There's beefsteak in mushroom and chocolate sauce ($13CUC) or deep-fried shrimps in mayonnaise ($9.50CUC) and plenty of more familiar dishes like the chef's special seafood paella ($15CUC). A cross between a workaday lunch venue and a refined restaurant, the office-building location and pavement café add to the identity crisis. Open 7am–midnight.

Café del Oriente Oficios no.112 esq. Amargura, Plaza de San Francisco ☏7/860-6686. A ritzy, high-class restaurant where the bow-tied waiters serve delicacies like deep-fried frogs' legs, calf's brain and thermidor lobster for up to $30CUC a main dish. The

lunchtime menu has cheaper, more familiar dishes like pasta and chicken, but the Orient Express-style decor, live piano music and 1930s aristocratic ambience make this place ideal for a late-night dinner.

Café Taberna Mercaderes esq. Brasil (aka Teniente Rey) ☏7/861-1637. Traditional Cuban food featuring set meals for $12–20CUC. An excellent seven-piece in-house band plays 1950s Benny Moré numbers, making this one of the best and loudest venues for music while you eat.

Castillo de Farnés Ave. de Bélgica (aka Monserrate) esq. Obrapía ☏7/867-1030. Low-priced, humble Cuban-Spanish restaurant tucked away behind a busy bar with decent specialities such as *fabada* ($4.50CUC), an Asturian stew made with beans, sausage and bacon, Chateaubriand steak ($12CUC) and smoked pork in a garlic and onion sauce ($10.50).

La Dominica O'Reilly esq. Mercaderes ☏7/860-2918. Fourteen varieties of generously topped pizzas ($4.50–12CUC), some reasonable pastas, like the smoked salmon fettucini ($10.50CUC) and a set of pricier but dependable seafood dishes ($9-35CUC), featuring a lot of squid and shrimp options. The classy mezzanine interior and black-suited waiters flatter to deceive, since the food is not high-class and is more in keeping with the outdoor cobbled-street café, where you can also dine.

Don Ricardo Hotel Palacio O'Farrill, Cuba esq. Chacón ☏7/860-5080. A refreshingly simple menu here is reflected in the extra attention paid to the food, *comida criolla* dining with a touch of class. The stylish dining room, formal service and location near the cathedral make the prices (mains $8–15CUC) seem even more reasonable.

El Floridita Ave. de Bélgica (aka Monserrate) esq. Obispo ☏7/867-1300. One of Habana Vieja's headline venues, where the quality of food is a bit hit and miss. Overpriced seafood, such as butterfly lobster ($40CUC), characterizes the menu, though alternatives like pork in chocolate ($20CUC) also catch the eye. A sense of exclusivity in the majestic circular dining area contrasts with the livelier sightseers bar (see p.134), on the other side of a separating velvet curtain.

Hanoi Brasil (aka Teniente Rey) esq. Bernaza ☏7/867-1029. This rustic place, with its dinky rooms and tightly packed trellis-roof courtyard, is one of the cheapest convertible-peso restaurants in Old Havana, with basic but acceptable set meals for $3.25CUC, lobster for $12CUC and side orders priced in cents. Oddly there is nothing discernibly Vietnamese about the food, but the speciality rice-based *Arroz Vietnamita* or *Sopresa Hanoi* will fill you up for the price of a cocktail at some other restaurants.

Jardín del Eden Hotel Raquel, Amargura esq. San Ignacio ☎7/860-8280. This supposedly Jewish restaurant, in an opulent hotel lobby, may not serve particularly Jewish food but is still a welcome break from the regular local fare. Starters include beetroot soup and amateurish hummus, while Hungarian goulash, fried fish in matzah breadcrumbs and *shashliks* feature among the main dishes, which average around $12CUC. Open 11am–11pm.

El Mesón de la Flota Mercaderes e/ Amargura y Brasil (aka Teniente Rey) ☎7/863-3838. Spanish-Cuban cuisine in a tavern-type restaurant, with nightly flamenco performances on a central stage. There's a tasty selection of cheap tapas ($1–5CUC), including fried chickpeas, squid and three types of tortilla, which double up as starters for the mostly seafood main dishes, among which is a good value lobster with tropical fruits ($12CUC).

▲ Dancers in El Mesón de la Flota

Los Nardos Paseo del Prado no.563 e/ Brasil (aka Teniente Rey) y Dragones ☎7/863-2985. Locals flock to this restaurant – hidden away on the windowless second floor of an old Asturian Society building – for the affordable Cuban food in huge portions and the chatty atmosphere. The queues for a table are, however, slightly misleading, since you will find better quality cooking at numerous less popular restaurants nearby. Still, there's a long list of lobster, fish, chicken and pork main courses, most of them less than $6CUC, and one of the largest wine racks in Havana. Note that an additional ten percent tax is added to all bills.

La Paella Hostal Valencia, Oficios no.53 esq. Obrapía ☎7/867-1037. It's hard to believe that the house special here has won a string of international awards, even if it was a few years ago, but the paella, of which there are several varieties, is nonetheless as tasty and authentic as it gets in Havana. The colourful picture- and plate-covered dining room is a large part of the draw. Main dishes cost between $8CUC and $25CUC. Open noon–10pm.

El Paseo Hotel Parque Central, Paseo del Prado esq. Neptuno ☎7/860-6627. The classier of the two ground-floor restaurants at this excellent hotel, with untypical seafood meals accompanied by live piano music. The fish dishes stand out: you'll find main courses such as needlefish fillet ($14.25CUC) and salmon carpaccio ($12.50CUC) prepared with relative skill, though the standard is below what you might expect from a five-star establishment.

El Patio Plaza de la Catedral ☎7/867-1034. The prices for the barbecued meat and fish dishes are as steep as you might expect at this ever-busy restaurant on one of Havana's most touristy squares. Housed in the opulent residence of an eighteenth-century marquis, you are certainly paying for the picturesque location more than the quality of the food, which is only slightly above average. Opt for a table in the serenity of the leafy courtyard as opposed to the seating out on the plaza itself.

Plaza de Armas Hotel Ambos Mundos, Obispo no.153 esq. Mercaderes ☎7/860-9530. An inviting restaurant on a plant-lined rooftop terrace, perfectly placed for a quick escape from the hustle and bustle in the heart of Habana Vieja. You can choose from standard grilled, fried and stewed meats, lobster in several different forms and one or two fish options, with most main dishes between $8.50CUC and $20CUC. Views take in the Parque Morro-Cabaña and the harbour.

Roof Garden "Torre del Oro" Hotel Sevilla, Trocadero no.55 e/ Paseo del Prado y Agramonte (aka Zulueta) ☎7/860-8560. One of the swankiest restaurants in the city, whose pseudo-French cooking, though well above average, takes a back seat to the regal setting: a cavernous balustraded hall with marble floors and towering windows offering superb views across the city. Dishes include lobster stewed in rum, sirloin steak, rabbit and some fine fish dishes. Prices per head are between $25CUC and $80CUC. Open 7–11pm.

Santo Angel Brasil (aka Teniente Rey) esq. San Ignacio, Plaza Vieja ☎7/861-1626. Delightful restaurant on the ground floor of a graceful colonial edifice, whose interesting dishes include *caldereta de mariscos* ($18.95CUC), a fish stew with tomato and white wine, pork *tostadas* in citrus fruit juices ($9.25CUC) and tuna salad with raisin and ginger vinaigrette ($5.55CUC). Choose from formal dining rooms, a snug and shady central patio or the café out on the square. Open 9am–11pm.

La Tasca Parque Morro-Cabaña ☎7/860-8341. Right on the rocky edge of the most attractive stretch of the bay, on a fabulous waterside terrace, this restaurant works equally well by day or by night, though after dark the lights of Habana Vieja on the opposite shore provide a particularly romantic backdrop. The three house specials – a paella ($19CUC), a mixed grill ($18CUC) and a kebab-style dish ($24CUC) – each combine seafood with meat and in general the food is prepared with a professional simplicity. Open noon–10pm.

El Templete Ave. Carlos Manuel de Céspedes (aka Ave. del Puerto) no.12–14 esq. Narciso López ☎7/866-8807. The gourmet seafood at this harbour-front restaurant is the finest and tastiest in Habana Vieja, thanks in large part to the Basque head chef. From delicious salads and starters like octopus *a la gallega*, to mouth-watering mains such as cod *a la vizcaína*, in a garlic, chilli and onion sauce, almost everything on the menu stands out and delivers. Mains around $14CUC.

▲ El Patio restaurant

Los Vitrales Paseo del Prado (aka Paseo de Martí) esq. Trocadero ☎7/862-4511. This enchanting restaurant overlooking El Prado used to be President José Miguel Gómez's house. The rather mundane *comida criolla* (set menus $10CUC) doesn't quite live up to the beautiful Neoclassical surrounds but it's a great spot nonetheless.

La Zaragozana Ave. de Bélgica (aka Monserrate) no.352 e/ Obispo y Obrapía ☎7/867-1040. Havana's oldest restaurant, established in 1830, specializes in Spanish-style seafood. The *zarzuela de mariscos* ($18CUC), a seafood stew, is a worthy alternative to more typical dishes like skewered lobster ($16.50CUC), which is nevertheless one of the top options here. The moody and fairly dimly lit interior, with its strikingly long bar, is a touch more authentically Spanish than the cuisine.

Paladars

Doña Blanquita Paseo del Prado no.158 e/ Colón y Refugio ☎7/867-4958. Prominently located paladar overlooking El Prado from the terrace balcony of a roomy first-floor apartment. Serves a wide selection of well-cooked, generously portioned *comida criolla* dishes ($7–12CUC), particularly pork and chicken. A good selection of vegetables too.

La Julia O'Reilly no.506a e/ Bernaza y Villegas ☎7/862-7438. This long-standing paladar has a justifiably good reputation for its flavourful *comida criolla*, particularly its pork dishes ($8–10CUC). The food certainly takes precedence over the exposed front-room location where you are almost dining on the curb and, for better or worse, there's a distinct lack of privacy.

La Moneda Cubana San Ignacio no.77 e/ O'Reilly y Empedrado ℡7/867-3852. This tiny spot near the cathedral, so narrow it almost spills onto the street, offers four set meals, each around $10CUC and all with *congrí*, salad, fried bananas and bread. Choose from ham, pork steak, omelette or fish, while you admire the walls plastered with banknotes and coins from around the world.

La Mulata del Sabor Sol no.153 e/ Cuba y San Ignacio ℡7/867-5984. The decent set meals ($6–10CUC) offered here, all classic Cuban combinations, include ham or liver as the main dish and, unusually, there's a vegetarian option and a wide range of egg-based courses. The bizarre and eclectic selection of ornaments and pictures reflects the effusive character of the sociable owner.

Centro Habana

Restaurants

Casa de Castilla Neptuno no.519 e/ Campanario y Lealtad ℡7/862-5482. Set well back from the entrance, what looks like a private club is in fact one of the cheapest places worth eating at in Centro Habana. This is way off the tourist circuit in terms of both character and location, but with fresh and well-prepared *comida criolla* main dishes starting at $1.70CUC, it's worth seeking out. Tues–Sun noon–10.30pm.

Los Dos Dragones Dragones no.311 altos e/ Rayo y San Nicolás, Barrio Chino ℡7/862-0909. This Chinatown restaurant is fantastically cheap and very popular with Cubans. The food is on the heavy side though, the meat-laced fried rice a meal in itself and the Tin Pan Chicken enough to feed a small family. To find it, look for the "Sociedad Chung Shan" sign hanging above the street entrance, leading up a staircase to a dining hall. Open noon–10.30pm.

Lava Día Malecón no.407-409 e/ Manrique y Campanario ℡7/864-4432. Well-presented tapas, most priced between $1CUC and $3CUC, in a casual stop-off spot over the road from the sea wall, under canvas-covered metal arches. The stuffed red peppers, tuna *empanadas*, fried chickpeas with sausage and the garlic mushrooms are all very appetizing.

Sechuan Plaza de Carlos Tercero, Ave. Salvador Allende (aka Carlos Tercero) e/ Arbol Seco y Retiro. Housed within the Carlos Tercero mall, this cheap and cheerful Chinese restaurant is popular with Cuban shoppers. It might be less than authentic, but dishes like chicken chop suey, clear soups and salads (all for under $5CUC) offer some surprisingly tasty budget options. Open Mon–Sat noon–7pm & Sun noon–2pm.

🏃 **Tien Tan Bulevar del Barrio Chino (aka Cuchillo) no 17 e/ Rayo y San Nicolás** ℡7/863 2081. Perhaps the best in Chinatown, Tien Tan has an extensive and well-priced menu with many authentic dishes expertly prepared by Shanghai-born chefs. Delicious starters like dumplings ($2CUC) and noodle soup with shrimp are equalled by mains like Foo Yung chicken ($7CUC). Pretty Chinese lanterns and red tablecloths, plus a good mix of Cubans and visitors, add to the pleasant atmosphere. Open daily 9am–midnight.

Paladars

Amistad de Lanzarote Amistad no.211 e/ Neptuno y San Miguel ℡7/863-6172. Jumbo helpings of *comida criolla*, with all the main dishes ($7–12CUC) coming with fried banana, *arroz moro* and salad. The chef has a typically Cuban penchant for covering things in breadcrumbs, but the presentation is simple and has an unusually subtle feel.

Asahi Lealtad no.364 e/ San Miguel y San Rafael ℡7/878-7194. Buried in the thick of Centro Habana, this simple front-room paladar has a photo-album menu full of all sorts of chicken, pork, fish and beef dishes (around $7–8CUC), many of them covered in breadcrumbs, and all served up with healthy portions of *congrí* and enough *tostones* to double your weight. Attracts a local neighbourhood crowd as well as tourists staying at nearby *casas particulares*.

🏃 **La Guarida Concordia no.418 e/ Gervasio y Escobar** ℡7/862-4940. This unbeat-able paladar is the only one in the city with an international reputation and worth every penny of its considerably higher prices (between $12CUC and $16CUC for mains). The meat and fish menu breaks with all the national norms, and the dishes – like rabbit lasagne, salmon in a spring onion sauce with bacon, and sugar-cane tuna glazed with coconut – brim with flavour and originality. Set in the aged apartment building where the acclaimed *Fresa y Chocolate* was filmed, the decor is eye-catchingly eclectic and the moody ambience in the three rooms perfect for a long-drawn-out meal. Reservations are essential and a meal here unmissable.

Torresson Malecón no.27 e/ Paseo del Prado y Cárcel ☎7/861-7476. Chicken, pork and fish dishes for average prices in a basic balcony spot overlooking the seafront with a good view of El Morro.

Vedado

Restaurants

1830 Malecón no.1252 esq. 20 ☎7/838-3090 to 92. A sumptuous colonial house complete with antique furniture, chandeliers and an expansive patio. The food lives up to the surrounds with well-prepared choices including duck in orange sauce and chicken breast with honey and lemon sauce. Cuban dishes like *ropa vieja* are also superb and at between $7CUC and $12CUC all are well worth the splurge. If the service were not so lamentable, this would be one of Havana's finest. Open daily noon–midnight.

Carmelo Calzada e/ D y E ☎7/832-4495. You can choose from a range of well-prepared dishes at this excellent vegetarian restaurant, including soya lasagne, croquettes and various salads. Dishes like steamed okra and fried aubergine make a welcome change from run-of-the-mill tomato and cucumber salad. Brightly lit and very clean, the only drawback here is the habitual overcharging. Dishes are priced individually and a meal for two with three or four dishes should come to around $7CUC. Open daily noon–10pm.

La Casona de 17 Calle 17 no.60 e/ M y N. ☎7/838-3136. Although this restaurant serves fairly average food at rather high prices, dishes like barbecued beef and fries ($9CUC), as well as the house specialty, a substantial paella, are dependable options. A worthier option in terms of quality is the grill and snack bar built alongside.

Comedor de Aguiar Hotel Nacional, Calle O esq. 21. The ritzy dishes match the surrounds in this regal restaurant serving suitably toothsome dishes, including lobster ($35CUC) and fresh fish ($15CUC), and mouth-watering desserts like profiteroles. One of two restaurants in the hotel (see p.130 for the other). Open daily noon–4pm & 7pm–midnight.

El Conejito Calle 17 esq. M ☎7/832-4671. Quirky, moderately priced restaurant with mock-Tudor panelling, staff inexplicably costumed in Teutonic regalia, live piano music and a house speciality of rabbit (a supposed favourite of Castro), prepared in several ways. Mains are $7CUC–12CUC; the rabbit in burgundy wine is particularly good. Open noon–11pm.

El Emperador Edificio FOCSA Calle 17 e/ M y N ☎7/832-4998. This dark and sultry restaurant has inlaid marble pillars, gleaming statues and a grand piano. With lobster cocktail and filet mignon on the menu, the food lives up to its fancy surrounds. Mains $6–17CUC.

Fabio Calle 17 esq J ☎7/836-3229. What *Fabio* lacks in atmosphere it makes up for in cheap plentiful food. The Italian cuisine here is not especially authentic – bruschetta sprinkled with raw garlic and grated parmesan is a case in point – but you can't go wrong with a bowl of pasta or pizza for under $6CUC.

Marakas Calle O e/ 23 y 25 ☎7/833-3740. Clean and friendly pizza parlour, close to La Rampa, with the feel of a North American diner. Large and tasty pizzas for around $6CUC make this good value.

El Rincón del Cine Hotel Nacional, Calle O esq. 21. Handy snack bar in the hotel's basement serving excellent hamburgers and thick milkshakes. It's also a good place for breakfast. Open 24hr.

La Torre Edificio FOCSA, piso 33, Calle 17 no.55 esq. M ☎7/838-3088. Mesmerizing views from atop the city's second-tallest building mean you don't really notice the plain interior here. The above-average prices are just about matched by the standard of cuisine, which tends towards choice meat and seafood prepared with successful simplicity. The pheasant in apple sauce ($25CUC) and oven-cooked cod ($16CUC) all hit the spot, while pork chops ($9CUC) are one of the few less expensive dishes.

Unión Francesa Calle 17 no 861, e/ 4 y 6, ☎7/832-4493. Set in a nineteenth-century mansion, this is possibly the most atmospheric and peaceful place to eat in the heart of Vedado. There are three floors to choose from, with al fresco tables overlooking Parque Lennon and a patio at the top lined with antique cabinets and a floral canopy. Friendly and attentive staff serve creative dishes like chicken with glazed pineapple and chicken in orange sauce. A main course and sides is around $8CUC. As a bonus the cocktails are freely poured too.

La Veranda Hotel Nacional, Calle O esq. 21. The large all-you-can-eat buffet restaurant in the hotel basement is one of Havana's best feeds, with an extensive range of fish and meat, a welcome array of green vegetables, all kinds of fruit, half-decent bread and a good selection of sweets. Breakfast 7–10am, $13CUC; lunch noon–3pm, $20CUC; dinner 7–10pm, $25CUC.

Paladars and street stalls

Casa de Adela Calle F no.503 e/ 23 y 21 ⊤ 7/832-3776. Filled with plants, cooing birds and ethnic artefacts, this gem of a restaurant has a throwback Bohemian feel. There's no menu here – instead, you pay $25CUC per person for a large selection of taster dishes, including delicious chorizo with coconut, meatballs, and malanga fritters with peanuts. Reservations essential. Open 6pm–midnight; closed Sun.

Decameron Linea no.753 e/ Paseo y 2 ⊤ 7/832-2444. The decor and ambience here are inspired and low-key, with pendulum clocks lining the walls, soft lighting and cane-backed chairs. A mix of Italian, Cuban and European food contributes to the cosmo-politan air. The giant pizzas are possibly the largest in town, the pasta is nicely al dente and there's a decent attempt at tuna nicoise. Prices are reasonable too, with most dishes falling in the $6–10CUC bracket. Strong and sweet *mojitos*, plus attentive service, round things off nicely. Open daily noon–midnight.

Doña Clara Calle 21 no.107 e/ L y N. One of the city's best stalls for lunch snacks at bargain prices. Ice-cold soft drinks, *papas rellenas* and hot pork rolls all available.

Doña Laura Calle H no.510 e/ 21 y 23. A rarity in the world of street stalls, *Doña Laura* has a seating counter at which to eat the tasty portions of smoked pork, *ropa vieja* and Italian liver all at rock-bottom CUP prices.

Gringo Viejo Calle 21 no.454 e/ E y F ⊤ 7/831-1946. Traditional Cuban dishes like garlic octopus, *ropa vieja*, *frijoles negros* and fried chickpeas perfectly complement

contemporary dishes like chicken with pineapple sauce and stewed lamb (mains $6–13CUC). There's a competent wine list too. Though the recent makeover (complete with noisy video screens) has removed some of its charm, it's still one of the better mid-range restaurants in town.

Monguito Calle L no.408 e/ 23 y 25. Even by Cuban standards, the portions of grilled fish, pork and fried chicken ($5–7.50CUC) are huge at this workaday spot almost hidden down an alleyway opposite the *Habana Libre*. Lunchtimes get busy but service is swift, so you don't usually have to wait long for a table. Closed Thurs.

Siete Mares Calle 23 s/n esq J. Though the main dishes in this open-air spot, such as grilled fish or shrimp with tomatoes, may seem slightly expensive at $9–10CUC, the food is elegantly prepared. A live band and curbside location make this a good place to watch the rest of Vedado drift past. Open daily noon–10pm.

Los Tres Amigos Calle M no.253 e/19 y 21 ⊤ 7/830-0880. Tasty lunchtime choices include rice and beans or *ajiaco* stew and possibly the best home-made chips in Havana. It's always busy so reservations are recommended (though you can wait on the patio outside if you prefer) and they also do a take-away service (you supply the container). Open noon–midnight.

Miramar and the western suburbs

Restaurants

El Aljibe Ave 7ma e/ 24 y 26, Miramar, Playa ⊤ 7/204-1583. In common with many other Miramar restaurants, *El Aljibe* is a place to head for a touch of luxury. The food pulls no surprises, but it is tasty. House specialities include the beef brocheta and roast chicken, and there's plenty of it. All this, an ambient open-air setting and a fabulous wine cellar make it a top choice for diners in the mood for pushing the boat out. Main dishes $15–30CUC.

La Casa Española Ave. 7ma esq. 26, Miramar, Playa ⊤ 7/206-9644. With a penchant for cooking food in alcohol, the kitchen here has given a twist to the otherwise standard Cuban restaurant ingredients. There are starters like chorizo a la cerveza, and mains such as salmon in cider, lamb in red wine sauce or slices of pork in sherry, with two courses averaging between $9CUC and

$16CUC. Only two of the fantastic rooms in this mock medieval fort, built in the Batista era, are open to diners but both are a real knockout, with beautiful mosaic tiled floors and Mudéjar motifs and furnishings.

La Cova de Pizza Nova Marina Hemingway, Playa ☎7/209-7289. Thin-crust pizzas ($5–11CUC) with the toppings of your choice (75¢–$1.75CUC each) are the best choice for food at the marina, perfect for a pre- or post-dive meal, but don't bother coming all the way out here just for this. Situated in between two canals, there is indoor and outdoor seating, the latter on a pleasant waterside terrace.

Don Cangrejo Ave 1ra e/ 16 y 18, Miramar, Playa ☎7/204-3837. Owned by the Fisheries Ministry, this plush seafood restaurant is every bit as good as it promises to be. Start with the crab cocktail ($6CUC) before choosing a fresh lobster ($20–25CUC) from the pit in the terrace, crab claws ($16CUC) or go for the *Mariscada*, the full seafood platter ($24CUC). A bar well-stocked with imported liquor and a wine store with a decent selection, two private dining rooms, a *humidor* and a swimming pool add to the general air of luxury.

La Ferminia Calle 182 esq. Ave. 5ta, Flores, Playa ☎7/273-6555. Upmarket gourmet restaurant in a posh Fifth Avenue mansion, with a number of splendid indoor and outdoor dining spaces. Serves modern and traditional Cuban food, much of it cooked on the open-air grill, plus some international options like spaghetti bolognese and juicy steaks, for suitably inflated prices. Main dishes $9–40CUC.

🏃 **La Finca Calle 140 y Ave. 19, Cubanacán, Playa** ☎7/208-7976. Among the countless top-quality lobster, shrimp and beef variations at this delightful restaurant are some more unusual Creole offerings, including *tasajo* ($12CUC), a filling dish of shredded and stewed beef, duck breast in apple sauce ($22CUC) and octopus fried in garlic ($18CUC). The head of the kitchen, Tomás Erasmo, lays claim to being Cuba's only celebrity chef, and the remote country house location provides a blissful and romantic treat, characterized by hanging Tiffany lamps, stained-glass windows and a split-level terrace sinking into luxuriant gardens.

El Gran Azul Acuario Nacional de Cuba, Ave. 3ra esq. 62, Miramar, Playa ☎7/203-6401 ext. 231 & 232. Though the fish, shrimp, lobster, ham and beef options ($4–12CUC) are perfectly adequate, the real point of eating at this novel restaurant is to enjoy one of the three daily sub-aquatic dolphin shows from your table. Three dolphins in a giant glass-fronted tank occupying almost an entire wall of a large dining hall entertain diners sat in what feels a little like the hull of a boat, staffed by waitresses in navy uniforms. Show times 1.30pm, 7pm & 9pm. Open noon–10.30pm, closed Mon.

El Rancho Calle 140 y Ave. 19, Cubanacán, Playa ☎7/208-9346. Also known as *Rancho Palco*, shrouded by tropical woodlands and on the edge of a lagoon, this large Taíno-style lodge is over the road from *La Finca* and run by the same organization, but lacks the distinction of its neighbour. Best suited to large parties and better in the day, the typical Cuban menu offers all-you-can-eat set meals for just $12CUC and inexpensive choices like *ropa vieja* ($4.50) and *ternera campesina* ($7CUC), a traditional veal dish. Open noon–11pm.

🏃 **El Tocororo Calle 18 esq. Ave. 3ra, Miramar, Playa** ☎7/204-2209. Atmospheric restaurant with first-class service and imaginative Cuban dishes, but no printed menu so you'll have to listen carefully to your waiter, who will suggest dishes such as smoked salmon in a tapenade dressing with okra and raisins or *cerdo a la camagueyana*, a traditional pork dish from Camaguey. A fantastic six-piece band perform in the evenings. In a separate room is a Japanese restaurant called *Sakura* serving a fairly limited selection of sushi, sashimi and tempura. Prices are generally upwards of $12CUC for a main course. Reservations advisable. Closed Sun.

Paladars

El Buganvil Calle 190 no.1501 e/ 15 y 17, Siboney, Playa ☎7/271-4791. On a garden patio in a secluded corner of the city, a five-minute drive from Club Habana and Marina Hemingway but out of realistic reach of public transport, this is one of the most affordable paladars in the western suburbs. It attracts a dedicated Cuban clientele who enjoy healthy portions of smoked pork loin ($4CUC), mutton in red wine ($8CUC) or any one of the other twenty or so hearty home-cooked dishes that appear on the printed menu here, most of them less than

$6CUC. There's a small car park on the house drive. Closed Sun.

La Cocina de Lilliam Calle 48 no.11311 e/ 13 y 15, Miramar, Playa ☏7/209-6514. Expats and ex-presidents (check out Jimmy Carter's thank you letter in the menu) patronize this discreet and luxurious restaurant, with tables set in a beautiful garden. The food is very good, with the malanga fritters, the lamb and the grilled fish particular standouts. Expect to pay around $70CUC for dinner for two. Open noon–3pm, 7–10pm; closed Sat.

El Diluvio Calle 72 no.1705 e/ 17 y 19, Almendares, Playa ☏7/202-1531. Cooked in a wood-fired oven, the pizzas ($8–12CUC) here are as authentic as you'll get in Havana – decent enough to attract honorary Neapolitan Diego Maradona, as the photo on the wall of him with the owners attests. The restaurant is in a kind of indoor, backyard terrace on an out-of-the-way street near the western edge of Miramar. Open noon–2.30pm and 6pm–midnight.

Doctor Café Calle 28 no.111 e/ 1ra y 3ra, Miramar, Playa ☏7/203-4718. Little touches like warm home-made bread, plus the big flavours in the exquisitely cooked seafood and meat dishes on a constantly changing menu, reflect the owners' insistence on the freshest ingredients. The professionalism extends to the service, which is friendly and attentive, and the setting is pleasant, split between a convivial garden patio and a small stone-floor dining room. Starters $4–6CUC; mains $8–12CUC.

La Esperanza Calle 16 no.105 e/ 1ra y 3ra, Miramar, Playa ☏7/202-4361. The owner of this fabulous restaurant has created a 1930s homage to the house's previous owner, the eponymous Esperanza. The creative menu is expertly prepared and offers dishes like chicken in

soy and ginger sauce or grilled aubergine with grated cheese and oregano. Prices for starters are between $4CUC and $12CUC and for main courses no more than $13CUC. Open 7–11pm; closed Sun. Reservations essential.

La Fontana Calle 46 no.305 esq. 3ra, Miramar, Playa ☏7/202-8337. A lively restaurant specializing in barbecued and grilled platters; equally popular with the Cuban bohemian set and foreigners. The food is almost as good as the atmosphere, with large portions of octopus ($10CUC), pork chops ($8CUC) and ribs ($8CUC) on the menu.

Mi Jardín Calle 66, no 517 esq. 5ta B, Playa ☏7/203-4627. This atmospheric Mexican/Italian paladar serves mains ($2.50–10CUC), such as *totopos con frjole* (refried beans with cheese, hot pepper sauce and tacos) and *pollo en mole* (chicken in a savoury chocolate sauce) come rich in complex flavours and perfectly presented. Seating is out in the pretty garden patio or in a dining room with marble floor and Mexican artwork.

El Palio Ave. 1ra esq. 24, Miramar, Playa. Extremely pleasant open-air paladar offering some unusual dishes cooked to a fairly high standard. Steer clear of the pasta and choose from *Pescado Walesca* (fish simmered with herbs), *Pescado Florida* (fish in orange sauce) or, best of all, the flavoursome chargrilled pork. Main dishes around $6CUC.

Vistamar Ave. 1ra no.2206 e/ 22 y 24, Miramar, Playa ☏7/203-8328. Relatively posh shorefront paladar with sea views from its first-floor dining room and around a dozen variations on the fresh fish, pork and chicken dishes that appear on the official menu (mains $8–10CUC). The unofficial menu, which can feature lobster, shrimp and beef, is equally good, as are the crisp and well-dressed salads.

Bars and cafés

he lines between **bars and cafés** are particularly blurred in Havana.
Most drinking venues are a mixture of the two, offering rum, beer,
coffee and tea in equal measure and open throughout the day, though
a significant number close around 6pm. They are invariably small,
single-room venues and tend to cater either to tourists or to Cubans but less
often to both – prohibitively expensive prices in tourist areas means a lack of
Cuban patronage, with some of the most famous bars little more than photo
opportunities. Conversely tourists rarely stray into Cuban-peso bars, and when
they do they tend to attract a lot of stares. Live music is often a feature as are
light meals. As with much of the entertainment and catering in the city, **hotels**
will feature prominently on any drinking itinerary.

A bar crawl in Havana can involve a lot of walking, as there are very few areas
with a concentrated buzz – it often makes sense to find a likeable venue and
stick there. Obispo in **Habana Vieja** can lay claim to the biggest concentration
of drinking spots (and *jineteros*), while the nearby Plaza de la Catedral district is
also quite lively at night. In **Vedado** the *Habana Libre* is the best starting point
for evening drinking, with the *Riviera* another good option. La Rampa in
Vedado has a good clutch of bars and clubs and heats up after 11pm. However,
for sheer *joie de vivre* you can't beat taking some beers or a bottle of rum down
to the **Malecón** and mingling with the crowds beneath the stars.

In **Miramar** a clutch of sophisticated bars, centred on the city's more
exclusive restaurants and business centres, is certainly worth exploring for a
completely different take on city nightlife. Unfortunately they are widely
dispersed, so you'll need transport to visit more than a couple in one night.
Waterfront Havana remains largely unexploited, with a surprising shortage of
bayside or ocean-view cafés and most of the existing choices pretty uninspired.
The **Centro Habana** section of the Malecón has a string of soulless outdoor
cafés and one or two places with a bit more character, while along the bay on
the Avenida del Puerto in Habana Vieja is a set of shacks dispensing cans of beer,
shots of rum and basic cocktails.

Bars

Habana Vieja

**Bar Asturias Paseo del Prado no.309 esq.
Virtudes.** A basic selection of rum, beer and
soda and one or two very cheap cocktails in
an Asturian society building. The upstairs

bar has window seats overlooking the
Prado, attentive staff and usually a small
collection of old timers sipping rum.
Bar Bilbao O'Reilly esq. Aguiar. An archetypal
locals' bar, with just enough room for a
couple of tables. The whole place is

bedecked in Bilbao colours, with flags and posters of the football team. Expect cheap rum and plenty of stares.

Bar Dos Hermanos San Pedro no.304 esq. Sol. A cool saloon bar opposite the more run-down section of the Terminal Sierra Maestra, where a blue-collar Cuban clietele often outnumbers tourists and imbues the place with a refreshing sense of local authenticity. Happily, newcomers are unlikely to feel like they are intruding.

Bar Havana Club San Pedro e/ Sol y Muralla. Attached to the rum museum, with a wide selection of excellent cocktails. It's a good place for some light food as well.

Bar Monserrate Ave. de Bélgica (aka Monserrate) esq. Obrapía. A traditional bar that, though on the tourist circuit, feels more like a local drinkers' haunt than many of the nearby alternatives. There is also a full and cheap *comida criolla* menu, but food definitely comes second to drink here.

La Bodeguita del Medio Empedrado e/ San Ignacio y Mercaderes. Ernest Hemingway was a regular member of the literary and Bohemian crowd that drank here, and his usual tipple, a *mojito*, has become the house speciality. One of the few places in town where you'll have to fight to get to the bar; the overcrowding makes it lively and atmospheric, but at $4CUC for a mediocre *mojito* and $5CUC for other cocktails, this is definitely a tourist trap.

Café de Paris San Ignacio esq. Obispo. Always packed with a mix of tourists and locals, many of the latter in pursuit of the former, this little bar has a worn simplicity that belies the party atmosphere stirred up each night by a live band.

El Floridita Monserrate esq. Obispo. Home of the Cuban daiquiri, this was another of Hemingway's favourite hangouts. A completely different experience to *La Bodeguita del Medio*, the comfy chairs, flowery wallpaper and velvet curtains make it feel like a posh living room, albeit one peopled by visitors on Hemingway pilgrimages sampling an expensive range of fifty-odd cocktails, including fifteen types of daiquiri.

El Gallo Obrapía esq. Habana. Set back from the main Habana Vieja drag by a couple of streets, this open-sided bar feels more authentic than some of the more touristy bars. High ceilings, marble-topped bar and walls signed by visitors give it a lively accessible feel.

Lluvia de Oro Obispo esq. Habana. One of the noisiest and busiest bars in Habana Vieja, usually with a live band and an enthusiastic clientele.

Los Marinos Ave. del Puerto. The location, on the end of a mock-up boat jutting out into the harbour, is the main draw of this miniature open-air bar, although there is a separate restaurant inside. Of all the water-front bars, this one provides the widest perspectives off the bay.

Plaza de Armas Hotel Ambos Mundos, Obispo no.153 esq. Mercaderes. This fabulous rooftop patio-bar gives a great perspective on the Plaza de Armas and the surrounding neighbourhood. Lolling on the tasteful garden furniture among the potted plants is as relaxing an option as you could wish for in Habana Vieja. There's a restaurant up here too.

Puerto de Sagua Ave. de Bélgica (aka Egido) esq. Acosta. This classy 1930s-style bar could easily be a set for a Hollywood gangster movie. The sleek black bar is a fantastic throwback and the drinks, including plenty of cocktails, are reasonably priced. Attached is a restaurant with nothing like the same character.

Taberna de la Muralla San Ignacio esq. Muralla, Plaza Vieja. Draught beer, a rarity in Havana, is not only served here but is brewed on the premises by the Austrian company that set the place up. It's the smoothest, best beer in the city and no doubt accounts for the buzz that usually surrounds this corner of the plaza, both inside the two large halls and outside on the square itself. You can order food, such as burgers, chorizo and fish, from the outdoor grill.

Centro Habana

Bar Nautilius San Rafael e/ Consulado y Paseo del Prado. This dark and shady-looking local hangout based on a submarine theme is surprisingly untouristy, given that it's right next to the *Hotel Inglaterra* (see p.111). There's a limited selection of drinks, though, and this is hustler headquarters.

Taberna El Galeón Malecón e/ Manrique y Campanario. The only real bar on the Malecón's best stretch, and one of the best places for a light meal or snack, you can sit out on a colonnaded porch or huddle into the tightly packed, understated interior.

Vedado

23 y 12 Calle 23 esq. 12. The open-air seating at this peso bar, situated on a lively corner of Vedado near the Chaplin Cine, is a great spot from which to people-watch. Micro-waved pizzas along with ham and cheese sandwiches make for half-decent snacks if you are peckish.

El Emperador Edificio Focsa, Calle 17 e/ M y N. This classy little 1950s bar hidden at the foot of the Focsa building succeeds where so many others fail in Havana with sultry lighting, hushed tones and a long marble bar serving perfect cocktails to a discreet clientele. Throw in the live piano music and this becomes one to return to again and again. Open until around 1.30am.

Fresa y Chocolate Calle 23 e/ 10 y 12. This unassuming bar, with a glass, arched roof and an entrance overgrown with greenery, is the hangout of choice for Cuban soap stars and musicians. Live bands play in the evening and attract an arty crowd.

La Fuente Calle 13 e/ F y G. The crowd is mostly Cuban at this open-air café/bar. Tables clustered around a water feature and musicians plucking out impromptu tunes add to the relaxed vibe.

Mesón La Chorrera Malecón e/ 18 y 20. An open-air bar in the seventeenth-century Torreón de la Chorrera, a squat fortified tower once part of the city's colonial defence system, with views over the mouth of the Río Almendares.

Opus Bar Teatro Amadeo Roldán Calzada esq. D. A good-looking, long bar with the air of a glam VIP departure lounge, all big squashy easy-chairs and sultry lighting. The available liquors include the 15-year-old Gran Reserva Havana Club, plus there's a good range of cocktails. While it gets busier between 8pm and 1am, it's not the place for a thumping night out but rather a sophisticated hide-out for those in search of a laid-back drink.

El Relicario Meliá Cohiba, Paseo e/ 1ra y 3ra. With its wide selection of luxurious cigars, this stylish little bar feels like a gentleman's drinking club, perfect for an expensive post-prandial Cohiba and scotch.

La Torre Edificio Focsa, piso 33, Calle 17 no.55 esq. M. Bar on the top floor of the tallest apartment building in the city, with floor-to-ceiling windows that negate the need for anything more than the long wooden bar, a couple of plants and simple seating. A wide selection of cocktails ($2–3CUC) and other alcoholic drinks plus bar snacks. There's a restaurant of the same name up here too (see p.129).

Miramar and the western suburbs

Amelia Miramar Trade Center, Ave. 3ra e/ 78 y 80, Playa. The contemporary style and DJ nights are a siren call here for the crowd of slick young Cubans who pack it out in the early evenings for drinks and short eats. As yet a rarity in Havana, there is a sense that this cosmopolitan bar is where the city's future lifestyle scene lies. $3CUC when there's live music/DJ. Open 6–11pm.

Bar Son de la Madrugada Calle 18 e/ Ave. 5ta y Ave. 7ma, Miramar, Playa. Within a large venue where live music is often on the agenda, this is one of the only places unattached to a restaurant where you can get a drink with some atmosphere in this part of Miramar.

Café Miramar Calle 28 esq. Ave. 3ra, Miramar, Playa. Attached to the *Cafetería Piropo*, a characterless outdoor café with a pool table, this more soulful little indoor bar has a jukebox and gets rammed with locals at the weekends, though it's pretty dead during the week. Sun–Thurs 10am–1am, Fri & Sat 10am–2am.

Café Rodney Calle 72 no.504 e/ 41 y 45, Marianao. The 1950s bar at the *Tropicana*, which you can visit without having to pay for the cabaret, has retained much of its original character, complete with chequered bar, swivel barstools and indoor trees. It makes it a good spot for an evening drink with a sense of occasion, though it's lacking in local clientele. Open noon–midnight.

Casa del Habano 5ta y 16 Ave. 5ta. no.1407 esq. Calle 16, Miramar, Playa. This impressive and upmarket cigar shop has a miniature bar, ideal for an afternoon smoke and drink. There's a restaurant here too.

Don Cangrejo Ave. 1ra e/ 16 y 18, Miramar, Playa. Well stocked with imported liquor and a wine store with a decent selection, this bar draws in the cool after-work crowd of Cubans and Miramar expats who gather to kickstart the weekend. The adjoining restaurant is excellent (see p.131).

Quinta Avenida Hotel Meliá Habana, Ave. 3ra e/ 76 y 80, Miramar, Playa. The loungey but elegant lobby bar of this plush hotel, with its eye-catching circular bar-counter and copious slump-back seats, make it a great place to get a drink, grab a snack and rest your feet after a day out.

El Tocororo Calle 18 esq. Ave. 3ra, Miramar, Playa. This superb restaurant has an equally alluring bar, in a separate room to the dining area, where musicians often play until late, entertaining drinkers having a post-meal *mojito*. One of the few proper bars in Miramar and non-diners are welcome. Open noon–2am.

Cafés

Habana Vieja

Café La Barrita Edificio Bacardi, Ave. de las Misiones e/ San Juan de Dios y Empedrado. Hidden away on the mezzanine level behind the foyer of the Bacardí building is this stylish Art Deco café, a comfortable and congenial little hideout and a great spot to take a break. Good-value snacks here too.

Café El Escorial Plaza Vieja. A dependable coffee shop with a covered terrace facing the square and a rustic interior decorated in earthy tones. As well as over 25 varieties of coffee, they serve coffee cocktails and coffee ice cream as well as other sweets, like cheesecake.

Café Habana Mercaderes esq. Amargura. A popular café-bar fuelling the caffeine cravings of a mostly Cuban clientele. Light snacks are served in the airy seating area and although the drinks list consists entirely of cappuccino and soda, at less than a peso a throw they won't get too many complaints. Open 10am–9pm.

Café O'Reilly O'Reilly no.203 e/ San Ignacio y Cuba. Sandwiches, fried chicken and burgers accompany the drinks menu in this informal, rustic café. Head up the spiral staircase to the narrow balcony and enjoy some people-watching from a laid-back vantage point.

Cafetería Bellas Artes Palacio de Bellas Artes, Trocadero e/ Agramonte (aka Zulueta) y Ave. de las Misiones (aka Monserrate). Escape the street strife and relax in this restful spot in Habana Vieja, the modern ground-floor courtyard of the Museo de Bellas Artes building. Teas, coffees, juices and beers can be enjoyed in almost complete calm.

Cafetería El Corojo Hotel Conde de Villanueva, Mercaderes esq. Lamparilla. A jungle of vegetation makes a coffee or cocktail at this colonial courtyard café, in one of the old town's most charming hotels, feel like having a drink in a tropical rainforest, cut off from the passing tour groups outside.

El Cañonazo Hotel Santa Isabel, Baratillo no.9 e/ Obispo y Narciso López, Plaza de Armas. Rooftop snack bar with the best available views of the Plaza de Armas and across the bay to the Parque Morro-Cabaña, though the latter are lost in the darkness at night. Cocktails ($4–5CUC), soft drinks, beers and coffee as well as a small selection of set meals ($15–25CUC).

Casa de las Infusiones Mercaderes e/ Obispo y Obrapía. Café serving herbal teas, iced tea and coffee, including some alcoholic versions such as the Napolitano, made with coffee, cream, cinnamon and brandy. The large main room, in a colonial-era building, is pleasant – but more charming still, hidden away through a stone arch at the rear, is a delightful little patio, perfect for an intimate chat.

La Casa del Café Baratillo esq. Obispo. A tiny place with a shop selling coffee downstairs and a cosy chat in the attic-style room upstairs, perfect for a quiet chat over a coffee cocktail – try the Daiquiri de Café. Open Mon–Sat 9am–7pm & Sun 9am–2pm.

Cremería El Naranjal Obispo esq. Cuba. A simple, conveniently located ice-cream café on a boisterous corner of Obispo, right in the heart of the action. There's not much to it but with ice creams starting at 50¢ and a five-scoop sundae for $2.20CUC, who's arguing. Open 9am–9pm.

Dulcería San Felipe Plaza de San Francisco. An outdoor café on the square with a small selection of cakes, sweets and sundaes.

La Logia Capitolio Nacional, Paseo del Prado. A great vantage point to view one of the liveliest cross-sections of Havana, high above the Prado on a balcony terrace. The drink selection is pretty basic, with rudimentary cocktails, coffee and soft drinks, but for a sense of the vibrancy of Havana, look no further.

El Louvre Hotel Inglaterra, Paseo del Prado no.416 esq. San Rafael, Parque Central. A classic stop-off for visitors to the Parque Central, this café on the hotel's colonnaded patio porch is at the centre of the hustle and bustle revolving around this side of the park. You can eat here too.

La Marina Brasil (aka Teniente Rey) esq. Oficios. This pretty patio café beneath a pergola of begonia and greenery is a welcome retreat from the crowds of nearby Plaza Vieja. Top choice is the Shrimp a la Habana ($7CUC) and the cocktails from the guarapo rum bar.

Museo del Chocolate Mercaderes esq. Amargura. Despite the name this is more a café than a museum, and one where they serve only chocolate drinks and sweets, all made from Cuban cocoa. Order a deliciously thick hot chocolate while you watch the sweets being made at the back.

El Patio Plaza de la Catedral. The waiters at *El Patio*, which spills out through the bold arches of an elegant eighteenth-century mansion's terrace onto the cathedral square, are kept constantly busy serving cocktails and coffees, plus a selection of food, at one of Habana Vieja's most visited cafés, which is also a restaurant.

El Pórtico Hotel Parque Central, Neptuno e/ Paseo del Prado y Agramonte (aka Zulueta), Parque Central. In the most enchanting hotel lobby in Habana Vieja, protected from the cacophony of the Parque Central, this is the perfect spot to recharge or wind down. Tea, coffee, alcoholic drinks as well as sandwiches, salads, tapas and sweets. Open 8am–3am.

Taberna del Galeon Baratillo no.53 e/ Obispo y Jústiz. Just off the Plaza de Armas and a good place to avoid the sometimes frenzied atmosphere of the Obispo bars and the plaza itself, on a dinky mezzanine floor above a rum and cigar shop. Open Mon–Sat 10am–7pm & Sun 9am–2pm.

Torrelavega Obrapía e/ Oficios y Mercaderes. Tree-shaded tables lined along a cobbled brick street at the back of the tiny Plaza de Simón Bolívar make this an attractive outdoor spot for a cold drink or a bite to eat. There are set-menu lunches too, with pork and beef dishes served with bread, side orders, dessert and coffee for $7CUC. Open 9am–9pm.

Centro Habana

Alondra Neptuno esq. Manrique. This branch of the ice-cream specialist is no different from any other but, like all of them, is one of the few places you can get more than a couple of flavours of ice cream and a good selection of sundaes.

Café Neruda Malecón e/ San Nicolás y Manrique. In a gap between seafront apartment buildings is this outdoor café, one of the most pleasant drinking spots on the Malecón. Features a lawn, park benches and tables protected from the wind by panes of glass sealing the place off from the street. Hot and cold drinks plus light snacks.

Plaza de las Columnas Ave. de Italia (aka Galiano) esq. Zanja. This simple outdoor cafeteria on the edge of Chinatown, suitable for a daytime break, is one of the few leafy spots in Centro Habana.

Vedado

Aire Mar Hotel Nacional Calle O esq. 21. Seasoned visitors swear a cooling daily *mojito* on the palatial terrace bar of this hotel is the way to beat the languid afternoon heat. The *Salón de la Fama* bar just inside is a bit tackier, but intriguing for all the photos of the hotel's famous guests.

Cafetería La Rampa Habana Libre, Calle 23 esq. L. This bright spot with a long diner-style counter overlooks the lively La Rampa junction. Great shakes and pasta along with some bizarre sandwich combinations like parmesan, parsley and Baileys liquor to tickle your fancy.

Coppelia Calle 23 esq. L. Havana's massive ice-cream emporium contains several cafés and an open-air area (you pay in Cuban pesos in the former, CUC in the latter), serving rich sundaes in exotic flavours like coconut, mango and guava.

▲ Café with Cuban confectionery on sale

G Café Ave de los Presidentes esq. 23.
Faux wicker chairs, an abundance of
greenery and the crowds of students from
the med school nearby give this lovely café
a bohemian feel. Lemon tea, cappuccino
and cocktails are all served (you pay in
pesos), while the poetry bookshop at the
back offers a lending service, for something
to read while you drink.

El Gran Añejo Meliá Cohiba lobby, Paseo e/ 1ra
y 3ra. Large comfortable sofas, wi-fi and
smooth service – plus a great selection of
cakes for afternoon tea – make this an
ideal place to catch a slice of luxury for a
few hours.

Pain de Paris Linea e/ Paseo y A. Heavenly
cakes, ice cream and croissants put this
little café top of the list for snacks and
breakfast. Plus it's open 24hr.

Sylvain Calle 21 e/ M y N. An excellent bakery
with a plentiful supply of custard-filled
éclairs, *senoritas* and biscuits.

Miramar and the western suburbs

La Casa Española Ave. 7ma esq. 26, Miramar,
Playa. There's a café, bar and rooftop views

to enjoy, spread around the five floors of
this mock fortress, one of them also the site
of a decent restaurant (see p.130). Café
open 7am–7pm.

Kasalta Calle 2 esq. Ave. 5ta, Miramar, Playa. A
block from the entrance to the Río
Almendares tunnel is this sports café
featuring pool tables and decorated in
sporting memorabilia. Popular with locals
and a good spot for an unfussy drink.

K Café Teatro Karl Marx, Ave. 1ra e/ 8 y 10,
Miramar, Playa. One of the most popular
drinking and casual-eating venues in
Miramar, this large and lively café in the
lobby of a huge theatre serves coffees and
cocktails as well as sandwiches and pizzas.
Child seats (and portions) are an added
bonus for parents.

El Pedregal Ave. 23 esq. 198, La Lisa. The
monolithic architecture of this huge building,
housing a nightclub, restaurant, bar and
café, make it one of the few easy-to-find
spots where you can stop for a drink or a
snack in this part of town.

Twenty-four-hour Havana

There is a common expectation among first-time visitors to Havana that the city is a
24-hour non-stop party. This couldn't be further from the truth, with most of the city
disarmingly quiet after about 2am. Equally scarce are all-night shops and eateries.
There are, however, various exceptions to these general rules. Listed below are some
of the 24-hour venues worth knowing about.

Cafeteria La Rampa Hotel Habana Libre, Calle 23 esq. L, Vedado. An American-
style diner, great for a bite to eat after a night on the tiles.

El Diablo Tun Tun Calle 20 esq 35, Miramar, Playa ☏7/204-0447. This excellent
music venue, above the *Casa de la Música de Miramar*, attracts a post-club crowd
and is a popular wind-down venue at weekends.

La Luz Obispo no.165 e/ San Ignacio y Mercaderes. A simple restaurant where the
bar, which attracts a good mix of locals and tourists, is open all night.

Pain de Paris Calle 25 e/ O y Calzada de Infanta, Vedado. One of the city's best
bakeries, just a couple of blocks from the *Habana Libre*, with better-than-average
sweets and cakes.

Pan.Com Ave. 7ma esq. 26, Miramar, Playa. A late-opening fast food café dishing out
sandwiches, burgers, milkshakes and sweet pastries on a leafy corner in Miramar. One
of the few oases of activity after dark in this generally quiet neighbourhood, with the
Casa Española restaurant and the *Complejo Dos Gardenias* nightspot over the road.

Panadería San José Obispo no.167 e/ San Ignacio y Mercaderes, Habana Vieja. A
24hr bakery in the heart of Habana Vieja.

Telégrafo Café Hotel Telégrafo, Parque Central. A distinctly soothing sense of space
and light pervades this hotel café-bar, one of the quieter spots in Habana Vieja, though
it lacks the lounge-style comfort that the atmosphere would suggest. Open 24hr.

8

Clubs, cabarets and music venues

Havana **nightlife** does not jump out at you but instead works its magic from isolated corners all over the city – in secluded clubs, hidden courtyards, theatre basements and on hotel rooftops. Spontaneous nights out are difficult as there's no single area with much of a buzz, but discovering world-class musicians performing in modest backstreet venues, or turning the corner of a quiet residential street to find a crowd gathering outside a club, has its own enchanting appeal. On the other hand, the headline venues, though set apart and widely dispersed, are big and brash affairs, many of them in the mansions and hotels of Vedado and Miramar. **Cabarets** are the least subtle of all, their flamboyant shows taking place in suitably stand-out venues and the most famous one, the Tropicana, occupying a huge outdoor site, though even this is found in a relatively far-flung corner of the city.

Whatever the venue, a night out almost always involves some form of **live music**, with numerous small concert venues, plenty of places where you can enjoy a meal with a performance and many club nights based around live acts. Restaurants are common venues for more traditional performances; among the best are *El Mesón de la Flota* (see p.126), *Café Taberna* (see p.125), *Santo Angel* (see p.127) and *El Tocororo* (see p.131). The **club scene** does not offer the range of music you might expect and tends to feature predominantly salsa, timba, reggaeton and pop; finding a funk, indie, hip-hop or electro night is a rarity and those that do exist tend to have little if any official backing, meaning they advertise via word-of-mouth only. For rumba performances see the dance venues section in Chapter 9 (pp.148–149) and for more on Cuban music genres see Contexts (pp.210–216).

You can pick up information on mainstream concert dates and club nights in the free monthly **listings** booklet *Guía La Habana*, usually in short supply but in theory available through the Infotur information offices, on Obispo in Habana Vieja and Avenida 5ta in Miramar, as well as through some hotel reception and information desks. Look out in these same places for fliers (usually cheap photocopies) advertising club nights and live musical performances, often the only way you will find out who is playing and where. As schedules are so unreliable it's wise to call the venue itself; likewise, **websites** can save you time. The few reliable ones include La Jiribilla (Ⓦ www.lajiribilla .cu), whose "Cartelera" section details monthly listings for classical music venues as well as theatrical productions and one-off concerts; Egrem (Ⓦ www.egrem .com), with listings for some of Havana's biggest clubs; Cuba Absolutely

(@www.cubaabsolutely.com) for concert dates, theatre listings and festivals information; and the "Cartelera" page of the Opus Habana site (@www.opushabana.cu) for Habana Vieja venues only.

A downside of Havana's nightlife is that you'll almost certainly encounter *jineteros* and *jineteras*, with the greatest concentration in the bars of Habana Vieja, clubs throughout town and along the Malecón after dark. If the attention is unwelcome then be firm but polite, and in the process try not to write off those locals who are just being friendly.

Clubs

Clubs in Havana almost always involve a live show, usually followed by recorded music – relying exclusively on DJs and turntables is rare. For a number of years now the most explosive club nights have tended to involve reggaeton and cubaton artists, and the frenzy whipped up by some of these acts means that even if the music doesn't get under your skin the atmosphere might. Salsa and timba are the other music styles attracting *la farándula*, a popular term referring to the fashionable clubbing fraternity.

For the liveliest nights out look for one of the **top performers** of these styles or for genre-busting all-time greats like Los Van Van, La Charanga Habanera and Adalberto Alvarez. For something a bit different, one of the most sought-after names by nightclub promoters is **PMM**, whose unique musical and visual shows, involving "electronic art", special effects and acrobatic performers as well as a DJ, have been a guarantee of big crowds in recent times.

For many venues you'll need to ring in advance or check at the club itself to find out what the **entrance cost** that night is, as prices vary according to the acts that are performing. Entrance costs at most places usually include at least one drink, normally a bog-standard cocktail like a Cuba Libre. This entitlement is known as *consumo* and you might see entrance costs expressed as, for example, "$10CUC inc. $2CUC consumo". **Dress codes** are common and most places do not allow shorts or vests.

Habana Vieja

Disco Galicia Agramonte no.658 e/ Apodaca y Gloria. For a taste of underground Cuban nightlife, and the antithesis of the visitor-friendly venues, this inauspicious club at the top of a battered neo-colonial building ticks most boxes. The crowd is 99 percent local, the music anything but traditional (usually consisting of R n' B and hip-hop), advertising and scheduling are strictly word-of-mouth, and the whole place is hidden so deep inside the building that there is no sign of its existence from the street. Turn up after 11pm on Wed, Fri or Sat and try your luck. Unofficial entrance $5CUC for non-Cubans.

Centro Habana

Cabaret Nacional San Rafael esq. Paseo del Prado ☎7/863-2361. Traditional cabaret shows are no longer the focus, as they were a few years back, at this popular if slightly seedy basement nightclub below the Gran Teatro, which now features live salsa, timba and reggaeton shows. The low ceiling, the street-smarts crowd and the abundance of dark red lend the place a clandestine flavour. Matinees 5–9pm, nights 11pm–3am. Entrance $5–20CUC.

Café América Trastevere Ave. de Italia (aka Galiano) e/ Neptuno y Concordia. Overshadowed by the larger and slicker Casa de la Música over the road, this cheaper alternative offers live and recorded salsa, son, rumba, hip-hop and reggaeton, with bands perched up on a little stage and just about enough room for a dance floor. Open 10pm–3am. Entrance $5CUC, including a drink.

Casa de la Música Habana Ave. de Italia (aka Galiano) no.155 e/ Neptuno y Concordia

☎7/860-8297. One of the top live music and club venues in Havana, with large and raucous queues forming outside every weekend and often during the week as well. All the biggest and most talked-about names in Cuban salsa, reggaeton and cubaton play here. You can enjoy the music from a table or on the sizeable dance floor. Afternoon performances 5–9pm except Fri 4–8pm; nights 11pm–3am. Entrance $5–25CUC.

El Palermo San Miguel esq. Amistad ☎7/861-9745. The nightly shows put on in this untouristy, no-frills venue vary from cabaret to live music; R n' B and hip-hop also feature. Doors open around 10.30pm and the entrance fee varies but shouldn't be more than $3–4CUC.

Piano Bar Habaneciendo Ave. de Italia (aka Galiano) e/ Neptuno y Concordia ☎7/862-4165. A relatively smart venue, though not snobbishly so, where punters can enjoy all types of Cuban music, both traditional and popular. Above the Casa de la Música Habana and under the same management, thus guaranteeing that big names such as Laritsa Bacallao and Coco Freeman perform here. Open Tues–Sun 11pm–6am. Fri matinees 4–8pm. Entrance $5–25CUC.

Vedado

Café Cantante Mi Habana Teatro Nacional de Cuba, Paseo y 39, Plaza de la Revolución ☎7/879-0710. One of the top clubs for salsa, timba and merengue enthusiasts. Top artists like Paulo FG and Los Van Van sometimes headline here, while regulars include Maikel Blanco y Su Salsamayor, one of the most popular Cuban salsa bands of recent years; prices depend on who's playing but are upwards of $10CUC, with a cheaper Thurs matinee. Arrive before 11pm at weekends when the small basement gets jam-packed and the queue can be enormous.

Club Scheherezada Calle M e/ 19 y 17 ☎7/832-3042. This dark and noisy club has a matinee session that starts at 4pm and is popular with locals. Open 4–8pm & 10pm–2am. Entrance $1–$2CUC/25CUP.

Club Imágenes Calzada esq. C ☎7/833-3606. Round tables and a red carpet give this suave little club some movie-set glamour. Performances of bolero and feelin', as well as karaoke, comedy and a late-night disco

draw a lively crowd of youngish Cubans and a smattering of foreigners. Open until 3am at weekends, making for a good late-night drop-in. Entrance $2–5CUC.

Club Tropical Calle F esq. Linea ☎7/832 7361. The cheap drinks ($1.50CUC for beer) are the primary draw at this sweatbox of a club. Cast iron furniture and loud reggaeton fill the small downstairs space; the crowd is more or less exclusively Cuban. Entrance $5CUC.

Delirio Habanero Piano Bar Teatro Nacional de Cuba, Paseo y 39, Plaza de la Revolución ☎7/878-4273. This sultry and atmospheric late-night jazz hangout is popular with Cuban sophisticates and visitors alike, with low-key piano music and live jazz bands like Sintesis nightly. Limited table space makes reservations essential at weekends. Bands play between 10.30pm and 3am, though the place stays open to 6am when it's busy. There's rumba on Sun. Entrance $5–15CUC.

El Gato Tuerto Calle O e/ 17 y 19 ☎7/838-2696. This pre-Revolution, beatnik jazz bar, whose name translates as "One-eyed Cat", has kept its cool edge despite a complete renovation. Excellent live feelin' is played nightly from midnight to 4am, making it one of the best nights out in the area, though for a slightly older crowd. There's a stylish eating area upstairs. Open 10pm–3am. Entry is free but subject to a $5CUC minimum *consumo*.

Habana Café Hotel Meliá Cohiba, Paseo e/ 1ra y 3ra ☎7/833-3636. The closest thing in Havana to a Hard Rock Café, offering an accordingly touristy environment, with a restaurant service for the fancy live music and cabaret shows. Most of the country's top mainstream musicians, from Los Van Van to Charanga Habanera, have graced this stage. The regular weekly programme includes the Rakatan cabaret on Tues, Thurs and Sat. Open 8pm–2.30am. Entrance $10–30CUC, which usually includes $10CUC *consumo*.

Jardines 1830 Malecón no.1252 esq. 20 ☎7/838-3090. The seafront setting in the landscaped gardens of a grandiose mansion, stood alone at the western end of the Malecón, provides much of the appeal here. The usual live and recorded salsa and reggaeton ensure decent crowds at weekends and the occasional fashion show takes place here too. Sundays are currently the liveliest evening. Open Mon–Sat 10pm–3am, Sun 6-11pm. Entrance $3–5CUC.

Karachi Calle K e/15 y 17 ☏7/832-3485. The action often spills out of this sweatbox disco onto the street outside, where an eclectic mix of foreigners, transvestites, *roqueros* (rockers) and straights mingles to gossip and eye each other up. Music is equally diverse – from reggaeton to rap and techno, and nights here are always good for a laugh. Entrance $2CUC. Open 10pm–2am.

La Madriguera Quinta de los Molinos, just off Calzada de Infanta at the end of Jesús Peregrino ☏7/879-6247. Although off the beaten track for locals, let alone tourists, this place is currently among the ever-changing venues to hear hip-hop and R n' B in the capital; held on irregular weekend nights in the backyard of a community building. Acoustic concerts are also performed here. Entrance $20CUP.

El Pico Blanco Hotel St John's, Calle O no.206 e/ 23 y 25 ☏7/833-3740. Entertainment here is twofold, with the early part of the evening (11pm–1am) commanded by excellent live feelin' and bolero. Arrive early to catch relaxed tunes complemented by panoramic views over the Malecón. Later is less laid-back, when the place turns into a disco. Entrance $5CUC.

Salón de los Embajadores Habana Libre, Calle L e/ 23 y 25. Cuba's finest music stars, including Chucho Valdés, Los Van Van and a host of hot salsa acts, play in this regal reception room, one of two salons in the hotel (see Cabaret Turquino, p.144). Well worth the costly price tag ($15–20CUC). Ask at reception for details of performances.

🏃 **Salón Rojo** Calle 21 esq. N ☏7/834-6560. Currently one of Havana's hottest night spots, the Salón Rojo plays host to big-hitting Cuban acts like Charanga Habanera and Havana d´ Primera. It's an atmospheric venue with seating sloping down towards the stage and a dance floor from which people spill over to dance in the aisles. Open 10pm–4am. Entrance $10–20CUC.

Sofía Calle 23 esq. O ☏7/832-0640. A lively, brightly lit spot on a busy Vedado corner. Excellent bands play between 10pm and midnight to a mixed crowd of locals and tourists. There's no cover and a shot of rum costs $2.50CUC.

Miramar and the western suburbs

🏃 **Casa de la Música de Miramar** Calle 20 esq. 35, Miramar, Playa ☏7/202-6147. It's worth the trip out to Miramar to visit this *casa de la música*, one of the most animated nightspots in Havana. The mansion itself is beautiful, and regular bands have included Bamboleo, Adalberto Alvarez and Paulo FG. If you want a table it's advisable to book in advance. Matinee 5–9pm. Nights 11pm–3.30am. Entrance $10–20CUC.

La Cecilia Ave. 5ta e/ 110 y 112, Miramar, Playa ☏7/204-1243. This large complex, also featuring a restaurant, bar and shop, is one of the city's largest outdoor music venues. The place has had its ups and downs in the last few years but it's always worth checking the performance schedules, as the huge dance floor and impressive stage have witnessed some of Havana's biggest salsa and timba parties in the last decade or so. Open Fri–Sun 10pm–3am. Entrance $5–10CUC.

El Chévere Club Almendares, Calle 49C esq. 28A, Kohly, Playa. Friendly, open-air salsa club with a large dance floor and stage under a high roof; a favourite venue for many of the city's salsa schools. Cubans and foreigners mix amicably here, with *jineterismo* frowned upon and a strict door policy. Cuban dance enthusiasts and learners should make a beeline here. Open Tues & Wed. Entrance $2CUC.

El Diablo Tun Tun Calle 20 esq. 35, Miramar, Playa ☏7/204-0447. A favourite of the all-night crowd, with its unusually late opening hours, connected to the *Casa de la Música de Miramar* but sometimes providing a more subdued atmosphere, especially during its weekend matinees. Hots up at night when salsa orchestras, reggaeton groups and upbeat recorded music dictate the pace. At any time the musicians are always excellent. Matinees 5–9pm. Nights 11pm–6am. Entrance $5–10CUC.

Macumba Habana Complejo La Giraldilla, Calle 222 y 37, La Coronela, La Lisa ☏7/273-0568. One of the brasher, most spectacular night-time venues in the city, with a weekly programme of live music, fashion and "special effects" shows on a giant screen. The huge open-air dance floor and stage is located within the grounds of a 1920s country estate, with a single-storey mansion at its heart. Live acts at weekends are followed by DJs spinning disco, dance, house, reggaeton and salsa until dawn. Some weeknights are more subdued, with trova groups performing on Wed until late. Open daily 5pm–4am. Entrance from $5CUC.

La Maison Calle 16 no 701 esq. 7ma, Miramar ℡7/204-1541 to 43. The Cuban penchant for including a fashion show in an evening's entertainment is best exemplified here, where the catwalk parade is the main event and the music secondary. The location is an elegant mansion containing patio gardens (where the shows are staged), a pool, piano bar, restaurant and shops. Ring for the weekly schedule as this place is dead when there's no show. Shows 9.45pm–midnight; piano bar 10pm–3am. Entrance $5–10CUC.

Río Club Calle A e/ Ave. 3ra y Ave. 3raA, Miramar, Playa ℡7/206-4219. Facing the mouth of the river and popularly known as *El Johnny*, this large split-level club currently attracts a boisterous college-age crowd sporting their best threads for sweaty nights on the dance floor to a soundtrack of international dance music and contemporary Cuban sounds. In the 1950s this was one of the jazz hotspots in Havana; it still looks like a classic jazz club but feels more like an end-of-term party at weekends. Open 10pm–3am. Entrance $5CUC.

Sala Atril Teatro Karl Marx, Ave. 1ra e/ 8 y 10, Miramar, Playa ℡7/206-7596. A

great venue for easy access to some of Havana's less well-represented music scenes in a relatively intimate stage venue attracting a diverse, trendy crowd. The programme of events represents an interesting cross-section of mostly modern and alternative Cuban music. The layout includes private booths and an outdoor terrace. Open daily 10pm–3am. Entrance $5CUC.

Salón Bolero Complejo Dos Gardenias, Ave. 7ma esq. 26, Miramar, Playa ℡7/204-2353. Upstairs in a restaurant and bar complex, the *Salón Bolero* is a saloon bar where exponents of bolero entertain subdued crowds seven nights a week. For a laid-back evening of music, enjoyed from tables gathered around a small stage, this is a good option. Open 10pm–3am. Entrance $5CUC.

Salón Rosado de la Tropical Ave. 41 esq. 46, Kohly, Playa ℡7/203-5322. Off the tourist track, this open-air concert venue doubles up as a kind of outdoor nightclub with live and recorded salsa, reggaeton and whatever else will keep the largely Cuban crowd dancing. Not a venue for the faint-hearted, with little security or regulation, but good for an unadulterated taste of local nightlife and a stomping ground for hardcore *timberos*. Daytime musical events take place here too but the scheduling for both night and day is haphazard. Also known as *Salón Rosado Beny Moré*. Usually Fri–Sun 8pm–2am. Entrance $1–2CUC/20CUP.

Cabarets

Cabaret shows tend to elicit strong reactions and are certainly not everyone's cup of tea. Some people revel in their sheer over-the-top flamboyance, while others are repelled by their perceived gaudiness. Either way they are an integral part of nightlife and entertainment in Havana. There are only a few cabaret-specific venues but a number of nightclubs feature cabaret shows in their weekly or monthly schedules, with the *Habana Café* (see p.141) among the most prominent. Notably there are no top-drawer cabaret venues in Habana Vieja or Centro Habana.

Vedado

Cabaret Parisién Hotel Nacional, Calle O esq. 21 ℡7/836-3564. The most renowned cabaret in the city after *Tropicana*, the show here takes place in a custom-built cabaret theatre with

a long history. The current productions are usually well attended and contain all the ridiculous costumes and musical styles you would hope for, and last for about two hours. Entrance $35CUC without dinner and from $55CUC with dinner. Open 9pm–2am.

Cabaret Turquino Habana Libre, Calle L e/ 23 y 25 ☎7/838-4011. On the top floor of the *Habana Libre*, one of two nightspots in the hotel, this expansive disco/cabaret ($10–20CUC) boasts a roll-back roof that reveals the stars, but even so, it still manages to look like a student bar with rather ordinary black chairs and tables. That said it puts on a cracking show, with live salsa on Mon, Tues, Thurs and Sat. Open 10pm–4am.

Copa Room Hotel Riviera, Paseo y Malecón ☎7/836-4051. One of the largest indoor venues for cabaret in the city and a good option for anyone seeking a classic cabaret venue and show, with the archetypal 1950s Las Vegas look and feel. Hasn't yet fully recovered the popularity and reputation it established in the 1990s, when it was the revered *Palacio de la Salsa*, and is sometimes a bit empty. Open 8.30pm–3am. Show usually 9–11pm. Entrance $20CUC without dinner, $25CUC with dinner, $10CUC after 11pm.

▲ Cabaret dancer in Tropicana

Miramar and the western suburbs

Tropicana Calle 72 no.504 e/ 41 y 45, Marianao ☎7-267-0110. Possibly the oldest and most lavish cabaret in the world, Cuba's unmissable, much-hyped open-air venue hosts a pricey extravaganza in which class acts such as Pablo Milanes, and a ceaseless flow of dancing girls, (under)clad in sequins, feathers and frills, regularly pull in a full house. Starts at 8.30pm with the show from 10 or 11pm. You can arrange all-inclusive bus trips from most hotels. Booking essential. Entrance $70–90CUC. Closed Mon.

Concert venues and music halls

Concert-only venues, as opposed to most live music venues, which often double up as nightclubs, tend to be either large theatres or idiosyncratic set-ups in quaint gardens, patios or parks. Many of the theatres are better known for staging plays and ballet and are listed in Chapter 9 (see p.148). All city boroughs, known as *municipios*, have their own **casa de la cultura**, a community centre where the local population can both be active participants in and audience to musical performances of all kinds, as well as other cultural activities such as plays and poetry. Some are better than others, but non-locals are welcome and they can be great places to catch veteran and up-and-coming musicians in a down-to-earth environment.

Habana Vieja

Casa de la Cultura Julián del Casal Revillagigedo e/ Gloria y Misión. Having moved from its long-time location on Aguiar in the heart of Habana Vieja, the municipal *casa de la cultura*, aimed primarily at local residents, is now found in one of the more run-down corners of the borough. It runs a programme of daytime and evening events which includes live music ranging from bolero and tango to rumba and reggaeton. Visit the building itself for the weekly programme. Entrance usually free.

Museo Nacional de Bellas Artes Trocadero e/ Agramonte (aka Zulueta) y Ave. de Bélgica (aka

Retro Havana

A short walk through the streets of downtown Havana reveals a city that exists in a chimerical state caught midway between the modern era and the glory days of post-war American design. Shop signs, cars, buildings – even household appliances like fridges and blenders – date back to the late 1940s and 1950s. What is all the more surprising is that in Havana they have been in constant use since their production date – which lends them a surreal workaday feel, unlike the showier reconditioned Americana popular elsewhere in the world.

El Floridita ▲

Habana Libre ▼

Art Deco door handle on the Bacardi building ▼

Cubamericana

The 1940s and 1950s was an era in which North American design dominated and shaped the design lexicon of the Western world. **US consumerism** was used to define the appearance of a nation but it was also a cultural ambassador: an example of the material riches that capitalism could bring. Nowhere was this more apparent than in Havana. While several companies like Coca-Cola, Colgate-Palmolive and Procter & Gamble operated under license in Cuba, most goods were made in the US and then exported to the island. By the mid-1950s the US represented over seventy percent of Cuba's import market so it's perhaps no surprise that its influence was, and continues to be, so widespread.

Today, some of the most eye-catching **relics of Cubamericana** are around Centro Habana. A walk along the classic shopping streets of Neptuno, the Avenida de Italia and San Rafael reveals vestiges of faded glory in the shop fronts, with doorways tiled in marble and inlaid with gilded metal. Inside, many still have their original wooden counters. The *Emperador* restaurant and bar, at the foot of Vedado's Edificio FOCSA, competes with the more famous *El Floridita* bar in Habana Vieja for 1950s underworld glamour. Many private houses are still furnished with original Modernist pieces, while it's not uncommon to find kitchens with their post-war fixtures and fittings intact. Ironically **1950s architecture** is some of the most monolithic and anonymous in the city, such as the former US embassy (now the US Special Interests Section). The lower floors of the *Habana Libre* are a notable exception, with an airy atrium inside and a stunning exterior ceramic mural by Cuban artist Amelia Peláez.

Art Deco

Though the 1940s and 1950s are a defining era in Havana's style, the **1920s and 1930s** also have a stake in the city's cultural heritage. Havana's most celebrated buildings from those years are on a par with other renowned Art Deco centres, such as Miami and New York. Sadly neglect has affected Havana's mainly concrete Art Deco masterpieces more than their nineteenth-century equivalents, with the result that they now look more grubby than romantically decaying. However, beneath their faded exteriors the variety and quality is endlessly surprising, with sleek concrete apartment blocks complete with vertical detailing, marble inlay and undulating balconies. Vedado has several private residences where the airy styles of the grand mansions marries with the clean lines and detailing of classic Art Deco.

Perhaps the finest example of Art Deco is Habana Vieja's **Bacardí Building** on the Avenida de Bélgica. Built in 1932 (when it was Havana's highest building) and restored in 2003, the exterior is strikingly tiled with yellow-and-white ceramics said to reference the white and gold rums the firm originally made. The interior has typical Art Deco pastels, lavish marble floors, impressive gilded wrought ironwork and a stylish mezzanine-level bar beyond the foyer (see *Café La Barrita*, p.136). Havana's first skyscraper, the Gotham City-like **López Serrano Building** on Calle 13 y L in Vedado, was also built in 1932 and modelled on similar buildings in New York. Other buildings to look out for include the **Moderna Poesía bookshop** on the corner of Obispo and the elegant **Casa de las Américas** (see p.93) with midnight-blue stained-glass windows.

▲ Edificio Barcardí, Habana Vieja

▼ Casa de las Américas, Vedado

▼ Moderna Poesía bookshop, Habana Vieja

Ford Fairlane ▲

Dodge Coronet ▼

Chevrolet Bel Air ▼

Classic cars

It's estimated that there are some sixty thousand classic cars in Cuba today – all of which were shipped to Havana from factories in Detroit during the 1940s and 1950s. Looking underneath the bonnet of these veteran vehicles reveals an engine that bears little resemblance to its manufacturer's original. With no possibility of buying spare parts, the owners have mended them with parts culled from everything from old tanks to Eastern Bloc Ladas – a testimony to both Cuban skill and US engineering. Nowadays some of the spruced-up models are used as tourist taxis by the Gran Car firm (see p.29). Most are more run-down and form the *rutero* taxi fleet, privately operated cabs that run regular routes around the city. A single journey usually costs each passenger $10CUP and drivers will load as many passengers as they can cram onto the two or three rows of broad seats that these huge cars come equipped with.

Car spotting

▶▶ **1950–53 Oldsmobile Rocket** The V8 engine was one of the most powerful of its time.

▶▶ **1951 Plymouth Belvedere** The first Belvedere hard-top had a wrap-around back mirror and two-tone body work.

▶▶ **1954 Chevrolet Bel Air** Possibly the most common classic car to be seen in Havana.

▶▶ **1956 Pontiac Star Chief** A low rider with two-tone trim and massive chrome bumpers.

▶▶ **1957 Chevrolet Bel Air** With two-tone tail fins and judicious use of chrome, this is one of the most iconic classic cars.

▶▶ **1958 Ford Fairlane** Wide, long and low, with stylish, long side fins.

Monserrate). This large Art Deco museum building contains an auditorium frequently used for jazz concerts by local and national artists, as well as folk, classical and orchestral productions. Concerts are usually staged Thurs–Sun and start between 5pm and 7pm. Entrance usually between $5CUC and $10CUC.

Salón El Gijonés Federación Asturiana, Paseo del Prado no.309 esq. Virtudes ☎7/862-3626. A little run-down and virtually unknown on the tourist circuit, the upstairs concert hall in this Asturian society building attracts an older crowd, mostly locals. The relatively humble Saturday night shows usually consist of musical ensembles playing traditional Cuban and Spanish music. Open Sat 9pm–late. Entrance $20CUP.

Vedado

Casa de las Américas Calle 3ra esq. Ave. de los Presidentes ☎7/838-2706. This cultural institution regularly hosts live music in its large first-floor function room, the Sala Che Guevara, with a strong tradition of putting on nueva trova acts and a tendency towards folk and classical music but sometimes hosting rap, salsa or rock groups. One of the nueva trova all-time greats, Silvio Rodríguez, performed his debut concert here aged 15. Concert start times tend to be between 4pm and 7pm. Ring for prices, which are generally quite cheap.

Casa de la Amistad Paseo no.406 esq. 17 ☎7/830-3114. Resident troubadour groups perform well-executed salsa, son and boleros in the majestic grounds of a Rococo building that was once a private house. Saturdays are livelier with old-school salsa. Tues–Fri 11am–midnight, Sat 11am–2am, Sun 11am–6pm. Closed Mon. Entrance $5–7CUC.

Casa de la Cultura de Plaza Calzada 909 esq. 8 ☎7/831-2023. There is no end to the activities at this off-the-beaten-track culture house, from theatre and poetry readings to every type of music Havana offers. Every week there's a choice of bolero, hip-hop, rumba and feelin'. With flamenco evenings and dance or art classes also available, this is a wonderful venue for those looking to immerse themselves in community-based culture. Closed Mon. Usually free.

Hurón Azul UNEAC (Unión de Escritores y Artistas de Cuba) Calle 17 no.351 e/ Ave. de los Presidentes y H ☎7/832-4551. It's always worth checking out the programme posted outside this beautiful Vedado mansion, home to the Writers' and Artists' Union. Regular events include bolero (Sat 9pm–2am), nueva trova alternated with rumba (Wed from 5pm) and son or rumba (Sun from 5pm). In addition, throughout the week there are various art exhibitions, fashion shows and festivals on the grounds, and you can sometimes catch such luminaries as Pablo Milanés in concert. Entrance $5CUC.

Pabellón Cuba Calle N no.266 esq. 23 ☎7/832-9056. Don't be put off by the monolithic appearance of this architectural monstrosity lurking at the foot of La Rampa, as you can catch a variety of live concerts in the large courtyard, ranging from rap, rock and reggae as well as the ubiquitous salsa. Run by the UJC (Union of Young Communists) and thus popular with a younger crowd. Entrance $1CUC.

Miramar and the western suburbs

Anfiteatro del Parque Almendares Parque Almendares, Kohly, Playa ☎7/205-1237. The gigs that take place at this small concert arena in the park are poorly promoted, but as one of the city's truly unique live music installations it's worth seeking out the latest info. The venue has a history as a space for non-mainstream artists and was a popular spot for the nueva trova scene in the 1970s and more recently guitar-playing singer-songwriters like Frank Delgado, Boris Larramendi and William Vivanco. Essential to ring or visit the venue in advance for latest performance details. Entrance usually no more than $5CUP.

Classical music and jazz venues

There are some fantastic **classical and jazz music** venues in Havana, oozing with atmosphere; several of Habana Vieja's religious buildings have been partially converted to classical concert auditoriums in the last decade or so. The city has one of the strongest traditions of jazz in the world outside of the US, marked every year by the Havana International Jazz Festival (see p.151), and fans of the genre should make a point of catching a live performance. The biggest name in Cuban jazz is still Chucho Valdés and his band Irakere, but other top names to look out for include Bobby Carcassés, Roberto Fonseca and his band Temperamento, and Harold López-Nussa.

Habana Vieja

Basilica Menor de San Francisco de Asis Plaza San Francisco ☎ 7/862-9683. Classical orchestras and sometimes solo vocalists perform in the main cloister of this church, on average three times a week. Entrance around $10CUC.

Chico O'Farrill Snack Bar Hotel Palacio O'Farrill, Cuba no.102–108 esq. Chacón ☎ 7/860-5080. This classy and cozy little lounge bar in an elegant hotel doubles up as a live music venue some weekends, visited by groups playing jazz, son and other traditional Cuban musical styles.

Iglesia de San Francisco de Paula Desamparado esq. San Ignacio ☎ 7/860-4210. Organ concerts, choir performances, chamber-music orchestras and symphonic works are all part of the sporadic scheduling at this eclectic and atmospheric church in southern Habana Vieja. There is rarely anything more than one concert a week here – often not even that – so it's essential to ring in advance. Entrance usually $6CUC.

Oratorio de San Felipe Neri Aguiar esq. Obrapía. This seventeenth-century church has gone back to its roots, having been converted to a bank in the mid-twentieth century, and is now the setting for the kinds of operatic and choral renditions that it was originally built to accommodate. Performances take place on a stage under the church dome and usually follow a Wed-to-Sat timetable. Matinees at 4pm, evening concerts at 7pm. Entrance usually around $5CUC.

Centro Habana

Centro Hispanoamericano de Cultura Malecón no.17 e/ Paseo del Prado y Capdevila (aka Cárcel) ☎ 7/860-6282. A seafront arts and cultural centre in a wonderful Neoclassical building, where the weekly programme usually features an operatic or classical performance of some kind, staged in the main hall. Films and theatrical productions are also shown here (see p.150). Musical performances are usually on Saturday afternoons, around 5pm. Entrance usually between $3CUC and $5CUC.

Vedado

Jazz Café Galerias del Paseo, Paseo esq. 1ra ☎ 7/838-3302. The top floor of a shopping mall (see p.161) may seem an unlikely venue, but this laid-back café is a must for jazz aficionados. The best Cuban jazz bands, including Irakere, often play here between 8pm and 2am, after which there's a disco. Food is served, so arrive early to bag a table. Entrance $10CUC.

Teatro Amadeo Roldán Calzada esq. D ☎ 7/832-4521. This is the home of the National Symphony Orchestra and one of the principal venues for the Havana International Jazz Festival. Accordingly, it is one of the best places to hear classical music and jazz in the city. The orchestra always plays at weekends (Fri 9pm, Sat 5pm, Sun 4pm). There are opera, choral, soloist or jazz programmes most weeknights between 6pm and 8pm, but you should check in advance. $10CUC.

La Zorra y El Cuervo Calle 23 no.155 e/ N y O ☎ 7/833-2402. A cool and stylish basement venue, with contemporary decor and a European feel, which puts on superior live jazz shows each night. Open 10pm–2am, though it doesn't heat up until the band starts at 11pm. Entrance $10CUC.

Performing arts and film

Supported and overseen by the state since the Revolution, film, theatre and dance have flourished in Havana. Happily, despite the high standards the cost of a ticket is comparatively low – affordable arts quickly became a national tenet in the early years of the Revolution. Note that Cubans pay in CUP while visitors are charged in CUC. Contrary to expectations, **theatre** and **film** are two areas in which political opinions are often fairly freely expressed. Though a good level of Spanish is needed to get the most out of performances, with inventive sets that are often a visual feast and highly physical performers, it's well worth checking out at least one performance on your trip.

Ballet, along with other forms of **dance**, is equally impressive, with world-class companies. Performances might be slightly shabbier round the edges than aficionados are accustomed to but they are still an enriching cultural experience. See the box on p.153 for help on where to find up-to-date listings information.

Theatre, ballet and opera

Havana has the cream of the country's **theatres**, where, especially during the international theatre festival in autumn you can catch excellent avant-garde and more traditional performances. Theatre and opera in Havana was firmly established in the nineteenth century but was generally soporifically romantic. Following the Revolution, under the helm of UNEAC (Union of Writers and Artists in Cuba), new writing and theatre companies flourished, with experimental works becoming popular alongside more traditional pieces. In the late 1960s ideological issues and censorship dogged the arts, theatre included, and many playwrights and theatre companies found themselves blacklisted. Just as the position was revised in the 1980s and theatre began to enjoy more creative freedom, the Special Period bit hard into theatres' budgets. The position now is somewhat rosier, with Havana's theatres able to put on regular shows of astonishing innovation and imagination given their still limited resources. Companies like Teatro Buendía (☎7/881-6689) and Teatro de la Luna (☎7/879-6011) have attracted international acclaim for their work.

Cuba also has one of the world's finest **ballet** companies, the Ballet Nacional de Cuba (ⓦwww.balletcuba.cult.cu), which was founded in 1948 by prima ballerina and Cuban heroine Alicia Alonso, who drew on traditional Russian and Western techniques as well as Cuba's own Latin American and Caribbean roots to pioneer a new ballet methodology. Ballet's universal language is particularly accessible in Havana, with regular performances making this one of the most enjoyable art forms to catch on a visit.

Venues

Anfiteatro de Habana Vieja Ave. del Puerto esq. Peña Pobre Habana Vieja ☎7/860-4311. Concerts, children's shows and the occasional theatrical production at one of the most novel theatres in Havana, an open-air amphitheatre built in 1936. Entrance $1–3CUC.

Centro Cultural Bertold Brecht Calle 13 e/ J y I, Vedado ☎7/832-9359. Two auditoria which feature theatre including musicals and farces (Fri & Sat 8.30pm) and a matinee (Sun), as well as performances for kids (Sat & Sun 11am) and comedy (Tues 8.30pm). Entrance $1–3CUC.

Gran Teatro Paseo del Prado esq. San Rafael, Habana Vieja ☎7/861-3096. This outstandingly ornate building on the Parque Central is the home of the Ballet Nacional de Cuba but also hosts operas and contemporary dance pieces. The biannual Festival Internacional de Ballet de la Habana (see p.153) takes place here in October, while every August the theatre plays host to a season of Spanish ballet. There are performances most weeks, usually from Fri to Sun, most starting around 8pm but usually a few hours earlier on Sundays. Programmes of opera, ballet and flamenco alternate, with each programme running for one or two weeks. Entrance $10–20CUC.

Teatro Amadeo Roldán Calzada esq. D, Vedado ☎7/832-4521. This is the home of the National Symphony Orchestra and accordingly one of the best places to hear classical music in Havana. The orchestra always plays at weekends (Fri 9pm, Sat 5pm, Sun 4pm). There are opera, choral, soloist and some jazz programmes most week nights between 6pm and 8pm, but you should check in advance. $5–10CUC.

Teatro América Ave. de Italia (aka Galiano) no.253 e/ Concordia y Neptuno, Centro Habana ☎7/862-5416. Smaller than its more renowned counterparts, this humble but happening theatre lends itself well to the comedy shows, live jazz and traditional music performances that are its mainstays. Entrance $3–5CUC.

Teatro Hubert de Blanck Calzada no.657 e/ A y B, Vedado ☎7/830-1011. This very small theatre has a good repertoire of contemporary Spanish and Cuban theatre. Entrance is a snip at $3–5CUC.

Teatro Karl Marx Ave. 1ra e/ 8 y 10, Miramar ☎7/830-0720. Havana's largest venue is an impressively ugly 1960s building hosting all kinds of music and dramatic arts events, including rock concerts and classical theatre. Definitely worth checking what's on. Entrance $5–15CUC.

Teatro El Sótano Calle K e/ 25 y 27 Vedado ☎7/832-0630. The home of the Teatro Rita Montaner company gives voice to a host of young up-and-coming playwrights and directors, with occasional visiting companies pitching in. Entrance $3–5CUC.

Dance

There are plenty of fine examples of **folklórico** dance (which celebrates Afro-Cuban culture) in Havana and the venues range from open-air street performances, particularly around Habana Vieja and Centro Habana, to minutely choreographed shows in theatres. In addition to those venues listed below, many of the major theatres listed above have regular performances of Cuban dance by companies like the state-funded Conjunto Folklórico Nacional de Cuba (Ⓦwww.folkcuba.cult.cu) and excellent contemporary dance company Danza Contemporánea de Cuba (Ⓦwww.cubaescena.cult.cu), which worked with Carlos Acosta on his internationally acclaimed Tocororo show. The annual Encuentro Mundial de Bailadores y Academias de Baile de Casino y Salsa, better known as **Baila en Cuba**, is an international celebration of all Cuban dance styles (see p.154).

Asociación Cultural Yoruba de Cuba **Paseo del Prado, e/ Máximo Gómez (aka Monte) y Dragones, Habana Vieja** ☎ 7/863-5953. A small roster of Afro-Cuban dance and percussion groups perform several times a week on the patio of this society building, a focal point for Havana's Santería community. Among the regular performers are Obini Batá, an all-female drumming and dancing outfit. Performances Wed, Fri and Sat 9–11pm. Entrance $5CUC.

Callejón de Hamel Hamel e/ Hospital y Aramburu, Centro Habana. The best-known Afro-Cuban location in the city is a quirky pedestrianized block of Centro Habana where rumba ceremonies spark off every Sunday and the narrow street is filled with drummers and dancers. There's still a sense of spontaneity here despite the crowds of onlookers. See p.84.

Casa del Tango Neptuno no.309 e/ Ave. de Italia (aka Galiano) y Aguila, Centro Habana ☎ 7/863-0097. Unusual for its domestic front-room location with walls choc-a-bloc with pictures and portraits, its promotion of the national dance of Argentina and its status as a more-or-less private venture with no official state sanctioning, this unique venue hosts regular dancing and singing performances of Cuban styles as well as tango. Dance classes are also held here and various dance schools catering to tourists incorporate it into their programmes. It's free to enter. Open daily 8–10pm.

El Gran Palenque Calle 4 no.103 e/ Calzada y 5ta, Vedado ☎ 7/833-4560. Home to the Conjunto Folklórico Nacional de Cuba, which puts on rumba and other Afro-Cuban dance performances on the patio. The regular Peña de la Rumba is a highly charged, energetic affair with group and individual dancers plus audience participation. It's well worth the entrance fee and takes place at 3pm on Sat. $5CUC.

Teatro Mella Linea no.657, e/ A y B Vedado ☎ 7/833-8696, ⓦ www.teatromella.cubaescena .cult.cu. This large theatre puts on many performances by the Conjunto Folklórico Nacional de Cuba as well as comedy, theatre and variety shows. Fri and Sat 8pm, Sun 5pm. $10CUC.

Film

Although Havana's first cinematic screening was in 1897, there were few films of note among the eighty or so made before 1959. However, within days of the Revolution the new government stamped its mark on Cuba's cinematic output with the creation of the Dirección de Cultura del Ejército Rebelde (Culture Division of the Rebel Army), which oversaw production of various documentaries celebrating the Revolution. A few months later this organization morphed into the ICAIC (Instituto Cubano del Arte e Industria Cinematográficos), which still funds film-makers and subsidizes cinemas today, and the golden age of Cuban cinema began. Throughout the 1960s the celebrated directors Humberto Solás and Tomás Gutiérrez Alea produced some of their seminal work and established Cuba as a main player on the international stage. Despite state funding and affiliation, Cuban films are often beautiful, progressive and surprisingly critical of the country's social problems.

Nowadays **cinema** is a popular form of entertainment, costing just a few pesos, and there are plenty of atmospheric fleapits dotted around Havana. They may be run-down – air conditioning often breaks and the smell of the toilets can be an unwelcome distraction – but a refreshing lack of anonymous multiplexes makes for an idiosyncratic experience. Case in point is the penchant for continuous screenings. Cubans often enter before one performance has ended and then watch the film up to the point at which they entered, making for a somewhat back-to-front viewing experience.

Although as a visitor you will probably be charged in convertible pesos ($2–3CUC), it's a small price to pay for the experience. Havana's cinemas usually screen a selection of Cuban, North American and European films, with the English-speaking ones generally subtitled in Spanish or, if you are unlucky, badly dubbed. Programmes at some venues change daily and cinema listings appear daily in *Granma* newspaper. The Festival Internacional de Nuevo Cine Latinoamericano (see p.154), which takes place every year in December, is an unrivalled opportunity to see new work from across Latin America and other countries, catch audiences and screenings with celebrated directors and producers, and even spot the occasional A-list actor.

Cinemas

Centro Hispanoamericano de Cultura Malecón no.17 e/ Paseo del Prado y Capdevila (aka Cárcel), Centro Habana ☎7/860-6282. This grand arts and cultural centre has screenings at least once a week and is one of Havana's most noteworthy alternative cinema venues. Call for further details. Theatrical productions are staged here too.

Cine Actualidades Ave. de Bélgica (aka Monserrate) no.362 e/ Animas y Virtudes, Habana Vieja ☎7/861-5193. Cinema offering one of the more varied monthly programmes, with performance times for the whole month usually posted in the front window.

Cine Chaplin Calle 23 e/ 10 y 12, Vedado ☎7/831-1101. The Chaplin may be small but it's one of Havana's most important cinemas, showing classic and modern Cuban films.

Cine Payret Paseo del Prado esq. San Martín (aka San José), Habana Vieja ☎7/863-3163. The best spot in Habana Vieja to see Cuban films and the occasional Hollywood blockbuster. One of the main venues for the Havana Film Festival.

Cine La Rampa Calle 23 esq. O, Vedado ☎7/878-6146. Although the auditorium is a bit run-down the entrance and atrium in brass and marble is rather stunning. Mostly North American and European films on show.

Cine Riviera Calle 23 e/ G y H, Vedado ☎7/830-9564. A stylish cinema painted cobalt blue

▲ Cine Payret

that shows a range of Cuban and international films.

Cine Yara Calle L esq. 23, Vedado ☎7/867-1374. A large, old-fashioned auditorium showing the latest Spanish and Cuban releases, with a small video room showing special-interest films. Also one of the main venues for the Havana Film Festival.

Festivals and events

C uba has some of the most highly regarded festivals in Latin America and events like the Festival Internacional del Nuevo Cine Latinoamericano continue to grow in prestige and attract visitors who time their trips accordingly. Despite this, it can still be frustratingly difficult to find accurate **information** on events. In Cuba itself, hotels like *Habana Libre*, *Hotel Nacional* and *Hotel Riviera* can be useful sources of information, particularly as each has served as the headquarters to a main event in the past. Some of the Cuban websites in this chapter are updated fairly regularly, more so close to an event, but it's wise to allow a certain amount of leeway when planning to attend something particular, as dates shift from year to year. Events can even be cancelled – although this fate is unlikely to befall the bigger ones.

Below are listings for the main festivals and a selection of smaller events. The excellent website **Cuba Absolutely** (ⓦ www.cubaabsolutely.com) has comprehensive listings regularly updated for festivals in Havana and across the country. The UNEAC website (ⓦ www.uneac.org.cu) is also a useful resource for lesser-known events.

January

Esteban Salas Early Music Festival (late Jan–early Feb; ☎ 7/860-4210, ⓦ www.arslonga.cu) Based largely in Habana Vieja, this annual festival celebrates the music of eighteenth-century Cuban composer Esteban Salas. Medieval, Renaissance and Baroque music is performed by Ars Longa, the early-music ensemble of the Oficina Historiador de la Ciudad. Key venues include the Basílica Menor of the San Francisco de Asís Convent, the Iglesia de Paula, and the Centro Hispanoamericano de Cultura.

February

Havana International Jazz Festival (mid-Feb; ☎ 7/862-4938, ⓦ www.festivaljazzplaza.icm.cu) Organized by the Cuban Institute of Music and veteran musician Chucho Valdés, this is the powerhouse event in Cuba's international jazz calendar. It consistently attracts an excellent line-up: Dizzy Gillespie, Charlie Haden, and Ronnie Scott have all played in the past, alongside Cuban luminaries such as Gonzalo Rubalcaba, Omara Portuondo

and of course Chucho Valdés himself. Venues across the city include Teatro Mella, Teatro Karl Marx, Teatro Amadeo Roldán, Teatro América and Casa de la Cultura de Plaza. The *Hotel Riviera* (☎ 7/833-4051) usually acts as the event headquarters and provides some information during the festival. Accreditation, which allows entry to all the performances, is around $120CUC, while entrance to individual events is around $20CUC.

Feria Internacional del Libro de La Habana (Havana International Book Fair) (mid/late Feb–early March; ✉ iroel@icl.cult.cu, ⓦ www.cubaliteraria.com) You'll find more books on Cuban politics and ideology at this country-wide festival than you can shake a stick at, as well as new fiction and poetry. Over one hundred publishers, largely from the Americas, present their catalogues at the main venue at the Fortaleza San Carlos de la Cabaña in the Parque Morro-Cabaña, as well as at several bookshops across the capital. Events include discussions, poetry readings, children's events and concerts.

There is a different guest country each year and the Casa de las Américas also presents its literary prize during the festival period.

March

Festival de Música Electroacústica "Primavera en La Habana" (mid-March; ⓔLnme@cubarte .cult.cu) Festival of electro-acoustic music held every even-numbered year in the bars, museums and cafés around Habana Vieja.

Bienal de La Habana (March–April; ⓔcontactobienal@wlam.cult.cu, ⓦwww .bienalhabana.cult.cu) This month-long biennale, which fans out in exhibitions and workshops throughout Havana, focuses on Cuban, Latin American, Caribbean, African and Middle Eastern artists. It takes place in several of the major commercial art spaces like Galería Habana and La Casona, as well as larger venues like Pabellón Cuba and Museo Nacional de Bellas Artes.

April

International Urban Dance Festival: "Old Havana, City in Motion" (mid-April; ☎7/860-4341, ⓦwww.netssa.com/retazos_theater.html) Rather than displays of break dancing and body popping, this festival, organized by the well-respected Retazos Dance Company, uses sites around Habana Vieja to show off contemporary dance choreography. Master classes, lectures, workshops and night-time jazz jams complement the dance programme.

May

Primero de Mayo (1 May) With a crowd of around twenty thousand waving painted banners and paper flags, and marching past dignitaries in front of the José Martí memorial at the Plaza de la Revolución, this quintessentially Cuban display in celebration of International Workers' Day is definitely worth catching.

Feria Internacional del Disco "Cubadisco" (mid-late May; ☎7/832-8298, ⓦwww .cubadisco.soycubano.com) A week-long annual event in which Cuban musicians who have released albums in the preceding twelve months compete for the title of best album of the year. As well as celebrating current releases, homage is paid to classics. Concerts take place in many of the city's major venues, including Teatro Karl Marx, with the finale held at Salón Rosado de la Tropical Benny Moré.

June

Festival Internacional "Boleros de Oro" (mid-late June; ☎7/832-0395, ⓦwww.uneac .org.cu) The siren song of bolero, a musical genre born in Cuba in the nineteenth century, draws singers from all over Latin America for this week-long festival organized by UNEAC. Cuban stars of the scene like César Portillo de la Luz, Mundito González, and Marta Valdés all regularly perform. Look out for concerts at Teatro Mella and Teatro América alongside the UNEAC's Hurón Azul, the Gato Tuerto and the *Hotel Nacional*, as well as elsewhere in the country. Entrance to individual events ranges from $5–20CUC.

July

Carnaval de la Habana (late July–early Aug) Held over the last two weekends of July and the first two weekends of August, carnival in Havana is a jubilant affair (if it's not cancelled as it has been in some recent years), with many of the country's top bands playing to packed crowds along the Malecón and throughout the city. On the final weekend a huge parade winds its way down the Malecón from Habana Vieja, an energetic display of costume and song.

▲ Carnaval de la Habana

Festival Internacional de Rock "Caiman Rock" (mid-July in odd numbered years; ☎7/832-3511) Organized by Asociación Hermanos Saíz, Caiman Rock showcases Cuban bands from soft to hard rock with homegrown bands like Anima Mundi, Zeus and Chlover. Concerts take place around Havana, with the Tribuna Anti-Imperialista the main venue. Prices to events vary from free to around $10CUC.

August

Festival de Rap Cubano (late Aug; ☎7/832-3511) Having developed significantly from its humble beginnings in the mid-1990s, this festival has now taken on an extra significance for the hip-hop community in Havana, as the overwhelming popularity of reggaeton has threatened to overshadow the more politically minded hip-hop artists. It's well worth the trip to the outer suburb of Alamar, where the main events take place, to witness a music scene still in tune with its less commercially minded origins; other events are held at venues around the city. Prices vary according to venue but are generally between $2CUC and $5CUC.

October

Festival de Teatro de la Habana (late Oct–early Nov; ☎7/861-3078, ⓦwww.cubaescena.cult.cu) Excellent ten-day theatre festival showcasing classic and contemporary Cuban works at various theatres around the city. As well as adult and children's theatre there's a solid programme of workshops, seminars and lectures.

Festival Internacional de Ballet (late Oct–early Nov every even-numbered year; ⓦwww.festivalballethabana.com) The highest calibre of Cuban and international dance luminaries pirouette into the limelight for this festival presided over by Alicia Alonso and the Cuban National Ballet. Highlights of recent years have included performances by visiting Cubans Carlos Acosta and José Manuel Carreño. Performances take place at the Gran Teatro and Teatro Mella. Entrance to individual events is around $5–10CUC.

November

Feria Internacional de la Habana (early–mid-Nov; ⓦwww.feriahavana.com) Not quite as dry as it sounds, this annual gathering at ExpoCuba of Cuban business and industry, alongside a host of its international counterparts, is an interesting insight into the state of modern Cuba and its aspirations.

Festival de la Habana de Música Contemporánea (mid–late Nov; ☎7/832-0395, ⓦwww.uneac.org.cu) Proving that Cuba's musical expertise extends well beyond the salsa stereotype, this festival offers the

Listings

Finding out about forthcoming events is a somewhat hit-and-miss affair in Havana. Although the free monthly **listings** booklets Bienvenidos, Guia La Habana and Cartelera – available only sporadically in the upmarket hotels and at branches of Infotur – carry information on festivals and other goings-on, they are far from comprehensive and many local events, particularly those organized principally by and for Cubans, don't get a mention. More detailed is the Opus Habana website (ⓦwww.opushabana.cu), also a quarterly magazine and whose Cartelera section is an excellent resource for the latest cultural events in Habana Vieja, as well as the Cartelera section of La Jiribilla (ⓦwww.lajiribilla.cu/cartelera_cultural.html), the "Magazine of Cuban Culture". The very best sources of information are the excellent websites of two independent foreign magazines: **Cuba Absolutely** (ⓦwww.cubaabsolutely.com) and **The H** (ⓦwww.thehmagazine.com), which carry week-by-week listings for a selection of key events across the city. The newspaper Juventud Rebelde publishes cultural listings in its Thursday edition. Radio Taíno often broadcasts details of major shows and concerts as well as advertisements for the tourist in-spots. For less mainstream events the principal method of advertising is word of mouth, with posters and flyers seldom if ever seen. For up-to-the-minute information it's also worth consulting hotel staff or casa particular owners. Better still, the staff at Infotur offices are usually very well informed.

chance to experience the latest direction in contemporary music with some of the genre's masters. Composer and conductor Guido López Gavilán, who presides, has been joined in the past by Krystof Penderecki and Marlos Nobre among others. The main venue is Teatro Amadeo Roldán but UNEAC is the best source of information. Entrance to individual events is around $5–10CUC.

Baila en Cuba – Encuentro Mundial de Bailadores y Academias de Baile de Casino y Salsa (late Nov; ☎7/836-2124, ⓦwww .bailaencuba.soycubano.com) Cuban dancers are fiercely proud of their version of salsa, known as *casino*, and since 2006 this festival has allowed them to promote it to an international audience. A week of concerts, workshops and classes draws in dance schools and aspiring *salseros* from around the world. There is usually an impressive line-up of salsa bands too.

December

Festival Internacional del Nuevo Cine Latinoamericano (early–mid-Dec; ☎7/838-2841, ⓦwww.habanafilmfestival.com) One of Cuba's top events, this ten-day film festival combines the newest Cuban, Latin American and Western films with established classics, as well as providing a networking opportunity for leading independent film directors and anyone else interested in film. Highlights from recent events included Benicio Del Toro arriving to promote the blockbuster two-parter *Che* and the premier of Cuban Juan Carlos Tabio's *El Cuerno de la Abundancia*. Information, accreditation and programmes are available at the event headquarters in the *Hotel Nacional*, from where the event is managed. It's well worth paying $40CUC for an accreditation pass, which gains you access to all screenings, seminars and talks and many after parties.

11

Shopping

Havana stands out, refreshingly for some, as one of the few capitals in the West whose centre is not dominated by a shopping district. **Obispo**, in Habana Vieja, is the most prominent shopping street, but even here there are plenty of residential apartments and as many eateries, museums and galleries as there are retailers. Elsewhere, although new **shopping malls** and **boutiques** are mushrooming steadily around the city, the general standard of merchandise is quite low. The effects of the US economic embargo are glaringly apparent in most of the city's shops, generally understocked and noticeably low on US brands.

Like the rest of Cuba, Havana specializes in non-specialist stores, with seemingly random selections of items appearing in many of them. That's not to say that from the visitor's point of view there is nothing worth buying – for rum, cigars, coffee and crafts this is a great city. For everything else the large hotels and the **Artex** and **Caracol** state chain stores have some of the best-quality products.

As far as basics like **toiletries** go, things have moved on since the Special Period and you can pick up most things easily providing you're equipped with convertible pesos. It's worth checking out the big-name perfumes available from hotels like *Cohiba* and *Habana Libre*, as they are often cheaper than back home.

There are still shops in Havana selling products in **national pesos**, mostly half-empty and stocking used, old or shoddy goods. Nevertheless these are a necessity for most Cubans and there are a few where you can pick up some absolute bargains, while others are worth a peek just for the twilight-zone feel to their time-warped interiors. It's particularly worth wandering up Centro Habana's **Avenida de Italia**, one of the classic shopping streets of pre-revolutionary Havana, when it was known as Galiano, and where the fading signs and barely stocked stores stand as testament to a bygone era.

Standard **opening hours** are Monday to Saturday 9am to 6pm; only a tiny minority of shops stay open after 7pm. Some shops are open all Sunday but most either don't open or close at lunchtime.

Food and drink

Fresh food markets, known as **agromercados**, where farmers are permitted to sell their excess produce, are dotted all around the city and are where the average Cuban buys most of their groceries. Everything is fresh and for sale in CUP, making them fantastically cheap – half a kilo of tomatoes will only set you back around $8CUP, while oranges go for $2CUP each. All the large *agros* have a Cadeca *casa de cambio* on hand where you can change convertible pesos into national currency. Make sure you take a plastic bag in which to carry your purchases as these are never provided.

Supermarkets do not generally stock fresh food, though some have meat counters. Other than the supermarkets listed below the food sections in the Harris Brothers and La Epoca department stores (for both see pp.160–161) are among the most central grocery suppliers.

Specialist **rum** shops are uncommon, though most shops selling alcohol have a bigger selection of rum than any other alcoholic drink. In fact, finding alternatives to rum (other than beer) can be tricky.

Agromercados

Calle 19 y A Vedado. The prettiest of Havana's *agros*, this picturesque market sells meat, flowers, honey and dry goods like rice and beans, alongside fresh heaps of fresh fruit and vegetables. Closed Mon.

Calle 21 y J Vedado. Small daily market with a permanent butcher. There's not a huge choice, but basics like salad ingredients, squash and potatoes are always available.

La Catedral Empedrado e/ Ave. de las Misiones (aka Monserrate) y Villegas, Habana Vieja. A large arched doorway leads into one of the best places in Habana Vieja for fresh fruit and vegetables. Open daily.

Egido Ave. de Bélgica (aka Egido), e/ Corrales y Apodaca, Habana Vieja. This is the daddy of food markets – a huge indoor space selling fruit and vegetables, spices, honey, rice, beans and meat as well as a few household goods like soap and razor blades. Open daily.

Tulipán Ave. Tulipán y Ave. de la Independencia, near Plaza de la Revolución. Large, daily open-air market selling mountains of fresh fruit and vegetables as well as other staples like rice and beans.

Supermarkets

Centro Comercial Palco Calle 188 esq. Ave. 5ta, Playa. It's a bit of a trek out here from Vedado or Habana Vieja but the trip might be worth it, as this place has the biggest stock of imported foods in the city plus hard-to-find items like cheese.

Supermercado 3ra y 70 Ave. 3ra e/ 66 y 70, Miramar. The biggest supermarket in Havana has slightly more variety than elsewhere but mostly has larger quantities of the same stuff. That said, this place does have one of the best fresh meat counters and a better-than-average selection of dairy products.

La Puntilla Calle A esq. Ave. 1ra, Miramar. The supermarket in this large and comprehensive mall is among the best, with a good range of pricey snack foods and imported liquor.

Herbs and spices

Farmacia La Reunión Brasil (aka Teniente Rey) e/ Compostela y Habana. This immaculately restored nineteenth-century pharmacy is a popular place to buy herbs and spices.

Marco Polo Mercaderes e/ Obispo y Obrapía. One of the only specialist suppliers of herbs and spices in the city.

Bakeries and sweet shops

El Laurel Obispo e/ Compostela y Habana, Habana Vieja. Gift-boxed sweets plus chocolates, rums and other liquors.

Pain de Paris Calle 25 e/ 0 y Infanta, Vedado. A few blocks from both the Malecón and La Rampa, this is a conveniently located branch of an excellent bakery chain with a lip-licking selection of cakes and treats.

Panaderia San José Obispo e/ Mercaderes y San Ignacio, Habana Vieja. With its upstairs café this place, at the heart of the tourist circuit, offers a pleasant spot to savour traditional Cuban sweets like *señoritas* and *pasteles de guayaba*.

Pastelería Francesa Paseo del Prado e/ Neptuno y San Rafael, Habana Vieja. Cakes, coffee, ice cream and sandwiches from this café-bakery on the Parque Central.

Rum and other liquors

Casa del Ron y del Tabaco Cubano Obispo e/ Bernaza y Ave. de Bélgica, Habana Vieja. One of the best selections of rum in Havana, and a decent range of cigars too.

Licorera Calle L esq. 25, Vedado. The small gallery of shops facing the street in the *Habana Libre* includes this liquor store, stocking six or so brands of Cuban rum and bottles of Bodegas San Cristóbal wine, one of the only Cuban winemakers.

Licorera Paseo e/ 1ra y 3ra, Vedado. A better than average selection of deli-style snacks, a good stock of spirits and some international wines at this shop on the side of the *Meliá Cohiba*.

Tienda Havana Club Museo del Ron, Ave. del Puerto no.262 esq. Sol. The only shop specialising specifically in Havana Club rum has everything from the potent Cuban Barrel Proof and Gran Reserva varieties to plain old Añejo Blanco plus gift-box bottles, branded cocktail kits, glasses, stirrers and shakers.

Specialist

Casa del Café Obispo esq. Baratillo, Plaza de Armas, Habana Vieja. Specialist coffee shop stocking a number of different Cuban coffee brands such as Cubita, sold in gift boxes, and lesser-known brands like Turquino Montañes and Monte Rouge.

Mercado Bethania Amargura esq. San Ignacio, Habana Vieja. One of the city's only health-food shops keeps a threadbare stock of cereals, lentils, beans, coffee, tea and preservative-free jams.

Cigars

The **Casa del Habano** chain of stores accounts for most of the cigars sold in Cuba and is well represented all over the city. Many of the top-class hotels have their own **cigar shops**; four of the best are in the *Meliá Cohiba*, *Habana Libre*, *Parque Central* and the Hotel *Nacional*. You'll need to show your sales receipts at customs to leave the country with more than fifty cigars.

Casa del Habano Mercaderes no.202 e/ Obispo y Obrapía, Habana Vieja. A dinky little store right next to the cigar museum in the heart of Habana Vieja, but the poor selection doesn't quite match the prime location.

Casa del Habano Conde de Villanueva, Mercaderes esq. Lamparilla, Habana Vieja. One for the connoisseurs, this place will also appeal to anyone attracted by the romanticized cigar smoker's image and lifestyle, with its moody smokers' lounge, low ceilings and private club atmosphere. The range of stock is above average.

Casa del Habano Partagás Fábrica de Tabacos Partagás, Industria e/ Dragones y Barcelona, Centro Habana. A busy, well-stocked cigar emporium and a must-visit for cigar aficionados.

Casa del Habano Quinta y 16 Ave. 5ta. no.1407 esq. Calle 16, Miramar. One of the most impressive of Havana's cigar shops, set in a posh mansion, selling an extensive range of brands in floor-to-ceiling cabinets. There are all kinds of smoking accessories, a "private sales" room where you can sit down and test your smokes, a bar and a restaurant.

Arts, crafts and antiques

When shopping around the **street markets** and **craft shops** in Havana be prepared to wade through the same Che Guevara-themed memorabilia, black-coral jewellery and wooden mantlepiece-sculptures over and over again. However, if you are prepared to put in the hours you can find the occasional sculpture, piece of jewellery or handmade item of clothing that stands out from the rest. Markets tend to close on a Sunday or a Monday, but rarely both, and generally trade between 9am and 6pm.

Privately run **art workshops and galleries** exhibiting the work of a single artist are increasingly conspicuous around the streets of Habana Vieja, providing an imaginative alternative to the garishly coloured paintings sold at markets.

Craft and art shops

Arte Malecón Calle D e/ 1ra y 3ra, Vedado. Quality paintings, ceramics and other handicrafts, including items engraved or printed with images from the Museo de Bellas Artes (see p.72), plus a decent DVD and CD department in a set of attractive little rooms also featuring a bar and café.

Colección Habana O'Reilly esq. Mercaderes, Habana Vieja. Great for browsing, this unique place specializes in a wide variety of pricey products based on high-class colonial-era designs. From chairs and dinner sets to ornaments, jewellery, bags and poster prints, you are unlikely to find many of the items here for sale anywhere else.

Galería Manos Obispo no.411 e/ Aguacate y Compostela, Habana Vieja. Run by the Asociación Cubana de Artesanos Artistas and therefore offering a reliably high quality of product, there's an eclectic mix of items for sale here including cigar boxes, bags, shoes, wood carvings, ceramics and jewellery. There's also a small patio and bar at the back.

Galería Victor Manuel San Ignacio no.56, Plaza de la Catedral, Habana Vieja. The location couldn't be more tourist-focused but this place does offer a good range of artesanía including pottery and paintings.

Palacio de la Artesanía Cuba no.64 e/ Cuarteles y Peña Pobre, Habana Vieja. A pleasant place to look around, with several floors of shops gathered around a central courtyard. You'll find the usual Cuban craftwork as well as units selling cigars, T-shirts, perfume, music, shoes, jewellery and toys.

Venecia Tacón no.17 e/ O'Reilly y Empedrado, Habana Vieja. One of the city's few half-decent stockists of art supplies, selling sketchbooks, oil paints, pastels and paint brushes.

Artist workshops and commercial galleries

Estudio de Pintura Julia Valdés Obispo no.517b e/ Bernaza y Villegas, Habana Vieja. The dinky front-room studio of Julia Valdés, a Santiago-born graduate of the Cuban National School of Art, is one of the more serene spots on Obispo and well worth a peek.

Estudio de Ronaldo Encarnación Muralla no.153 e/ San Ignacio y Cuba, Habana Vieja. The abstract art in this attractive little workshop-gallery comes in all kinds of shapes and sizes. The artist, born in Pinar del Río, describes his work as "metaphors of my soul".

Estudio Taller de Pintura Reinaldo Juan Martínez Mercaderes no.268 e/ Brasil (aka Teniente Rey) y Amargura, Habana Vieja. Energetic and highly original abstract paintings by a Havana native who has exhibited his work all over the city.

Galería Habana Linea no.460 e/ E y F, Vedado. This place always has an impressive collection of contemporary art on display and for sale. See p.93 for more.

Taller de Papel Manufacturado Mercaderes no.120 e/ Obispo y Obrapía, Habana Vieja. Small but interesting shop selling pretty handmade crafts alongside an exhibition of talented local artists, which changes every month.

Markets

Feria de Arte Obispo Obispo e/ Compostela y Aguacate, Habana Vieja. Around fifteen stalls in the ruins of an old building on the main shopping street in the old town. Ornamental gifts, clothing, jewellery and ceramics.

Mercado de la Catedral Tacón, outside the Plaza de la Catedral, Habana Vieja. Among the highlights on the two hundred or so stalls at the largest crafts market in the city are leather baseballs, wooden jewellery boxes decorated with cigar labels, hand-embroidered dresses and some accomplished artwork. Closed Mon.

Mercado del edificio Fin de Siglo San Rafael e/ Ave. de Italia (aka Galiano) y Aguila Centro Habana. On the ground floor of the otherwise vacant Fin de Siglo department store, once a Havana classic, is an arts, crafts and book market stuffed with brightly coloured paintings, wooden statuettes and countless knick knacks.

Mercado de la Rampa La Rampa e/ M y N, Vedado. A small craft market, its miscellaneous merchandise includes pumpkin-seed necklaces, handmade leather items and imported clothes. Closed Mon.

Books and stationery

Secondhand **bookstalls** are very popular in Cuba, especially Havana, with plenty around the central tourist areas and the best in the Plaza de Armas, selling books in Spanish and other languages, some of them rare editions which pre-date the Revolution. **Bookshops** themselves are generally disappointing, as the publishing industry in Cuba is still trying to find its feet after the Special Period. That said, they are the place to look for the distinctive movie posters that are one of the trademarks of the Cuban film industry and increasingly collectible; they are also the main stockists of stationery.

Bella Habana Palacio del Segundo Cabo, O'Reilly esq. Tacón, Plaza de Armas, Habana Vieja. A good place to find collectors' editions and rarities, particularly from the 1950s and 1960s, such as the 25-volume *Complete Works of José Martí*. There's another bookshop across the hall.

Ediciones Boloña Mercaderes esq. Obispo. The publishing arm of the Oficina del Historiador de la Ciudad has its own specialist shop carrying the best selection of books, magazines and pamphlets on the history and reconstruction of Havana, particularly Habana Vieja.

La Internacional Obispo no.526 e/ Bernaza y Villegas, Habana Vieja. Among the better bookshops in the city, and with a reasonably good travel section and a tiny selection of novels in English by the likes of Stephen King and Danielle Steel.

Librería Centenario del Apóstol Calle 25 no.166 e/ 0 y Calzada de Infanta, Vedado. With piles of books everywhere and shelves crammed with tatty, out-of-print and secondhand stock, this is a good shop for keen browsers, despite the slightly cramped space. Alongside countless political and academic works on Marxismo and such, there are old Cuban magazines and plenty of Cuban fiction, plus a few old English-language paperbacks.

Librería Fernando Ortiz Calle L esq. 27, Vedado. One of the widest selections of history and politics titles in English and Spanish, as well as a decent selection of novels.

Librería Rayuela Ave. de los Presidentes esq. 3ra. The bookshop of the Casa de las Américas struggles to reflect the rich cultural life of this respected arts and cultural institution, though it does stock a reasonably highbrow selection of literature and academic works. This is the best place for the house's own periodicals including *Boletín Música* and *Conjunto*. Closed weekends.

🏃 **Mercado de Libros** Plaza de Armas, Habana Vieja. Market with plenty of stalls full of fascinating old books, a few dating back to the nineteenth century, with some asking prices going past the $100CUC mark. There are newer titles as well and, as always, numerous revolutionary publications such as transcripts of Fidel Castro's speeches. Closed Mon.

La Moderna Poesia Obispo esq. Bernaza, Habana Vieja. Some worthwhile specialist guides to Cuban architecture, as well as maps. Also has one of the better selections of magazines and a good stock of Cuban film posters.

Papelería O'Reilly Tacón esq. O'Reilly, Habana Vieja. One of the only dedicated stationery and art-supplies shops in the capital, and probably the best.

🏃 **Tienda de Museo de Bellas Artes** Trocadero e/ Ave. de las Misiones (aka Monserrate) y Agramonte (aka Zulueta), Habana Vieja. Unsurprisingly, given the location, this little shop sells books on Cuban art and artists you are unlikely to find anywhere else. It also holds one of the best collections of Cuban films and documentaries on DVD, plus a good choice of posters.

▲ Typical book stall

Music and film

Music stores in Havana are all relatively small and the range of CDs a little disappointing for a city so intrinsically associated with music and musicians. That said, as stock tends to consist only of music recorded on the island by Cuban labels, much of which is not internationally distributed, you will find not only obscure gems in the more niche genres but numerous salsa, son, bolero and reggaeton albums you're unlikely to come across anywhere else. Conversely you're unlikely to see any foreign-label releases, such as the official Buena Vista Social Club recordings (though there have been innumerable Cuban-released spin-offs released since) and music by foreign artists is almost non-existent.

Music shops double up as the city's principal suppliers of **DVDs** and videos, though these are also stocked in some bookshops and there is a particularly fine selection in the Tienda del Museo de Bellas Artes (see p.159). Bootleg CDs and DVDs are commonplace but street vendors openly selling them can be hard to find.

Casa de la Música Habana Ave. de Italia (aka Galiano) e/ Concordia y Neptuno, Centro Habana. Run by Egrem, the nation's principal record label, this small store has a slightly more discerning selections of CDs than some other music stores in Havana. Also has above-average listening facilities.

Casa de la Música Miramar Calle 20 esq. 35, Miramar, Playa. One of the best nightclubs in Havana also has a music shop with a good stock of CDs plus musical instruments for sale.

Galeria Juan David Cine Yara, Calle L esq. 23, Vedado. Tiny commercial outlet for the Cuban film industry selling videos, film-poster art and similarly decorated souvenirs.

Habana Sí Calle L esq. 23, Vedado. This store has one of the widest and best-organized ranges of CDs in town, divided into genres more precisely than elsewhere. Also carries books and a decent collection of Cuban films on video and DVD.

ICAIC Centro Cultural Cinematográfico Calle 23 no.1155 e/ 10 y 12, Vedado. An excellent source of cool screen-printed film posters, the Cuban Film Institute also sells cult films on video, including many by Tomás Gutiérrez Alea, and some specialist film publications mainly in Spanish. Closed Sun.

Longina Obispo no.360 e/ Habana y Compostela, Habana Vieja. The most conveniently located music shop for sightseers, though the choice is much narrower than elsewhere. Does better with its array of musical instruments.

Seriosha's Shop Neptuno no.408 e/ San Nicolás y Manrique, Centro Habana. A little crate-diggers' paradise for collectors of Latin and easy listening music on vinyl. Located at the back of a larger shop. Everything is sold in Cuban pesos.

Shopping malls and department stores

Havana's modern **shopping malls**, though unimpressive by international standards, are where you'll find some of the best-quality merchandise outside of the hotel shops. Most of the more upmarket complexes are found in Miramar and Vedado, while Centro Habana and Habana Vieja have some of the city's best-known **department stores**. All over Havana there are a number of more distinctly Cuban shopping centres, typically located in old mansions divided into five or six units, sometimes all part of the same chain. The hotels themselves are common locations for commercial centres, notably the *Habana Libre* and *Meliá Cohiba*.

Arte Habana San Rafael no.110 esq. Industria, Centro Habana. A relatively slick commercial complex with products representing various aspects of Cuban culture – music, literature, art, clothing, etc. The quality is generally higher than average.

La Epoca Ave. de Italia esq. Neptuno, Centro Habana. The biggest department store in town is nevertheless a pretty uninspiring place, with a supermarket in the basement, branded sports clothing and perfumes on the ground floor and on the floors above electrical goods, home furnishings and Cuban-brand clothing departments.

Focsa Calle 17 y L Vedado. The clutch of decent shops here includes a photography shop, an Adidas sportswear outlet, a cheap shoe shop and two general stores, one selling household goods and the other groceries.

Galería Comercial Comodoro Ave. 3ra e/ 80 y 84, Miramar. Havana's largest and most upmarket shopping mall is also the most pleasant to shop in, flanked by lawns, pavement cafés and outdoor eateries. There are around thirty stores here, many of them clothes shops, as well as specialists in jewellery, watches, perfume and cigars.

Galerías Amazonas Calle 12 e/ 23 y 25, Vedado. The best thing about this shopping precinct is the delicatessen selling olives and other delicacies and an array of fancy chocolates. Other shops worth a mention include a florist and a fairly good shoe shop, Peletería Claudia.

Galerías de Paseo Paseo esq. Calle 1ra, Vedado. The clothes and homeware shops in this flashy mall are more run-of-the-mill and number far fewer than you might expect from the size and look of the place. The excellent Jazz Café (see p.146) is the highlight here.

Harris Brothers Monserrate e/ O'Reilly y San Juan de Dios, Habana Vieja. Although the selection and quality of products inside this classic department store don't live up to the expectations raised by the grand exterior, it does have one of the better supermarkets and widest choice of products in Habana Vieja.

La Maison Calle 16 no.701 esq. 7ma, Miramar. Housed in a graceful colonial mansion and more upmarket than the larger department stores in the older parts of the city. Most notable for the choice of watches, jewellery, cosmetics, shoes and clothing, as well as the fashion shows which are frequently held here.

Plaza de Carlos Tercero Ave. Salvador Allende (aka Carlos Tercero) e/ Arbol Seco y Retiro, Centro Habana. This four-floor mall is usually swarming with customers and has a food court on the ground floor, a cigar shop, a large shoe shop and a number of clothes shops scattered around.

Clothing, jewellery and accessories

The quality of Cuban-made **clothing** is generally very poor, though the numerous T-shirt specialists, most of them found in hotels such as the *Habana Libre*, tend to offer a better cut of cloth. For reliable quality you'll have to seek out the foreign brand names, only a few of which have their own stores in Havana. Well-made, good-quality **jewellery** tends to be easier to find, while there are several one-off shops, particularly on Obispo in Habana Vieja, like the bag-seller Novator, that offer high-grade merchandise.

La Bella Cubana Oficios esq. Lamparilla, Habana Vieja. Women's beauty and fashion shop geared up to the Italian-influenced side of contemporary Cuban styles, with flashy Alex Max handbags, Rifle jeans and a selection of tops and dresses.

Casa del Abanico Obrapía no.107 e/ Oficios y Mercaderes. Artistically embroidered hand-held fans, with made-to-order designs on offer, too.

Casa de la Obrapía Obrapía esq. Mercaderes Habana Vieja. The goods here warrant the heftier price tag due to the quality of the traditional *guayabera* dresses ($60CUC) and shirts ($30CUC). Patchwork bags, bedspreads and wall hangings are sold alongside, and you can order made-to-measure clothes in the adjoining workshop, which is open Tues–Fri.

El Clip Obispo no.501 e/ Villegas y Bernaza, Habana Vieja. Watch shop selling mostly Cuban brands.

Galería Amelia Peláez Hotel Habana Libre, Calle 23 esq. L, Vedado. One of the best selections of tack-free jewellery, with some surprisingly affordable pieces given the five-star location.

Guayabera Habanera Tacón no.20 e/ O'Reilly y Empedrado. The place to come for an authentic *guayabera*, the classic Cuban shirt with four pockets and two rows of pleats.

Novator Obispo no.365 e/ Compostela y Habana, Habana Vieja. Smart-looking bags, handbags, belts, hats, wallets and purses.

Optica El Almendares Obispo no.364 e/ Compostela y Habana. This touristy optician is the best place in Havana to look for sunglasses.

Ropa Rampa Calle 23 e/ O y P Vedado. Has a surprisingly good, if random, collection of pretty cotton and linen dresses for women and children, men's shirts, tea towels and place mats, all designed and made on site.
San Eloy Obispo no.115 e/ Mercaderes y Oficios. The five cabinets here contain the

city's best selection of gold and silver jewellery, from $10CUC silver bracelets to $3000CUC gold rings.
Vía Uno Oficios esq. Obrapía. This shoe shop has one of the better selections of women's footwear, from formal shoes to trainers.

Hairdressers, beauty salons and perfumeries

Travellers with 220-voltage hair dryers and straighteners may find they are unable to use them where they are staying, given the prevalence of 110-voltage sockets in Cuba – a common reason for the foreign patronage of the city's hairdressers and beauty salons.

Estilo Obispo no.510 e/ Bernaza y Villegas ☎ 7/860-2650. A professionally run and reputable hair stylists and beauty salon where you'll pay $10CUC for a cut, $15CUC for a blow dry and $5CUC for a manicure or pedicure.

Habana 1791 Mercaderes no.156 e/ Obrapia y Lamparilla, Habana Vieja. This unique shop sells what it bills as "aromas coloniales de la Isla de Cuba": handmade perfumes like those used during the eighteenth and nineteenth centuries in Cuba. Made from flowers and plant oils, they are sold in ceramic or glass bottles; prices range from around $5CUC to $20CUC.

La Nouvelle Miramar Trade Center. One of the best-stocked perfumeries in the city, with a decent choice of international brands including Armani, Elizabeth Arden, Chanel and Bulgari.
Peluqueria Mercedes Beltrán San Miguel no.573 e/ Padre Varela (aka Belascoaín) y Gervasio ☎ 7/878-2047. A neighbourhood women's hairdressers in an apartment building, offering good rates. Popular with locals.
Salón Correo Brasil (aka Teniente Rey) e/ Mercaderes y Oficios, Habana Vieja. Friendly little barbers in the heart of the old town.

Photography

There are small photographic suppliers and developers all round the city and many of the shopping malls have photography shops or kiosks.

Foto Habana Tacón no.22 e/ O'Reilly y Empedrado. The most professional photography specialist in Habana Vieja.
Fotovideo Ave. 5ta e/ 40 y 42, Miramar. Photographic equipment and supplies as well as videotaping accessories.

Photoservice Calle 23 esq. L. This branch of the national chain based in the *Habana Libre* sells digital cameras, memory cards and flash drives. There are also facilities to issue prints straight from cameras or drives.

Sporting goods and clothing

Sports clothing is readily available in Havana and you'll see several Adidas and Puma outlets around the city. Among the malls and department stores, the Galería Comercial Comodoro has the most comprehensively stocked sports store.

Adidas Neptuno no.460-462 e/ Campanario y Manrique, Centro Habana. The largest Adidas outlet in the city is one of the few sports stores that actually sells a bit of equipment as well as clothing, including basketballs, footballs and baseball gloves.

D' Primera Calle 1ra y B, Vedado. A collection of sportswear shops stocking New Balance, Puma, Vans, Converse and Fila gear.
Puma Miramar Trade Center, Ave. 3ra e/ 78 y 80, Playa. Predominantly clothing and trainers.

Sports

S
port plays a prominent role in the lives of habaneros. Rarely will you see an open space not hosting a game of **baseball**, the national sport, and in the last decade **football** has become equally visible on the city streets. Vedado is where you'll find much of the action, with cement **basketball** and racquetball courts scattered around, plus a couple of run-down sports complexes, most notably the Parque Martí (see p.169), hosting neighbourhood clashes every evening.

With professional sport in its strictest sense non-existent in Cuba, there's a distinctly different look and feel to top-class sport in Havana. Teams don't have sponsors, merchandising, websites or any of the other trappings of modern sport elsewhere in the world. Unfortunately, however, Havana struggles to provide the city's plethora of sporting stars with the stadia and arenas they deserve – the economic hardships of the last two decades having taken their toll on the city's sporting infrastructure. There are very few single-sport venues outside of baseball, with most arenas used for several sports or more. This, however, is more than balanced out by the entrance costs, no more than a plain old peso or two in most cases, offering fantastic value.

Booking a ticket for a sporting event in advance is rarely possible and usually unnecessary. The flip side to this is that finding advance **information** is absurdly difficult and usually involves consulting one of the few Cuban sports websites or contacting the venues themselves, though not many have official information lines. The best place to start for a general idea of the latest goings on in Cuban sport is the website run by INDER (Ⓦwww.inder.cu), the National Institute for Sport and Recreation, which includes a yearly schedule of events. INDER also publishes an online newspaper called JIT (Ⓦwww.jit .cu), which is well worth checking. The only printed information you are likely to find on sport will be in one of the national newspapers, with *Juventud Rebelde* and *Granma* carrying a very limited amount of information on fixtures and results.

Baseball

Cubans are fanatical about baseball, with a history of the sport on the island going back to the nineteenth century. The city has two major baseball teams, **Industriales** and **Metropolitanos**, both of which play at the 55,000-capacity **Estadio Latinoamericano** (Ⓣ7/870-8175) at Pedro Pérez no.302 e/ Patria y Sarabia in Cerro, the city borough south of Centro Habana and Vedado. Industriales, traditionally the most successful team in Cuba, attracts the biggest crowds, especially when they play their arch-rivals Santiago de Cuba. Both teams compete in the national league, the **Serie Nacional de Béisbol**, which takes place between October and May, consisting of a ninety-game regular season followed by the play-offs. Matches usually take place on Tuesday, Wednesday, Thursday and Saturday at 9pm and Sunday at 1.30pm. There is always plenty of banter in the crowd and a relaxed vibe, but with so many games the stadium is often half-empty, the big crowds usually only coming out for the most important confrontations. This means to catch a game all you need do is turn up and pay at the gate.

The best sources for **game schedules**, and Cuban baseball in general, are the Federación Cubana de Béisbol Aficionado (Ⓦwww.beisbol cubano.cu) and Radio Coco (Ⓦwww .radiococo.icrt.cu). Also check the back pages of *Granma* newspaper for details of forthcoming games.

Basketball

Though among the most popular sports in Cuba, basketball has not yet produced any world-class players or teams. Despite this, the smaller arenas make for a more animated atmosphere than at baseball matches. **Capitalinos**, the local team, spends the winter months, usually January to April, in weekly combat with the other seven teams in the **Liga Superior de Baloncesto** (LSB), the national league. This is preceded by the Torneo Nacional de Ascenso (TNS), an annual national qualifying tournament for the LSB, which begins in November. Ciego de Ávila has been the team to beat in recent years, collecting six league titles in the last decade, defeating *Los Azules*, as Capitalinos are known, in the final on four of those occasions.

Advance **information** on games is even harder to find than baseball listings, a situation not helped by the irregular timing of the league from season to season. Your best bet is either to ask around or to contact one of the relevant arenas. Over the years games have been played variously at the Sala Polivalente Ramón Fonst, the Ciudad Deportiva and the Sala Polivalente Kid Chocolate (for details of all three see p.169). Games usually begin around 6pm.

For a pick-up game head to Vedado, the spiritual home of **street basketball** in Havana. There are numerous courts dotted around but the best-known are on the corner of Calle 23 and Calle B and in the Parque Deportivo José Martí (see p.169).

Boxing

Cuban boxing, with its amateur ethos, has no box-office names but the country has a rich tradition in the sport, before and since the Revolution, and has been a dominant force in the amateur game for decades. Names such as Teofilo Stevenson, Felix Savón and Mario Kindelan have gone down in Olympic boxing history and would doubtless have been successful in the professional game had they defected. There have been high-profile defections in recent times, memorably in 2007 when three Olympic gold medalists – Yan Barthelemy Varela, Yuriorkis Gamboa and Odlanier Solis – fled to the US to pursue professional careers. Most Cuban champions, however, have chosen to remain in Cuba and current boxers to look out for include Yordenis Ugás, Emilio Correa and Osmay Acosta, while the Havana Boxing Academy in Mulgoba, near the airport, subject of a fantastic recent feature-length documentary called *Sons of Cuba*, ensures that the fine boxing tradition will continue.

The most famous boxing arena in Havana is the **Sala Polivalente Kid Chocolate** (see p.169), named after Eligio "Kid Chocolate" Sardiñas, a Havana-born boxer and one of the most successful Cuban fighters from the professional era. Local and national boxing tournaments are held here, while international bouts tend to take place at the Ciudad Deportiva. The highly regarded national championship, the **Campeonato Nacional Playa Girón**, take place every January, with the location rotating around the

▲ Sculptures of boxers at the Complejo Panamericana

country on an annual basis. Also staged on a rotation basis is the prestigious **Giraldo Córdova Cardín** tournament, an annual international event held in Cuba every April or May, pitting Cuban boxers against foreign fighters, usually from Latin America.

For a taste of grassroots boxing head for the **Gimnasio Rafael Trejo** (℡7/862-0266; open Mon–Fri 8am–5pm; $1CUC) at Cuba no.815 e/ Merced y Leonor Pérez (also called Paula) in Habana Vieja, where you can catch neighbourhood bouts in a small but historic outdoor arena,

one of the oldest in the country. There are no fixed schedules but there's usually something going on and even if it's just training this place is still worth a peek.

Diving, fishing and boating

Havana has two marinas, the **Marina Hemingway** at Ave. 5ta y Calle 248 (℡7/204-5088) in the far western suburbs of Santa Fe in Playa, and **Marina Tarará** at Vía Blanca Km 18 in Habana del Este (℡7/796-0242). Most of the fishing, diving and sailing in the waters around Havana is arranged through one of these two marinas, both of which are run by **Marlin** (Ⓦwww.nauticamarlin.com), offering a very similar set of packages and the same prices.

The **diving** clubs at the marinas use over thirty dive sites off the Havana coastline, with depths of 5m to 30m. The dive centre at the Marina Hemingway is called La Aguja (daily 10am–5pm; ☎7/204-1150) and you'll need your passport for dive trips from here, as it is an international port of entry. For all diving enquiries at Marina Tarará contact the marina itself. Many of the dives, particularly from the Marina Hemingway, take place at the twenty or so dive sites that line the Playa coastline, including a couple of shipwrecks, coral walls and small caves. Both charge $40CUC for one dive or $60CUC for two on the same trip. There are various certified ACUC courses offered, including a two-day beginner's course for $170CUC, a four- to five-day open water course for $340CUC and a similar course for more experienced divers for $280CUC. There is another Marlin-run dive club at the *Copacabana* hotel (☎7/204-1037 ext. 6191) in Miramar at Ave. 1ra no.4404 e/ 44 y 46.

Both marinas offer regular **deep-sea fishing** (pesca de altura) and **bottom-fishing** (pesca a fondo) trips. The set price for a deep-sea fishing trip for four people is $300/400/500CUC for four/six/eight hours. This includes all equipment and bait, a fishing instructor and crew plus some on-board drinks. Non-fishing companions are charged an extra $20CUC per person up to a maximum of ten people. All the same stuff is included on bottom-fishing trips but the prices differ and start at $170CUC for four hours.

There are also one or two non-fishing **organized excursions** by boat. These excursions are aimed at groups and as such depend upon a certain number of punters, unless you

are prepared to fork out for the whole cost yourself, making their frequency somewhat irregular and ringing ahead essential. The Puesta del Sol excursion, for example, a three-hour sunset cruise along the entire length of the Havana shoreline, is priced at $180CUC for six people and an additional $40CUC per person above this number up to a maximum of ten.

All the best-known **fishing tournaments** are based at the Marina Hemingway – including the most prestigious one, running since the 1950s, the annual **International Billfish Tournament** (Torneo Internacional de la Pesca de la Aguja), which usually takes place in June. The most celebrated of the other yearly competitions are the International Wahoo Fishing Tournament, which takes place in November, and the International Blue Marlin Fishing Tournament in September.

Yacht owners wanting to dock in Havana from international waters must head for Marina Hemingway, where there are immigration services and where you can dock in one of the four hundred berths along the four canals, each canal 4.5m deep and 6m wide. If you are docking you should notify your arrival through VHF channel 16 or 72, or alternatively HF channel 7462 or 7821. If you want to **charter** your own boat this is also the marina to call in at. Most charters from here are motorboats (to charter a sailing boat you'll need to head for the south coast) and have a capacity for four people plus an assigned crew, usually no more than a captain and a chef. Typical destinations are Varadero to the east and the network of cays off the northern coastline of Pinar del Río to the west. The price is currently $500CUC per day.

Football

Football has never been more popular in Cuba, with an explosion in participation over the last decade, and you'll see evidence of its growth in replica kits, crowds around TV sets when a World Cup is on and football games played all around Havana, in places where previously you would only have seen kids swinging baseball bats or bouncing basketballs. Despite its overall popularity, the national league is still struggling for recognition by the general public, with attendances and atmospheres at live games often quite disappointing.

The home of football in Havana is the **Estadio Pedro Marrero** (℡7/209-5428) at Ave. 41 no.4409 e/ 44 y 46 in Marianao in the western suburbs, where one of the city's two league teams, **Ciudad de la Habana**, and the national team play most of their matches. The other Havana team competing in the national league, the **Campeonato Nacional de Fútbol**, is **Industriales**, who play their home games in the **Estadio La Polar**, a very modest stadium next to the Río Almendares about a kilometre south of the Estadio Pedro Marrero in a neighbourhood called La Ceiba. The regular league season concludes in March and is followed by a knockout competition in April between the top two teams from each of the four regional groups. Compared to the local baseball and basketball teams, Ciudad de la Habana has had limited success over the last decade or so and Industriales even less so. Match schedules have been highly irregular in recent seasons, with games taking place on any day of the week and the league breaking altogether for most of December and January. Games tend to kick off between 3pm and 5pm. By far the most comprehensive and up-to-date **website** for Cuban football fans is FutCuba (ⓦwww .telepinar.icrt.cu/futcuba).

If you fancy joining in, head for the university stadium, the Estadio Juan Abrantes, one of the most reliable places for a game with several going on almost every evening.

Golf

Prior to the Revolution, Cuba was a popular golfing destination and had nearly a dozen golf courses. All except one were bulldozed once the revolutionaries took over and though a new course was built 140km away in Varadero in 1998, the sole survivor of pre-1959 Cuba, the **Club de Golf Habana** (daily 8am–9pm; ℡7/649-8918), remains the only course standing in Havana today. Located on the Carretera de Vento just off the road linking the city to the airport, the Avenida de Rancho Boyeros, this basic nine-hole course covers an area less than a kilometre in length and less than half a kilometre in width. Green fees are $20/30CUC for nine/ eighteen holes with caddy hire at $3/6CUC respectively; trolley hire is $5CUC and club hire is $10CUC, while for another $10CUC you can get yourself a golf lesson. The complex also features a *cancha* court ($2CUC per person), which doubles up as a tennis court (same price), a bowling alley, a pool and a restaurant, called *La Estancia*, serving basic pizzas and Cuban cuisine.

Swimming

There are only a few **public pools** in Havana, all of them outdoors but not all of them containing water. They are so unreliable, in fact, that you're almost always better off aiming for one of the hotel or tourist-complex pools dotted around the city, mostly in Vedado and Miramar. Habana Vieja currently has three hotels with pools: the *Sevilla*, the *Parque Central* and the *Saratoga*. You may be asked to show a passport – and sometimes refused entrance – if you are not a guest at the hotel. For more pools see box on p.168.

Tennis, squash and cancha

Tennis is not a particularly popular sport in Cuba and public tennis courts are a rarity in Havana. The Federación

Havana's top swimming pools

Best for views: Hotel Saratoga (see p.112) Access for non-hotel residents depends on how busy the pool is with hotel guests. The pool itself is rather small but worth it for extensive views over the Capitolio building and beyond to the sea. No official fee but you may be asked to make a minimum spend at the bar.

Best for style: Hotel Riviera (see p.113) The stunning three-tier diving board towering over the expansive saltwater pool exudes 1950s style, while the poolside area is perfect for lounging in the sun and people-watching. $10CUC minimum spend.

Best for leisurely lengths: Hotel Nacional (see p.113) The rectangular pool overlooking the lawn is the quieter of the *Nacional*'s two pools, particularly early in the morning; it's also a good spot for those looking to exercise rather than sunbathe. $15CUC minimum spend.

Best for kids: Panorama (see p.114) This giant oasis of a pool is one of the largest in the city and has shallower areas for paddling, a bridge and a bar you can swim up to. $15CUC minimum spend.

Best beach alternative: Club Habana (see p.105) *Club Habana* boasts an elegant pool and given the ample sports facilities and restaurants – not to mention its distance from Habana Vieja – it's an ideal place to head to for a day of relaxing. Day pass $20CUC.

Cubana de Tenis (℡7/766-2121) is based in the **Centro Nacional de Tenis 19 de Noviembre** (℡7/795-2121), in the Complejo Panamericano in Habana del Este, where the facilities include ten hard courts. International tournaments are occasionally held here, such as Davis Cup regional qualifiers and ITF Junior events. The other specialist tennis venue in the city is the *Occidental Miramar* hotel, which has six synthetic courts as well as a squash court; non-guests can sometimes rent courts. It stages one of the few regular international tennis tournaments that take place in the city, the Copa Occidental Miramar, held here every December. The hotel also runs a members' **squash club** open to anyone prepared to pay the $50CUC monthly fee. Other hotels with tennis courts include the *Nacional*, the *Meliá Habana* and the *Comodoro*, while the *Meliá Cohiba* is one of the only other hotels with a squash court. Outside of the hotels the most accessible place to play tennis is Club Habana (see p.169), which has four synthetic-surface courts.

Far more popular than tennis among Habaneros themselves is **cancha**, versions of which elsewhere in the world are known as racquetball or frontenis, similar to squash but played on outdoor courts. There are *cancha* courts all over the city, including in the Parque Deportivo José Martí (see p.169), and they are free to use, though you'll probably need to befriend some locals to have any chance of getting a game.

Multi-sport spectator venues

Havana's lack of sporting infrastructure means that numerous sports have to share the same arenas. There are a number of multi-sport arenas and stadiums around the city and with event information so hard to get hold of and individual team websites all but non-existent, one of the best ways to stay informed is to contact the venues themselves. Entrance is sometimes free and rarely more than a peso or two.

Coliseo de la Ciudad Deportiva ☎7/648-5000. This 15,000-capacity arena, built in 1957, is part of a huge sports complex of the same name used predominantly by students of physical education and home to INDER. It's located just off the roundabout where the airport road meets the Vía Blanca in Cerro. Volleyball is most frequently played here, though gymnastics, martial arts, boxing and occasionally basketball also take place.

Complejo Panamericano Ave. Monumental Km 4½, Habana del Este. Flanking both sides of the road to the Playas del Este, just before you reach Cojímar, this huge sports complex, not all of it open to the public, was originally built to host the 1991 Panamerican Games. There's a tennis centre (☎7/795-2121), a velodrome (☎7/797-3773), an Olympic-sized swimming pool and diving pools (☎7/795-2333) and the centrepiece, the Estadio Panamericano (☎7/795-4140), an athletics stadium that has also staged football matches in recent years. Much of

the time these facilities are used only for training purposes by national teams, though occasionally they host competitions on view to the public.

Sala Polivalente Kid Chocolate Paseo del Prado e/ Brasil y San Martín ☎7/862-8634. Opposite the Capitolio Nacional, this rickety old sports hall is best known for hosting boxing matches and takes its name from a great of Cuban boxing. A number of international tournaments have been held here in recent years but there are no regularly scheduled bouts. It also hosts basketball, wrestling, badminton and five-a-side football among other sports. Check the notice board posted behind the bars at the entrance for the daily and weekly programmes.

Sala Polivalente Ramón Fonst Ave. de Rancho Boyeros e/ Bruzón y 19 de Mayo, Plaza de la Revolución ☎7/881-4296. Used predominantly for basketball but this arena has also hosted volleyball, handball, gymnastics and fencing.

Gyms and sports centres

There are no staffed or professionally organized public sports centres as such in Havana; instead, the best places for participatory sports are the local neighbourhood courts and pitches where all-comers are usually welcome. At the other end of the spectrum are the hotel gyms and one or two members' clubs.

Club Habana Ave. 5ta e/ 188 y 192, Reparto Flores, Playa ☎7/204-5700. The best-equipped sports centre in the city has its own beach and three swimming pools, four tennis courts, outdoor hard courts with equipment for basketball or football, *cancha* courts, a sauna and gym, plus facilities for table tennis, martial arts classes, aerobics classes, chiropody and reflexology treatments. Non-members pay the daily entrance cost (Mon–Fri $10CUC, Sat & Sun $15CUC) and are then free to use any of the facilities assuming they have not been booked by members and pending the cost of any equipment rental. Open daily 7.30am–9pm.

Estadio Juan Abrantes Ave. Universidad, Vedado. The university stadium has an athletics track, an outdoor pool, basketball courts, a rudimentary gym and a sports hall. Access is sometimes denied to the public but the locals from the surrounding neighbourhoods

have been playing baseball, basketball and football here for years.

Occidental Miramar Fitness Center Hotel Occidental Miramar, Ave. 5ta e/ 72 y 76, Miramar, Playa ☎7/204-3584. Members of this sports and fitness centre, one of the best in the city, have access to a gym, sauna, swimming pool, tennis courts, badminton and table tennis; for an added charge on top of membership you can use the squash court. Membership costs $60CUC per month.

Parque Deportivo José Martí Ave. de los Presidentes esq. 5ta, Vedado. Known locally as the Parque Martí, this is a popular but poorly maintained public facility with a dusty athletics track, baseball field, basketball courts and small-sided football pitches, *cancha* courts, an outdoor swimming pool (which occasionally has water in it) and a sports hall.

Gay Havana

Despite a very poor overall record on gay rights since the Revolution, there has been marked progress in the social standing and acceptance of homosexuals in Cuba since the early 1990s and Havana has become, by Latin American and Caribbean standards, a relatively gay-friendly city. That said, in a country where almost everything needs state-sanctioning to exist publicly, there is still only one official gay venue in Havana – Playa Mi Cayito (see below) – though the gay community has established a number of their own locations – some of them well known, most still rather clandestine affairs. Furthermore, police harassment of gay men and particularly of transvestites is still quite common. Despite this, there are now significant numbers of openly gay men on the streets of Havana, though gay women are far less visible. There is still a strong stigma attached to same-sex hand-holding or similar displays of sexuality, but freedom of expression for gay people is greater now than at any point since 1959.

Mariela Castro, the daughter of President Raúl, has emerged as a champion for gay rights in Cuba in recent years. As director of **Cenesex**, the National Centre for Sex Education (Ⓦ www.cenesex.sld.cu), she has been instrumental in a number of initiatives designed to increase tolerance and awareness of gay issues. In 2007 Cenesex was behind the country's first official recognition and celebration of the International Day Against Homophobia. Attended by important government dignitaries and personalities from the Cuban arts, and covered on television with a closing gala starring transvestites, this was a significant development. On the same day in 2009 the first **gay march** took place on Calle 23 in Vedado. The inaugural Gay Pride Parade in 2008 was cancelled following the arrest of two of its organizers – affirmation that the issue of gay rights remains a politically sensitive issue in Cuba.

The only state-sanctioned gay venue in Havana is a section of beach at the Playas del Este known as **Mi Cayito**. Located on the edge of Boca Ciega, this five-hundred-metre stretch of coastline is normally patrolled by police who tend to stop any displays of homosexuality considered to be too provocative, including same-sex kissing. The beach is also popular with young Cuban men looking to pick up tourists.

There is no **pink press** in Havana. The only magazine in which gay issues are regularly discussed is the rather academic *Sexología y Sociedad*, the quarterly magazine published by Cenesex.

Festivals and events

Since 2005 there has been an annual **Festival de Cine Gay**, which lasts for a week, usually in November, and takes place at Cine 23 y 12 (℗7/833-6906) in Vedado. Despite receiving virtually no coverage in the Cuban press, the festival has proved successful and spawned a popular monthly film club, open to the public, known as Cine Club Diferente. It meets on the third Thursday of every month at Cine 23 y 12 for screenings of films exploring "sexual diversity" followed by discussions. Check the Cenesex website for more details (℗www .cenesex.sld.cu/webs/diversidad/cineclub.htm).

The **International Day Against Homophobia** continues to be celebrated every year at the Pabellón Cuba, found at Calle N esq. 23 in Vedado (for more on this venue see p.145).

Accommodation

Although gay couples or individuals shouldn't have any problems staying in any of the establishments listed in Chapter 5 (see pp.109–121) there are a number of **casas particulares** around the city that have declared themselves gay-friendly.

Casa Aleido San Rafael no.108, apto. 1, e/ Consulado y Industria ℗7/861-3455, ℮malinamc@infomed.sld.cu. A few metres from the Parque Central on a busy pedestrianized street, both rooms here are sumptuously decorated by *casa particular* standards and have their own private bathrooms. In the larger room doors open onto the street scene below.

Casa de Armando R Menéndez Castiñeiras Neptuno no.519, apto. 4, e/ Campanario y Lealtad, Centro Habana ℗7/862-8400, ℮neptuno519@yahoo.es. Quiet flat, tucked away at the back of an apartment building, artistically and uniformly decked out with well-preserved Art Deco furniture, most of it here since the 1940s. An extremely likeable, laid-back option run by an astute landlord.

Casa de Ray Aguila no.309, piso 2, apto. 2, e/ Neptuno y Concordia, Centro Habana ℗7/863-5107, ℗www.raycasaparticular.com. The hosts here are a very hospitable gay couple who run their large, stylishly kitsch apartment, which is full of wonderful antique furniture including chandeliers in the guest rooms, with professionalism and friendliness.

Nightlife, bars and cafés

There are no gay nightclubs as such in Havana but there are nights when certain clubs tend to attract a predominantly gay crowd. Not surprisingly, given these restricted state-sanctioned options, much of the **gay nightlife** and social scene in Havana is organized in private locations around the city and advertising is strictly by word of mouth. The scene as a whole is known as **la movida**. These locations, however, are not altogether inaccessible to visitors, though they change with relative frequency. The unwritten rule for anyone looking to attend is to head for the corner of Calles 23 and L in Vedado, outside the Cine Yara, from where taxi drivers in the know will pick up anyone looking for a "taxi a la fiesta", the accepted code, and ferry them to the latest location. They can reliably be assumed to take place at weekends and the taxi ride is normally charged at $1CUC to Cubans, though as a foreign visitor you will probably have to haggle to get it down to this price and should expect to pay a peso or two extra. Entrance to these "private" parties is between $1CUC and $3CUC and they often feature a transvestite show followed by recorded music into the early hours of the morning.

The Cine Yara is at the heart of the best-known and liveliest gay and lesbian **cruising area**, the section of Calle 23 between the Malecón and the Avenida de los Presidentes. The action is usually most concentrated near to and on the Malecón itself opposite the foot of La Rampa.

Clubs

Atelier Calle 17 esq. 6, Vedado ☎7/830-6808. This small but lively club in the heart of Vedado hosts a gay-friendly night every Monday with an almost exclusively Cuban clientele. Entrance $2CUC.

El Bonsai Calle 10 de Octubre esq. Colina, Diez de Octubre. Right off the mainstream circuit, this nightclub has an unofficial gay night every Wednesday. Entrance $40CUP.

El Cabaret de las Estrellas Casa de Rogelio Conde, Calle A e/ 15 y 16, Lawton, Diez de Octubre ☎7/698-6129. The third floor of a residential block in the neighbourhood of Lawton is the renowned yet undercover venue of the best-known transvestite show in the city. Bookings essential. $25CUC for a table for four.

Bars and cafés

Bim Bom Calle 23 esq. Calzada de Infanta, Vedado. Given its location so close to the best-known gay cruising area, this branch of an ice-cream chain has effectively become a gay café.

Cafetería 23 y P Calle 23 esq. P, Vedado. Long-established meeting spot for gay men and women in the heart of the action on La Rampa, but otherwise nothing to mark this fairly ordinary café out as a particularly worthwhile place for a drink.

Castropol Malecón no.107 e/ Genios y Crespo, Centro Habana. One of the only fixed lesbian venues, where on Thursdays there is usually a live show featuring resident singer Yenisey del Castillo, a well-known Cuban pop star. There's a small outdoor patio and a dance floor inside.

Kids' Havana

H avana is a city that loves children but doesn't really provide for them; with a few notable exceptions, most of what will amuse the kids is incidental rather than tailor-made. Practically speaking you'll be able to find most things like **nappies** in the department stores and some of the hotel shops, though the quality might not be what you're used to. Baby wipes and nappy bags are less common so it's wise to bring your own. **Baby food**, while not impossible to come by, might require some searching out in the larger supermarkets (see p.156). The only milk widely available is UHT.

Make sure your **first-aid kit** has child-strength fever reducers, diarrhoea medicine, cold remedies, plasters and other medicines. These are available in Havana but not always readily so and tend to be more expensive than at home. Plenty of **sunscreen** is essential; the Caribbean sun is very hot, particularly during the rainy season (May–Oct). Pack lots of loose cotton clothing, remembering a few long-sleeved tops and trousers to combat the brutal air conditioning in restaurants and buses. It's also a good idea to pack a raincoat and appropriate footwear, as sudden downpours are common even outside of the rainy season. Bear in mind that with limited laundry facilities you may be hand-washing many garments, so take items that are easy to launder and dry.

Children should stick to **bottled water** or water that has been boiled as there are parasites in some areas of the country. Avoid eating uncooked food or food sold on street stalls. You should also apply the same principle to **ice cream** sold on the street, as water quality cannot be guaranteed.

Public **toilets** are scarce in Cuba and those that do exist are rather unpleasant. You are better off heading to a hotel or, at a pinch, a nearby restaurant, although these are sometimes no better. Many of these will not be equipped with toilet paper so make sure you carry your own supply. There are few places with dedicated baby-changing facilities; again your best option is the women's bathrooms in larger hotels like *Habana Libre* or *Parque Central*.

In terms of **accommodation**, children under 12 can stay for half price in many hotel rooms and if no extra bed is required they may be able to stay for free. Staying in a *casa particular* is a great way to give children a taste of Cuba beyond the tourist belt. Rooms often have extra beds for children and many households have pets and courtyards where children can play.

Eating out, children are made very welcome pretty much everywhere. Children's menus are on the rise but generally still scarce. Places with high chairs are similarly rare – most children sit on their parents' laps. Discreet breast-feeding in public is fine.

If you plan on **renting a car** to go further afield, bring your own child- or baby-seat, as rental companies never supply them. Newer cars are fitted with three-point seat belts in the front and seat belts in the back.

Museums and sights

In general, museums in Havana are of the stand-and-look variety rather than offering much interaction, which means that children might get bored quickly. Two visitor attractions are aimed squarely at children: the **Museo Nacional de Historia Natural** (see p.53), which has a separate activity room with stuffed animals to pet and crayoning tables; and the **Acuario Nacional** (see p.102), offering dolphin and sea lion shows throughout the day. The **Museo Castillo de la Real Fuerza** (see p.54) tells Cuba's naval history through displays brimming with treasures, including gold bars and models of Spanish galleons that kids may find exciting. Meanwhile the **Maqueta de la Habana Vieja** scale model of the old city (see p.59) will appeal to kids' interest in miniatures. Further afield, the **Parque Zoológico Nacional** (see p.188), the **Botanical Gardens** and **ExpoCuba** (see p.188) offer short day-trips with scope to run wild.

Activities and entertainment

The most accessible of Havana's modest assortment of activities for kids is Habana Vieja's **Parque Infantil La Maestranza**, with bouncy castles, slides and toy trains. More lavish is the Isla del Coco **theme park** at Calle 112 e/ 5ta y 3ra in Miramar. Opened in 2008, this Chinese-designed park has over twenty separate rides and attractions including a rollercoaster, a looping pirate ship and various themed play areas. There's a similar theme park, the Parque Mariposa, in Parque Lenin (see p.186). Next door to Isla del Coco is a circus tent where shows take place at weekends. Also in Miramar is Havana's only proper **city park**, the Parque Almendares (see p.103), just over the river from Vedado, which offers run-down but endearingly traditional activities for children, such as pony and playground rides, crazy golf and boating, some of them available only at weekends. And if all else fails you can always pack them into a taxi and head to the Playas del Este **beaches** (see p.180), where sandy swathes and shallow waters make for low-maintenance holiday fun.

While theatre might be beyond the reach of non-Spanish-speaking children, **puppet shows** are visually entertaining enough to jump the language barrier; the best is at **Teatro Nacional de Guiñol** at Calle M y 17 in Vedado.

Shops

There are few shops dedicated to children, but you can buy cheaply made imported **clothes and toys** at the Galería Comercial Comodoro (see p.161) in Miramar and Trasval on Avenida de Italia (also called Galiano) in Centro Habana.

Out of the City

Out of the City

www.roughguides.com

East of Havana

T aking the tunnel in Habana Vieja under the bay and heading east on the Vía Monumental, past El Morro and parallel to the coast, leads you straight to **Cojímar**, a fishing village famed for its Hemingway connection. Past here the road dips inland to become the Vía Blanca and passes Villa Panamericana, the village built to support the 1991 Pan American Games, and runs south towards **Guanabacoa**, a quiet provincial town with attractive churches and a fascinating religious history. For many, the big attraction east of Havana will be the boisterous **Playas del Este**, the nearest beaches to the city 18km away, where clean sands and a lively scene draw in the crowds. In contrast, **Playa Jibacoa**, 32km further east, offers a quieter, less glitzy beach resort, while the inland hills of the **Escalera de Jaruco** present a scenic diversion. The hippie retreat at **Canasí**, tucked away on the cliffs overlooking the ocean, is perfect for a back-to-basics camping experience and represents the province's final outpost before the border with Matanzas.

Both the Habana Bus Tour (see pp.25–26) and the Metrobús network (see p.26) traverse the eastern outskirts of Havana allowing direct, though slow, access from the centre of the city to most of these sights.

Cojímar

Just 6km east of Havana, the tiny fishing village of **COJÍMAR** is a world apart from the bustling city – tailor-made for enjoying such simple pleasures as watching fishing boats bob about in the calm, hoop-shaped bay, or wandering the tidy, bougainvillea-fringed streets. Cojímar is served by the #58 **bus** from the Paseo del Prado, by the mouth of the tunnel in Habana Vieja, while a taxi will cost around $10CUC.

Cojímar's sole claim to fame revolves around one of its late residents, Gregorio Fuentes, the first mate of Ernest Hemingway's boat *The Pilar*, who also claimed to be the old man upon whom Hemingway based Santiago, the protagonist of his Pulitzer- and Nobel Prize-winning novel *The Old Man and the Sea*. There is some doubt surrounding this, as Fuentes was actually only in his forties when Hemingway started writing the tale in 1951, and Hemingway himself asserted that Santiago was based on no-one in particular. However, up until the late 1990s Fuentes could be seen sitting outside his house or in *La Terraza de Cojímar* restaurant, charging US$10 for a consultation with fans eager for Hemingway stories. When Fuentes died in 2002, aged 104, it marked the end of an era and one of the last personal links with Hemingway.

▲ Playas del Este (15km), Jibacoa (45km) & Canasí (55km)

RESTAURANTS	
El Golfito	1
El Palenque	3
La Terraza de Cojímar	2

EAST OF HAVANA

0   500 m

Monumento a Hemingway
Torreón de Cojímar

ZONA 14
ZONA 12
ZONA 8
ZONA 22
ZONA 4
ZONA-3
ZONA-2
ZONA 7
ZONA-6
ZONA-10
ZONA 5
ZONA 9
ZONA 11

ALAMAR

BERROA

VÍA MONUMENTAL

La Ceiba

COJÍMAR

Río Cojímar

VÍA-BLANCA

ROTONDA COJÍMAR

VILLA-PANAMERICANA

VÍA-MONUMENTAL

AVENIDA COJÍMAR

ANTONIO GUITERAS

EDUARDO CHIBÁS

Iglesia Parroquial Mayor

GUANABACOA

Iglesia de Santo Domingo

Iglesia de San Francisco

Museo Histórico de Guanabacoa

Complejo Panamericano

CAMILO CIENFUEGOS

CARRETERA-DEL-MORRO

REGLA

CARRETERA-CASABLANCA

Bahía de la Habana

CASABLANCA

Hershey Train Terminal

El Cristo de la Habana

Fortaleza de San Carlos de la Cabaña

Parque Morro Cabaña

Castillo de los Tres Reyes del Morro

Canal de Entrada

HABANA VIEJA

N

The village pays homage to the writer in the **Monumento a Hemingway**, a weatherbeaten construction close to the small *malecón*, which looks a bit like a tiny circular Acropolis. In the middle is Hemingway himself, represented by a rather meagre brass bust, made from boat fittings donated by local fishermen. The whole thing has the air of a misplaced garden ornament and manages to invest the nearby **Torreón de Cojímar** with a similarly spurious air. Overhanging the water's edge, the fort, built between 1639 and 1643 as part of the Spanish colonial fortification, is so small it looks rather like a well-crafted toy. A squat and sturdy building, with sharp, clean angles and Moorish sentry boxes, it was designed by the engineer Juan Bautista Antonelli – who also designed the not-dissimilar El Morro castle in the Parque Morro-Cabaña (see p.75) – as an early-warning system for attacks on Havana harbour, and only needed to accommodate a couple of sentries rather than a whole battalion. Even so, it was usually left unmanned, a defensive weakness fully exploited by the British in 1762, who bombarded it with cannon-fire, routed the peasants' and slaves' attempts at retaliation and romped off to capture the city. The fort is still in military use, so there's no access to the building, although you are free to examine the outside.

Eating

Cojímar's flagship **restaurant**, *La Terraza de Cojímar*, on the east side of the village on Real (☎7/766-5150), is airy, pleasant and full of black-and-white photos of Hemingway and Fuentes, although the food isn't all it could be: go for the simple dishes and avoid the soggy paella and over-salted lobster thermidor. Reservations are recommended as the place is often booked out by bus tours. Otherwise, there's a café on the *malecón* serving chicken and chips, and *El Golfito* on the east side of the river offers basic eats for Cuban pesos.

Guanabacoa

Less than 2km inland from the Vía Monumental turnoff to Cojímar is **GUANABACOA**, a little town officially within the city limits but with a distinctly provincial feel. The site of a pre-Columbian community and later one of the island's first Spanish settlements, it is historically important, though its disproportionately large number of churches and the strong tradition of Afro-Cuban religion, a result of its position as an important centre for slave trade, hold the most appeal for visitors. The #P15 bus from the Parque de la Fraternidad in Habana Vieja cuts right through the centre of town.

The town's most coherent and impressive attraction is the **Museo Histórico de Guanabacoa**, at Martí no.108 e/ Quintin Bandera y E.V. Valenzuela (Mon–Sat 9.30am–4.30pm, closed Tues; $2CUC; ☎7/797-9117, worth calling ahead), two blocks from the understated main square, Parque Martí. The museum's interest lies in the collection of cultish objects relating to the practices of Santería, Palo Monte and the Abakuá Secret Society. One room is moodily set up to reflect the mystic environment in which the *babalao*, the Santería equivalent of a priest, would perform divination rituals, surrounded by altars and African deities in the form of Catholic saints. Equally poignant are the representations of Eleggúa, one of the most powerful of Afro-Cuban *orishas*, with their almost threatening stares. There are also some interesting bits and pieces, including furniture and ceramics, relating to the town's history.

The town's five churches make up the remainder of its sights, and though none has reliable opening times there's usually a staff member on hand willing to let you take a wander inside. The most accessible and intact are the run-down **Iglesia Parroquial Mayor** on Parque Martí, with its magnificent, though age-worn, gilted altar; the eighteenth-century **Iglesia de Santo Domingo** and adjoining monastery, on the corner of Lebredo and Santo Domingo, with a lovely leafy courtyard; and the huge monastery, now a school, attached to the still-functioning **Iglesia de San Francisco**, a block south of Martí on Quintin Bandera. Otherwise, once you've checked out the Afro-Cuban-style knick-knacks in the Bazar de Reproducciones Artísticas, two blocks down from the museum at Martí no.175, and eaten at *El Palenque*, the basic outdoor restaurant next door, you've done the town justice.

Playas del Este

Fifteen kilometres east of Cojímar, the Vía Blanca reaches Havana's nearest beaches – Playa Santa María del Mar, Playa Boca Ciega and Playa Guanabo, collectively known as the **Playas del Este**. Hugging the Atlantic coast, these three fine-sand beaches form a long, twisting ochre ribbon that vanishes in the summer beneath the crush of weekending Habaneros and tourists. There's not a whole lot to distinguish between the beaches, geographically, although as a general rule the sand is better towards the western end.

If you're based in Havana, the excellent self-catering and hotel accommodation here makes this area a good choice for a mini-break. Those craving creature comforts should head for the big hotels in Santa María, while budget travellers will find the best value in the inexpensive hotels and *casas particulares* in Guanabo. Other than the run-down and forbidding all-inclusive *Club Blau Arenal* (☎7/797-1272; $110CUC), there's nowhere to stay in Playa Boca Ciega. Although a number of restaurants serve cheap meals, these all tend to be much the same, and your best bet is to eat at one of the two paladars in Guanabo; otherwise, see if one of the *casas particulares* can recommend somewhere.

In terms of **transportation**, a metered taxi from the centre of Havana to Guanabo will cost around $15–20CUC. The excellent Habana Bus Tour company's #T3 runs a regular service that picks up and drops off at several hotels along the Santa María strip roughly every 30min from 9am to 9pm. An unlimited-use day ticket costs $3CUC.

Playa Santa María del Mar

Due to its proximity to Havana, **Playa Santa María del Mar**, usually just called Santa María, is the busiest and trendiest of the eastern beaches, with boombox reggaeton, watersports and beautiful bodies on sun-loungers. It extends for about 4km from the foot of Santa María Loma, a hill to the south of the Río Itabo, with the bulk of hotels dotted around the main **Avenida de las Terrazas**, just behind the beach. Arguably the most beautiful of the three beaches, with golden sands backed by grasslands and a few palm trees, it's also the most touristy and can feel a bit artificial.

The beach has plenty of sun-loungers ($2CUC a day) and is patrolled by eager beach masseurs (roughly $5–7CUC for 30min). Santa María is the best of the beaches for **activities** and you can play volleyball or rent a catamaran ($8CUC for 30min) or snorkelling equipment ($3CUC per hour) – though sadly you'll see more empty beer cans than fish. With thatch-hut beach bars at intervals along the beach and roving vendors selling rum-laced coconuts, there's no shortage of **refreshments**. A big convertible-peso shop on Avenida de las Terrazas sells the makings of a picnic, although the prices are higher than goods in Havana, so you'd do well to bring what you need with you.

Accommodation

Hotel Atlántico Ave. de las Terrazas, no.10 ☎ 7/797-1085, ⊕ www.hotelesc.es. Although the building is a bit outdated, this large and friendly all-inclusive (drinks included too) is your best choice for Santa María accommodation. Facilities include tennis courts, a beachfront pool with kids' area, gym and internet. There's also a free shuttle to Havana. $150CUC.

Las Terrazas Ave. de las Terrazas e/ 11 y 13 ☎ 7/797-1203. Spacious and airy apartments in a complex of somewhat run-down buildings with views over the beach. Each room has a TV and fridge, and there are two pools in the grounds. Good value for groups. Offers moped rental. $75CUC.

Eating

La Caleta Ave. de las Terrazas. Central to the beach, this open-air restaurant has a thatched-palm roof, music at weekends and a lively air. The decent menu includes lobster brochette for $8CUC and pork dishes for $5CUC.

Costarena Villa Los Pinos, Santa María. An average restaurant with beach views, mediocre service and typical Cuban fare for around $6CUC for mains.

Playa Boca Ciega

A bridge across the Río Itabo connects Santa María to **Playa Boca Ciega**, also known as Playa Mi Cayito. A paucity of public facilities and just one rather grubby café, *Mi Cayito*, make this the least user-friendly of all the beaches here. However, the beach itself is beautiful and open to all, and the waters around the

▲ Playa Santa María del Mar

ACCOMMODATION

Bernardo y Adelina	F	Casa de René y Esperanza	E
Casa de Mercedes Muñiz López	I	Club Blau Arenal	D
Casa de Mileydis y Julito	G	Hotel Atlántico	A
Casa de Raisa García Güell	C	Playa Hermosa	H
		Las Terrazas	B

estuary mouth are usually quite busy and cheerful, with kids and adults paddling and wading in the river currents. Further west, towards Santa María, the beach is popular with the gay community.

Playa Guanabo and Brisas del Mar

Far more pleasant than Playa Boca Ciega is laid-back **Playa Guanabo**, roughly 2.5km further east, where the sun-faded wooden houses and jaunty seaside atmosphere go a long way to compensate for the slightly poor brownish-sand beach. With fewer crowds and no big hotels, it feels much more authentic than Santa María, especially towards the east end of town where tourism has hardly penetrated at all. While not idyllic, it still has its charms: palm trees offer welcome shade, and if you're not bothered about the odd bit of seaweed, this is a refreshingly unaffected spot to hang out.

As most tourists stay on the better beaches further west, Guanabo is pretty much left to the Cubans, with many residents commuting daily from here to Havana. Avenida 5ta, the appealing main street, has a clutch of cafés and shops, including a convertible-peso shopping precinct selling sweets, toys and sportswear, while around the side streets and near the beach are a couple of excellent paladars. The Banco Metropolitano on Avenida 5ta has a cash machine. Other than the *Playa Hermosa* hotel all accommodation is in *casas particulares*, giving the area a pleasant homespun feel.

Further east of the beaches, another 4km or so from Guanabo, is the virtually deserted **Brisas del Mar**. Were it not for the outstanding *casa particular* practically built on the strand, this lovely stretch of clean sand would make for an awkward day-trip. However, it's well worth making an overnight stay to experience the near solitude so rare in Playas del Este and to enjoy the hospitality of one of the best *casas particulares* in the entire province.

Accommodation

Bernardo y Adelina Calle 478 no.306 e/ 3ra y 5ta, Guanabo ☏ 7/796-3609, ℮ bernardo @infomed.sld.cu. One a/c room with a private bathroom, an adjoining sitting room, a dining area and a kitchen with a fridge. The balcony with a sea view is a bonus. $35CUC.

Casa de Mercedes Muñiz López Calle F no.4 e/ 24 y Lindero, Brisas del Mar, Guanabo ☏ 7/796-5119, ℮ waldo.suarez@infomed .sld.cu. The two simple but thoughtfully decorated rooms in a *casa particular* that backs onto an almost private stretch of beach make for the perfect coastal idyll. One room

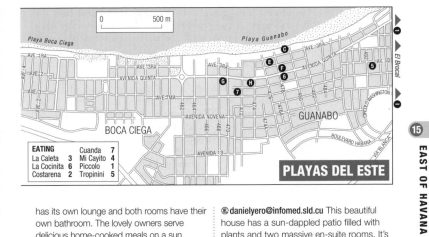

EATING
La Caleta	3
La Cocinita	6
Costarena	2
Cuanda	7
Mi Cayito	4
Piccolo	1
Tropinini	5

PLAYAS DEL ESTE

has its own lounge and both rooms have their own bathroom. The lovely owners serve delicious home-cooked meals on a sun terrace and will come and collect you from Guanabo centre when you arrive. There's even an outdoor shower to wash sand off as you leave the beach. $35CUC.

Casa de Mileydis y Julito Calle 468 no.512 e/ 5ta y 7ma, Guanabo ☎7/796-0100. One a/c apartment in a *casa particular*, close to the beach, with TV and small bathroom. Has a pretty garden and a porch where you can relax, plus extremely hospitable owners. $30CUC.

Casa de Raisa García Güell Ave. 3ra no.47801 e/ 478 y 480, Guanabo ☎7/796-2878,

ⓔdanielyero@infomed.sld.cu This beautiful house has a sun-dappled patio filled with plants and two massive en-suite rooms. It's close to the beach and there's space for parking too. $35CUC.

Casa de René y Esperanza Ave. 3ra no 47607 e/ 476 y 478, Guanabo ☎7/796-3867, ⓔjcparra @infomed.sld.cu. The double room, with its own kitchen, boasts a wide terrace with a sea view. $30CUC.

Playa Hermosa Ave. 5ta e/ 472 y 474 ☎7/796-2774. Basic but pleasant hotel, popular with holidaying Cubans. Has simple rooms, a swimming pool and daily cabaret. $30CUC.

Eating and drinking

La Cocinita Calle 5ta e/ 178 y 180. This open-sided bar is the liveliest spot in town, with a live band most nights. It's safe enough but can feel a little edgy at times due to the groups of raucous men who patronize it.

Cuanda Calle 472 esq. 5ta D. A basic restaurant dishing up reasonable meals on the pork, salad, rice and beans theme. At $3.50CUC for a main meal, it's good value.

Piccolo Calle 5ta, no.50206 e/ 502 y 504 ☎7/796-4300. Exposed brick work and a stone floor give this Italian paladar a rustic

feel. A decent stab at Italian food has been made with highlights including spaghetti and pesto sauce ($7.50CUC) and pizzas. Open daily noon–midnight.

Tropinini Calle 5ta Avenida no.49213 e/ 492 y 494. Excellent paladar open until 2am. Breakfast is a wholesome combination of eggs, toast and fruit juice, while lunch and dinner consist of pork, chicken or spaghetti served with fried green bananas and salad for $5–6CUC. Easily the best choice in the area.

Playa Jibacoa and around

Forty kilometres east from the Playas del Este, tucked behind a barricade of white cliffs, is **Playa Jibacoa**, a stretch of coastline basking in relative anonymity. Approaching from Havana on the Vía Blanca road, the first turning after the bridge over the Río Jibacoa leads down onto the coastal road that runs the length of this laid-back resort area. Predominantly the domain of Cuban holidaymakers, the beach here is mostly small and unspectacular but pleasantly protected by swathes of twisting trees and bushes, with an appealing sense of privacy. There are modest coral reefs offshore and basic **snorkelling** equipment can be rented at the *campismos* (see below).

For better **diving** opportunities, though, as well as boat trips and fishing facilities, you're better off heading 12km further east along the Vía Blanca to the nautical centre at **Puerto Escondido**. The Centro de Buceo Puerto Escondido (☎7/866-2524), operated by Cubamar, is a relatively small outfit but it does run a ten-man dive boat used to visit the five coral reefs that provide all the centre's dive sites. Prices can be negotiated, especially if you intend several dives, but a single dive usually costs $30CUC, or two dives for $40CUC.

There's only one fully developed, international-standard **hotel** in these parts, the *Superclub Breezes Jibacoa* (☎47/29-5153; $150CUC), an attractive all-inclusive on a private patch of coastline, predominantly reserved for tourists on pre-booked packages; kids under 14 aren't allowed. More suitable for the casual visitor are the *campismo* sites along the shoreline – while several are used to accepting foreign guests, many are quite scrappy, while others are for Cubans only or closed in winter. Among the more developed options is *Villa Loma* (☎47/28-3316; $40CUC), which sits up on a small hill at the Havana end of this stretch of coastline, overlooking one of the widest sections of beach. The twelve-house site is simple, rather than basic, with a charming little restaurant, a pool and a fantastic bar in a stone watchtower. Two other decent, good-value options are *Villa Los Cocos* (☎47/29-5231; $30CUC), with a pool, video room and small library, and the more recently renovated *Cameleón Villas Jibacoa* (☎47/29-5206; $50CUC), featuring two restaurants, several modest bars and a pool. For $35CUC you can buy a day pass here, which gives you access to everything in the resort as well as drinks, lunch and dinner. Both have above-average accommodation for *campismos*, made up of pleasant-looking bungalows with air conditioning and TV.

Canasí

Around 10km east of Playa Jibacoa, high upon a cliff-like precipice overlooking the narrow Arroyo Bermejo estuary, the tiny hamlet of **CANASÍ** doubles as the informal weekend campsite for a hippie-chic crowd of young Habaneros. In the summer, scores of revellers descend every Friday to set up camp in the tranquil woodland around the cliff's edge, spending the weekend swimming and snorkelling in the clear Atlantic waters, exploring the woods and nearby caves, singing folk songs and generally communing with nature. It's a refreshingly uncontrived experience with a peace-festival kind of atmosphere. There are no facilities, so you'll have to bring everything you need, most importantly fresh water.

Regular visitors take the late-night **Hershey train** ($3CUC) from Casablanca to Canasí on Friday night; this is not the most reliable form of transport, though, and you might be better off driving. The road down to the water's edge is badly signposted but look for a left turn off the Vía Blanca (a 5min walk from the station) and take the dirt track to the estuary mouth, where the fishermen who live in the waterside cottages will row you across the shallow waters to the site for about $2CUC a head, though the hardy can wade.

South of Havana

H eading south of Havana, the city fades in fits and starts, the buildings dying out only to reappear again almost immediately among the trees and green fields which bind this area together. Numerous satellite towns dot the semi-urban, semi-rural landscape, distinctly provincial in character yet close enough to Havana to be served by municipal bus routes. The best of what there is south of the city is all within a thirty-kilometre drive of the city centre.

The airport road, the **Avenida de Rancho Boyeros**, also known as the **Avenida de la Independencia**, is the easiest route to most of the day-trip destinations this side of the capital. It makes sense to visit at least a couple of these on the same day, since they are all difficult to get to by public transport and in many cases the distances between them are short. A near-perfect preservation of the great writer's home in Havana, the **Museo Ernest Hemingway**, is the most concrete option and one of the few that stands up well by itself; the views from the house alone are enough to justify the trip. The relative proximity of **Parque Lenin** to the **Parque Zoológico Nacional** and the sprawling **Jardín Botánico Nacional**, over the road from **ExpoCuba**, makes these a convenient combination for anyone looking for a full day out. Just beyond the southern end of the Avenida de Rancho Boyeros, past the airport, the town of **Santiago de las Vegas** and the nearby **Santuario de San Lázaro** make good stopping-off points on the way to **San Antonio de los Baños**, a 25-kilometre drive further south, which, with its unique Museo de Humor and its picturesquely located hotel, make it the only town in provincial Havana worth spending more than a day in.

Museo Ernest Hemingway

Eleven kilometres southeast of Habana Vieja, in the suburb of San Francisco de Paula, is **Finca La Vigía**, an attractive little estate centred on the whitewashed late-nineteenth-century villa where Ernest Hemingway lived for twenty years until 1960. Now the **Museo Ernest Hemingway** (Mon–Sat 10am–5pm, Sun 10am–1pm, closed Tues; $3CUC; ☎7/91-0809), it makes a simple but enjoyable excursion from the city. On top of a hill and with splendid views over Havana, this single-storey colonial residence, where Hemingway wrote a number of his most famous novels, has been preserved almost exactly as he left it – with drinks and magazines strewn about the place and the dining-room table set for guests. Brimming with character, it's a remarkable insight into the writer's lifestyle and personality, from the numerous stuffed animal heads on the walls and the bullfighting posters to the bottles of liquor and the thousands of books lining the shelves in most of the rooms, including the bathroom. The small room where his

▲ Hemingway's writing room in the Museo Ernest Hemingway

typewriter is still stationed was where Hemingway did much of his work, often in the mornings and usually standing up. Frustratingly, you can't actually walk into the rooms but must view everything through the open windows and doors; by walking around the encircling veranda, however, you can get good views of most rooms. In the well-kept gardens, which you can walk round, Hemingway's fishing boat is suspended inside a wooden pavilion and you can visit the graves of four of his dogs, located next to the swimming pool.

The museum closes when it rains, to protect the interior from the damp and to preserve the grounds, so try to visit on sunny days. To **get there** by car, head south down Padre Varela (also called Belascoain) and then Avenida de México (also called Cristina) from Centro Habana to the Vía Blanca, which you should then follow on its course around the bay until the turnoff for the Carretera Central. This section of the Carretera Central is called Calzada de Guines and cuts straight through San Francisco de Paula. To get there by **public transport**, take the #P7 bus from the Parque de la Fraternidad in Habana Vieja or the #P2 from the junction between Calle 23 and Avenida de los Presidentes in Vedado. Either way it's a ten-minute walk from the bus stop in San Francisco de Paula. Alternatively, you can visit on an organized excursion: the San Cristóbal travel agency on the Plaza de San Francisco in Habana Vieja offers a special Hemingway-themed day-trip that includes the museum for $20CUC per person.

Parque Lenin

Roughly a twenty-minute drive south of the city, about 3km west of the José Martí airport, are the immense grounds of **Parque Lenin** (June–Sept Wed–Sun 9am–5pm, July & Aug Tues–Sun 9am–5pm; free; information ☎7/643-1165, switchboard ☎7/644-3026), a cross between a landscaped urban park and a rolling tract of untouched wooded countryside. Founded in 1972, this was once a popular escape for city residents who came here to picnic, ride around on horseback or on the park's own steam train, and enjoy the other facilities,

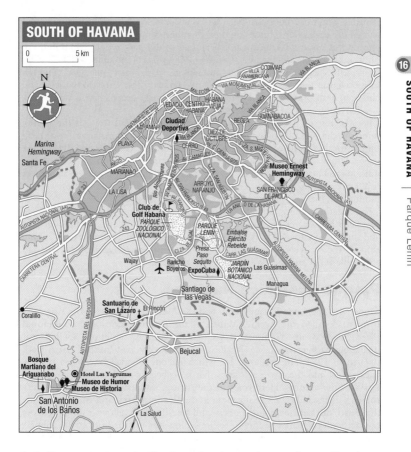

including restaurants and cafeterias, swimming pools, a small art gallery, boats and fairground rides. The deterioration in public transport since the early 1990s led to a sharp drop in visitors, and today a pervasive air of abandon blows around the park, many of the facilities, including the train and pools, now closed and in disrepair. Nonetheless, its sheer size (almost eight square kilometres) and scenic landscape make Parque Lenin a great place for a picnic, a wander or just a breath of fresh air. The park's attractions are spread quite sparsely, so it can be a tiring place to explore on foot.

There are a couple of very inconvenient **bus routes** to the park, the #P13 and the #PC (see colour maps), neither of which drop you in the park, though the latter goes closest. To get to the park by car, head towards the airport on Avenida de Rancho Boyeros, and take the signposted left turn onto Avenida San Francisco (also called Calle 100), which, within 5km, leads to the park's main entrance, marked by a large billboard. You can drive into and around the park, though the main through-road leads straight over to the far side where the park boundaries are less clearly marked and it's easy to drive out without knowing you've left.

A more exciting way to explore is on horseback; the **Centro Ecuestre** is signposted at the first right-hand turn as you enter from the city side. Here you can hire horses for $3CUC an hour, assuming the centre is open and has horses available. This uncertainty has been seized upon by locals, who hang around this part of the park offering rides on their own horses; be prepared to haggle if you choose this option. It's in this northern half of the park where you'll find the only new development, the **Parque Mariposa** (entrance $1CUP, rides $1–6CUP), a Chinese-designed amusement park built in 2007. Though unspectacular this is nonetheless one of Havana's best attractions for young children, with over twenty different rides including bumper cars, a water slide, a rollercoaster and a 42-metre-high Ferris wheel.

For the rest of the park's more tangible activities, head towards the central reservoir, the Presa Paso Sequito. You can take a **boat** out on the water or head for the southern side of the lake, where you'll find the **Galería Amelia Peláez** (free), a small art gallery for temporary exhibitions; the semi-abandoned and quite surreal **aquarium** where, in over sixty small tanks, you can see all sorts of fish, crabs, turtles and even a couple of crocodiles; or the park's most famous monument, the nine-metre-high marble **bust of Lenin**.

For the time being, reliable **eating options** are limited to ramshackle *El Dragón*, a patio eatery just off the main road, and *Las Ruinas*, an incongruous and surprisingly formal hulk of a restaurant south of the reservoir, built among ruined, moss-covered walls and specializing in expensive seafood, though affordable pizza and *comida criolla* are also available.

Parque Zoológico Nacional

Sandwiched between Parque Lenin and the Avenida de Rancho Boyeros, off a main road called the Avenida Varona, is the **Parque Zoológico Nacional** (Wed–Sun 9.30am–3.30pm; $3CUC adults, $2CUC children, $5CUC car including passengers; ☎7/643-8063), a perpetually half-finished safari park opened in 1984. The spacious site, which includes a small lake, has a suitably natural feel and the two enclosures that have been completed do allow good views of the animals. Herbivores of the African savannah, including elephants, rhinos, giraffes and zebras, roam about in the **Pradera Africana** enclosure, while the **Foso de Leones**, a huge grass- and tree-lined pit, allows excitingly close contact with the park's twenty or so lions. However, the majority of the animals, mostly big cats and apes, are kept in cramped conditions in the so-called Area de Reproducción. The zoo opened in 1984, partly in response to the need for improved conditions for the animals cooped up in Havana's smaller, inner-city zoo, but there is still some way to go before these ambitions are fully realized. If you don't want to walk or drive about the park, you can ride one of the free **buses** that leave from just inside the main entrance every thirty minutes or so on tours of the park; they include guides, but don't count on an English speaker.

A couple of kilometres north of the zoo, approaching the Avenida de Rancho Boyeros on the route back into the city, off the Carretera de Vento, is the unmarked turning for the **Club de Golf Habana**, where a swimming pool, bowling alley, restaurant and nine-hole golf course make for a neatly packaged stop-off point. For more details, including green fees, see p.167.

Jardín Botánico Nacional and ExpoCuba

Three kilometres south of the entrance to Parque Lenin, along the Carretera del Rocío, is the entrance to the **Jardín Botánico Nacional** (Wed–Sun 9am–4pm; $1CUC, $3CUC for guided tour with own vehicle, $4CUC for train tour; ⓦwww.uh.cu/centros/jbn/index.html), a sweeping expanse of parkland showcasing a massive variety of plants and trees.

Laid out as a savannah rather than a forest, the grounds are split into sections according to continent. Highlights include the collection of 162 surprisingly varied species of palm, the cacti collection in the **Pabellones de Exposiciones** greenhouse-style buildings and the meticulously landscaped **Japanese Garden**, donated by the Japanese government on the thirtieth anniversary of the Revolution in 1989. The Japanese Garden also has the best place to stop for **lunch**, at *El Bambú* (1–3.30pm; ☎7/54-7278; reservations advised), with a tasty $14CUC vegetarian buffet.

Though you can explore the park yourself, a lack of printed literature and plaques means you'll learn far more by booking an organized excursion from the city or taking the **guided tour**, whether in the trackless train or having a guide in your own car. There's usually at least one English-speaking guide available, but it's worth noting that the tractor-bus tours, which generally last from one to two hours, do not necessarily cover the whole park. Tours leave every hour or so from just inside the main entrance, near the useful **information office**. There's also a small shop selling ornamental plants; at weekends a bus takes passengers from here directly to the Japanese Garden (every 30min; $1CUC).

ExpoCuba

On the other side of the Carretera del Rocío, directly opposite the gardens, what looks like a well-kept industrial estate is in fact **ExpoCuba** (Wed–Sun 9am–5pm, closed Sept–Dec, except for special events; $1CUC), a permanent exhibition of the island's endeavours in industry, science, technology and commerce since the Revolution. Despite its impressive scope, displays are a little dry and the hordes of children here on school trips tend to be more interested in riding on the mini rollercoaster ($0.50CUC) and boating on the small lake ($1CUC). There's a seafood **restaurant** by the lake and various cafeterias, including the *Bar Mirador*, a circular revolving café from where you get an excellent perspective on the layout of ExpoCuba and views across to the Jardín Botánico.

For one week every year, usually the first week in November, ExpoCuba hosts the **Feria Internacional de la Habana** (Ⓦwww.feriahavana.com), an international trade fair (see p.153). This is by far the best time to visit, as commercial enterprises from around the world come to exhibit their products and promote their services, creating a livelier atmosphere and a more exciting range of exhibits. There are fashion shows, concerts and all kinds of goods on display, as well as a pitch for many of the capital's more famous restaurants.

Santiago de las Vegas and the Santuario de San Lázaro

With a history dating back to the late seventeenth century and a population of around 35,000, **SANTIAGO DE LAS VEGAS**, 2km south of José Martí airport, is one of Havana's more noteworthy satellite towns. That said, there are few specific sights beyond the attractive central square and the modest national hockey stadium, both just off the main street, but if you're on your way to the church and pilgrimage point in El Rincón (see p.190) it makes sense to stop here for a bite to eat or a stroll to get a feel for Cuba beyond the big city. Calle 409, leading off the square, is full of cheap snack stalls, but for something more substantial head for *Tanokura* at Calle 403 no.1803 e/ 180 y 184 (☎7/683-2173), a popular paladar with a vast array of pork, chicken, rabbit and fish dishes as well as pizzas (mains $50–200CUP). There are several **buses** connecting the town with the centre of Havana, among them the #P12, which

El Día de San Lázaro

On December 17, the road between Santiago de las Vegas and El Rincón is closed as hordes of people from all over Cuba come to ask favours of San Lázaro in exchange for a sacrifice, or to keep promises they have already made to the saint. Some have walked for days, timing their pilgrimage so that they arrive on the 17th, but the common starting point is Santiago de las Vegas, 2km down the road. The most fervent believers make their journey as arduous as possible, determined that in order to earn the favour they have asked for they must first prove their own willingness to suffer. In the past people have tied rocks to their limbs and dragged themselves along the concrete road to the church, while others bring material sacrifices, often money, as their part of the bargain.

leaves from the Parque de la Fraternidad in Habana Vieja, and the #P16 from the Hospital Ameijieras in Centro Habana. El Rincón is a couple of kilometres further south of the town on the Carretera Santiago de las Vegas, the main road running through it.

Ten kilometres south of central Havana, the **Santuario de San Lázaro** (daily 7am–6pm), on the edge of the tiny village of **EL RINCÓN**, is the final destination of a pilgrimage made by thousands of Cubans every year, culminating on December 17. Amid scenes of intense religious fervour, pilgrims come to the church to ask favours of San Lázaro, whose image appears inside, in exchange for sacrifices (see above). Whatever the month, though, people come here to cut deals with the saint, and the road through the village, like the car park next to the church, is always busy with people selling flowers and statuettes of the saints. Sitting peacefully in the grounds of an old hospital, the church itself is striking only for its immaculate simplicity, though there are several fine altars inside, usually surrounded by flowers and candles, and topped respectively with images of San Lázaro, Santa Barbara, the Virgen de Regla and the Virgen de la Caridad, four of the most popular saints in Cuba.

San Antonio de los Baños

Of all the small towns in Havana province, **SAN ANTONIO DE LOS BAÑOS**, about 20km south of the capital's western suburbs and a 45-minute drive from Habana Vieja, is the only one with the right ingredients to merit more than a fleeting visit. A riverside hotel with good opportunities for swimming and boating, an engaging museum and a lovingly created countryside park all combine to provide at least a day's worth of laid-back activity. The town itself has the undisturbed, nonchalant feel that characterizes so much of Cuba's interior, with an archetypal shady town square and residential streets largely free of traffic.

The simplest **route from Havana** is to follow the Avenida de Rancho Boyeros to the first major junction heading south from the city, then turn west onto the Pinar del Río road, the Autopista Nacional, and head west for 9km until, at another major junction, you reach the Autopista del Mediodía heading due south. After around 17km on this road you will reach San Antonio de los Baños.

Museo de Humor and Museo de Historia

Based in a colonial home at Calle 60 e/ 41 y 45, the excellent **Museo de Humor** (Tues–Sat 10am–6pm & Sun 9am–1pm; $2CUC; ☎47/38-2817), founded in 1979, has a small permanent exhibition charting the history of graphic humour in

Cuba. The museum also illuminates the tradition of political satire in Cuban newspaper art, with a couple of old anti-Spanish cartoons, anti-imperialist drawings and some Punch-style creations; unfortunately, none of it is presented with much context. The museum has a dynamic calendar of temporary **exhibitions** and the best time to visit is when one of these is taking place. The two most prestigious of these, the Salón de Humorismo y Sátira and the Bienal Internacional del Humorismo Gráfico, take place in alternate years starting every March or April and lasting as late as August. Both follow similar lines, with entries drawn from a large number of countries, falling under categories such as political satire, caricatures, photography and comic strips. Also worth catching is the Evento de Caricatura Personal Juan David (Dec–Feb), a national competition attracting the best caricaturists in the country; and the Salón Nacional de Humor Juvenil, a competition for young Cuban comic illustrators that first took place in September 2008. If you are coming all this way specifically for the museum it's worth ringing in advance as it sometimes closes for days at a time to mount exhibitions.

A few blocks away is the modest **Museo de Historia**, at Calle 66 e/ 41 y 45 (Tues–Sat 10am–6pm, Sun 9am–1pm; $1CUC), whose relatively diverse collection includes some great photographs of local bands from the 1920s and 1930s as well as a room of colonial furniture.

Bosque Martiano del Ariguanabo

The principal ringroad that cuts through the southern side of the town enters San Antonio de los Baños from the northeast and leads back out into the countryside at the southwestern corner. A few hundred metres beyond is the inviting **Bosque Martiano del Ariguanabo**, an enclosed tract of land with landscaped gardens and a small man-made forest. The site is the proud creation of Rafael Rodríguez Ortiz, an elderly local man, every bit the rural Cuban revolutionary and passionate student of José Martí (see p.71). Rodríguez's vision of transforming what was once a rubbish dump into a small nature reserve, in which young Cubans could learn about the natural world through the teachings of Martí, was realised in May 1994 when the site was officially inaugurated. Visitors are welcome and are free to wander around the lawns, dotted with boulders and other features such as a huge mechanical wheel from a sugar refinery, many of which are inscribed with quotes from Martí's writings. The principal source of inspiration was his *Diario de Campaña*, written by Martí in 1895, and every one of the 54 species of tree, bush and shrub here are mentioned in that diary.

Practicalities

On the northern border of the town, the side closest to Havana, is *Las Yagrumas* (☎47/38-4460, ✉gerencia@yagrumas.co.cu; $40CUC), a family-oriented **hotel** catering predominantly to Cubans, who are usually here in large numbers. Based around a large pool, the palm-fringed grounds slope down to a bend in the Río Ariguanabo where, from a café on a riverside terrace, you can rent rowing boats ($1CUC per hour), motorboats ($3CUC per hour) and pedalos ($1CUC per hour) between 9am and 5pm daily. Other activities include organized excursions, nature trails and a full programme of evening entertainment.

For **refreshment** in the town there's a branch of the fast-food chain *El Rápido* on Calle 68, but for a more atmospheric setting follow Calle 68 uphill to its conclusion on the edge of town, where a right turn leads to *La Quintica*, a simple peso restaurant leaning over the river, serving standard *comida criolla*. The tree-lined banks of the river lend this spot a delightfully relaxing ambience, occasionally shattered by music blaring out from the restaurant itself.

West of Havana

Most of the tourist traffic travelling west out of Havana is heading for **Pinar del Río**, Cuba's westernmost province and home to some of its most visually striking countryside, characterized by low mountain ranges. The nearest such range to Havana is known as the **Sierra del Rosario**, covered in thick forest; further west the Sierra de los Organos is dotted with unusual limestone hillocks that look like giant boulders and are known as *mogotes*. Just over the provincial border are two of the most worth-while day-trip destinations from the capital, the hillside resorts of **Las Terrazas** and **Soroa**, either of which is well suited for an overnight stay.

There are some scrappy beaches out this way, on the northern coastline of Havana province, and a number of sleepy towns further inland, but none warrants more than a stop-off on the way to Pinar del Río. Most buses, including all the Víazul services, head straight for the Autopista Nacional and none actually stop at Las Terrazas, Soroa or anywhere else of particular interest until they reach the provincial capital. The nearest you can get to either of the hillside resorts by **public transport** is to take the train from Havana to Candelaria, but it's still another 8km to Soroa from the station and over 20km to Las Terrazas – a distance you will almost certainly have to either walk or hitch a lift to cover. With a **car** you can afford to take a more scenic route from the city, such as driving west through Miramar and the western suburbs, one of the easiest and most pleasant drives in the whole city, following Avenida 5ta along the northern coastline and out to **Playa El Salado**, or travelling inland from the south of the city along the Carretera Central. Alternatively, all the national travel agents in Havana offer day-trips to Soroa and Las Terrazas. Cubanacán, for example, offers a daily day-trip to both for $50CUC.

Western Havana province

Fifteen kilometres west of the capital, straight along Avenida 5ta from Miramar and then onto the Autopista La Habana-Mariel, is the only coastal resort of any significance on this side of Havana province, **Playa El Salado**. Just five minutes' drive to the west of the lazy seafront hamlet of Baracoa, itself host to several scrappy little beaches, it's an unspectacular place with a sporadically open hotel and an eyesore of a gutted restaurant but the secluded, rather rocky beach, nestling inside a tree-lined inlet, is a relatively pleasant spot and a good place for a paddle or a bit of relaxation. The only other attraction here of any note is the

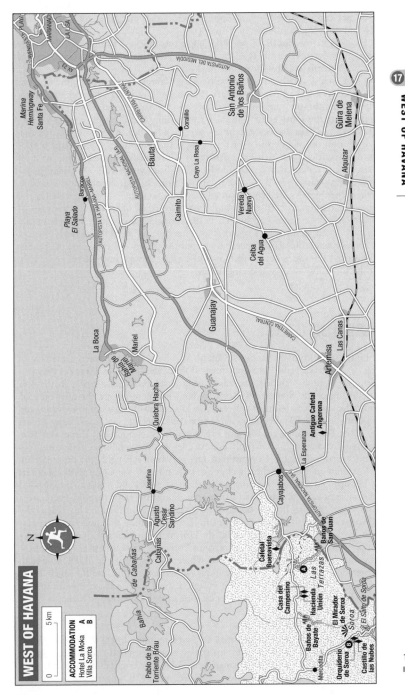

WEST OF HAVANA

ACCOMMODATION
Hotel La Moka   **A**
Villa Soroa   **B**

0   5 km

N

Bahía
de Cabañas

Pablo de la
Torriente Brau

Bahía
de Cabañas

Cabañas

Merceditas

Orquideario
de Soroa

Castillo de
las Nubes

Baños de
Bayate

El Mirador
de Soroa

Soroa

El Salto de Soroa

Casa del
Campesino

Hacienda
Unión

Las
Terrazas

Cafetal
Buenavista

Baños de
San Juan

Josefina

Agusto
Cesar
Sandino

Quiebra Hacha

La Boca

Mariel

Bahía de
Mariel

Cayajabos

La Esperanza

Antiguo Cafetal
Angerona

Artemisa

Las Canas

Güira de
Melena

Alquizar

Guanajay

Caimito

Ceiba
del Agua

Vereda
Nueva

Cayo La Rosa

Baracoa

Playa
El Salado

Bauta

Coralillo

San Antonio
de los Baños

Marina
Hemingway
Santa Fe

LA LISA

MARIANAO
PLAYA

AUTOPISTA DEL MEDIODÍA

CARRETERA PANAMERICANA

CARRETERA CENTRAL

AUTOPISTA LA HABANA–MARIEL

AUTOPISTA NACIONAL A4

AUTOPISTA NACIONAL A4

MN 32

go–cart track (Mon–Sat 9am–5pm; $5CUC for 10min, $25CUC for an hour; 16 and older only), a rarity in Cuba.

Five kilometres south of Avenida 5ta is the quickest route out of the city heading west to Pinar del Río, the four-lane **Autopista Nacional**, also known as the **Autopista Este-Oeste** (marked on most road maps as **A4**). For a closer look at rural Cuba head along the twisting **Carretera Central**, which begins its route west in La Lisa, the western suburb south of Playa. The going is mostly flat, cutting through sugar-cane territory and pleasant croplands with occasional glimpses of the south coast. The small towns along this animated route – principally Bauta, Guanajay and Artemisa – are all quite similar, with little of interest.

The most distinct detour worth making before crossing the provincial border into Pinar del Río is to the **Antiguo Cafetal Angerona**, 6km west of Artemisa, a nineteenth-century coffee plantation where 750,000 coffee plants once grew. Here you'll find the derelict ruins of the Neoclassical mansion where the owner – a German named Cornelio Souchay – resided, as well as the slave quarters and a ten-metre-high watchtower, all of it now in the grip of advancing vegetation. Legend has it that Souchay used the seclusion of the plantation to engage in a clandestine interracial affair with a black Haitian woman named Ursula Lambert, away from the gossip and prejudice of the city. Nowadays the site is occasionally visited by tour groups, but you're more likely to be the only visitor wandering about.

Las Terrazas

About 10km from the Antiguo Cafetal Angerona, at the western extremity of Havana province, is the signposted turn off the *autopista* for **Las Terrazas** (Ⓦwww .lasterrazas.cu), a secluded but substantially developed visitor resort in the low mountains of the **Sierra del Rosario**. Four kilometres along the turn-off road from the *autopista*, a left turn will lead you to a **tollbooth** marking the eastern end of Complejo Las Terrazas, situated in a protected area that costs $4CUC per person to enter. The resort is actually just over the provincial border in **Pinar del Río**, and is spread around a relatively compact set of valleys, hillsides and woodlands with a small village, the **Comunidad Las Terrazas**, at roughly the central point.

Just a few metres past the checkpoint is the turn for the **Cafetal Buenavista**, a hilltop colonial coffee plantation with great views and a restaurant. Beyond the village, a few kilometres further west along the main through-road, are a couple of simple little retreats, ideal for a daytime break. The **Casa del Campesino** offers restaurant meals from a delightfully tranquil vantage point just a few paces away from **Hacienda Unión**, the remains of one of the area's numerous colonial-era coffee plantations. You can escape the main road again at the turning for **Baños de Bayate** where, deeper into the thick mountain vegetation, you can cool off at a natural swimming spot or stop for lunch at the waterside restaurant. South of the village, a small road leads to the **Baños de San Juan**, another set of natural pools and a beautiful riverside hangout.

Comunidad Las Terrazas

At the heart of the resort is a small valley community living in red-tile-roofed bungalows and white city-style apartment blocks perched on terraced, grassy slopes, at the foot of which is a man-made lake. This unusual-looking village, of around a thousand people, was founded in 1971 as part of a massive government-funded **reforestation project** covering some fifty square kilometres of the Sierra del Rosario. The local residents formed the backbone of the workforce employed to build the village itself and to plant trees along terraces dug into the hillside, thus guarding against erosion and giving the place its name. This was all part of a grander scheme by the government to promote self-sufficiency and education in rural areas, one of the promises of the Revolution. Today a large proportion of the community work in tourism, some as employees at *Hotel La Moka* (T 48/57-8600, E alojamiento@hotel.terraz.co.cu; $85–110CUC), a peaceful hillside hideaway sculpted into the landscape and the resort's only hotel. Nestling on wooded slopes looking over the village, the hotel grounds mingle with the trees in the shadow of the Loma del Salón, one of the highest peaks hereabouts. There's a swimming pool ($3CUC for day visitors) and tennis court area, set further back, providing the only open spaces within the complex.

Steps from the hotel lead down the slopes into the village, where there is a small set of simple distractions, including **artists' workshops**, a tiny local museum and the small village square, the **Plaza Comunal**, a pleasant and sociable spot in the evenings with its benches, trees and modest views of the lake and valley.

Down on the edge of the lake, in one of the residential cabins, is a small but engaging museum, the **Peña de Las Terrazas Polo Montañez** (9am–5pm daily; $2CUC). This simple four-room place was where one of Cuba's most heralded musicians of recent times, Polo Montañez, lived before he was killed in a car accident in November 2002. His personal effects, including his guitars, are on display while his bedroom has been left as it was when he lived here. Some of his CDs are on sale too.

Eating and outdoor activities at the village

The two best **restaurants** in the resort are in the village, both in the apartment buildings at the foot of the slopes on which the hotel sits. Nearest to the steps leading down from the hotel is *El Romero* (daily 9am–9pm; main dishes $3–14CUC), with its unique menu of organic, predominantly vegetarian dishes such as cold pumpkin and onion soup, bean-filled crepes and chickpea burgers. More traditional meals are served a few buildings along, at the open-air *Fonda de Mercedes* (9am–9pm daily; main dishes $5–8CUC), where top-notch, home-cooked Cuban cuisine is served up on a spacious roof-covered balcony. In between the two restaurants is the *Café de María*, a lovely little spot for a **drink**, on a balcony with pleasant views.

There's more to do around the village than might at first appear to be the case given the laid-back feel of the place. A kind of novelty gondola-lift called the **Canopy Tour** (daily 9am–6pm; $25CUC), offers 800-metre aerial journeys over the village. **Horseriding** is also possible and can be arranged through the hotel. There are a number of set rides, lasting between an hour and four hours and generally costing $5CUC an hour. For a more subdued pastime, you can rent out rowing **boats** on the lake for $3CUC an hour. The Casa de Botes, where boats are moored, is just off the main road through the village and easy to find.

Cafetal Buenavista

Immediately inside the checkpoint at the Havana end of the resort is the turning for the **Cafetal Buenavista** (daily 9am–4pm; free), an excellent restoration of a nineteenth-century coffee plantation. French immigrants who had fled Haiti following the 1791 Revolution established over fifty coffee plantations across the sierra, but this is the only one that has been almost fully reconstructed. The stone house, with its high-beamed ceiling, now shelters a restaurant, while the food is

Rancho Curujey and hiking at Las Terrazas

All **hiking** around Las Terrazas must be done with a guide and this can be arranged through the Oficinas de Reservaciones y Coordinación at **Rancho Curujey** (☎48/57-8555 or 57-8700, ⓔreserva@terraz.co.cu), the reserve's visitor and information centre, where you can also can get a map and help with almost any activity around Las Terrazas. To reach Rancho Curujey arriving from Havana and the west, take the signposted right-hand turn off the main through-road just before the left turn that leads to the village and hotel. Most hikes take place along one of the official **hiking routes** or **nature trails** mapped out around this protected area, either on tailor-made programmes or one of the regular pre-booked excursions. For groups of six people or more, guides usually cost around $10CUC per person, though prices vary depending on group size and your specific needs and can reach $30–40CUC. You may be able to join another visiting group if you call a day in advance, or if you arrive on or before 9am. The *Hotel Moka* works closely with Rancho Curujey and can arrange hiking packages for guests.

Hiking routes and nature trails

Cascada del San Claudio (20km) The longest hike offered here lasts a whole day, or around eight to ten hours, and is a gruelling affair scaling the hills looming over to the northwest of the complex and down the other side to the Río San Claudio.

El Contento (8km) This pleasant, easy-going hike descends into the valley between two of the local peaks and joins the Río San Juan. It passes the La Victoria ruins, another of the area's old coffee plantations, as well as fresh and sulphurous water springs, and reaches its limit at the Baños del San Juan, a beautiful little set of pools and cascades where you can bathe.

Loma del Taburete (7km) One of the tougher hikes, this route climbs some relatively steep inclines on the way up a 453-metre-high hill, from the peak of which there are views all the way over to the coast, and slopes down to the Baños de San Juan on the other side where the hike concludes.

Sendero Las Delicias (3km) This trail finishes up at the Cafetal Buenavista and takes in a *mirador* at the summit of the Loma Las Delicias, where there are some magnificent panoramic views.

Sendero La Serafina (4km) A nature trail ideal for birdwatching, leading uphill through rich and varied forest. Guides are able to point out some of the more notable of the 73 bird species that inhabit the sierra, such as the red, white and blue tocororo, the endemic catacuba and the enchanting Cuban nightingale.

Valle del Bayate (7km) On the road to Soroa, 6km from Las Terrazas, a dirt track next to the bridge over Río Bayate follows the river into the dense forest. Passing first the dilapidated San Pedro coffee plantation, this undemanding trail arrives at the Santa Catalina plantation ruins, a peaceful spot where you can take a dip in the natural pools.

cooked in the original kitchen building behind it. The terraces on which the coffee was dried have also been accurately restored and the remains of the slaves' quarters are complete enough to give you an idea of the incredibly cramped sleeping conditions that the plantation's 126 slaves would have experienced. You can drive here quite easily by taking the side road at the tollbooth; this is also the final destination for some of the official hikes in the area (see box above).

Baños de San Juan

From the south side of the village, at the junction where the road to the hotel begins, another road leads off in the opposite direction for the **Baños de San Juan**, a delightfully pleasant spot featuring natural pools, riverside picnic tables, a simple restaurant and some even simpler cabins providing rudimentary accommodation. If you have a receipt from the toll gate at the entrance to the reserve, you'll need to show it at the riverside car park, located about 3km from the village, to avoid another charge. Zig-zagging pathways along the river's edge lead downstream to the focal point here, a small set of clear, **natural pools** fed by dinky waterfalls and ideal for a bit of midday bathing. On the riverbank looking over them is *El Bambú* (daily 9am–7pm) a rustic **restaurant-caféteria** serving simple Cuban food. Set back from the river, at the foot of some grassy slopes breaking up the surrounding woodlands, are five rooms (known as *cabañas rusticas*) for rent via *Hotel Moka* ($15CUC/$25CUC single/double). They're no more than roof-covered platforms on stilts, aimed squarely at the backpacker set, with no furniture and about enough space to lay a couple of sleeping bags down.

Casa del Campesino and Hacienda Unión

A kilometre or so past the village, heading west on the main through-road, a sign indicates the way down a short dirt track to **Casa del Campesino**, a lazy, secluded little woodland ranch housing a **restaurant** (daily 8am–9pm) serving wholesome *comida criolla*. On a mound overlooking the immediate area, concealed from the main road and melting into the surrounding forest, this rural retreat is a great place to spend a couple of hours unwinding, so long as you have some bug repellent, as the mosquitoes can be fierce.

From the restaurant you can see, through the trees, the neighbouring **Hacienda Unión**, one of the area's partly reconstructed nineteenth-century coffee plantations. You're free to take a look around the broken stone walls of the plantation, which has at least kept enough of its structure to be recognizable for what it once was two centuries ago. The circular grinding mill, with its cone-shaped roof and stone base, is the most intact section and the easiest to spot, whilst much of the space here has been divided up into small, rock-lined plots forming an attractively laid out if somewhat rudimentary **garden**.

Baños de Bayate

Back on the main road, 3km past the turning for the *Casa del Campesino*, another dirt track, this one more of a bone-rattler than the last, winds down about a kilometre to a section of forest-shrouded river known as the **Baños de Bayate**. The depth and clearness of the water at this delightful spot provide a perfect opportunity to cool off from the jungle's humidity, although its tranquillity is sometimes broken by the screams and shouts of young swimmers leaping into the river. Stone paths run 50m or so along one side of the mostly very shallow river, linking the several rustic barbecue grills built on the water's edge. There's also an outdoor **restaurant** here, perfect for a post-swim plate of grilled pork or chicken.

The final stretch of the main road leads up to the western-end **tollbooth** (where you won't get charged if you already paid at the other end), immediately after which a left turn will take you on the road to Soroa.

Soroa

Sixteen kilometres southwest from Las Terrazas, the tiny village of **Soroa** nestles in a long narrow valley. The turning from the *autopista* is marked by the first gas station in Pinar del Río province from Havana, but you can also get there direct from Las Terrazas without returning to the motorway. Although a cozy spot, access into the hills is limited and the list of attractions brief, meaning the resort is best suited for a short break. If you do decide to stay the night, the place to do so is **Villa Soroa** (☎48/52-3534 & 52-3556, ⓔreserva@hvs.co.cu; $82CUC), a well-kept complex of neatly trimmed lawns encircling a swimming pool, featuring comfortable, modern-looking cabins.

El Salto de Soroa

A stone's throw from the hotel is a car park marking the start of the path through the woods to **El Salto de Soroa** (daylight hours; $3CUC), a twenty-metre waterfall and Soroa's most publicized attraction. It's not as spectacular as tourist Cuban literature tends to paint it, often describing it as one of the area's great natural marvels, but it's a pleasant spot and worth visiting for a dip in the water and a picnic.

El Mirador de Soroa

Back at the car park, a sign close by indicates the route up to one of the two overlooks, **El Mirador de Soroa**, at the summit of the more challenging of the two easy-going hills in the area. While there are a number of possible wrong turns on the way up, you can avoid getting lost by simply following the track with the horse dung – if you'd rather ride up, horses can be arranged at *Villa Soroa* for $3CUC per person. At the summit you'll find vultures circling the rocky, uneven platform and the most impressive views to be had around Soroa.

Castillo de las Nubes

El Castillo de las Nubes is the more developed of Soroa's two hilltop viewpoints and reached, either by car or on foot, by following the same side road which leads past the Orquideario. It shouldn't be more than a twenty-minute walk to reach the hilltop **restaurant**, housed in a building resembling a toy fortress with a single turret. The standard Cuban cuisine is nothing special but it's worth stopping for a meal, as the views from the window-side tables are fantastic. Beyond the restaurant the road ends at a deserted stone house – from here you can see all the way to the province's southern coastline.

Orquideario de Soroa

At the foot of the side road which begins between the car park for El Salto and the hotel is the **Orquideario de Soroa** (daily 9am–4pm, ☎48/57-2558; $3CUC), a well-maintained botanical garden specializing in orchids and spread across 35,000 square metres. It was originally constructed in 1943 by Tomás Felipe Camacho, a wealthy lawyer and botanist from the Canary Islands who, from then on, dedicated his time to the expansion and glorification of the orquideario, travelling the world in search of different species, until his death in 1960. The obligatory tours are a little rushed, but you get to see flowers, plants, shrubs and trees from around the globe, including some seven hundred species of orchid, in grounds radiating out from a central villa, where Camacho lived.

Contexts

Contexts

History

Beginnings

Havana's success and riches were founded on the strength and position of the **harbour** – the largest natural port in the Caribbean – spotted by Sebastián de Ocampo in 1509, when he took advantage of its deep and sheltered waters to make repairs during his circumnavigation of Cuba and named it the Puerto de Carenas (careening port). The original **San Cristóbal de La Habana** settlement, one of six *villas* founded by conquistador Diego Velázquez, was established on July 25, 1515, St Christopher's Day, on the south coast at Batabanó, 50km from where the city now stands. This first outpost was an unmitigated disaster zone of swampland rife with mosquitoes and tropical diseases, with a flat coastline and shallow port that left ships unable to drop anchor close to shore. The settlement limped along under these testing conditions before finally relocating in 1519 to the north coast, at the mouth of the freshwater Río Chorrera (now called the Almendares), until rising seas and the lack of a sheltered harbour forced another move less than a year later. On November 25, 1519, Havana's pioneers shifted again a few kilometres east to the banks of the large deep-water bay, backed by heavy forests, which is now known as the **Bahía de la Habana.**

Taking advantage of the high ground near the harbour, the early settlement began to ripple out from the newly established Plaza de Armas into what is now Habana Vieja. The first streets established down on the seafront were between the present-day Plaza de Armas and Plaza de San Francisco, with the earliest *bohío* houses made of mud and daub quickly outlawed – one of the earliest dictums issued by the governing council was to decree that houses be made of stone. This early incarnation of Havana was not yet Cuba's capital, which was still in the east of the island (initially Baracoa and subsequently Santiago de Cuba). Life revolved around the port, which Spanish settlers and conquistadors used as a base from which to set forth into other areas of the Americas. The land on the east bay was used as farmland, tilled by the captured indigenous population who were put to work under an *encomienda* system little different to slavery, working what was formerly their own land for the benefit of Spanish overlords.

Although the settlement had established itself as a firm base, between 1520 and 1540 the fledgling city's population declined by eighty percent. The supplies of what little gold was to be found had been exhausted and so the rapacious conquistadors had moved on to pastures new; the indigenous population had been worked to death and virtually extinguished; and with the establishment of towns elsewhere in the Spanish empire now complete, Havana's role as the base from which other Latin American and Caribbean settlements were established was growing defunct.

The profitable trade routes

Havana took off again following the discovery of a deep, navigable channel through the treacherous shallow waters between Cuba and the Bahamas, which represented a major step in the establishment of **trade routes** between Spain and the New World. Although the **Gulf Stream**, the warm and swift Atlantic ocean current running through the Straits of Florida, had been discovered in 1519 by ship's pilot Antón de Alaminos, its true value became apparent when the Spanish started shipping bounty from the Americas back across the

Atlantic to Seville. Helped by Havana's marvellous harbour, which could hold hundreds of ships simultaneously, Cuba quickly rose in global importance. Havana became a convenient **port of call** for conquistadors, with captains of the Spanish fleet steering their galleons in to have sails stitched and hulls remade, and sailors allowed to let off steam one last time before departing for Seville. Brothels, inns and gambling houses sprang up to cater for the seamen, and prostitution and syphilis were rife. So popular were these last hurrahs that the nascent town struggled to sustain the transient populations of sailors who came to restock their ships. By the mid-sixteenth century Havana was one of the most important centres of the Americas, its destiny as Cuba's most important city sealed in 1553 when Gonzalo Pérez de Angulo – the governor of the island – moved his residence to Havana from his headquarters in Santiago. In his entertaining history *Havana, Autobiography of a City*, Alfredo José Estrada estimates that in the first two decades of the seventeenth century alone the Spaniards sent back some fourteen tons of gold from Havana.

Pirates and corsairs

With ships disgorging new sailors and merchants daily, **pirates** drawn by tales of wealth were able to wander anonymously through the crowded town, planning their attacks with admirable precision. Inadequately armed and with few resources, Habaneros were often forced to hand over town riches under threat of having their homes razed to the ground. Though a provisional fort, the Fuerza Vieja, had been erected in Plaza de Armas, it was not well manned and there were few soldiers to defend it in the event of an attack.

In 1555 this was made manifestly apparent by a devastating attack from the French Huguenot pirate **Jacques de Sores**. Nicknamed the Exterminating Angel, as the viciousness of his wrath was matched only by his religious fervour, de Sores was unlikely to let Havana off lightly. When his two ships were spotted off the coast on the morning of July 10, 1555, the alarm was sounded throughout the city but the vessels did not drop anchor and, as they sailed past the harbour, the soldiers in the Fuerza Vieja breathed a sigh of relief. But de Sores merely sailed up the coast, disembarked and, with two hundred soldiers in tow, attacked Havana from the west. The governor Gonzalo Pérez de Angulo fled with his family to Guanabacoa and it fell to Juan Lobera, Havana's military commander, to mount the defence. From the comparative safety of the fort he manfully kept the French ships out of the harbour for two days as de Sores ransacked the city and desecrated the churches. Then disaster struck as Lobera was shot and wounded: left with little resources he was forced to surrender. Meanwhile de Angulo had had time to gather his mettle. With a motley crew of Guanabacoan Indians and slaves pressganged into service, he mounted a futile counter-attack. De Sores's retaliation was swift – he killed the remaining military prisoners and demanded a ransom for Lobera. When de Angulo declined to deliver, the Avenging Angel razed the city to the ground. Lobera was then unaccountably released and the corsairs sailed away. The devastation of the city had taken just under a month.

The city is fortified

Though the attack had left Havana a smoking ruin, the destruction was also to be the city's making. Given the ease with which de Sores and his men had been able to overpower the city, the Spanish crown realised that future attacks were inevitable if Havana was not adequately protected. Flush with money from its recent conquest of Mexico, Spain plumbed some of its proceeds into fortifying

Havana. In 1558, after consolidating shipping operations by making Havana the only Cuban port authorized to engage in commerce, Spain started a long period of fortification with the construction of the first stone fort in the Americas, the impressive **Castillo de la Real Fuerza**, which stands today set back from the harbour mouth on the site of the destroyed Fuerza Vieja. Although never attacked it did prove itself a useful deterrent: even Sir Francis Drake sailed past in 1586 instead of mounting the attack for which he had apparently come equipped.

Before the end of the sixteenth century Havana had become the fastest-growing city in the Americas, with hospitals, monasteries, a shipyard and three forts bristling with soldiers. Once the second fortification, the Castillo de San Salvador de la Punta, was completed in the 1590s, a huge cedar-log chain extending from the Castillo to the opposite side of the harbour was stretched through the water across the harbour mouth. Every night this was erected to deter enemy ships stealing into the harbour under cover of darkness. The formidable **Castillo de Los Tres Reyes del Morro** itself was also started in 1589 and finally completed in 1630. And in 1663, after more than a hundred years of discussion, a ten-metre-high protective wall to encircle the city was begun. By its completion in 1740 Havana was already bulging beyond its newly erected confines and was manned by some 3400 men, with gates drawn tight from dusk to dawn. Its establishment marked Havana as a city of military substance, fully staffed by the most competent soldiers serving under the Crown.

The British occupation

The defence lived up to expectation and further serious attacks were seen off until 1762 when the **British**, led by the **Earl of Albemarle**, made a successful two-pronged assault on the city. The British saw Havana as more than just a rich city ready to be sacked: its seizure would allow them to extend their own operations in the Caribbean and disrupt the Spanish shipping trade lines at the same time.

While part of the British fleet sailed up the Río Almendares to lure Spanish forces there as a decoy, the rest of the fleet landed to the east of El Morro castle at Cojímar and attacked a Spanish force already weakened by an epidemic of yellow fever. This cunning tactic paid off, and from the Cabaña headland opposite the city, the British subjected Havana to a ruthless artillery bombardment. Spanish naval captain Luis de Velasco defended the El Morro castle so valiantly that even today there is always a ship in the Spanish fleet named Velasco in his honour, but it was to no avail. After a six-week siege Albemarle and his men had the city surrounded and Havana fell to the British.

In the event British influence was limited to Havana; the terms of the surrender agreement decreed that the British would not extend their attack beyond the city itself – a situation perfectly agreeable to them, as a complete conquest of Cuba had never been their goal. Indeed, British plantation owners in Jamaica were wary of the threat the untapped Cuban market represented and were resistant to any suggestion that Albermarle and his men might begin to colonize the rest of Cuba. In the event the British only held Havana for eleven months, eventually deeming it more profitable to swap Havana back to the Spanish in exchange for Florida.

However, the free trade that the port enjoyed during its brief period of occupation kick-started Havana as a centre of commerce. When Albemarle abolished the constricting taxes that prevented Havana from trading with anywhere but Seville and Cádiz and reformed the corrupt judiciary, merchants from around the world flooded in to sell their wares. Ultimately it was **slavery** that was to be the most enduring legacy that the British bequeathed to Cuba. A staggering forty thousand slaves were sold into Havana during the occupation. By the time the British withdrew, the unhappy destiny of several generations of Africans was sealed.

In January 1763 the British left and the returning Spanish troops were led back into Havana with much fanfare by one Alejandro O'Reilly, an Irish mercenary brigadier general, for whom the eponymous street in Habana Vieja is named. Spain wisely kept British trade policies intact and the consequential influx of wealthy Spanish sugar families and slaves to man their plantations propelled Havana into a new age of affluence.

The age of elegance

The **nineteenth century** was a period of growth, when some of the most beautiful buildings around Habana Vieja were constructed and the city enjoyed a new-found elegance. At the same time, prostitution, crime and political corruption were reaching new heights, causing many of the new bourgeoisie to abandon the old city to the poor and to start colonizing what is now the district of Vedado. By the 1860s the framework of the new suburbs stretching west and south was in place. The city walls were pulled down in 1863, less than two centuries after their completion, because of the overcrowding and subsequent outbreaks of cholera. Taking no further chances with the city's defences, the Spanish also built the **Fortaleza San Carlos de la Cabaña** on the very ridge upon which the British launched their attack.

By the middle of the century Havana had a population of 130,000 and a fully cultivated taste for luxury. Life in the city grew languorous and refined; ladies traversed the Prado, remodelled by the governor Capitán General Miguel Tacón, in elegant *volante* carriages, and attended operas and theatre performances escorted by the city's wealthy merchants. **Tobacco** was an important component of city life – originally sold by free slaves before laws by the Spanish outlawed the practice, it became a lucrative plinth in Havana's economy as Havana cigars were exported around the world.

Unusually nineteenth century Havana was a city with much less social segregation than other Caribbean cities. Under Spanish law slaves were permitted to marry, own property and buy their own freedom piecemeal, and as many free slaves migrated to the city this led to a much greater social mix. In his diary of 1859 American tourist Joseph J Dimock remarked that the palatial houses of the richest white Habaneros stood side by side with the very poorest of black families. North Americans were drawn by the convivial way of life, but Havana was enticing to more than just tourists: it was also the era in which US foreign policy turned its attention to Cuba, the ripe fruit waiting to be plucked from the Spanish.

The war years

The lust for independence from Spain had come slowly to Cuba – and in particular Havana – where a period of prosperity, coupled with a fear that slaves would gain influence and power under Cuban rule, tempered the desire of the *criollos* (Cubans of Spanish descent) for self-government. By 1868, however, support for the cause in the east and centre of the island resulted in the first **War of Independence**, which lasted ten years until the revolutionary movement began to flounder following the battlefield death of the movement's leader, Carlos Manuel de Céspedes. The Pact of Zanjón was signed between most of the rebels and Spanish authorities, but fifteen years later, when Spain had failed to fulfill the promises made, war broke out again in 1895.

The US had been paying keen attention to the developments of its close neighbour, and when intense fighting broke out in Havana it seized the opportunity to send in the warship *Maine*, ostensibly to protect US citizens in the capital. When the *Maine* blew up in Havana harbour in 1898, the US accused the Spanish of sabotage and so began the **Spanish-American War** – and with it the start of US political involvement in Cuban home affairs.

The rise of tourism

In 1902, after the Wars of Independence, **North American influence and money** flowed into the city. When the Volstead Act in 1919 outlawed the sale and consumption of alcohol in the US, tourism in Cuba was given fresh impetus. The first half of the twentieth century saw the building of tower blocks, magnificent hotels and glorious Art Deco palaces, many bankrolled by North American companies, to serve the booming tourist industry. The mid-1920s were peak years, and between December 1925 and March 1926 nearly 45,000 North Americans holidayed in Cuba, most of them bound for Havana. The exotic colonial charm of Habana Vieja was matched with plush new attractions in the west of the city as suburbs like Marianao developed around the Havana Country Club, a race track and a casino – all designed to draw the tourist dollar.

It is difficult to overstate the influence that North America business interests had on Havana and the rest of Cuba at this time – the fates of the two countries were well and truly intertwined. In the 1920s places like the Havana Country Club were the centre of operations for many business deals and numbered among its members some of the Hershey family and the president of Coca-Cola (Cuba's sugar was a major ingredient for both businesses), plus a host of sugar barons. Many US investors sat on the board of Cuban interests. While the population of poverty-stricken Cubans languished, the money that American investment brought into the country enabled the building of roads, trams and electricity plants, and largely allowed Havana to far outstrip the rest of the country in terms of urban and social development.

1930s: political turbulence

Yet behind the scenes of gaiety, political unrest seethed – with protests led by students at Havana University and elsewhere in the capital contesting President Machado's corrupt regime. Away from the developments for tourists, Havana was a poor city with bad accommodation, little education and a lot of crime. Backhanders were rife and Cuban politicians lined their pockets with the boom, while low wages and lack of unions for workers ensured an unequal distribution of wealth. Even the cash cows of the casinos themselves were prey to petty corruptions, as gambling bosses devised systems to trick clients into ever-increasing losses. **Political activism** was growing and sympathizers with a range of ideologies – including Communism – grew increasingly frustrated with successive governments' empty promises to reform a corrupt system. In 1933 a general strike followed by loss of military support brought Machado to his knees and he fled the country.

Meanwhile within the army, a young sergeant named **Fulgencio Batista** staged a coup that year and used a powerful military position to became the decision-maker behind a series of puppet presidents. Demonized more than any other pre-Revolution leader by the current regime, Batista was not, at least during the first of his two tenures as president of the country (from 1940 to 1944), the hated man the Communist Party would have people believe and some of his policies were met with widespread support. For example, in 1934 he presided over the dissolution of the Platt Amendment that had chained Cuban sovereignty to the US since the Wars of Independence. And in 1937 he released all political prisoners and used the army to institute health and education programmes in the countryside and among the urban poor. But his progressiveness did not extend to rising above corruption: throughout the mid-1930s Batista used the lottery as a personal source of income and cultivated ties with the bosses of organized crime syndicates.

The hour of the Mafia

Though the Great Depression of the 1930s wounded Havana's tourist industry, it was too strong a beast to kill and as affluence returned to the Americas so tourists returned to Havana. North American **organized crime** bosses had long had an interest in developing Havana and by the late 1930s already managed many of the gambling interests there. Using Havana as a key location in their Prohibition alcohol-smuggling trade, when alcohol was produced in the Caribbean and smuggled to the US, cemented their interest.

Meyer Lansky, the overlord of Jewish organized crime in New York, was instrumental in making Havana a key Mafia interest and sealed the deal with his associates at the infamous Havana Conference held at the *Hotel Nacional* in December 1946. Feasting on flamingo, turtle, caviar and manatee, Lansky, Vito Genovese and Lucky Luciano among others formulated plans on how to make Havana more profitable to them than Las Vegas. When Batista returned to power in 1952 – by cancelling the elections and staging a military coup to oust the Auténtico Party's equally corrupt Carlos Prío Socarrás – he formally put Lansky in charge of gambling in Havana. Lansky's ostensible role was to clean up an industry which, ironically, had grown increasingly corrupt under the auspices of organized crime, and create a place in which North American tourists could spend their money knowing that they were not being unduly fleeced. In exchange for kickbacks, Batista offered Lansky and the Mafia control of Havana's racetracks and casinos, and offered to open Havana up to large-scale gambling. Batista also offered to match any hotel investment made by Lansky and his associates dollar for dollar.

1950s: Corruption and the rise of Castro

Beyond the world visible to tourists Havana was in turmoil, as the pace of development in the west of the city was matched by the **urban decay** to the east in Habana Vieja. In the 1950s many of Habana Vieja's colonial palaces had become multiple housing units, and by the end of the decade less than twenty percent of the neighbourhood's accommodation was considered to be in good condition. There was no structure for preservation and the only plans for urban improvement were deeply insensitive. José Luis Sert, a contemporary of Le Corbusier, drew up dramatic plans to raze many of the narrow streets and buildings of Habana Vieja and replace them with glass-and-concrete towers. These plans, which would have resulted in the destruction of what is now a UNESCO Heritage Site, did not come to fruition.

Fed up with living in a city that had been ravaged by two decades of corrupt leaders, and now faced with the dissolution of a fragile republic in the face of Batista's military junta, Habaneros took matters into their own hands. Guns brought from the army or smuggled in from abroad were abundant and *gangster-ismo* was rife, with different political factors backing up political jockeying with attacks by violent goon squads. **Terrorist attacks** in the capital staged by different insurgency groups became a frighteningly common factor of city life. According to the constitution of 1940 the University of Havana was an area in which civil and military police were not allowed, and now political gangs joined student activists to take advantage of this and use the university as a refuge from authority. One such activist was the charismatic lawyer **Fidel Castro**.

Castro had hoped to run for congress in the 1952 elections but his hopes were dashed by Batista's military coup. Effectively frozen out of constitutional politics by Batista's intolerance of organized opposition, Castro was one of several would-be politicians to challenge the authority of the new regime with armed action – in his case an ill-fated attack on 26 July, 1953 on Santiago's **Moncada barracks**, which failed due to the bungled execution of a reasonably well-laid plan and resulted in Castro giving the order to retreat, leaving behind two dead and one wounded. This relatively light casualty count was overturned within 48 hours when Batista's officers captured, tortured and executed between 55 and seventy of the original rebels. Castro's week-long avoidance of capture, by hiding out in the countryside around Santiago, probably saved his life: outrage at the army brutality helped raise Castro to hero status and, fearing public uprising, Batista arrested and tried Castro rather than secretly executing him. Alongside 31 other rebels, Castro was tried in October and sentenced to fifteen years, although he was released into exile in 1955 after serving only two.

In exile in Mexico later that year, Castro formed the **26 July Movement** (M-26-7), raised funds and coordinated his return to Cuba. It was during this time that many of the significant players of the Revolution were drawn together, most notably **Ernesto Che Guevara**, to whom Castro was introduced by Raúl Castro and M-26-7 member Nico López. Castro was anxious to return to Cuba and by October 1956 had gathered enough support and money to declare himself ready. On November 25, 82 rebels crammed onto a 58-foot leaky yacht called **Granma**, slipped past the Mexican coastguard and headed for Cuba's Oriente. Thanks to foul weather, cramped conditions and a malfunctioning engine, what was supposed to be a five-day journey ended up taking eight, and they ran out of petrol and capsized several miles from where their coastal contacts were waiting to receive them. Batista's men had been tipped off about their arrival and staged an attack. Though several were killed, the rest of the rebels escaped into the mountains and were able to regroup two weeks later and head to the Sierra Maestra to establish their base.

Despite this, Batista initially refused to take the threat of Castro's M-26-7 insurgency seriously, believing that censoring news of the struggle would be enough to starve it of support. Instead he concentrated his brutal police forces on subduing the movements of Havana's politically active Federation of University Students.

Under the leadership of the personable architecture student **José Antonio Echevarría**, students had demonstrated against the regime on the steps of the Vedado university site in 1955. Reprisals by Batista's secret police were bloody and Echevarría himself was badly beaten. Reaching the conclusion Castro had reached two years earlier that there was to be no peaceful political solution to the situation, Echevarría started the direct action group **Directorio Revolucionario** to oust Batista from power. In March 1957 the DR staged an assassination attempt on Batista at the Presidential Palace but Batista was tipped off and left the building minutes before the gang arrived. The would-be assassins fled the palace but were stopped by the police mid-flight and Echevarría died in a shoot-out. Had he lived it is possible that Echevarría would have eventually rivalled Castro for power, but following his death the DR, Auténticos and the M-26-7 insurgency movement formed the **Cuban Liberation Junta**, a loose alliance of anti-Batista groups.

Meanwhile, waging a war based on guerrilla tactics, the rebels had been able to gain the upper hand against Batista's larger and better-equipped forces. They had also built up a large base of support for the cause among local peasantry and enlisted new recruits into their army. At the same time an insurrectionary movement in Havana and other cities began a campaign of sabotage, including bombings and strikes aimed at disabling state apparatus. By the end of 1958 the majority of Cubans had sided with the rebels.

On January 1, 1959, crushed by the twin blows of withdrawal of US military support and demoralized troops, many of whom refused to continue fighting, Batista fled to the States.

Castro arrived in Havana a week later, borne in on the wave of goodwill that he had ridden on his epic journey across the country. His M-26-7 men swiftly established civil order, putting an end to the minor looting and smashing of casinos that had marked Batista's departure. A government was quickly assembled with **Manuel Urrutia**, a popular judge, as president and **José Miró Cardona** as prime minister. Castro was appointed commander in chief of the armed forces. In his short tenure, Urrutia's most significant act was to shut down the casinos. But when Castro protested, citing the income and jobs that would be lost, the decision was revoked. Cardona resigned in protest and Castro assumed the role of prime minister and with it all the major decision-making, rendering Urrutia little more than a puppet president. Amid increasing tension between himself and Castro – due in part to Urrutia's avowed denouncement of Cuban communists, Urrutia resigned in July 1959. Castro appointed Osvaldo Dorticós, the Minister of Revolutionary Law, to the post, in which he remained until Castro became head of state in 1976.

The Revolution

Following the Revolution the social fabric of Havana changed irrevocably. Throughout the 1960s the new regime cleaned the streets of crime, prostitution and general debauchery, laying out the basis of a socialist capital. Initially the Revolution was well received by Havana's middle classes, with whom Batista's corrupt regime had been unpopular. But with the advent of the progressive and radical agrarian reforms, nationalization of US-owned industries and the move towards communism, the largely urban middle class came to see the Revolution as a threat to their established way of life. Between 1960 and 1962 droves of Habaneros fled the city bound for Miami, where they hoped they would wait but a few months for Castro's overthrow and a return to a pre-1959 way of life. Fine houses, abandoned by owners fleeing to the US, were left in the hands of erstwhile servants, and previously exclusive neighbourhoods changed face overnight.

The **Patrimonio Cultural** or Cultural Heritage department was set up in the 1960s to allocate unoccupied houses to newly formed government bodies as offices – and to revolutionary figures as palatial homes. Although the casinos were eventually reopened, anti-American feeling, the nationalization of key industries and an increase in hostility between Cuba and the US meant that tourism never regained its pre-Revolutionary popularity and the era of glittering Havana drew to a close.

As the nature of the Revolution became clearer, the relationship between Cuba and the US continued to worsen. The US government froze purchases of Cuban sugar, restricted exports, backed counter-revolutionary forces within Cuba and then in 1961 broke off diplomatic relations. In April that year a military force of Cuban exiles, trained and equipped in the US, landed at the

Bay of Pigs in southern Matanzas. The revolutionaries were ready for them and the whole operation ended in failure within 72 hours.

In December that year, in the face of complete economic and political isolation from the US, Castro declared himself a Marxist-Leninist and allied himself with the Soviet Union. Concerned by the prospect of another attack from the US, in 1962 Castro asked the Soviets to install over forty missiles on the island. Angered at this belligerent move, President John F Kennedy declared an embargo on any military weapons entering Cuba, which went ignored by Soviet Premier Nikita Khrushchev. Neither side appeared to be backing down and weapons were prepared for launch in the US. A six-day stalemate followed, after which a deal was struck and the **Cuban Missile Crisis** passed. Khrushchev agreed to withdraw Soviet weapons from Cuba on the condition that the US would not invade the island.

Reduced to non-military intervention, the US response was to tighten the trade embargo. Cuba's isolation from the US was firmly in place.

Urban development

While Havana was the headquarters for the wave of social and economic reforms, city development itself was haphazard. With the emphasis on improving conditions in the countryside, the **post-Revolution years** saw many fine buildings crumble while residential overcrowding increased. Habana Vieja was declared a UNESCO Heritage Site in 1982 and a year later a campaign was launched to start safeguarding its architecture. The modern-day saviour of Habana Vieja has been city historian **Eusebio Leal**, who has worked tirelessly to restore the city to its colonial glory through raising funds abroad and lobbying for money in Cuba. Though it is estimated that three buildings reach the point of irreparable repair every day in Havana, there has been tremendous improvement and by 2001 Leal's office had funded 76 restoration projects, opened fourteen hotels and a host of other tourist facilities.

Havana today

Today there is a growing prosperity in Havana evident from a new bus infrastructure, commercial ventures selling Western goods in convertible currency, increasingly well-fed citizens and a rash of new cars on the roads. Managing the redistribution of the wealth that tourism brings to the city is the biggest challenge facing the state. Measures like heavy taxation and stringent checks on private entrepreneurs are unpopular but relatively effective ways of furthering the Revolution's aim. While the changes that Fidel's brother **Raúl Castro** has tentatively ushered in since assuming the role of president in 2008, including allowing citizens to own mobile phones and discussing performance-related pay rises, are among the most progressive moves the city has seen in decades, the sense of frustration, particularly amongst the city's wealthier citizens, is clearly apparent. With increased access to the internet, Havana-based bloggers who are critical of the government give an insight into a city behind the party headlines in state-sanctioned papers like *Granma*, while clued-up Habaneros beat the restrictions of information with texting networks on their phones.

Life in Havana is a balancing act between the benefits of free state education and health care and the system of petty corruption, black-market dealing and backhanders essential to what Habaneros refer to as *la lucha* or daily struggle. Yet despite the rumblings of discontent there is no sense that this is a city poised to throw the Revolutionary baby out with the bath water. Habaneros want a change to their way of life rather than a complete change at the highest level. It looks like the fates of Havana and the Revolution will remain intertwined for some while yet.

Music and musicians in Havana

Havana bounces with rhythm and hums with melody: it is a city where music is woven into the fabric of everyday life in an unusually prevalent way. Parks and squares are frequent hosts to concerts and few bars, restaurants or hotel lobbies stay silent for long, with live bands striking up constantly. The music in nightclubs especially, however, does not always fit with visitors' preconceived ideas of what popular music is in Havana. At the most prestigious nightspots you are as likely to find live reggaeton or pop-oriented salsa as guitar-strumming trova groups or bolero singers. But even at its most commercial, music in Havana is most often performed live, and this is one of the best cities in the world for experiencing musicians at the top of their game, especially if you want to hear specifically Cuban styles.

The origins of most traditional Cuban musical styles are found in the east of the country, particularly in and around Santiago de Cuba. Havana, however, can not only itself claim to be the birth place of a number of influential music genres but has played a vital role in the development, popularization and spread of all Cuban music. The city has a fantastically rich history of outstanding musicians, while it remains a hotbed of musical talent for artists of Cuban and non-Cuban genres.

Rumba

Not to be confused with the rumba of ballroom dancing, the frenetic rhythms and dances of Cuban **rumba** are the closest contemporary Cuban music has to a direct link with the music brought to the island by African slaves. A raw music driven by drums and vocals, it emerged from the docks in Havana and Matanzas and from the sugar mills in the eponymous provinces in the late nineteenth century. Black workers developed songs and dances by playing rhythms on cargo boxes and packing cases. These rudimentary instruments were subsequently replaced, once the music became more popular, with conga drums of several different sizes and tones along with two different kinds of wooden sticks (*claves* and *palitos*), a metal shaker (*maruga*) and specially manufactured boxes (*cajones*). Rumba is very distinct and can sound like a cacophony of rhythm to the uninitiated, making it perhaps one of the less accessible musical styles to the foreign ear, with so many percussive elements and an absence of brass, string or wind instruments. On the other hand rumba performances are among the most engaging and energetic and the vocal sections, involving a leader and a responder, can be quite hypnotic. Improvisation is an integral part of the art of rumba, as is call-and-response, while the dance calls on its performers to display explosive levels of energy.

Modern rumba divides into three main dances. The **guaguancó** is a dance for a couple in a game of seduction and sexual flirtation; the **yambú** is slower and less overtly sexual, while the **columbia** is a furiously energetic solo male dance.

There are several venues around Havana where rumba is now performed for the benefit of mostly foreign audiences. The best-known is at the Callejón de Hamel in Centro Habana but also El Gran Palenque in Vedado (see p.149 for both), and though rumba at its most authentic is informal and spontaneous, these venues do offer something completely different to the kind of thing you will see and hear at most live music venues. **Los Muñequitos de Matanzas, Claves y Guaguanco** and **Los Papines** are all legendary rumba groups still going strong, while the musicians and dancers of the **Conjunto Folklórico Nacional** perform more regularly and are based at El Gran Palenque. Members of this collective have formed one of Havana's most successful rumba groups of recent times, **Rumberos de Cuba**.

Danzón

In contrast to rumba, danzón is a more formal strain of Cuban music, less spontaneous and with none of the improvisations of rumba; it best represents the musical traditions brought to Cuba by the Europeans. Danzón was born out of the instrumental music known in Cuba as **contradanza**, a style performed in ballrooms and at formal events during the nineteenth century by recreational versions of military bands. The contradanza was adapted and reinterpreted during the course of the nineteenth century until, in 1879, a Cuban band leader in Matanzas, Miguel Failde, composed what is generally considered to be the very first danzón, though there is some dispute over this. More upbeat and tuneful than contradanza, danzón orchestras nevertheless maintained the same basis of brass and string instruments, though the flute was given greater prominence. Various other innovations were made as the style developed during the early decades of the twentieth century, developing alongside and influencing the sound of jazz in New Orleans and elsewhere in the US. The piano later became an essential ingredient, while congas have also been incorporated, taking the style closer to what is now known as son. Danzón is still popular with elderly Cubans who meet up at weekends in dancehalls, but it was son that really took off and came to define the Cuban sound.

The best time to experience danzón in the city nowadays is during the annual Festival Danzón Habana, which usually takes place in February, when groups such as Charanga de Oro and the Orquesta Barbarito Diez demonstrate that this traditional style is still very much alive.

Son

Son is the blood running through the veins of Cuban popular music. More than any other music style it represents an intrinsically Cuban blend of African and European musical elements, though it has undergone so many innovations and spawned so many sub-genres that it is difficult to talk of it as an individual musical style at all. Though a large proportion of bands making music in Cuba today could legitimately be described as son groups, references to son nowadays tend to be to traditional son with its signature sound provided by the Cuban guitar, known as the **tres**, the upright double bass and vocals; *claves*, maracas, a scraper and bongos also feature in this traditional sound.

Son had its origins in eastern Cuba in the late nineteenth century and arrived in Havana around the first decade of the twentieth century. The earliest groups to popularize the sound were sextets and subsequently, with the addition of a trumpet in the 1920s, septets. The sound was transformed in the 1940s and

1950s by **Arsenio Rodríguez**, considered by many to be the father of the modern Afro-Cuban sound. He added extra trumpets to his son band, brought in the piano and added a conga drummer, moving son closer to the sound produced by modern salsa bands, a transformation which was cemented in the 1970s by pioneering groups such as Los Van Van (see p.214). Bands consisting of this larger, expanded line-up became known as *conjuntos*. This same period marked the rise of **Benny Moré**, cited by many as Cuba's greatest ever *sonero*, who was known as the Barbarian of Rhythm. With traditional son now en vogue again thanks to the Buena Vista Social Club, there is no shortage of traditional son groups performing in Havana today.

Chachachá

The first ever chachachá, "La Engañadora", was composed by Enrique Jorrín, one of the early innovators of danzón, who, it is said, wanted to provide Americans with something they would find more manageable on the dance floor, having seen them struggle with other more complex Cuban dance rhythms. This music and dance craze, along with mambo, took Europe and especially the US by storm in the 1950s. A modification of the danzón, the name is said to have been born out of the sound made by the dancers' feet at the Silver Star club in Centro Habana when they danced to this new rhythm, their feet grazing the floor on three successive beats.

You are most likely to hear chachachá around Habana Vieja, as performed by the duos and trios providing the soundtrack in hotel lobbies and restaurants.

Mambo

Mambo emerged in the 1940s, another product of the danzón tradition. It is associated with big bands and is a racier, louder, less elegant and more Africanized sound than danzón. Congas and *timbales* drums were added to danzón line-ups to create mambo orchestras, which were actually a bigger hit abroad than they were on the island itself; mambo is one of the lesser performed styles in contemporary Cuba. The classic Cuban mambo bands belong to the 1940s and 1950s; bands led by greats such as pianist Pérez Prado, singer Benny Moré and the originators of the mambo, Arsenio Rodríguez and Antonio Arcaño.

Trova

Another Cuban musical tradition to have emerged from the east of the island, **trova** grew out of the troubadour tradition. Troubadours were travelling musicians who would disperse news or tell stories through song. The early Cuban troubadors relied on nothing more than their voice, guitar and imagination, composing lyrics based on both romantic and patriotic themes. Nowadays it is typically sung with two voices in harmony and one or two guitars. Although no longer at the forefront of Cuban music, it can still be heard in Havana and throughout the island in Casas de la Trova and to a lesser

extent Casas de la Cultura, community-focused venues providing a performance space for predominantly local musicians. This simple guitar-based musical
tradition gave birth to the song *Guantanamera*, perhaps the best-known Cuban
song, and certainly the most familiar to tourists who have spent any time in
Habana Vieja's bars and restaurants.

Sindo Garay, a leading trova singer during the General Machado dictatorship
in the 1930s and 1940s, was a fixture at the *Bodeguita del Medio* bar and restaurant in Habana Vieja (see p.125), historically a meeting place for trova singers.
Other greats of Cuban trova like Carlos Puebla played there and in the run-up
to the Revolution it was a popular meeting place for intellectuals and critics of
Batista. Trova musicians can today be heard in touristy spots all around Havana,
usually working in duos or trios, and if you eat out regularly in Havana you will
inevitably become familiar with some of the most popular songs in the trova
repertoire. Modern concert performers of traditional trova in Havana include
Heydi Igualada and Manuel Argudín.

Bolero

An offshoot of trova, Cuban **bolero** is another guitar-based style derived from
trova but has a more lyrical, poetic and romantic slant. Like trova it is typically
performed by guitar duos and two voices in harmony. It arrived in Havana
around the same time as trova, in the late nineteenth century, and has been
performed in cafés and music halls ever since.

Ibrahim Ferrer, one of the original Buena Vista Social Club singers, was an
expert exponent of the bolero, as is Omara Portuondo, whose renditions of one
of the classic bolero songs, *Dos Gardenias*, has seen a resurgence in popularity
following the Buena Vista explosion. An excellent venue for live bolero is
Hurón Azul, the UNEAC headquarters in Vedado (see p.145).

Feelin'

Feelin', also known as filin, combined the bolero tradition with jazz in the
1940s to create a Cuban version of the kind of music being produced and
performed by the likes of Frank Sinatra, Nat King Cole and Ella Fitzgerald.
Where the backing track for the bolero singer is supplied by a guitarist, the
archetypal feelin' soundtrack is provided by a pianist.

Compared with trova and bolero, the two styles with which it shares the
closest heritage, feelin' gets less exposure in Havana or indeed anywhere in
Cuba nowadays. *El Gato Tuerto*, a restaurant and nightclub in Vedado, is one of
the best places to hear feelin' performed.

Salsa and timba

Arguably **salsa** is not a musical style at all but a catch-all term for music born
and bred in the Spanish-speaking Caribbean and the Latin communities of
the eastern United States. Though there are countless definitions of what salsa
actually is, the term was popularized as a description of a specific kind of music

in the 1960s and 1970s in New York, Puerto Rico and Cuba and is undeniably a product of son. By that time son groups had already created a branch of Cuban son sufficiently different from traditional son to warrant a new name. This distinguishable sound was cemented in the 1970s when modern salsa was created following innovations to son bands made by **Adalberto Alvarez**, and his band **Son 14, and by Juan Formell** and his legendary group **Los Van Van,** introducing changes by adding a trombone, synthesizer and drum. The modern salsa band may be unrecognizable from the son sextets of the 1920s but there is a common thread, that unique Afro-Cuban blend, running down the decades. Cuban salsa has been tweaked in recent years to create **timba**, a version of salsa strongly associated with Havana, as opposed to San Juan, New York or any of the other major salsa centres.

Salsa and timba bands dominate Cuban popular music. Los Van Van remains at the forefront of the scene and still draws huge crowds, while fellow all-time greats La Charanga Habanera and Adalberto Alvarez are still relevant. Pioneers of a new wave of louder, more aggressive salsa bands, with grittier lyrics and a more streetwise vernacular, include **NG La Banda,** founded in 1988 but still going strong. In common with many modern-day salsa bands, they have combined salsa with elements of hip-hop, reggaeton and jazz. The group **Bamboleo** and the charismatic female vocalist **Haila** are also great performers and have been headline timba acts for a few years now. **Maikel Blanco** and **Habana D'Primera** are two of the more recently established salsa acts to cause a real buzz.

Cuban jazz

There have been **jazz bands** in Havana almost as long as they have existed in New Orleans but quintessentially Cuban jazz, as opposed to jazz made by Cubans, emerged in the 1940s, marked by the success of the band Afro-Cubans and their lead singer Frank "Machito" Grillo. The Afro-Cubans, however, moved to New York to establish themselves in the wider consciousness of American jazz, leaving Cuban jazz as performed and developed on the island to really find its feet in the 1970s with the formation, in 1973, of the great Cuban jazz pioneers **Irakere**. Without doubt the godfather of Cuban jazz is composer and pianist Jesús "Chucho" Valdés, who, along with Paquito D'Rivera and Arturo Sandoval, formed the backbone of Irakere. Cuban jazz tends to incorporate elements of son and other Afro-Cuban music styles. Percussion is an integral part of the sound, with the conga and bongo drums lending it its unmistakable trademark rhythm.

Though D'Rivera and Sandoval both defected from the island in the 1980s, Havana-based Irakere is still going strong and regularly perform live. Among the leading lights of the newer generation of Cuban jazz artists in Havana is Roberto Fonseca, a virtuoso composer and master of several instruments, and Rembert Duharte, who regularly performs at locations around Vedado.

Nueva trova

Nueva trova refers to the post-Revolution generation of folksy singer-songwriters who first came to prominence in the late 1960s and 1970s on a basic template of vocals and solo acoustic guitar. Nueva trova artists nowadays are a mix of solo acoustic guitar players in the traditional trova and folk moulds and bands producing a slightly harder-edged sound, crossing over into rock. The style is sometimes referred to as **nueva canción** (new song).

Nueva trova songs encompass protest and politics as well as romance and relationships, in keeping with the trova tradition. Artists have tended to be patriotic but reflective and sometimes critical of the regime. The two giants of nueva trova, both considered amongst the founders of the movement, are **Pablo Milanés** and **Silvio Rodríguez**, both hugely popular throughout the Spanish-speaking world and still active today. Though at times critical of the regime, Milanés and Rodríguez have in fact been staunch supporters of the Revolution.

The Casa de las Américas in Vedado (see p.93) and its founding director, Haydee Santamaría, played an important role in the nurturing and development of nueva trova and it remains a good place to check for performances. Among the biggest names on the current nueva trova circuit are **Carlos Varela**, whose songs express some of the frustrations of the younger generation in Cuba, and **Sara González**.

Cuban rock

Rock music was actively discouraged and heavily frowned upon by the Cuban authorities in the early years of the Revolution, perceived as yankee music and anti-revolutionary. This attitude mellowed very slowly and had softened sufficiently enough by 2001 for Welsh rockers the Manic Street Preachers to be able to perform at the Teatro Karl Marx in Miramar, a significant breakthrough at the time. Havana today has its share of rock musicians, and though one or two Cuban rock bands have been given record deals, on the whole they are underexposed and perform at low-key venues. As elsewhere they can be split into numerous sub-genres from soft rock to heavy metal, though the most characteristically Cuban take on rock takes its influence from the nueva trova movement. Many nueva trova artists, including Silvio Rodríguez, have written what could be described as cross-over rock songs.

Havana natives Santiago Feliú and Carlos Varela are among the rockier of the nueva trova artists still performing today, while Gerardo Alfonso and David Blanco are worth a listen for the latest Cuban twists on the rock formula. For something a little closer to classic rock look out for Los Kent, long-time performers on the Havana rock scene.

Cuban hip-hop

Cuban hip-hop represents a refreshing alternative to the violence, misogyny and bling that have come to dominate modern hip-hop in the US and elsewhere. The music and particularly the lyrics are generally closer to the political and socially conscious rap of late 1980s and early 1990s New York hip-hop, and nothing like the ultra-polished formulaic sound of the current hip-hop celebrity. A lack of resources has, to some extent, dictated this Cuban take on hip-hop, with bedroom producers and pre-recorded tracks providing the music. Scratch DJs are pretty much non-existent – as are turntables.

Havana is the undisputed home of Cuban hip-hop. The annual **Festival de Rap** has been, since its inception in 1995, the biggest event in the Cuban hip-hop calendar. Its main venue, a concrete amphitheatre, is in Alamar on the eastern outskirts of Havana. Among the groups that performed at the inaugural festival were Amenaza, members of which went on to form Orishas, the only Cuban hip-hop group to date to have an international following and, significantly, based abroad. Most of the more innovative Cuban hip-hop artists remain outside of the mainstream. Among the privileged few groups to have recorded with Cuba-based record labels are Obsesión, Telmary Díaz, Fres K and Papo Record. The vast majority of groups still rely on home-made recordings and live performance to get their music heard, and some of the most respected names within the Cuban hip-hop community, such as Los Paisanos, Ogguere, Doble Filo and the controversial Los Aldeanos, perform regularly around Havana.

Reggaeton and cubaton

For a while it looked as though the explosion of Cuban hip-hop groups over the last decade was going to put hip-hop firmly on the Cuban musical map. However, the momentum built up by the initial surge of rappers in Havana and elsewhere on the island was seized upon by **reggaeton** artists and it is they who have gained the recognition and radio air-play the hip-hop artists so craved. The sound is a combination of modern Rn'B, watered-down commercial reggae and rapped lyrics. A home-grown, salsified version of reggaeton, known as **cubaton**, is equally popular and this kind of music is now a staple on the Havana club scene.

The first wave of Cuban reggaeton artists were led by Eddy K, who is still a superstar in Havana, whilst more recently established top performers of both reggaeton and cubaton are Clan 537 and Gente de Zona.

Books

ot only does Havana have a fine literary heritage but it has also been the inspiration for many evocative works by exiled Cubans and non-Cubans, most famously Ernest Hemingway and Graham Greene. Secondhand books are widely available in Havana, with a cluster of bookstands in Habana Vieja in particular. At these you can often find core Cuban texts about the Revolution: transcripts of interviews with Castro, for example, sometimes translated into English. Sadly, these interesting tomes are often let down by poor translation and proofreading but are worth a browse none the less.

Most of the books listed are currently in print, but those that aren't should be available on websites such as ⓦwww.abebooks.com or ⓦwww.amazon.com. Titles that are out of print are marked "o/p". The 🏃 symbol indicates titles that are especially recommended.

History, politics and biography

Carlos Acosta *No Way Home.* Acosta excels as a writer almost as much as he does as one of the world's best ballet dancers. This detailed autobiography covers his early life in Cuba, including his childhood in the suburbs of Havana, and subsequent successes in dance companies throughout the world. The chapters that capture the feel of life in Cuba for a child in the '80s are particularly enjoyable.

🏃 **Simon Calder and Emily Hatchwell** *Cuba in Focus: A Guide to the People, Politics and Culture.* A succinct overview of the country and its history, touching on a lively variety of different subject areas, from race to tourism, all dealt with intelligently and in just enough detail to be informative. Small enough to read from cover to cover on the plane.

Dick Cluster and Rafael Hernández *The History of Havana.* One of the few books in English to cover the history of the Cuban capital specifically, it provides a history of Cuba too. This engaging, people-centred account takes a social and cultural perspective as much as an economic and political one. It's peppered with lively personal testimonies helping to make the facts of the past more pertinent and more real.

🏃 **Leycester Coltman** *The Real Fidel Castro.* Succeeds where so many biographies of the man fail, in being both a balanced and highly readable account of Castro's extraordinary life. Refreshing in its political neutrality and its animated, non-academic style, this is also a highly accessible insight into the Cuban Revolution itself.

TJ English *The Havana Mob.* Despite the somewhat artless writing, English's meticulous research into the Mafia is a fascinating account of how the corruption and interrelations between pre-revolutionary politicians dominated Havana's tourist trade and how the Revolution itself dismantled their money-spinning industry.

🏃 **Alfredo José Estrada** *Havana (Autobiography of a City).* Although at times the writer lets his anti-Castro bias flavour his outlook, that doesn't detract from this meticulously researched social and architectural history, rich in fascinating vignettes in which the author traces the lineage of the city from its earliest incarnation to modern times.

Guillermo Cabrera Infante *Mea Cuba.* A collection of writings on Cuba from 1968 to 1993 by a Cuban exile and opponent of the current regime. His vehement criticisms of Fidel Castro are uncompromising and can make for rather heavy reading, but there are plenty of thoughtful and eyebrow-raising commentaries from a man who is clearly passionate about his subject matter.

Isaac Saney *Cuba: A Revolution in Motion.* An accessible and intelligent account of the mechanics behind the Revolution written from a Marxist standpoint. This is an essential read for anyone wishing to see how the Revolution estimates itself. It also provides up-to-date information on how Cuba expects to carry the Revolution forward over coming decades.

Rosalie Schwartz *Pleasure Island – Tourism and Temptation in Cuba.*

A must for anyone bemused by the stark contrast between evident *jineterismo* throughout the island and the upstanding ideals of the Revolution. Schwartz's readable and lively history charts the history of tourism in Cuba during its pre-Revolution days and draws a few comparisons with its modern-day incarnation. The book cuts to the heart of the matter, analysing the political and economic benefits and backhanders as well as giving a fascinating account of the role played by the Mafia. Essential reading for those wishing to be clued-up visitors.

Jaime Suchlicki *Cuba: From Columbus to Castro and Beyond.* Now in its fifth edition, this is one of the best up-to-date complete histories of the country and should be one of the first books to read for anyone interested in the subject matter, though it does have a distinct anti-Castro bias. Concise yet comprehensive, extremely well informed yet not too wordy or academic.

Culture and society

Roberto González Echevarría *The Pride of Havana: A History of Cuban Baseball.* Painstakingly detailed, this exhaustive history of Cuba's national sport may prove a little too detailed for the casual reader. Aficionados of the game, however, will appreciate this passionate attempt to record and explain Cuban baseball's role in the history of the game itself as well as its unique evolution on the island.

Stephen Foehr *Waking Up In Cuba.* An entertaining and fascinating portrait of contemporary Cuba as reflected in its music and musicians. This lively account is based on the author's own experiences on the

island and his encounters with a wide and intriguing range of music makers, from ground-breaking rappers and reggae artists to pioneers of the nueva trova movement and the Buena Vista Social Club.

Guillermo Cabrera Infante *Holy Smoke.* A pompous and entertaining tribute to the Havanan cigar, full of painful puns and obscure references.

Ian Lumsden *Machos, Maricones and Gays.* One of the few available books that discusses homosexuality in Cuba. A thorough and sensitive treatment, covering the history of homophobia in Cuba and such complex issues as the Cuban approach to AIDS.

Robin D. Moore *Nationalizing Blackness: Afrocubanismo and Artistic Revolution in Havana, 1920–1940*. A clear and compelling analysis of the cultural and artistic role of black Cubans during an era of prejudice. A good introduction to black culture in Cuba.

Pepe Navarro *La Voz del Caimán*. This engaging collection of short encounters with Cubans from all walks of life aims to portray the lives, opinions and aspirations of a society in all its complexity. This is an ideal book to dip into at any page and the cast really does make up an impressively diverse set of occupations and lifestyles within modern Cuba.

Pedro Peréz Sarduy and Jean Stubbs (eds) *AfroCuba: An Anthology of Cuban Writing on Race, Politics and Culture*. Essays and extracts written by black Cuban writers covering religion, race relations, slavery, plantation culture and a fascinating variety of other topics. This anthology contains a wide variety of writing styles with excerpts from plays, novels, poems and factual pieces, but some of the quality of the texts is lost in the occasionally stilted translations.

Sue Steward *Salsa: Musical Heartbeat of Latin America (o/p)*. Tracing the roots of salsa and examining its place in its various home territories, from Miami to London, with three chapters concentrating specifically on Cuba.

Travel writing

John Duncan *In The Red Corner: A Journey Into Cuban Boxing (o/p)*. The story of an English journalist's attempt to go to Cuba and arrange the fight of the century, between the great Cuban heavyweight Felix Savón and Mike Tyson. Effectively two books in one, around half the chapters are dedicated to the history of Cuban boxers and can become a little dry, but the observations of contemporary life in Cuba and all its idiosyncrasies are both perceptive and witty, and should strike a chord with most Westerners who have visited Cuba.

John Jenkins (ed) *Travelers' Tales of Old Cuba*. A worthy collection of eighteen stories and accounts of Cuba by travellers through the ages. What's fun about this book is comparing old Havana with your own experiences today. Although many of the authors may be unheard-of, a smattering of renowned writers make an appearance, with a delicate description of Havana

and Santa Clara by Anaïs Nin and a Hemingway appearance by proxy.

Louis A. Pérez (ed) *Impressions of Cuba in the Nineteenth Century: The Travel Diary of Joseph J. Dimock*. An elaborate first-person account of many aspects of Cuba, including the lives of slaves, Spanish and Creoles and daily life in Havana. At times unwittingly comic, it is as revealing of Cuba as it is of the opinionated stuffed-shirt author.

Alan Ryan (ed) *The Reader's Companion to Cuba*. Twenty-three accounts by foreign visitors to Cuba between 1859 and the 1990s, including trips to Havana and Santiago de Cuba by Graham Greene and fascinating observations on race relations by Langston Hughes. A broad range of writers, from novelists and poets to journalists and naturalists, covers an equally broad range of subject matter, from places and people to slavery and tourism.

Photography and architecture

Juliet Barclay and Martin Charles *Havana: Portrait of a City (o/p).* A graceful social history of the city filled with intriguing vignettes complemented by skilful photography.

Alexandra Black and Simon McBride *Living in Cuba.* Essentially a photographic portrait of the interiors of houses and other preserved colonial buildings around Cuba. The book does a fine job of displaying Cuba's vibrant architectural heritage but, despite its title, shows very little of the environment in which everyday life unfolds. A little like a museum handbook, in nonetheless splendid style.

John Comino-James *A Few Streets, A Few People.* Depicting everyday street scenes and people in the Cayo Hueso district of Havana, this photo collection captures the essence of Centro Habana life, so much of it lived outdoors and on view.

Gianni Costantino *Cuba: Land and People.* Sold in bookstores throughout Cuba, this collection of mostly postcard-style photography is a relatively dispassionate depiction of Cuban society, predominantly covering cities, landscapes and architecture, with the occasional street scene.

Walker Evans *Havana 1933 (o/p).* An exceptional set of photographs taken by Walker Evans, a US photographer commissioned to visit Cuba to supply pictures for a book entitled *The Crime of Cuba* by Carleton Beals. A highly evocative portrayal of 1930s Havana, illustrating, among other facets of the culture, the poverty of the time.

Tania Jovanovic *Cuba ¡Que Bola! a photographic essay (o/p).* Through lucid and evocative black-and-white portraits Jovanovic perfectly captures the exuberance, camaraderie and *joie de vivre* of Cuba.

Christophe Loviny *Cuba by Korda.* Alberto Korda was the man who photographed the iconic portrait of Che Guevara and unwittingly created the most popular T-shirt image of all time. This collection of his work includes numerous other classic shots, such as those of Castro and his rebels in the Sierra Maestra during the Revolutionary War. There are lesser-known photos here too, from dramatic scenes during the Bay of Pigs invasion and the Cuban Missile Crisis to a picture of Castro and a tiger at the Bronx Zoo.

Fiction

Edmundo Desnoes *Memories of Underdevelopment.* In this novel set in 1961 the jaded narrator takes the reader through early revolutionary Cuba after his family has fled for Miami. Its bleak tone and unflinching observations are in stark contrast to the euphoric portrayal of the era generally offered by the state.

Cristina García *Dreaming in Cuban.* Shot through with wit, García's moving novel about a Cuban family divided by the Revolution captures the state of mind of the exile in the States and beautifully describes a magical and idiosyncratic Cuba.

Graham Greene *Our Man in Havana.* Greene's atmospheric 1958 classic is a satirical romp through the world of espionage and despotic duplicity in the run-up to the Revolution. Unequalled entertainment.

Pedro Juan Gutiérrez *Dirty Havana Trilogy* and *The Insatiable Spiderman*. Disturbingly sexy and compelling, this is the story of life under Castro through the eyes of poverty-stricken Gutiérrez. Unlikely to ever be acclaimed by the Cuban Tourist Board, *Dirty Havana Trilogy* is as candid as it gets, airing untold stories of vice and poverty in the heart of Cuba. *The Insatiable Spiderman* continues the theme of poverty and deprivation but is more muted in tone and as such is a less visceral – and assaulting – read.

Ernest Hemingway *To Have and Have Not; The Old Man and the Sea*. The first is a stark novel full of racial tension and undercurrents of violence, with a plot concerning rum-running between Cuba and Key West in the 1930s. The second is the simple, powerful account of an epic battle between an old fisherman and a giant marlin. Set in Cuban waters and the fishing village of Cojímar, this novella won Hemingway the Nobel Prize for literature in 1954.

Pico Iyer *Cuba and the Night*. Against a backdrop of the Special Period, Iyer's bleak and claustrophobic tale of a jaded Western man's affair with a Cuban woman captures the pessimism, cynicism and ambiguity of such relationships in Cuba.

Ana Menéndez *In Cuba I Was a German Shepherd*. Set in the nether land between Miami and Havana inhabited by displaced Cubans, this collection of short stories comprises sensitive and achingly melancholic accounts of jealous husbands, old dreamers and fading wives. Menéndez is skilled in evoking the nostalgia felt by old Cubans pining for a lost homeland and that of a generation of young US Cubans living in the shadow of a never-seen Shangri-la. A promising debut.

Leonardo Padura *Havana Red; Havana Black; Havana Blue*. Published a decade ago but only recently translated into English, these award-winning detective novels broke new ground in Cuba with their gritty and very real depictions of Havana life and their flawed protagonist, Lieutenant Mario Conde, revitalizing a genre characterized previously by party line-towing plots and detectives. *Havana Black* is the most captivating of the series. Against a backdrop of an approaching hurricane, Mario Conte investigates government corruption. For a writer living in Cuba, Padura is refreshingly outspoken as he creates a sombrely metaphysical depiction of a city of disillusionment, corruption, friendship and passion.

Juana Ponce de León and Esteban Ríos Rivera (eds) *Dream with No Name*. A poignant and revealing collection of contemporary short stories by writers living in Cuba and in exile. Mixing the established talent of Alejo Carpentier, Reinaldo Arenas and Onelio Jorge Cardoso with the younger generation of writers represented by Jacqueline Herranz Brooks and Angel Santiesteban Prats, the anthology covers a diversity of subjects from rural life in the 1930s to lesbian love in modern Cuba.

Language

Language

Spanish

Though you are very unlikely to witness any hostility for speaking English to Habaneros, and you will usually find plenty of locals willing to attempt a conversation in English, it makes sense to learn a few basic phrases in Spanish as proficient English is not widely spoken. This is especially true if you are using local buses, as the complete lack of information means you will almost certainly have to ask for help.

Cuban Spanish bears a noticeable resemblance to the pronunciation and vernacular of the Canary Islands, one of the principal sources of Cuban immigration during the colonial era. Students of Castilian Spanish may find themselves a little thrown by all the variations in basic vocabulary in Cuba. However, though the language is full of Anglicisms and Americanisms, like *carro* instead of *coche* for car, or *queic* instead of *tarta* for cake, the Castilian equivalents are generally recognized. Be prepared also for the common Cuban habit of dropping the final letters of words and changing the frequently used -ado ending on words to -ao.

Despite these areas of confusion, the rules of pronunciation for all forms of Spanish are straightforward and the basic Latin American model applies in Cuba. Unless there's an accent, all words ending in d, l, r and z are stressed on the last syllable, all others on the second last. All vowels are pure and short.

a somewhere between the A sound in "back" and that in "father".

e as in "g**e**t".

i as in "pol**i**ce".

o as in "h**o**t".

u as in "r**u**le".

c is soft before E and I, hard otherwise: *cerca* is pronounced "serka".

g works the same way: a guttural H sound (like the ch in "loch") before E or I, a hard G elsewhere: *gigante* becomes "higante".

h is always silent.

j is the same sound as a guttural G: *jamón* is pronounced "hamon".

ll is pronounced as a Y: *lleno* is therefore pronounced "**ye**no".

n is as in English, unless it has a tilde (accent) over it, when it becomes NY: *mañana* sounds like "man**ya**na".

qu is pronounced like the English K.

r is, technically speaking, not rolled but you will frequently hear this rule contradicted.

rr is rolled.

v sounds more like B: *vino* becomes "beano".

z is the same as a soft C: *cerveza* is thus "servesa".

Idiom and slang

Cuban Spanish is rich in idiosyncratic words and phrases, many borrowed from English. Some of the slang is common to other Latin American countries, particularly Puerto Rico, while there are all sorts of *cubanismos* unique to the island.

The following lists of words are a cross section of some of the more common idiosyncrasies of Cuban Spanish. Some of the terms, such as *barbacoa*, have emerged because of uniquely Cuban practices, while others reflect aspects of Cuban culture. A number of everyday Cuban words, particularly for items of clothing, differ completely from their Castilian equivalent. These are not slang words, but equate to the same kind of differences that exist between North American and British English. See the "Public transport and taxis" and "Cuban menu reader" sections for more local vocabulary.

Clothing

el blúmer	knickers	el overol	dungarees
la camiseta	vest	el pitusa	jeans
el chubasquero	cagoule	el pulover	T-shirt
el chor	shorts	el saco	a suit
la guayabera	a traditional lightweight shirt, often with four pockets	los tenis	trainers, sneakers
		el yin	jeans

Money

baro	dollar/s, convertible peso/s	kilo/s	cent/s or centavo/s.
		un medio	five cents or centavos
divisa	hard currency (used in an official capacity, eg in a bank or shop)/dollars/ convertible pesos	moneda efectivo	cash, convertible pesos
		moneda nacional	national currency, Cuban pesos
fula	dollar/s, convertible peso/s	una peseta	twenty cents or centavos

Miscellaneous

asere	similar to "mate" or "buddy" (usually used as an exclamation)	chino/a	a person with facial characteristics commonly found in Chinese people
barbacoa	two rooms created from one by building in a floor halfway up the wall to create an upper level that is about four feet high, used for sleeping (a popular Cuban practice)	chivatón	grass, informer
		chopin	convertible-peso shop, often a supermarket (an appropriation of the English "shopping")
		coger lucha	to get stressed out or upset
bárbaro/a	excellent, great	¿Cómo andas?	How's it going?
bolsa negra	black market	compañero/a	comrade (formal); friend, mate, pal (informal)
chance	chance; often used in the expression ¡Dame un chance! - Give me a chance!	coño	an exclamation that denotes surprise or amazement (often shortened to ño)
chao	goodbye (never hello)		

empatarse	to get it together with someone romantically or sexually	papaya	literally pawpaw or papaya fruit though never used in this sense in Cuba; female genitalia
en candela	messed up or useless		
estar puesto/a	to fancy or be attracted to someone; *¿Estás puesto pa' ella?* - Do you fancy her?	peña	musical group, jam or small concert
		pepe/a	tourist
guapo	criminal or street hustler	pila	a lot; *Hay una pila de gente aquí* – "There's a lot of people here"
gusano/a	Cuban refugee or counter-revolutionary (pejorative)		
		prieto/a	dark-skinned
¿Gusta?, ¿Gustas?	Would you like some?, Would you care to? (in reference to meals and food)	ponchera	puncture repair and bicycle maintenance workshop
		posada	short-term hotel renting rooms for sex
irse para afuera	to go abroad		
jinetera	female hustler who specifically targets tourists; prostitute	¿Qué bolá?	What's up?, How's it going?
		reparto	neighbourhood or area of a city
jinetero	male hustler who specifically targets tourists	sala de video	venue where films are shown to public on a television screen
maceta	a player or hustler (indicates wealth acquired illegally)		
		socio/a	mate, buddy
monada	a group of policemen (pejorative)	¿Te cuadra?	Does that suit you?, Is that OK with you?
moña	hip-hop music	tonga	a lot
pa'	for (shortened version of para)	trigueño/a	light-brown-skinned
		Voy echando	I'm out of here, I'm off
paladar	privately-run restaurant located in the owner's home	yuma	foreigner
		yunta	close friend

Spanish language basics

Essentials

yes	sí	Miss	señorita
no	no	here	aquí/acá
please	por favor	there	allí
thank you	gracias	this	esto
sorry	disculpe	that	eso
excuse me	permiso, perdón	open	abierto/a
Mr	señor	closed	cerrado/a
Mrs	señora	with	con

without	sin	the toilets	los baños
good	buen(o)/a	ladies	señoras/damas
bad	mal(o)/a	gentlemen	caballeros
big	grande	I don't understand	No entiendo
small	pequeño/a, chico/a		
more	más	I don't speak Spanish	No hablo español
less	menos		
the toilets	los servicios	I don't know	No sé

Numbers and days

0	cero	70	setenta
1	uno/una	80	ochenta
2	dos	90	noventa
3	tres	100	cien(to)
4	cuatro	101	ciento uno
5	cinco	200	doscientos
6	seis	201	doscientos uno
7	siete	500	quinientos
8	ocho	1000	mil
9	nueve	2000	dos mil
10	diez	first	primero/a
11	once	second	segundo/a
12	doce	third	tercero/a
13	trece	fourth	quarto/a
14	catorce	fifth	quinto/a
15	quince	Monday	lunes
16	dieciséis	Tuesday	martes
20	veinte	Wednesday	miércoles
21	veitiuno	Thursday	jueves
30	treinta	Friday	viernes
40	cuarenta	Saturday	sábado
50	cincuenta	Sunday	domingo
60	sesenta		

Greetings and responses

goodbye	adios/chao	My name is…	Me llamo…
hello	hola	What's your name?	¿Cómo se llama usted? or ¿Cómo te llamas? (informal)
Good morning	Buenos dias		
Good afternoon/ night	Buenas tardes/ noches		
		I am English	Soy inglés(a)
See you later	Hasta luego	…American	americano(a)
Pleased to meet you	Mucho gusto	…Australian	australiano(a)
How are you?	¿Cómo está (usted)? or ¿Cómo andas? (informal)	…Canadian	canadiense(a)
		…Irish	irlandés(a)
		…Scottish	escosés(a)
		…Welsh	galés(a)
Not at all/You're welcome	De nada/por nada	…a New Zealander	neozelandés(a)

Public transport and taxis

airport	el aeropuer to	train station	la estación de ferrocarriles
bicycle taxi	el bicitaxi/el ciclotaxi	truck (a commonly used alternative to long-distance buses)	el camión
bus (usually a local city bus)	la guagua		
bus (used more to refer to long-distance bus)	el ómnibus	I'd like a (return) ticket to...?	Quisiera boleto/pasaje (de ida y vuelta) para...
bus station	el terminal de ómnibus	Is this the stop for...?	¿Es está la parada para...?
bus stop	la parada	Is this the train for Havana?	¿Es éste el tren para La Habana?
communal taxi (operates more like a bus service)	el taxi colectivo	Take us to this address	Llévenos a esta dirección
every other day (seen on bus and train timetables)	días alternos	What time does it leave (arrive in...)?	¿A qué hora sale (llega a...)?
		When is the next bus to...?	¿Cuándo es la próxima guagua para...?
to hitchhike	coger botella	Where can I get a taxi?	¿Dónde puedo coger un taxi?
juggernaut-style bus	el camello		
state-run taxi charging in convertible pesos	el turistaxi	Where does the bus to...leave from?	¿De dónde sale la guagua para...?
		Where is a good place to hitchhike?	¿Dónde hay buen lugar para coger botella?

Car rental, driving and roads

car	el carro	Is the petrol/ gasoline included?	¿Está incluida la gasolina?
Could you check...?	¿Puede usted comprobar...?	main road	la carretera principal
...the oil	...el aceite	map	el mapa
...the water	...el agua	motorway	el autopista
...the tyres	...los neumáticos	petrol station	la gasolinera
crossroads	el cruce	pothole	el bache
driver's licence	el carné de conducir	railway crossing	el crucero
Fill it up please	Llénelo por favor	road	la carretera
Give way	Ceda el paso	roundabout	la rotonda
I'd like to rent a car	Quisiera alquilar un carro	traffic light	el semáforo

Asking directions

Carry straight on	Siga todo derecho/ recto	Is this the right road to…?	¿Es esta la carretera para…?
How do I get to…?	¿Por dónde se va para llegar a…?	Next to	Al lado de
		Opposite	Frente/enfrente
How far is it from here to…?	¿Qué distancia hay desde aquí hasta…?	Turn left/right	Doble a la izquierda/ derecha
Is it near/far?	¿Está cerca/lejos?		
Is there a hotel nearby?	¿Hay un hotel aquí cerca?	Where does this road take us?	¿A dónde nos lleva esta carretera?
		Where is…?	¿Dónde está…?

Needs and asking questions

Can you help me please?	Por favor, ¿me puede ayudar?	I'd like	Quisiera
		I want	Quiero
Could you speak slower please?	Por favor, ¿puede usted hablar más despacio?	(one like that)	(uno así)
		There is (is there)?	(¿)Hay(?)
		What…?	¿Qué…?
Do you accept credit cards/traveller's cheques here?	¿Aceptan aquí tarjetas de crédito/ cheques de viajero?	What does this mean?	¿Qué quiere decir esto?
		What is there to eat?	¿Qué hay para comer?
Do you have…?	¿Tiene…?	When…?	¿Cuándo…?
Do you know…?	¿Sabe…?	What's that?	¿Qué es eso?
Do you speak English?	¿Habla usted inglés?	What's this called in Spanish?	¿Cómo se llama esto en español?
Give me…	Deme…	Where…?	¿Dónde…?
How much is it?	¿Cuánto cuesta?		

Time

a day	un día	night	la noche
a month	un mes	now	ahora
a week	una semana	quarter past two	Dos y cuarto
afternoon	la tarde	quarter to three	Tres menos cuarto
half past two	Dos y media	today	hoy
It's one o'clock	Es la una	tomorrow	mañana
It's two o'clock	Son las dos	tonight	esta noche
later	más tarde or después	What time is it?	¿Qué hora es?
morning	la mañana	yesterday	ayer

Accommodation

air conditioning	aire acondicionado	Do you have a room?	¿Tiene una habitación?
balcony	el balcón	…with two beds/ double bed	…con dos camas/ cama matrimonial
boutique hotel	el hostal		
cabin complex	el campismo	…facing the sea	…con vista al mar
Can one…?	¿Se puede…?	…facing the street	…con vista a la calle
…camp (near) here?	¿…acampar aqui (cerca)?	…on the ground floor	…en la planta baja
		…on the first floor	…en el primer piso

Do you have anything cheaper?	¿No tiene algo más barato?	key	la llave
fan	el ventilador	laundry service	el servicio de lavandería
hot/cold water	agua caliente/fria	reception	la carpeta
house with rooms to rent	casa particular	room service	el servicio de habitación
It's fine, how much is it?	Está bien, ¿cuánto es?	safety deposit box	la caja de seguridad
		swimming pool	la piscina
It's for one person/ two people	Es para una persona/ dos personas	The TV/radio doesn't work	No funciona el televisor/el radio
...for one night	...para una noche	toilet/bathroom	el baño
It's too...	Es demasiado/a...	village complex	la villa
...expensive	...caro/a	We have booked a double room	Hemos reservado una habitación doble
...dark	...oscuro/a		
...noisy	...ruidoso/a		

Shopping, banks and exchange

agromercado	market selling fresh produce for Cuban pesos	casa comisionista	Cuban equivalent to a pawnbrokers
		en efectivo	in cash
artesanía	arts and crafts	guardabolso	cloakroom for bags (usually outside shops)
bodega	a general store only open to those with a corresponding state-issue ration book		
		habanos	Cuban cigars
		humidor	box for storing and preserving cigars
bolsa negra	black market		
cambio	bureau de change		
casa de cambio	a bureau de change for changing convertible peso into Cuban pesos		

Cuban menu reader

Food and restaurant basics

aceite	oil	comidas ligeras	light foods
ají	chilli	cuenta	bill
ajo	garlic	desayuno	breakfast
almuerzo	lunch	ensalada	salad
arroz	rice	entrantes	starters
azúcar	sugar	entremeses	starters
bocadillo/bocadito	sandwich	guarnición	side dishes
cena	dinner	huevos	eggs
cereal	cereal	huevos fritos	fried eggs
combinaciones	set meals	huevos hervidos	boiled eggs
comida criolla	Cuban/native food	huevos revoltillos	scrambled eggs

mantequilla	butter or margarine	platos fuertes	mains
mermelada	jam (UK); jelly (US)	potaje	soup, stew
miel	honey	queso	cheese
mostaza	mustard	sal	salt
pan	bread	sopa	soup
perro caliente	hot dog	tortilla	omelette
pimienta	pepper	tostada	toast
platos combinados	set meals	vinagre	vinegar

Table items

botella	bottle	mesa	table
carta	menu	plato	plate
cuchara	spoon	servieta	napkin
cucharita	teaspoon	tenedor	fork
cuchillo	knife	vaso	glass
cuenco	bowl		

Cooking styles

al ajillo	fried with lots of garlic	empanadilla	puff pastry/pie
a la brasa	braised	enchilado/a	cooked in tomato sauce
a la jardinera	with tomato sauce	estofado/a	stewed/braised
a la parrilla	grilled	frito/a	fried
a la plancha	grilled	guisado/a	stewed
agridulce	sweet and sour	grillé	grilled
ahumado/a	smoked	hervido/a	boiled
al horno	baked	lonjas	slices/strips
asado/a	roast	poco cocinado/a	rare (meat)
bien cocido/a	well done (meat)	regular	medium (meat)
cazuela	stew, casserole	revoltillo	scrambled
churrasco	grilled meat	tostado/a	toasted
crudo/a	raw		

Cuban dishes

ajiaco	rich stew featuring corn and varied meats and vegetables	lechón	roast pork suckling
		moros y cristianos	rice and black beans
bistec uruguayo	steak covered in cheese and breadcrumbs	palomilla	steak fried or grilled with lime and garlic
		ropa vieja	shredded stewed beef
chicharrones	fried pork skin/pork scratchings	tamale	Mexican-influenced local dish made with steamed cornflour
congrí	rice and red beans (mixed)	tasajo	shredded and jerked stewed beef
langosta enchilada	lobster in a tomato sauce	tostones	fried plantains

Fish (pescados) and seafood (mariscos)

anchoas	anchovies	langosta	lobster
arenque	herring	merluza	hake
atún	tuna	pargo	red snapper (tilapia)
bacalao	cod	pulpo	octopus
calamares	squid	salmón	salmon
camarones	prawns, shrimp	tetí	small fish, local to Baracoa
cangrejo	crab		
espada	swordfish	trucha	trout

Meat (carne) and poultry (aves)

albóndigas	meatballs	masas de	cubed (pork)
bistec	steak	oveja	mutton
brocheta	kebab	pavo	turkey
buey	beef	pato	duck
cabra/chivo	goat	pechuga	breast
carnero	mutton	picadillo	mince
cerdo	pork	pierna	leg
chorizo	spicy sausage	pollo	chicken
chuleta	chop	rana	frog's meat
conejo	rabbit	res	beef
cordero	lamb	ropa vieja	shredded beef
costillas	ribs	salchichas	sausages
escalope	escalope	sesos	brains
hamburguesa	hamburger	solomillo	sirloin
hígado	liver	ternera	veal
jamón	ham	tocino	bacon
lacón	smoked pork	venado	venison
lomo	loin (of pork)		

Fruits (frutas) and nuts (frutos secos)

aguacate	avocado	maní	peanut
albaricoque	apricot	manzana	apple
almendra	almond	melocotón	peach
avellana	hazlenut	melón	melon (usually watermelon)
cereza	cherry		
ciruelas	prunes	naranja	orange
coco	coconut	pera	pear
fresa	strawberry	piña	pineapple
fruta bomba	papaya	plátano	banana
guayaba	guava	toronja	grapefruit
lima	lime	uvas	grapes
limón	lime/lemon		
mamey	mamey (thick, sweet red fruit with a single stone)		

Vegetables (verduras/vegetales)

aceituna	olive	lechuga	lettuce
berenjenas	aubergine/eggplant	malanga	starchy tubular vegetable
boniato	sweet potato		
calabaza	pumpkin	papa	potato
cebolla	onion	papas fritas	french fries
champiñón	mushroom	pepino	cucumber
chícaro(nes)	pea (pulse)	pimiento	capsicum pepper
col	cabbage	quimbombó	okra
esparragos	asparagus	rábano	radish
frijoles	black beans	remolacha	beetroot
garbanzos	chickpeas	tomate	tomato
habichuela	string beans/green beans	yuca	cassava
		zanahoria	carrot
hongos	mushrooms		

Sweets (dulces) and desserts (postres)

arroz con leche	rice pudding	queik	cake
churros	long curls of fried batter similar to doughnuts	queso	cheese
		merengue	meringue
		natilla	custard/milk pudding/ mousse
cocos	sweets made from shredded coconut and sugar		
		pasta de guayaba	guava jam
		pay	pie (fruit)
...en almíbar	in syrup	pudín	crème caramel or hard-set flan
galleta	biscuit/cookie		
empanada de guayaba	guava jam in pastry	torta de queso	cheesecake
		torta Santiago	almond tart
flan	crème caramel	tortica	shortbread-type biscuit
helado	ice cream	tres gracias	three scoops of ice cream
jimaguas	two scoops of ice cream		

Rums (rones) and cocktails (cocteles)

Cuba Libre	rum and Coke	Daiquirí Frappé	white rum, maraschino (cherry liqueur), white sugar, lemon juice and crushed ice
Cubanito	white rum, lemon juice, salt, Worcester sauce, hot sauce and crushed ice		
		Habana Especial	white rum, maraschino, pineapple juice and ice
Daiquirí	white rum, white sugar, lemon juice and crushed ice		

Mulata	dark rum, white sugar, lemon juice and cacao liqueur	…carta blanca (ron blanco)	white rum, aged three years
Presidente ron…	white rum, curaçao, grenadine and sweet white vermouth	…carta oro	dark rum, aged five years
…añejo	dark rum, aged seven years	…gran reserva	dark rum, aged fifteen years
		Ron Collins	white rum, lemon juice, white sugar and soda

Other drinks (bebidas)

agua	water	leche	milk
agua mineral	mineral water	limonada natural	lemonade (fresh)
…(con gas)	…(sparkling)	prú	fermented drink flavoured with spices
…(sin gas)	…(still)		
batido	milkshake		
café	coffee	refresco	pop/fizzy drink
café con leche	coffee made with hot milk	refresco de lata	canned pop
		té	tea
cerveza	beer	té manzanillo	camomile tea
chocolate caliente	drinking chocolate	vino tinto	red wine
guarapo	sugar cane pressé	vino blanco	white wine
ginebra	gin	vino rosado	rosé wine
jerez	sherry	vodka	vodka
jugo	juice	whisky	whisky

Small print and
Index

A Rough Guide to Rough Guides

Published in 1982, the first Rough Guide – to Greece – was a student scheme that became a publishing phenomenon. Mark Ellingham, a recent graduate in English from Bristol University, had been travelling in Greece the previous summer and couldn't find the right guidebook. With a small group of friends he wrote his own guide, combining a highly contemporary, journalistic style with a thoroughly practical approach to travellers' needs.

The immediate success of the book spawned a series that rapidly covered dozens of destinations. And, in addition to impecunious backpackers, Rough Guides soon acquired a much broader and older readership that relished the guides' wit and inquisitiveness as much as their enthusiastic, critical approach and value-for-money ethos.

These days, Rough Guides include recommendations from shoestring to luxury and cover more than 200 destinations around the globe, including almost every country in the Americas and Europe, more than half of Africa and most of Asia and Australasia. Our ever-growing team of authors and photographers is spread all over the world, particularly in Europe, the US and Australia.

In the early 1990s, Rough Guides branched out of travel, with the publication of Rough Guides to World Music, Classical Music and the Internet. All three have become benchmark titles in their fields, spearheading the publication of a wide range of books under the Rough Guide name.

Including the travel series, Rough Guides now number more than 350 titles, covering: phrasebooks, waterproof maps, music guides from Opera to Heavy Metal, reference works as diverse as Conspiracy Theories and Shakespeare, and popular culture books from iPods to Poker. Rough Guides also produce a series of more than 120 World Music CDs in partnership with World Music Network.

Visit www.roughguides.com to see our latest publications.

Rough Guide travel images are available for commercial licensing at www.roughguidespictures.com

Rough Guide credits

Text editor: James Rice
Layout: Anita Singh
Cartography: Ed Wright
Picture editor: Mark Thomas
Production: Rebecca Short
Proofreader: Helen Castell
Cover design: Chloë Roberts
Photographer: Greg Roden
Editorial: Ruth Blackmore, Andy Turner, Keith Drew, Edward Aves, Alice Park, Lucy White, Jo Kirby, James Smart, Natasha Foges, Róisín Cameron, Emma Traynor, Emma Gibbs, Kathryn Lane, Monica Woods, Mani Ramaswamy, Harry Wilson, Lucy Cowie, Amanda Howard, Lara Kavanagh, Alison Roberts, Joe Staines, Peter Buckley, Matthew Milton, Tracy Hopkins, Ruth Tidball; **Delhi** Madhavi Singh, Karen D'Souza, Lubna Shaheen
Design & Pictures: **London** Scott Stickland, Dan May, Diana Jarvis, Nicole Newman, Sarah Cummins, Emily Taylor; **Delhi** Umesh Aggarwal, Ajay Verma, Jessica Subramanian, Ankur Guha, Pradeep Thapliyal, Sachin Tanwar, Nikhil Agarwal, Sachin Gupta
Production: Vicky Baldwin

Cartography: **London** Maxine Repath, Katie Lloyd-Jones; **Delhi** Rajesh Chhibber, Ashutosh Bharti, Rajesh Mishra, Animesh Pathak, Jasbir Sandhu, Karobi Gogoi, Alakananda Bhattacharya, Swati Handoo, Deshpal Dabas
Online: **London** George Atwell, Faye Hellon, Jeanette Angell, Fergus Day, Justine Bright, Clare Bryson, Aine Fearon, Adrian Low, Ezgi Celebi, Amber Bloomfield; **Delhi** Amit Verma, Rahul Kumar, Narender Kumar, Ravi Yadav, Debojit Borah, Rakesh Kumar, Ganesh Sharma, Shisir Basumatari
Marketing & Publicity: **London** Liz Statham, Niki Hanmer, Louise Maher, Jess Carter, Vanessa Godden, Vivienne Watton, Anna Paynton, Rachel Sprackett, Laura Vipond, Vanessa McDonald; **New York** Katy Ball, Judi Powers, Nancy Lambert; **Delhi** Ragini Govind
Manager India: Punita Singh
Reference Director: Andrew Lockett
Operations Manager: Helen Atkinson
PA to Publishing Director: Nicola Henderson
Publishing Director: Martin Dunford
Commercial Manager: Gino Magnotta
Managing Director: John Duhigg

SMALL PRINT

Publishing information

This first edition published January 2010 by
Rough Guides Ltd,
80 Strand, London WC2R 0RL
14 Local Shopping Centre, Panchsheel Park, New Delhi 110017, India

Distributed by the Penguin Group
Penguin Books Ltd,
80 Strand, London WC2R 0RL
Penguin Group (USA)
375 Hudson Street, NY 10014, USA
Penguin Group (Australia)
250 Camberwell Road, Camberwell, Victoria 3124, Australia
Penguin Group (Canada)
195 Harry Walker Parkway N, Newmarket, ON, L3Y 7B3 Canada
Penguin Group (NZ)
67 Apollo Drive, Mairangi Bay, Auckland 1310, New Zealand
Cover concept by Peter Dyer.

Typeset in Bembo and Helvetica to an original design by Henry Iles.

Printed in Singapore

© Fiona McAuslan and Matt Norman, 2010

Maps © Rough Guides

No part of this book may be reproduced in any form without permission from the publisher except for the quotation of brief passages in reviews.

248pp includes index

A catalogue record for this book is available from the British Library

ISBN: 978-1-84836-258-1

The publishers and authors have done their best to ensure the accuracy and currency of all the information in **The Rough Guide to Havana**, however, they can accept no responsibility for any loss, injury, or inconvenience sustained by any traveller as a result of information or advice contained in the guide.

1 3 5 7 9 8 6 4 2

Help us update

We've gone to a lot of effort to ensure that the first edition of **The Rough Guide to Havana** is accurate and up-to-date. However, things change – places get "discovered", opening hours are notoriously fickle, restaurants and rooms raise prices or lower standards. If you feel we've got it wrong or left something out, we'd like to know, and if you can remember the address, the price, the hours, the phone number, so much the better.

Please send your comments with the subject line "**Rough Guide Havana Update**" to ©mail @roughguides.com. We'll credit all contributions and send a copy of the next edition (or any other Rough Guide if you prefer) for the very best emails.

Have your questions answered and tell others about your trip at ®www.roughguides.com

www.roughguides.com

239

Acknowledgements

Matt Norman wishes to thank: Miriam Rodríguez, Sinai Solé, Ricardo Morales, Hildegard Milian and her daughter Nimueh plus Hector and Etienn for all their love and support. Thanks also to Armando R Menéndez for advice on the gay scene in Havana and Miri for doing everything with a smile. A special thank you and much love to Sophie Madden for being supportive, good humoured and for driving in the face of adversity. Finally thanks to James Rice and Ed Wright for being so thorough and so easy and enjoyable to work with.

Fiona McAuslan wishes to thank: Diana and Pavel for their support, generosity and friendship. Also much love to Aurora, Luís and Nelson for their enduring support, encouragement and love over many years. Thanks to Armando for swift and fantastic work on the Gay Havana chapter and a huge thanks to Toby Brocklehurst for introducing me to an unexpectedly chic side of the city. In England thanks to all at the Cuban Embassy, particularly Igor Caballero and Maribel, for making the research trip possible. Finally thanks to all those at Havana's Centro de Prensa.

SMALL PRINT

ROUGH GUIDES

Index

Map entries are in colour.

F

G

H

I

J

K

L

M

Map symbols

maps are listed in the full index using coloured text

Symbol	Description	Symbol	Description
▬▬▬	Highway/autopista	ⓘ	Tourist information
═══	Main road	⊠	Post office
───	Minor road	Ⓒ	Telephone
)═══(	Tunnel	@	Internet access
▨▨▨	Pedestrianized street	⊞	Hospital
------	Path	⊙	Statue/memorial
━━●━━	Railway	🅿	Parking
━━━━	Electric railway	⛽	Fuel station
───	River	──	Wall
·■·■·■	Municipal boundary	⤞	Bridge
·■·■·■	Provincial boundary	◉	Accommodation
♦	Point of interest	■	Restaurant/café/bar
⚱	Waterfall	▬	Building
⚘	Viewpoint/mirador	✛	Church/cathedral
⚶	Spring	⬭	Stadium
⚑	Golf course	▨	Beach
⚵	Church (regional map)	⊹	Cemetery
✈	International airport	▨	Park
♟	Museum (regional map)	⌇	Mangrove swamp

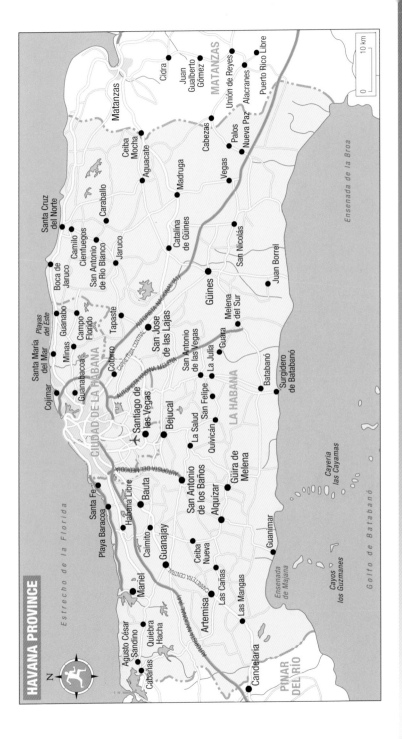

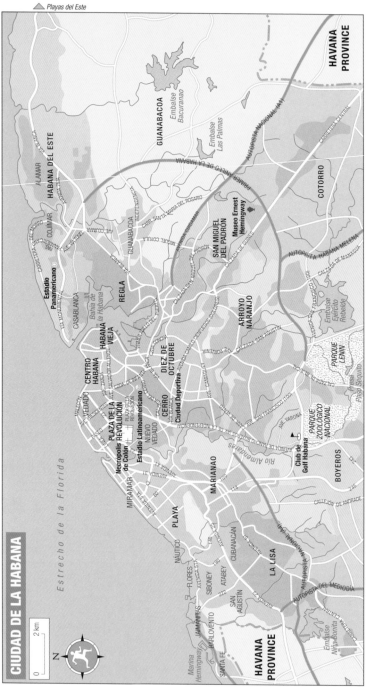

CIUDAD DE LA HABANA

0   2 Km

N

Estrecho de la Florida

Playas del Este

HAVANA
PROVINCE

GUANABACOA

Embalse Bacuranao

Embalse Las Palmas

HABANA DEL ESTE

ALAMAR

COJIMAR

Estadio Panamericano

CASABLANCA

Bahía de la Habana

REGLA

GUANABACOA

Museo Ernest Hemingway

SAN MIGUEL DEL PADRON

ARROYO NARANJO

COTORRO

AUTOPISTA HABANA MELENA

PRIMER ANILLO DE LA HABANA

AUTOPISTA NACIONAL (A1)

CARRETERA CENTRAL

HABANA VIEJA

CENTRO HABANA

VEDADO

DIEZ DE OCTUBRE

Necrópolis de Colón

PLAZA DE LA REVOLUCIÓN

Estadio Latinoamericano

CERRO

NUEVO VEDADO

Ciudad Deportiva

MIRAMAR

PLAYA

MARIANAO

Río Almendares

Club de Golf Habana

PARQUE ZOOLÓGICO NACIONAL

Embalse Ejército Rebelde

PARQUE LENIN

Presa Paso Sequito

BOYEROS

NAUTICO

FLORES

SIBONEY

ATABEY

SAN AGUSTIN

CUBANACAN

LA LISA

AUTOPISTA DEL MEDIODIA

Embalse Niña Bonita

HAVANA
PROVINCE

JAIMANITAS

BARLOVENTO

SANTA FE

Marina Hemingway

Las Terrazas

San Antonio de los Baños

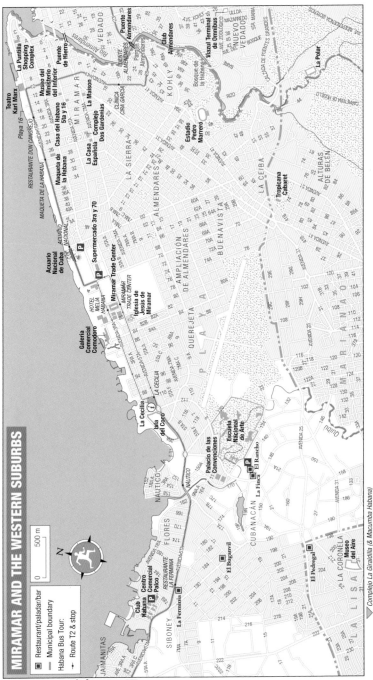

MIRAMAR AND THE WESTERN SUBURBS

- ■ Restaurant/paladar/bar
- — Municipal boundary
- Habana Bus Tour:
- + Route T2 & stop

0 — 500 m

N

▽ Marina Hemingway & La Cova de Pizza Nova

▽ Complejo La Giraldilla (& Macumba Habana)

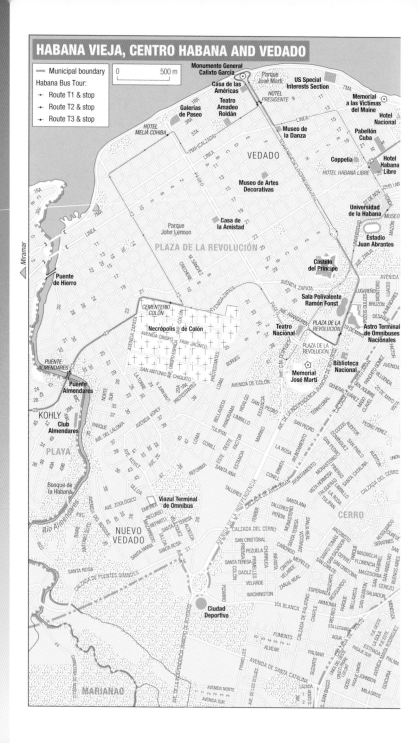

HABANA VIEJA, CENTRO HABANA AND VEDADO

Municipal boundary
Habana Bus Tour:
→ Route T1 & stop
→ Route T2 & stop
→ Route T3 & stop

0   500 m

Monumento General Calixto García
Casa de las Américas
Parque José Martí
US Special Interests Section
7MA
Memorial a las Víctimas del Maine
HOTEL PRESIDENTE 9
Teatro Amadeo Roldán
Galerías de Paseo
Hotel Nacional
HOTEL MELIÁ COHIBA
Museo de la Danza
Pabellón Cuba
VEDADO
Coppelia
Hotel Habana Libre
HOTEL HABANA LIBRE
Museo de Artes Decorativas
Universidad de la Habana
MUSEO
Puente de Hierro
Casa de la Amistad
Parque John Lennon
PLAZA DE LA REVOLUCIÓN
Estadio Juan Abrantes
Castillo del Príncipe
AVENIDA ZAPATA
PUENTE ALMENDARES
Sala Polivalente Ramón Fonst
Astro Terminal de Ómnibuses Nacionales
CEMENTERIO COLÓN
Puente Almendares
Necrópolis de Colón
Teatro Nacional
PLAZA DE LA REVOLUCIÓN
PLAZA DE LA REVOLUCIÓN
KOHLY
Club Almendares
Biblioteca Nacional
PLAYA
Memorial José Martí
Bosque de la Habana
CERRO
Río Almendares
Viazul Terminal de Ómnibus
NUEVO VEDADO
CALZADA DEL CERRO
SANTA ROSA
CALZADA DE PUENTES GRANDES
Ciudad Deportivo
VÍA BLANCA
MARIANAO
AVENIDA NORTE
AVENIDA SUR
Miramar

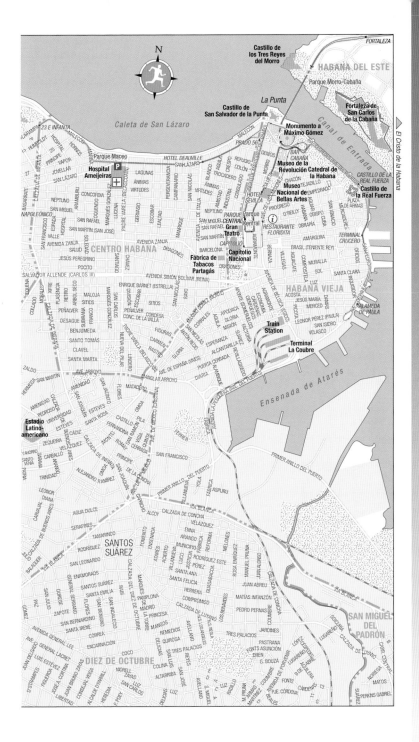

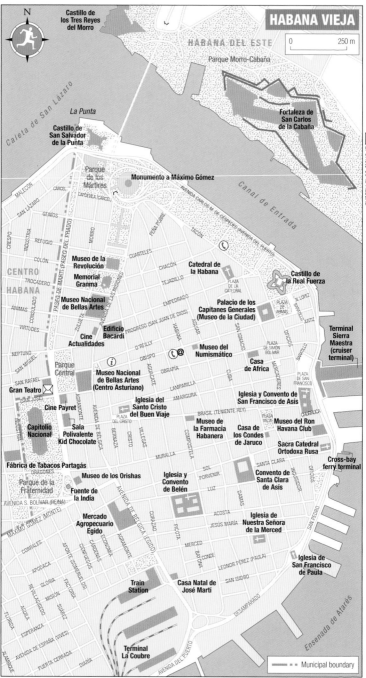

HABANA VIEJA

N

0   250 m

Castillo de
los Tres Reyes
del Morro

HABANA DEL ESTE

Parque Morro-Cabaña

La Punta

Caleta de San Lázaro

Castillo de
San Salvador
de la Punta

Fortaleza de
San Carlos
de la Cabaña

El Cristo de la Habana

Parque
de los
Mártires

Monumento a Máximo Gómez

Canal de Entrada

AVENIDA CARLOS M DE CÉSPEDES (AVENIDA DEL PUERTO)

MALECÓN

CÁRCEL

CAPDÉVILA (CÁRCEL)

PEÑA POBRE

TACÓN

SAN LÁZARO

GENIOS

CUARTELES

CHACÓN

Catedral de
la Habana

PLAZA
DE LA
CATEDRAL

Castillo de
la Real Fuerza

CRESPO

INDUSTRIA

REFUGIO

COLÓN

MORRO

Museo de la
Revolución

Memorial
Granma

TEJADILLO

EMPEDRADO

PLAZA
DE
ARMAS

N. LÓPEZ

BRETILLA

JUSTIZ

CENTRO
HABANA

TROCADERO

ÁNIMAS

Museo Nacional
de Bellas Artes

PASEO DE MARTÍ (PASEO DEL PRADO)

AVENIDA DE LAS MISIONES

Palacio de los
Capitanes Generales
(Museo de la Ciudad)

SAN IGNACIO

OFICIOS

Terminal
Sierra
Maestra
(cruiser
terminal)

CONSULADO

VIRTUDES

ZULUETA

Cine
Actualidades

Edificio
Bacardí

PROGRESO (SAN JUAN DE DIOS)

HABANA

AGUIAR

Museo del
Numismático

PLAZA
DE SIMÓN
BOLÍVAR

Casa
de Africa

BARATILLO

PLAZA
DE SAN
FRANCISCO

NEPTUNO

SAN MIGUEL

Parque
Central

O'REILLY

OBISPO

OBRAPÍA

CUBA

MERCADERES

Iglesia y Convento de
San Francisco de Asís

CHURRUCA

SAN RAFAEL

Gran Teatro

Museo Nacional
de Bellas Artes
(Centro Asturiano)

AGUACATE

LAMPARILLA

SAN JOSÉ

Cine Payret

AMARGURA

PLAZA
VIEJA

Museo del Ron
Havana Club

Capitolio
Nacional

AGRAMONTE

AVENIDA DE BÉLGICA

Sala
Polivalente
Kid Chocolate

PLAZA
DEL CRISTO

BERNAZA

Iglesia del
Santo Cristo
del Buen Viaje

CRISTO

VILLEGAS

BRASIL (TENIENTE REY)

Museo de
la Farmacia
Habanera

COMPOSTELA

Casa de
los Condes
de Jaruco

Sacra Catedral
Ortodoxa Rusa

Cross-bay
ferry terminal

OFICIOS

Fábrica de Tabacos Partagás

INDUSTRIA

DRAGONES

MURALLA

SOL

SANTA CLARA

Convento de
Santa Clara
de Asís

INQUISIDOR

SAN PEDRO

Parque de la
Fraternidad

Museo de los Orishas

Fuente de
la India

AVENIDA DE BÉLGICA (EGIDO)

CURAZAO

Iglesia y
Convento
de Belén

PORVENIR

LUZ

DAMAS

AVENIDA S. BOLÍVAR (REINA)

MÁXIMO GÓMEZ (MONTE)

Mercado
Agropecuario
Egido

AGRAMONTE

ECONOMÍA

ACOSTA

JESÚS MARÍA

Iglesia de
Nuestra Señora
de la Merced

CORRALES

CÁRDENAS

CIENFUEGOS

PICOTA

MERCED

APODACA

GLORIA

FACTORÍA

APONTE (SOMERUELOS)

SUÁREZ

MISIÓN

BAYONA

CONDE

LEONOR PÉREZ (PAULA)

SAN ISIDRO

Iglesia de
San Francisco
de Paula

FLORIDA

ÁGUILA

REVILLAGIGEDO

ESPERANZA

Train
Station

Casa Natal de
José Martí

DESAMPARADO

ALAMBIQUE

AVENIDA DE ESPAÑA (VIVES)

PUERTA CERRADA

DIARIA

Terminal
La Coubre

AVENIDA DEL PUERTO

Ensenada de Atarés

Municipal boundary

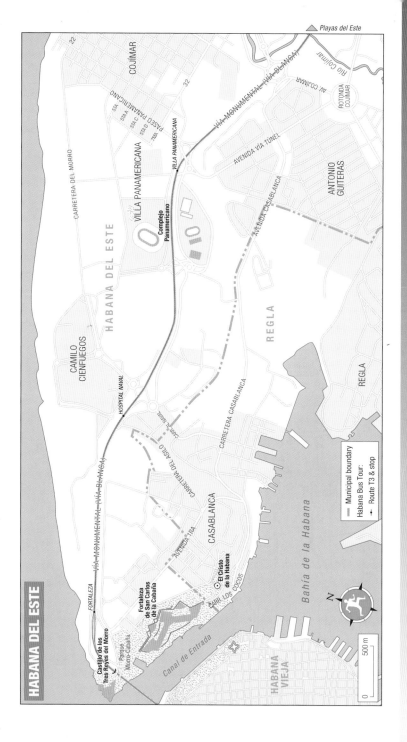

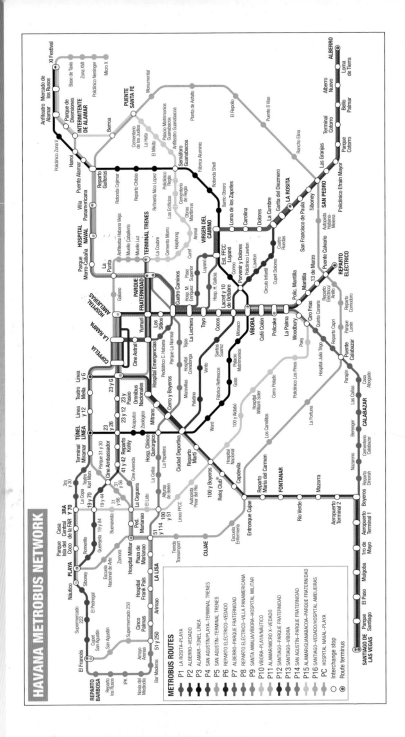